# BANNERS
OF THE
# DURHAM
# COALFIELD

## NORMAN EMERY

SUTTON PUBLISHING

First published in 1998 by
Sutton Publishing Limited · Phoenix Mill
Thrupp · Stroud · Gloucestershire · GL5 2BU

British Library Cataloguing in Publication Data
A catalogue record for this book is available from the British Library

ISBN 0 7509 1708 3

Cover picture: The NUM (NE Area) banner, with images of the 1984–5
strike, 'We Struggle for Justice and Freedom'.

Endpapers: *front*, The Durham County Colliery Enginemen's and Boiler
Minders' Association banner being carried over Elvet bridge at the 1933
Gala; *back*, The 1996 Trimdon Grange DMA banner paraded around the
streets of the village after the formal unfurling and dedication.

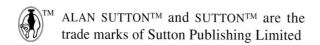
™ ALAN SUTTON™ and SUTTON™ are the
trade marks of Sutton Publishing Limited

Typeset in 11/13 pt Times.
Typesetting and origination by
Sutton Publishing Limited.
Printed in Great Britain by
Butler & Tanner, Frome, Somerset.

# Contents

# Foreword

Norman Emery, through his patient research, has captured the valuable role played by the banners of the miners' lodges in the history and development of the culture of the Durham coalfield. Each banner represents a page in that history, which covers a wide spectrum from politics to religion, including the struggles to build a better society through the aims and objects of the mining unions, their achievements, failures and, on occasions, the disasters and atrocities endured.

From the middle of the nineteenth century the banners were used to unify and rally the communities in the coalfield. The illustrations on each side of them give a graphic picture of the changing social and political scene during this period. Passages used from renowned writers and poets such as Burns, Bunyon, Byron, Pope and Shakespeare, quotations from the Bible, as well as established clichés, were used to depict and reflect the founding principles of the trade union movement and the miners in particular. The skill and artistry of painters such as Norman Cornish were used, indicating the high esteem and pride in which they were held by the lodges.

The Durham Miners' Gala has been, and still is, the principal event when the banners have been paraded. In addition to marches and rallies organized during times of struggle, during the major strikes which took place in the 1880s, 1920s, 1930s, 1970s, 1980s and, most recently, in the 1993 pit closure campaign, the banners have played a vital role in rallying the support of members of the union and the mining communities. They were used on picket lines to help deter would-be strike breakers and on some of these occasions the women in the community commissioned their own banners and marched and campaigned in unity.

They were also used on social occasions, displayed in miners' halls and working men's clubs and carried on sad occasions at funerals when requested by the family.

In 1985, after the epic year-long strike, banners in the coalfield were carried by the members as they returned to work as a symbol of defiance and to demonstrate the continued unity in defiance of the colliery closures and in the protection of jobs and their community. At Dawdon Colliery on Monday 5 March 1985 the whole of the community of miners and their families, local business people, the retired and unemployed marched through the pit gates behind their banner and promptly turned round and marched back out for a further day's strike to underline their determination to continue the struggle. At Monkwearmouth the miners were faced with hundreds of police under instruction not to allow the banner through the pit gates, an indication of how important the employers saw the role of the banner in the struggle. In the melée that ensued as the police applied force, the banner was damaged, leaving bitterness and resentment on the part of the workforce towards the management and the forces of the state at the perpetration of such a wilful act.

Alas, due to political dogma, shortsightedness and the overwhelming use of state machinery, aided and abetted by the management of British Coal and the media, all of the collieries of County Durham have now been closed and miners' jobs taken away. Perhaps the motto on the Marsden Lodge banner, which chose the lines from Oliver Goldsmith's *The Deserted Village* of 1770, is a fitting comment on the folly of the destruction of the collieries:

> Ill fares the land to hastening ills prey
> Where wealth accumulates and men decay
> Princes and lords may flourish or may fade
> A breath can make them, as a breath has made
> But bold peasantry their country's pride
> When once destroyed can never be supplied.

The heritage of our communities will however live on, partly in the form of our banners, which depict the magnificent role of our forefathers, partly in volumes such as *The Banners of the Durham Coalfield*, but mainly in the communities themselves and the men, women and children of today and of the future, as the values forged in the past and depicted on our banners are passed on to each generation.

Miners united will never be defeated.

David Guy
President
National Union of Mineworkers (North East Area).

# Acknowledgements

The banner archive was produced for the National Union of Mineworkers (NE Area), and it is a great pleasure to acknowledge the invaluable assistance of Mr Dave Guy and Mr David Hopper, president and general secretary of the union.

When the research was being carried out, a number of NUM lodge and other coalfield union branch officials arranged access to, or provided information on, banners, for which I am extremely grateful: Alan Cummings, Easington lodge; Alan Mardghum, Monkwearmouth lodge; Ed Malcolm, Westoe lodge; the National Association of Colliery Overmen, Deputies and Shotfirers; Jim Perry, Westoe Mechanics branch; and A. McGough, Houghton Mines Rescue Brigade.

Access to other banners was given by Mr and Mrs E. Atherton, Blackhall Rocks; Mr and Mrs C. Bainbridge, Clara Vale; J.W. Brown, Kibblesworth; Eileen Carnaffin, Gateshead Central Library; Lawrence Claughan, Sacriston; John Cook, Gilesgate; Alan Craythorne, East Hetton; Faye Cunningham, South Shields Town Hall; John Cunningham, Wear Valley District Council; Mr Dowgray, Bowburn; Revd Desmond Hall, St Ive's Church, Leadgate; R.C. Duffy, Ferryhill Town Council; Revd Kevin Dunne, South Hetton; Arnold Ellis, South Hetton; Lena Fairless, Byers Green; Ralph Hughes, Shotton; Caroline Imlah, Tyne and Wear Museums; Jim McManus, Cassop County Junior and Infants School; Gordon Penman, Durham Aged Mineworkers' Homes Association; Tom Renny, Hetton-le-Hole; Lily Ross, Burnhope; Arthur Scorer, Chester-le-Street District Council; G. Shaw, Seaham; George Shield, Ferryhill; Gerry Steinberg MP, Durham; Revd John Stephenson, All Saints' Church, Eppleton; John Sudder, lodge chairman, Bradley Shops; John Taylor, No Place; John Temple, South Shields Labour Party; Dave Wallace, Chilton; Terry and Tony Watson, Kibblesworth; and John Williams, Haswell.

Officials and members of staff of Murton Welfare; Washington 'F' Pit Museum; Durham Heritage Centre; Gateshead Civic Centre; Spennymoor Town Hall; Durham Town Hall; Castle View County Secondary Modern School, Sunderland; Deaf Hill, Esh Winning, Harraton and District, Trimdon Grange and Wheatley Hill Community Associations; and the stewards and committees of North Road Social Club, Boldon colliery; Kibblesworth Working Men's Club; Usworth and District Workmen's Club; Usworth and Washington Gardeners Club; and Westwood Club also allowed access to banners.

Information on banners, and assistance with locations, was provided by Errol Black, Brandon University, Brandon, Manitoba, Canada; Billy Calvert, Silksworth; John Foster, Hartlepool; Myrtle MacPherson, Easington; Million Makepeace, Butterknowle; Barbara Morrow, High Shincliffe; Spennymoor & Newton Aycliffe Trades Union Council; O. Tchoubar, Consulate General of the Russian Federation; and Jim Tuck.

Comparative material was made available in other parts of Britain thanks to the staff of the National Museum of Labour History, Manchester; the Timothy Hackworth Victorian and Railway Museum, Shildon; Hazel Edwards, Woodhorn Colliery Museum, Northumberland; Rosemary Preece, Yorkshire Mining Museum, Caphouse colliery; Jeanette Harbron, Dorman Museum, Middlesbrough; and Mrs J. Flynn, Tow Law Community Association.

The staff of Paradise Silk Mill Museum, Macclesfield, were of great assistance in explaining the technicalities of the Jacquard loom.

During the documentary and photographic research I received invaluable help from Jennifer Gill, David Butler and the staff of Durham County Record Office; the staff of the Public Record Office (Kew and Chancery Lane); the Greater London Record Office; the British Library, Newspaper Library; Somerset House; Companies House; the library staff at Bishop Auckland, Darlington, Durham City, Durham University, Ferryhill, Spennymoor, Newcastle and Manchester; Sandra Morrison, Sedgefield Borough Council; Bob Davis, the Northern Film and Television Archive; the library staff of the *Northern Echo* and *Sunderland Echo*; and the staff of Beamish Museum, particularly Rosemary Allen and Jim Lawson.

I would like to thank the Dean and Chapter, Durham Cathedral for permission to reproduce part of the 1995 Miners' Service sheet; and the Revd Martin King, for permission to quote from his sermon at the 1996 dedication of the Trimdon Grange banner.

I am extremely grateful to Beamish, The North of England Open Air Museum; British Coal; The British Library; Mr W. Calvert; Durham County Record Office; Durham University Library; Gateshead Libraries and Art Service; Newsquest (North East) Ltd; Northeast Press Ltd, *Sunderland Echo*; Scorpion Cavendish; Mr D. Scott; Sedgefield Borough Council; and Miss A. Thompson for permission to reproduce photographs.

Dr Jan Rhodes, Mr Trevor Wood, Anne Sayers, Bob Davis, and Fine-Cut Facilities helped to bring the work to completion.

Particular thanks also go to John Gorman, and Ann Clwyd MP for their interest in the research; and to my parents for their help and support.

It is a particular pleasure to thank Dame Catherine Cookson for her generous help and support. Without her assistance this book might not have been published. I am extremely grateful.

# Introduction

The second half of the nineteenth century saw the rapid expansion of coalmining in the north-east of England, reaching a peak just before the First World War. Coal was exported, or used in this country, and the high-rank coals of western Durham were converted to coke for blast-furnace use. The limited reserves of iron ore in west and north-west Durham were exploited by a number of inland iron works, but the exploitation of the ore in the Cleveland Hills, from the 1840s, saw the rise of iron and steel production around Teesside. The workers for these industries were housed either in new settlements or in terraces around existing villages. As these new communities developed, so the features of village life appeared – the school, institute, Co-op store, pub, church and chapel – some to survive, some to decay, as the years went by and the patterns of life and work changed.

Groups and societies were formed – the trade union at the work-place, the Friendly Society, the Sunday School, temperance groups, or political parties. Many of these groups chose to make, or purchase, a banner, a distinct emblem, the symbol of their identity. Banners were also produced to proclaim a very visible message, on some political, industrial, or social question, and were numerous and wide-ranging. Many of these were designed for, and related to, a particular event, and were only expected to be used for a short period. In 1872, for instance, there was considerable agitation among women throughout the colliery villages over sudden increases in the cost of butchers' meat, just as their menfolk had received a pay rise. The women linked together in a virtual union, and held mass meetings at which they fixed the prices they were willing to pay, and some offending butchers were assaulted. Tudhoe women acquired a blue-and-white calico banner inscribed:

> Live and let live.
> The wives are first class union men.
> The butchers they'll defeat;
> As sure as 5 and 5 make ten
> They'll bring down butchers meat.
> For ever.[1]

In the North-East, the Durham Miners' Association, the Northumberland Miners' Mutual Confident Association, the Cleveland Miners' and Quarrymen's Association, and a number of allied unions, all purchased large and ornate banners, as did several earlier northern unions which did not survive. Although the banner might not be used very often, it was the lodge or branch symbol and a rallying point, equivalent to the battle standard of a regiment. During the 1879 county coal strike, Mrs Sharp spoke of this aspect at a solidarity mass meeting of miners' wives on Pelton Fell. She spoke of the struggle and urged, 'Let us be like soldiers' wives and stick to our colours and our banners. Never let us lose heart and give in.'[2]

While the majority of historic trade union banners in the North-East relate to the coal industry, a number of other old banners have survived, including examples from the Cleveland Miners' and Quarrymen's Association, the Iron and Steel Trades Confederation, National Union of Agricultural Workers, and National Union of Railwaymen. In churches and chapels around the country, banners were also present. Most Anglican churches, for instance, had a Mothers' Union bannerette, with an embroidered Marian image. The Methodist Big Meeting in 1957 had a procession of witness to Durham Cathedral, and the groups certainly carried large, professionally made banners.[3] In 1880 seventeen Anglican, Wesleyan, New Connexion, Presbyterian and Congregational schools came to Durham to celebrate the centenary of the Sunday School movement: 'There were only two bands, but each school carried neat and artistic banners, containing the name of the school to which they belonged and other suitable inscriptions, such as "forward be our watchword", and "simply to the cross I cling".'[4] Some Church of England schools still have banners today.[5] Also, closely associated with the religious groups was the temperance movement, and several Bands of Hope around the region possessed banners.

Many banners were also produced for the Women's Sections of the Labour Party, which developed after 1918, and which, like the miners, held important, well-attended annual demonstrations in Durham from 1923. The banners, like those of the Women' Suffrage movement,[6] and the Co-operative Women's Guilds,[7] were smaller than the trade union banners, and were usually locally made, of appliqué or embroidered work, or with paintings. The green-and-white colours of Labour and the Labour Party badge were common elements, while the designs were either textual, thematic paintings, or portraits.[8] New banners, with distinctive illustrations, were produced for the Miners' Support Groups at the time of the 1984–5 strike.

The woven silk banner, hung on a carrying frame and blown in the wind like a sail, was prone to damage. Tears were common, while the conditions of storage and the effects of displaying a banner by leaving it hanging for long periods of time have created a whole range of restoration and conservation problems.

Rule 40 of the 1980 NUM (Durham Area) Rules indicated that when a lodge closed, it was a requirement that 'All books, accounts, papers or other documents or goods of the lodge . . . shall be sent or returned to the registered office of the Union' (p. 22). In the 1988 NUM (North-East Area) rule book, rule 38.D covered the question of a lodge closure and the transfer of goods to Red Hill, and more specifically included within this category, 'emblems' (p. 34). Some banners sent to Red Hill were later transferred to other lodges which required one, with the result that the lodge name, and sometimes other details, were overpainted. A group of banners from Red Hill were passed to Beamish Museum: The North of England Open-Air Museum, principally in 1984. Several banners, however, were not sent to Red Hill, but were retained and given pride of place in a community building. Others, unfortunately, were stored away and 'lost'. Some have since been found, like the Tanfield Lea banner, located under a hall stage. Workmen, removing slates during the demolition of Sunnybrow welfare hall, discovered the nineteenth-century Rough Lea banner, covered in dust, in the roof-space. As the coalmining industry in Durham has now been destroyed by the last Conservative government, there is a policy to have the remaining banners, held at Red Hill, restored and sent back to the communities which once owned them, and to have them securely and sensitively displayed in community buildings, like chapels, community centres and workmen's clubs.

The study of banners and their history was stimulated by the publication of *Banner Bright*, by John Gorman, in 1973. This pioneering work, with an important introduction by Gwyn Williams, covered a wide range of British trade union banners. This book was re-published, with additions, in 1986, and includes a number of Durham banners. Banners also appeared in two books which looked at the broader subject of 'folk art' – Anthony Lewery's *Popular Art Past and Present*, published in 1991, and Emmanuel Cooper's *People's Art. Working Class Art from 1750 to the Present Day*, which followed in 1994.

In County Durham an exhibition of lodge banners was mounted in the Durham Light Infantry Museum and Arts Centre at the beginning of 1973, and was accompanied by a book by William Moyes, *Banner Parade*. This served as an introductory work and was followed in 1974 by *The Banner Book*, which drew together photographs and banner details while highlighting the problem of locating 'lost' banners. This book went out of print, but, as part of a display of banners at the 1986 Gala, a souvenir brochure, *Durham Miners' Banners*, was produced by David Jones, in collaboration with the DMA. This work detailed forty-one Durham banners. Since then an attempt has been made to establish a record of banners, surviving and long gone, as an archive of Durham's mining heritage. This book incorporates the collected record and examines the banner – their makers, the techniques of production, the designs and mottoes, their history and use.

# CHAPTER 1

# Banner Makers

In the latter half of the nineteenth century Durham miners' lodges purchased their banners principally from the south of England. In London, George Tutill, W. Elam, and H. Hales supplied banners for the earliest Galas in the 1870s. H. Slingsby in Nuneaton, West Midlands, H. Whaite in Manchester and Messrs Riley & Co. in Leeds, West Yorkshire, also supplied early banners, as did a small group of north-eastern firms: S.M. Peacock and R. Hodge of South Shields and Bainbridges and George Cooper & Co., both of Newcastle.

Of these manufacturers, George Tutill was to dominate the market. He was born in 1818 at Howden, Yorkshire, and it is thought that, in his early years, he had showground connections, where there was a long tradition of banner art, going back at least to the eighteenth-century fairs.[1] These canvas show-cloths were used to advertise the different exhibits, waxworks, boxing-booths and freak shows, and were often elaborately painted. He set up in business in 1837, and was married and living in London when his daughter, Georgina, was born in 1855. In 1857 he was living at 8 Angel Terrace, St Peter's Street, Islington, operating as an artist,[2] but in 1859 he moved to 14 Douglas Road, Canonbury.[3] In the same year he concentrated his business at 83 City Road, on the east side of the thoroughfare, between Cowper Street and Leonard Street, on the borders of the East End of London.[4] The location of the factory in this area was probably influenced by the fact that it had a long association with silk weaving.

The British silk industry had a medieval origin, but the arrival of Protestant Huguenot silk workers to England, particularly to London, as a result of religious persecution in France following the revocation of the Edict of Nantes in 1685 and economic necessity, boosted its production and quality.[5] These émigrés settled principally in the area of Bishopgate, Shoreditch, Bethnal Green, Mile End, Whitechapel and Spitalfields. By the late eighteenth century measures were being taken to protect the industry in London. In 1766 importation of French silks was prohibited; and as silk manufacture gradually began to move out of London to counties like Lancashire and Somerset, affecting employment among silk

Day's Menagerie, at
Hull Fair in 1892,
displaying the large
painted showcloths.

workers in the Metropolis, the 1773 Spitalfields Act was introduced, whereby magistrates regulated the wages of journeymen weavers. The Act kept labour prices high and caused discontent among the employers, forcing many to buy in cheaper thrown silks from the country operators. By 1821 around 48–50,000 silk workers were employed in Spitalfields, out of a total UK figure of 500,000. From 1826 these measures were repealed.

Three types of silk were imported into Britain: bulk waste, principally from France; raw silk; and thrown silk. Raw silk had mainly come from France and the Empire (through the development of a production system linking the British East Indies and India). In 1842 1,156,498 lb were imported from the former country, and 1,359,599 lb from the colonies; however, with fluctuations, the imports fell markedly over the next ten years.[6] This was compensated for by a substantial increase in the purchase of Chinese silk, rising from 180,124 lb in 1842 to 4,576,706 lb by 1855. Thrown silk imports fluctuated in the 1840s and 1850s, with a series of peaks and troughs. France had been the principal supplier to Britain in the early 1840s, but an outbreak of silkworm disease resulted in her goods falling to almost a third of British requirements by the mid-1850s. However, the Free Trade movement, and particularly the Cobdens–Chevalier treaty with France in 1860, removed the protection which the home industry had enjoyed since 1766, with serious results. Continental silk goods flooded the market, and in Britain unemployment levels rose, leading to an inevitable decline in many parts of the East End of London, where there were areas of acute poverty and dereliction. There was also substantial emigration from other centres, like Macclesfield, where around 15,000 left for America, principally to the silk works of Patterson, New Jersey.[7]

Banner production continued, but Tutill undertook two major developments which were to increase the quality and prestige of his products. Firstly, he had been carrying out experiments on the treatment of the banner, particularly to create a more pliable paint. This he achieved using india-rubber, a substance which began to be commercially exploited around 1800, using latex from the forests of the Amazon basin, and which had increased in importance and output in the 1830s with the development of vulcanized rubber. Tutill patented his technique on 6 July 1861, reporting that 'the materials are rendered more durable, pliant, flexible and elastic, and that the paint is not liable to crack, or become detached from the banner or flag or other article, thus causing the design to last for a much longer time than is at present the case; and also that by this method a banner or flag can be produced in a much less space of time than by the ordinary process'.[8]

The second improvement occurred with the introduction of a Jacquard loom to the City Road factory, produced by Henry Maddox, a silk machine manufacturer of 479 Bethnal Green Road. This loom, the product of an amalgamation and development of a series of existing French designs, was created by J.M. Jacquard in 1804, and used punch cards, carrying the design data, to operate the shedding. This type of loom appeared in Britain around 1818, and was gradually taken up by the fabric and carpet industries during the 1820s, and particularly from 1837.[9]

By 1861 Tutill was a widower, but he remarried, and moved to Red House, Upton Lane, West Ham.[10] He died in 1887 and was buried in the family grave at Howden. His will allotted Red House, and the business, to his daughter, Georgina, who had by that time married Charles Henry Lewis.[11] Arrangements were made that William Henry Smith, Tutill's clerk, should manage the business on Georgina's behalf, but not as a partner. Georgina appears to have remarried, for by the 1930s the business was in the hands of Tutill's grandson, Lewis Henry Storey. He operated the firm under the name 'George Tutill & S.W. Wolff & Co'.

During the Second World War the City Road area was bombed and although the block between Cowper and Leonard streets (nos 73–95) generally suffered minor and general blast effects, no. 83 received such serious damage that it was not considered repairable.[12] The Jacquard loom

An advert showing the nations of the world coming to Tutill for banners and regalia.

was recovered, though never used again, and a quantity of woven silk banner blanks survived.

The banner makers, Turtle & Pearce, took on the operation of the George Tutill & S.W. Wolff business, but by an agreement of 1941, Turtle & Pearce sold it on to a new company, George Tutill Ltd, a banner-making business based at 9 Higham Road, Chesham, Buckinghamshire.[13] The directors of the new company, Henry M. Killik, W.S. Chandler and Eric M. Killik, were also directors of Turtle & Pearce.

The firm of Turtle & Pearce Ltd was founded in 1872 and operated from 13 Duke Street. In 1900 they were manufacturing printed and

The Edmondsley (later Blackhouse) banner by William Elam, showing William Crawford, Joseph Cowen and William Patterson.

'pattern dyed' flags, banners and bunting, and supplying to the Board of Trinity and Colonial Port Trusts, the principal shipping companies, and yacht clubs. Around 1964–5 the company moved to 31 Tanner Street. In the early 1980s they made banners for Dawdon, Eppleton, Sacriston, Monkwearmouth and Murton lodges.

Of the other London makers, William Elam started up as a flag maker in 1866, at 58 Pollard Row, Bethnal Green Road, where he produced banners in the 1870s for Byers Green, Edmondsley and Lizzie lodges.[14] In 1874 he moved to 257 Hackney Road, where the banner of the Durham Colliery Enginemen's and Boiler Minders' Association was painted in 1900.[15] He continued as a silk banner maker until 1904.[16]

Also in London, Henry Hales began as a masonic and theatrical trimmings manufacturer, at 16 Marquis Court, Drury Lane, in 1857.[17] He moved briefly, around 1861, to 20 Bow Street, Covent Garden, but in 1863–4 he transferred his operations to 40 Wellington Street, the Strand.[18] It was here that he produced a number of Durham banners in

The Good Samaritan on
the Westerton banner,
by Henry Hales.

the early 1870s, including one for Westerton. Hales described his trade
as a 'manufacturer of regalia for all societies and stage and tinsel
trimmings, gold embroidery, silk banner painter, caterer for talent at
fêtes, and costumier'.[19] A newspaper correspondent at the 1873 Gala
was not, however, terribly complimentary about the quality of the banner
painting:

> Not a few of the metropolitan productions were execrable as works of
> art, and it was difficult to say whether the poverty of ideas displayed,
> or the clumsiness of the execution were the most deserving of
> reprobation. One of the banners we are referring to was from
> Wellington Street, Strand, and while the banner itself was of the

richest and most costly material, the artistic portion of it would have been considered a disgrace to any Durham house painter.[20]

Henry continued in business up to 1886, but by 1887 Thomas Hales had taken over. He ran the firm up to 1901, when he was joined by Thomas Gardiner Hales, who normally ran a livery stable at King's Head Yard, Russell Street, Covent Garden. T.G. Hales operated both businesses, but dropped the tinsel lace making in 1908, running the livery stable until 1913.

Henry Whaite of Manchester produced banners for Philadelphia, Thornley and Houghton lodges, which were carried at the 1872 Gala. Whaite began in business as a carver and gilder at Bridge Street in 1823, but by the 1830s had also moved into print selling and fancy stationery. He began painting banners around 1845, and to sell artists' materials – watercolours, oils, brushes, pencils and paper. This led to the establishment of the 'Fine Art Gallery' at 64 Bridge Street in 1856, which, four years later, became the venue for a series of exhibitions and sales of works by many artists.[21] In 1887 the operation moved from Bridge Street into the adjoining thoroughfare of Deansgate, and soon afterwards additional premises were taken in Blackfriars Street. It continued with fine art dealing, and flag and banner making, while diversifying into the supply of tents for fêtes and the decoration of bazaars and ballrooms. By 1910, however, the addresses were considered to be a fine art repository,[22] and in 1911–12 the business was taken over by Jeremiah Bibby & Co., a firm set up in 1843. Their early history seems to have been as tent dealers, but by the 1870s they were making flags, banners and bunting.

In Warwickshire, silk ribbon weaving was a staple industry, at centres like Coventry, Nuneaton, Bedworth and Foleshill. At the beginning of the nineteenth century Coventry had 2,260 engine looms and 1,008 hand looms, while Nuneaton had 500 engines and 1,000 hand looms.[23] The weaving industry had three levels – masters, middlemen or undertakers (although their role was on the decline) and operative weavers. The undertaker received the manufacturing order from a master, and the silk for the job. He passed this to the weaver to make up, but was responsible for the quality of the work, the payment for the warping and winding, and the looms and shop room. The weavers were divided into two classes: single breadth, making single figured ribbons on a loom, and engine weavers, who produced from eight to twenty-eight plain ribbons per loom.

In 1843 Henry Slingsby founded a ribbon-weaving business in Nuneaton, but the Free Trade treaty of 1860 seriously affected Nuneaton's staple industry. Slingsby survived by diversifying into the manufacture of 'regalia, emblematical scarfs, collars, badges, ribbons, banners etc' for the Friendly Society and trade union market.[24] Slingsby's took skeined and hanked Chinese and continental silk and wove it at the Seymour Road works, using Jacquard looms. Among their work was the huge 1909 banner of Randolph lodge. The firm passed from father to son, Henry, and

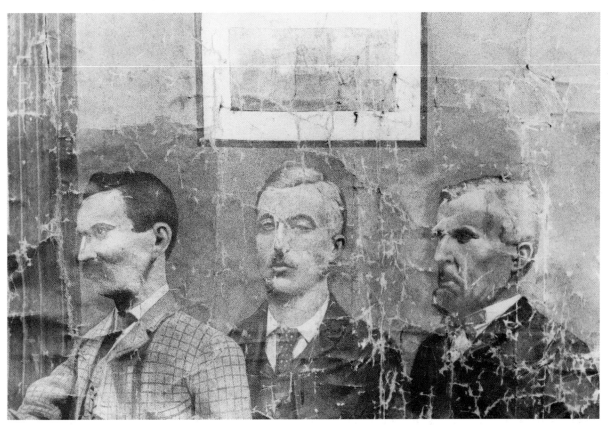

A fragment of the 1892
Deaf Hill banner, by
Bainbridge of
Newcastle.

on to grandson, M.C.B. Slingsby. It became a limited liability company in
1912, but the mill was closed down in 1942 under the government scheme
for the concentration of materials and labour during the war.[25] It was
reopened, under William Franklin & Son of Coventry, in 1947.

Edward Riley & Co. of Leeds produced the 1909 Littleburn banner.
This firm is recorded in directories from 1900 to 1955, producing bunting,
flags and banners at Providence Mills, in Providence Street. They were
one of three such firms listed in the 1913 Leeds Chamber of Commerce
Year Book, and were considered, there, as a branch of the clothing
industry.

The Bewicke Main, Hebburn and Wallsend, and Hetton collieries
banners, carried at the 1872 and 1873 Galas, bore the mark of Bainbridge
of Newcastle. The firm was established by Emerson Muschamp
Bainbridge in 1841, as silk mercers and drapers.[26] Although they were
principally involved with fashion goods, buying in from principal
manufacturers, which did include British and foreign silks, they must have
purchased woven banner silk grounds. The paintings were done by T.S.
Bowman, at his studio at 50 Grainger Street, or by William Gowdy.
Gowdy also painted the Townley banner, in use in 1873, which was

supplied by George Cooper & Co., of 83 Clayton Street, Newcastle. Cooper was a paper stainer, painter and manufacturer of looking-glasses, but also did house and church decorating.[27]

An early Lambton banner bears the mark of S.M. Peacock of South Shields. The commercial directories first record an S.M. Peacock – Samuel Morley Peacock – in 1894, but as a Prudential agent, at 35 Baring Street.[28] However, by 1897 an S.M. Peacock was running two businesses – as a fine art dealer at 4 Albion Terrace and as a china dealer in Ocean Road.[29] The business seems to have been principally concerned with the glass, china and 'fancy goods' trade, but this may have been a sideline while he acted as a commission agent for the Prudential. Both activities were being pursued in 1914, but are not recorded by 1921.

Another South Shields artist, Robert Hodge, produced the 1901 Browney banner. Post Office directories suggest that between 1890 and 1894 he started operating at 13 Baring Street,[30] but by 1897 was at 18 Victoria Terrace.[31] No reference is made to him in directories from 1902. Hodge is also known to have produced a banner for the South Shields branch of the Boilermakers' and Iron and Steel Shipbuilders' Society.[32]

Some of the early banners were made and painted on site. The Pelton Fell banner at the 1872 Gala, for instance, had been drawn out and painted by a local miner – his first attempt. John Pickett, the lodge secretary, wrote to the editor of the *Durham Chronicle* objecting to a reporter's criticism of the quality and accuracy of the painting, and won some free publicity when his letter was published: 'any of your numerous readers who may want banners or paintings might give him a trial.'[33]

In the 1960s two banners were produced for Durham lodges by Sharp Studios in Hitchin – the 1962 Washington 'F' pit banner and the 1966 Horden banner. In both cases the central designs were painted by Pauline Traill.

After the 1984–5 strike a small number of new banners were purchased. The banners of the NUM North East Area, and Murton and Westoe lodges were produced by Chippenham Design, of Overstrand, Norfolk, and were heavily influenced by the experiences of that great struggle.

CHAPTER 2

# The Banner

## *Construction, Form and Layout*

Silk is formed as a development stage in the life cycle of the moth *Bombyx mori*. The moth's eggs are laid on the leaves of the mulberry, which becomes the principal food source when the eggs develop into worms. The worm consumes the leaves, expanding and bursting out of its skin several times, before beginning to spin a cocoon of silk threads around itself, glued together with sericin, from which it will eventually emerge as a moth. The cocoons are gathered before this final stage and the worms are killed (or stifled). By soaking in warm water, the sericin is broken down, and the silk thread of the cocoon can be drawn out.

The raw silk is then 'thrown'. The hanks of silk, set up on reels, or 'swifts' (a form of six-spoked wheel), are drawn out into bobbins, before undergoing a twisting process which strengthens the yarn. Two or more filaments, on their separate bobbins, are then wound together and further twisted, before being wound onto another bobbin. The silk is subsequently scoured to remove any remaining gum, leaving it in a state ready for dyeing.

Before the latter part of the nineteenth century most dyes were vegetable extracts, like madder, turmeric, lichens and indigo, which came from the East, principally Bengal, fixed to the fabric with a mordant, like alum. In the eighteenth century indigodisulphonic acid, a man-made indigo derivative was introduced as 'Saxe Blue', but was not truly synthetic. The first synthetic dye, mauveine, was derived from aniline, a coal-tar product, in 1856. New dyes followed rapidly onto the market, like aniline black in 1863, and synthetic indigo, invented in 1880 but not commercially viable until after 1897.

In the weaving of cloth, the warp threads are laid parallel, longitudinally, on the loom, and the weft thread is passed, by means of a shuttle, in an arranged order, under and over various warp threads. For the weft thread, a full bobbin was hung in a frame, and the thread drawn out and wound onto a 'pirn', which is fixed onto a winder, like a spinning

A wheel used to wind
threads onto a pirn
ready for the shuttle.
Paradise Silk Mill,
Macclesfield.

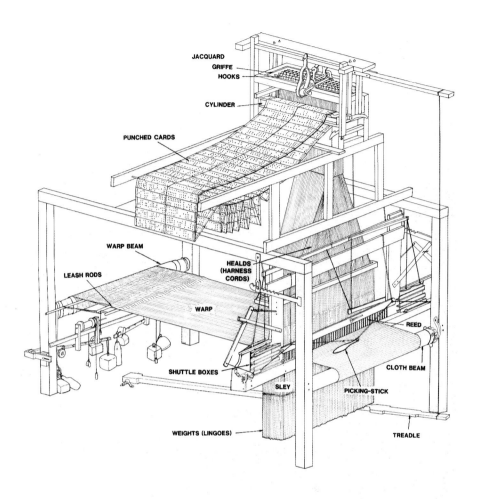

The elements of a Jacquard loom.

wheel. By turning the wheel, the pirn is spun and the thread is wound onto it. Two completed pirns will then fit into a shuttle, and the thread is drawn through an eye in the side of the shuttle. For the warp, bobbins are set up on a frame, or 'creel', and the threads are drawn through a frame and a comb, or 'reed', onto a wood-framed roller and wound in sections. From this frame the threads are passed over a 'stretcher roller' and onto an empty wooden 'warp roller' or 'warp beam', the layers separated by sheets of paper. This is then set up at the back of the loom. From here the warp threads are passed between 'leash rods' and laboriously threaded through the eyes of the harness cords (healds). The threads pass through the 'splits' or gaps in the teeth of a comb, also known as a 'reed', before being attached to the 'cloth beam' at the front of the loom. The reed hangs from a frame on which is fixed a shelf, or 'sley', with shuttle boxes at each end.

Tutill used the Jacquard system to create elaborate designs in the woven silk. The pattern to be woven was first laid out on 'point paper' (a form of

The Jacquard operating system, with the griffe, hooks and cylinder at the top, and the punch-cards which influence the movement of the warp threads. Paradise Silk Mill, Macclesfield.

graph paper design sheet) and the arrangement for raising particular warp threads was marked on it. These details were then transferred by punching the data into strips of millboard card using a piano-card cutter. These punched cards were leashed together, just like continuous computer paper, racked in a card cradle on top of the loom and set onto the take-up sprockets of a square-sectioned 'cylinder', forming part of the Jacquard mechanism.

A series of hooks, from which were hung the healds holding the warp threads, were pivoted on spring-mounted needles. When the weaving process was in operation and a card tracked through, over the cylinder, it would be held against the ends of the needles. The needles either engaged holes in the card, or hit and were deflected by an unpunched part of the card, so that when the weaver pressed down the foot treadle, it would raise a multi-bladed knife beam, or 'griffe', which, in turn, would lift up the vertical hooks and the associated healds and warp threads, while the deflected hooks would remain unmoved and the associated warp threads would stay horizontal. The creation of the space between the flat and the raised warp threads was called a 'shed', providing a route through which the shuttle (carrying the weft thread or 'pick') passed.

The flying shuttle, developed by John Kay in 1733, was propelled though the shed when the weaver pulled a 'picking stick', hung on cords in front of him and linked to a mechanism which pulled the 'picker'. This knocked the shuttle from its box and sent it the length of the sley, to a box at the other end. As it ran through, the weft thread was drawn out. The weaver then released the treadle and pulled the sley towards him, so that the reed comb beat, or 'bumped up', the newly laid weft thread, before the process started again. Thus the fabric for the banner was gradually built up.

Two early banners of the Tursdale branch of the Durham Miners' Association survive, where the construction comprised two sheets, each with its own design, stitched together, back-to-back. George Tutill, and other makers, advanced from this type to the large single sheet banner. This type of banner comprised a woven silk ground – either the 'patent-woven' form of damask silk done on the Jacquard loom, or a plain silk, on which was applied a painted design – a border, trimmed at the base with a fringe of one or two colours, sometimes interwoven, and a tough top heading braid with a series of loops, usually from eleven to fifteen in number. These loops took the cross pole and were generally nailed to it. This pole was then secured to two carrying poles.

The design to be placed on the silk was done in stages. The increasing sub-division of labour in the manufacture of goods in late nineteenth-century Britain, seen from porcelain painters to the sweatshop jobs in tailoring and the boot trade, also extended to banner making, with artists specializing in particular aspects of the design. Tutill noted that among his staff 'are clever artists who excel in special branches of art; for instance, an architectural subject would be painted by a man who thoroughly understands such work, but a portrait or a figure subject would be executed by other artists, who make such work their exclusive study'.[1] The firm's artists included Herbert Sharpe, who painted the 1935 Chopwell 'Red' banner; and Barry Clarke and Barbara Salford, who worked at Chesham in the 1960s.[2] Fred Mann, the studio manager at Chesham, did much of the signwriting.

The decoration on the banner increasingly followed a fairly standard pattern. At the top of the silk ground was a long, usually curved ribbon. This carried the name of the organization: initially 'Durham Miners' Association' and later 'National Union of Mineworkers'. In some cases the name of the lodge would be included at this stage. The letters tended to be roman-based, generally in yellow or white and shaded to give a raised, three-dimensional effect. They were set on a bordered ribbon which was usually reddish-orange, light blue or green. In some cases transfer gold was used on the border. The ribbon was usually surrounded by elaborate scrollwork, like curling foliage, which hung down, flanking the main illustration. This feature was sometimes associated with flower-heads, tasselled cords, or even putti with cornucopia. The ribbon was set above the main illustration, painted within a roundel, on a shield, or a moulded panel. This sometimes incorporated a top label recording the name of the lodge and, in the case of an NUM banner, the area. Alternatively these details might be placed on strips or ribbons between the main top ribbon and the panel. The panel might also incorporate a base label indicating the title of the illustration, or a motto. The reverse side tended to follow the basic layout of the obverse, but with a different central illustration. Sometimes the inscription on the top ribbon would be changed to incorporate a title or motto relating to the subject of the painting.

At Tutill's City Road works the artists worked in long studios, including a gallery added in about 1895, with high windows and skylights providing natural light. Work benches were set up over pipes which ran down the centre of the studios, on which were kept the paints, thinners, brushes and other materials needed by the artists. The silk sheet was stretched tightly in a wooden frame and, after the design and drawing out stages, the painting started with the basic central roundel, shield or panel, and the ornamentation; the principal central painting was then added, followed by the lettering, and fine touching, including bordering and shading.

The paintings on Tutill banners were built up in stages. First, a thin solution of india-rubber was brushed on, and allowed to dry. A second coat, mixed with linseed oil, was then applied. Once that was dry, a paint undercoat was added to form a ground on which the design could be painted. This was done using a standard palette, brushes and maulstick. Tutill advised his customers, 'Banners painted at my leisure in the autumn and winter months are far more durable than those hurriedly executed in the busy season, because sufficient time is allowed for the work to get thoroughly dry and properly set before the Banner is used.' A more recent example, Barry Ormsby's Tursdale Mechanics' banner, was produced using acrylics.

The fabric for the bordering of traditional banners was around 6 in (15 cm) to 8 in (20.5 cm) in width, woven on a small loom, and stitched to the main ground. The heading braid fixed to the top of the banner was a stout fabric, around 1.75 in (3.2 cm) wide, with loops of similar width. A silk twisted bullion fringe, from 3 in (7.5 cm) to 5 in (12.7cm) in height, was then stitched to the base of the banner. At the City Road works this trimming was added by women in an upper gallery.

The loops of the heading braid took the cross pole. This was a circular-sectioned wooden pole, occasionally silvered, with brass end caps, each of which held a steel swivel loop. This formed a means of attachment to the two vertical carrying poles, usually stained and varnished. Again, these had a brass top cap with a socket which took the screw shaft of the lacquered brass spearhead, threaded through the steel loops of the cross pole. The spearhead was around 9.25 in (23.5 cm) long, and cast in a mould, either solid or hollow. Several forms of head were used. One type used with Tutill banners was decorated with a plain shield, a curling foliage design and the name and address, 'G TUTILL LTD CITY ROAD LONDON'. The carrying poles were either single shafts, or in two sections which were slotted together. Most of the poles were wood, but some recent examples, like the 1980 South

Hetton banner, had plastic poles. The rounded or reduced ends of the banner poles fitted into the brass cups of the carrying harness. The tubular cup was 73 mm high and 35 mm in diameter, with a brass loop through which a leather belt was threaded. Two types of harness were used. The simplest was a looped belt hung around the neck. A modified form, used by lodges like Harton and Westoe, incorporated a linked waist belt.

From the top of each carrying pole hung guide ropes, usually woollen cords, one run out and held ahead of the banner, the other behind. These ropes were finely produced, with elaborate finishings and tassels, often exquisitely bound with intricate threadwork. On some banners guide tapes were attached at the bottom corners of the main silk ground, either with a fabric rosette, or threaded through the loop at the bottom of a brass disc. The brass type is usually found on Tutill banners. They are 1.5 in (4 cm) in diameter and are inscribed 'G TUTILL / 83 CITY ROAD / LONDON' across the centre, with 'SOLE MANUFACTURER OF PATENT BANNERS' around the rim. The tape is around 1.5 in (4 cm) wide, and often up to 5 ft 8 in (1.73 m) long, though generally reduced to a suitable length by the person holding the tape, by looping and knotting it.

Manufacturers' details appear on many of the banners. Some of the earlier Tutill City Road marks are found on the silk, below the central illustration. Later, the City Road address appears in threadwork at a corner of the damask silk banners. On the banners of Eden, New Herrington, Pittington and Sacriston (1919), TUTILL LONDON is inscribed at the base of the scene. This practice continued when Tutill moved to Chesham, with TUTILL–CHESHAM appearing in the painting, sometimes with a record number. Where damask silks, woven at the City Road works and bearing that address, were painted at Chesham, a discreet Chesham address label was stitched onto the top braid of the banner. This is usually a small rectangular piece of white fabric, 1.25 in × 0.75 in (3 × 2 cm), with red lettering: 'George Tutill Ltd. / 9 Higham Road / Chesham, Bucks'. Examples can still be seen on the Eden, Monkwearmouth, Whitworth Park and Witton banners. Occasionally Tutill banners incorporate the date of manufacture, discreetly painted on miners' tokens, often found lying beside a safety lamp, and used as infill at the borders of a central scene. Turtle & Pearce banners are usually marked on the edge of the central painting: 'TURTLE & PEARCE LTD. LONDON S.E. 1', with a code number and the last two digits of the year. They may also carry an attached maker's label on a guide tape. These are white fabric, 1.75 in × 1 in (4.4 × 2.5 cm), with the details in red lettering: 'TURTLE & PEARCE LTD. FLAG MAKER 31, TANNER STREET LONDON SE1 3GQ TEL. NO. 014071301'. With the details is a witty logo showing a turtle pierced by an arrow. Banners by Chippenham Design carry a discreet manufacturer's label on the fabric ground, inscribed simply 'CHIPPENHAM'.

# Banner Illustrations and Images

The choice of banner design was made either by using a manufacturer's pattern-book or by holding a competition among the membership to produce a design, from which the best image was chosen by the lodge committee, or both. A few of the designers are known and are recorded in the catalogue of lodge banners in Chapter 5. Both men and women submitted designs for the competition.

The pattern-book images are discussed below in the next section of this chapter (Pattern-book designs). One lodge is also known to have used a design originally devised for another trade union. Two early Tursdale banners repeated, in modified form, an emblem produced for the Friendly Society of Iron Founders in 1857 by James John Chant and John Saddler.[3] The image was originally based around an architectural framework with three iron founding scenes divided by columns. Surmounting it is a stepped cornice on which stand two men holding tools, while an iron ore

The Tursdale banner design based on a Friendly Society membership card.

miner is shown hewing with a pick. Accompanying them are three women representing Art, Justice and Industry, with a knotted serpent, a beehive and a phoenix. Flanking the main structure are industrial, rural and marine scenes. On the left are factories by a river and a train crossing a bridge, while on the right is a horse-drawn plough at work and a steamship with sails. The Tursdale design replaced the iron ore miner with a huge beehive, and placed a set square and sextant with the knotted serpent.

Two banner designs were painted by the respected pitman-artist Norman Cornish. He worked at Dean and Chapter colliery, starting as an underground datal lad.[4] Art increasingly played an important part in his life; he attended a sketching club in Spennymoor, became a proficient draughtsman and his paintings contained evocative scenes of pit village life. His one-man show at the People's Theatre in Newcastle was followed by increasing involvement in exhibitions, paintings for the NCB and also the production of designs for the Westerton and Tudhoe Mill Drift banners.

Photographs were used on a few occasions in the preparation of the artwork. The design for the 1949 Brandon lodge banner, for instance, was taken from a photograph of the Gala gathering on the Racecourse by Charles Hodgson. The image for the Craghead banner, showing the 'traditional view' of Durham Cathedral, was submitted as a slide, with unfortunate consequences. The painted design on the banner was reversed! A slide taken at Westoe colliery during the 1984–5 strike, looking towards the Crown winder tower, was used to produce the Westoe mechanics' banner. The scene was projected onto the banner fabric, marked out in charcoal and then painted.[5]

The designs used on the banners are wide ranging, illustrating the aims, struggles and achievements of the union. They reflect the struggles for safety in mines, the nationalization of the industry, education, better housing, and general social improvement and development. The themes of fraternity extend from the unity of miners to international brotherhood. There is, in many, an idealism, a belief in a better world, a new world which could be achieved.

Portraits are predominantly male, representing lodge officials, DMA, MFGB and NUM leaders, or national political figures. Three icons dominate – John Wilson, Keir Hardie, and A.J. Cook. Unusually, a small group of literary figures are also to be found. Shakespeare's portrait appeared within a laurel wreath on the Wingate banner, probably produced by S.M. Peacock of South Shields. The portrait of Scotland's national poet, Robert Burns, appears on the Lambton lodge banner, also produced by S.M. Peacock. The illustration is taken from the portrait by Alexander Nasmyth, of 1787, now in the Scottish National Portrait Gallery. It is shown over the main painting of the cottage at Alloway, Ayrshire, where Burns was born on 25 January 1759. A small portrait also appears on the Wingate banner, alongside that of Shakespeare.

The Tudhoe Mill banner designed by Norman Cornish. The drift operated from 1954 to 1965.

The workplace does appear on banners, though colliery scenes illustrated in detail are not numerous. There are good examples of pitheads and associated buildings, for instance, on the banners of Eppleton (Jane shaft), Randolph and Silksworth, but underground scenes are comparatively rare. Associated with mining industry scenes is the image on the 1981 Eppleton

The 1962 Craghead banner, showing the reversed image of Durham Cathedral.

banner, based on a photograph dating from about 1903 of a rebuilt George Stephenson engine, designed to work on the Hetton railway in 1822, 'The Oldest working Locomotive in the World'. Middridge Drift lodge banner has a fine painting of a pony, without its harness, standing in a field, with the appropriate message, 'Lest we forget'. In 1937 there were 10,336 horses and ponies toiling alongside the miners in Durham pits, and the last 7 ponies retired from Sacriston colliery in 1984.

Common pattern-book images are representations of friendship, love, truth and justice, with the associated themes of caring for the sick and the bereaved. Some aspects of these themes are derived from the Bible, from both the Old and New Testaments, like the Good Samaritan, but other Biblical banner images have a hidden or alternative interpretation. An example is where David and Goliath are used to represent Labour and Capital. Other popular Biblical themes include 'Suffer the little children', 'O thou of little faith', and David and Goliath. The religious revival during the nineteenth century no doubt influenced the choice of these images and mottoes. While attendance at church and chapel was by no means universal, as the 1851 Religious Census of England and Wales has shown, in County Durham nonconformity, and particularly Methodism, had come to dominate the religious scene. Many of the DMA leaders, from William Crawford and John Wilson to Jack Lawson and Sam Watson, were Methodists, and in the lodges the officials were frequently members of a Methodist sect, with Primitive Methodism, in particular, being associated with radicalism and the development of trade unionism. Through time, however, two changes occurred: Methodism moved from pioneering missionary zeal to established respectability and gradual decline; and the union and its leadership made the political change from Liberalism to Socialism. However, religious images and mottoes continued to be chosen by lodges well into this century. Sometimes this may have been the lodge simply repeating an old and familiar design, or perhaps there was a mixing of Christian and Socialist themes, where the 'World for the workers' included social responsibility, with the caring image of the Good Samaritan and its motto, 'Go thou and do likewise', sitting well alongside the promised land of 'The Sunshine of Liberty', the 'Economic Commonwealth', and mottoes of 'Many can help one, where one cannot help many' (Greenside), 'Each for all, all for each' (Handon Hold), and 'Shield the Oppressed' (on a Westoe mechanics badge).

Many banners, including post-1945 NUM examples, incorporated ancient symbols. Life and death are portrayed, represented by the open book, the book of life, the corn stalks of life and fertility, the skull and crossbones and the hour-glass, the symbolism of passing life and death. God is portrayed as an all-seeing eye (usually a right eye), often set within rays of light. Other Christian symbols include the cross, the dove (sometimes crowned), as the life spirit, and the lamb, as innocence and purity. The themes of friendship, love, truth and justice are represented throughout by female figures, with associated symbols. Love and piety are also represented by the heart-and-hand design, most noticeably on the Rough Lea banner. Unity and labour are illustrated by clasped hands, the wheatsheaf and the beehive.

Buildings are frequently illustrated. Not surprisingly, one of the most popular buildings to appear on lodge banners is Durham Cathedral, the spiritual heart of the county. Begun in 1093 by William of St Calais, replacing a Saxon church, it was to house the remains of St Cuthbert and, later, those of Bede. The illustrations are predominately the 'traditional view', popular with artists for centuries, showing the west end towering above the River Wear and the wooded banks of the peninsula.

Two other churches, both Anglican, have achieved pride of place on banners – All Saints', Lanchester, on the Fenhall Drift banner and St Mary's, on the Horden banner. Lanchester church, with its west tower and clock, standing by the village green, is a twelfth-century structure, possibly incorporating pre-Conquest remains, including some stone from the Roman fort. Horden church was designed by Joseph Potts & Sons and built by William Pearson of West Hartlepool. It is massive in form, of artificial stone and pressed brick, with nave, transepts, lantern tower and chancel. Col. R. Burdon of Castle Eden, who owned the Horden estate and the coal royalty, gave the church as a gift to the people of Horden and it was consecrated on 26 April 1913. It is described on the banner as the 'Miners' Cathedral'.

Specific local structures are also depicted, like the fourteenth-century Hylton Castle on the local banner, the pier at South Shields, which appears

NATIONAL UNION OF MINEWORKERS

DURHAM AREA
RAMSHAW LODGE

DURHAM CATHEDRAL

A popular view of the west end of Durham Cathedral on the Ramshaw banner.

on the St Hilda (later South Moor No. 1) banner, or the long-since demolished Hetton Hall, at one time the home of the mining engineer Nicholas Wood, on the Eppleton lodge banner. Grahamsley lodge banner at the 1872 Gala actually showed the Wood Memorial Hall in Newcastle. The building, in Italian Gothic, to the designs of Archibald Dunn, was erected by public subscription in 1870, five years after Wood's death. Other illustrations of buildings are associated with mining and the pit village. The union's county headquarters in Durham, at North Road and Red Hill, appear on several banners, while Boldon and Seaham show their own miners' halls. Conishead Priory and The Hermitage were popular choices; the Sam Watson Rest Home at Richmond appears on the Langley

Park and NACODS banners; Easington has its welfare hall; and Brandon, the pavilion of the welfare ground. Depictions of aged miners' homes are particularly common, while the banner of Waterhouses illustrates the communal hall and homes at Esh Winning. County administration is also represented by a fine painting of the front of County Hall which appeared on the Langley Park (later East Hetton) banner. County Hall was built in reinforced concrete by John Laing & Sons Ltd, to the designs of G.R. Clayton, and opened on 14 October 1963. Set on a wall in the main public reception area is a large mural showing 'A Durham Miners' Gala Day' by Norman Cornish.

Roddymoor chose Burnhope reservoir for its banner illustration. The reservoir was created through the driving force of Peter Lee. Work began on 6 January 1930, and it was completed on 15 September 1937, enabling up to 1,357 million gallons of water to be made available to the people and industries of the county. One natural structure depicted is the limestone sea stack, Marsden rock, which appears on several versions of the local lodge banner.

## Pattern-book Designs

In the eighteenth and early nineteenth centuries, paintings and a number of publications of illustrations and designs were being used as pattern-books by craftsmen in, for instance, the production of particular styles of furniture. Banner and regalia manufacturers, like George Tutill, were also producing illustrated catalogues of their products. Certainly by the 1890s Tutill had gathered together a number of designs which would be suitable directly, or with minor modifications, for any trade union or group banner, and these pattern-books were sent out to prospective customers, with a price-list.

Many of the banner designs incorporate allegorical or mythological figures, and often a hotch-potch of symbolism. The use of allegorical figures with traditionally distinct attributes, or figures modified and carrying craft or other items, had appeared in dictionaries, like Cesare Ripa's *Iconologia* of 1593. Such figures had also moved onto English church monuments in the sixteenth century, increasing in popularity in the eighteenth century.[6] The figures, with created arms and emblems, spread to pottery in the late eighteenth century, with mugs or similar items produced for particular trades or groups decorated with coats of arms and doggerel verses, and onto banners, regalia, and a wide range of ephemera in the nineteenth century, providing an air of tradition and respectability.

Personalized paintings on banners would be produced, but the additional design work required tended to force up the price. Some of the pattern-book themes are described below, although titles and mottoes were frequently interchangeable. There is also a complexity of variations with many of them, and there are examples where more than one theme may appear on a banner.

The 'Friendship, Love and Truth' design on the Eden banner.

### 'FRIENDSHIP, LOVE AND TRUTH'

The image is presumably derived from the three Graces – Thalia, Euphrosyne and Aglaia, the daughters of Zeus and Euryname.[7] Several banners show the figures under the gaze of an all-seeing eye, with a central circular panel containing a sick-bed scene. The panel has a broad border, sometimes rope-edged, which carries a standard motto, 'United we stand, divided we fall'. The panel is set on a raised base and is supported by two miners, one standing, the other sitting. Below the panel is, normally, an architectural feature with a semicircular opening, through which can be viewed a small underground scene of a driver with a pony and tub. This is flanked by shields with the national symbols of England, Scotland, Ireland and Wales.

The three female figures invariably hold a long ribbon scroll inscribed 'Amicitia Amor et Veritas' (Friendship, Love and Truth), and are usually shown wearing symbolic necklaces, decorated with a cross, fouled anchor and a red heart respectively – the cross of truth, the anchor of faithfulness and friendship and the heart of love. These attributes can be traced back to iconographies and sculptural images and are more frequently related to the virtues of Faith, Hope and Charity; the anchor, for instance, derives from Hebrews 6.19, 'Which hope we have as an anchor of the soul, both sure and steadfast'. Generally Friendship and Truth are shown bareheaded, while Love has either her head covered or her right breast bared. The image may also carry the motto, 'We unite to assist each other'. Common on Durham miners' banners, this design is also found on the Prospect Lodge No. 4 Skelton banner of the Cleveland Miners' and Quarrymen's Association.

Simplified versions were available by the 1930s, with the Latin title reset in English and the supporting miners removed. Consequently the principal figures were emphasized and modified. Love, for instance, is sometimes shown as a mother holding a baby, with her cloak draped around a second child. This design was used on the Blackhall NUM banner. Another variant is seen on the Browney lodge DMA banner where the figures are set around a lyre and an incense-burner. Truth and Love are seated on either side of the burner, Truth with a book and cross, Love with a small, naked child and a baby. Behind them is Friendship, represented by two women standing together, and the new character, Justice, shown with sword and scales.

### 'BEAR YE ONE ANOTHERS BURDENS'

The title sometimes varies, but the illustration shows one or two lodge officials visiting a sick member confined to bed, and distributing financial aid to his wife, who is usually accompanied by her children. This image of the union providing assistance was very popular and there are examples from other trades, such as Tutill's damask banner for the Cardiff, Penarth and Barry Coal Trimmers' Protection and Benefit Association,[8] or the Kentish Town branch of the Operative Bricklayers' Society, produced by L. Boughton, 'working banner painter' of New Cross.[9] It was also used by Friendly Societies, like the Druids and Oddfellows. Other titles used by unions for this type of illustration include 'All Men are Brethren' and 'I was Sick and ye Visited Me'.

### 'WE SUCCOUR THE WIDOW AND ORPHANS'

There are two principal forms. One shows a weeping widow kneeling at the grave of her husband, with her children around her and a union official arriving to give assistance. Sometimes a pithead is shown in the background. Another form, found on the Marley Hill banner, shows the widow and orphans at a grave, accompanied by three angels. One of the angels, draped with a cornucopia, carves on the tombstone, 'Sacred to the memory of a brother'.

The first form is found on other trade union banners, like those of the United Society of Boiler Scalers and Stoke-hold Labourers,[10] and the Amalgamated Society of Railway Servants.[11] It was also a popular theme

A sick-bed scene, 'Bear ye one anothers burden', on the Lambton banner.

used for the National Union of Railwaymen, such as the Bath, Maze Hill and Richmond branches.[12]

### 'UNITY IS STRENGTH'

The bundle of sticks image, commonly found on the reverse side of banners, is taken from Aesop's 'Unity is Strength' fable.[13] Although this Greek story was written around the mid-sixth century BC, the banner illustration generally shows the figures as Anglo-Saxons. A Germanic-style chieftain is normally shown seated in an elaborate chair or throne on the right side of the painting. He is usually shown as either a venerable figure with a long beard, or a warrior, with his sheathed sword lying close by him. In front of him, on the far left, a young man dressed in a tunic and furs kneels and attempts to break a bundle of sticks over his knee. Meanwhile, in the centre of the scene, a young boy is shown triumphantly breaking a stick. Variations on the standard form are found. On the Trimdon Grange banner, the small boy was dispensed with and the young

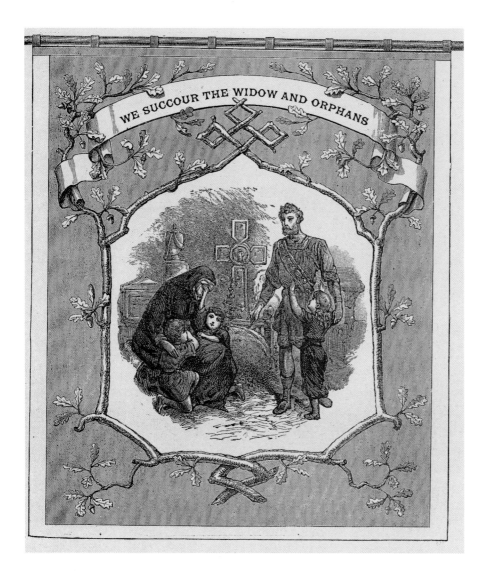

The Tutill pattern-book design, 'We succour the widow and orphans'.

Saxon continued his attempts to break the bundle, while an old man, sitting on a step and dressed in more Biblical costume, snaps one of the sticks. Butterknowle updated the figures, showing the old man, in fact John Wilson, dressed in a black frock coat, while the young man and boy are in work clothes. The fable's symbolism of strength in union was reduced to its most basic form on an early Tursdale banner, where a single workman is shown attempting to break the bundle of sticks.

### 'ALL MEN ARE BRETHREN'

The Tutill pattern-book form shows a blacksmith and a carpenter standing either side of a low stone block, shaking hands. The scene is set on grassland in front of a factory and the stone block is bedecked with an

Aesop's bundle of sticks fable, 'Unity is Strength'.

anvil, tongs, a plane, a scroll and dividers, a mason's mallet and a wheel. Behind the two figures, and floating in the air, is an angel holding a ribbon inscribed 'Unity is strength'. The scene is given the broad title, 'Workers of the world unite'. The blacksmith and carpenter form was taken up by Shotton lodge and was also used on the Tutill banner of Barnsley Main branch of the Yorkshire Miners' Association.[14]

The design more common in Durham is a variant of the standard Tutill form and usually shows two miners standing either side of the low stone block, shaking hands. They are normally dressed in their pit clothes and hold a shovel or safety lamp in their left hand. Around the stone block are

The union theme of 'All Men are Brethren', or 'United to Obtain the Just Reward of Our Labour', on the South Moor No. 1 lodge banner.

roses and a beehive, while floating in the air is the angel holding a ribbon inscribed 'Unity is Strength' or 'All Men are Brethren'. Background scenes include pitheads, bridges, or busy rivers with merchant ships and barges.

Esh Winning broke from the accepted form of two workers shaking hands and showed a miner and an owner; the angel displayed the more appropriate appeal, 'Let us work together'. The Ipswich Dockers' Union also followed this theme, where a docker, standing with a barrow, shakes hands with an employer with a money bag and cash box at his feet.[15] The banner of Tanfield Lea also modified the image, transferring it to a dockside with merchant ships in the harbour. A miner is shown, wearing a cap, sleeveless vest and short trousers (known as 'pit hoggers'), and holding a pick over his left shoulder. At his feet is a pile of coal and a safety lamp. He shakes the hand of a sailor, who is standing by a crate and holding a looped length of rope.

Nationally, a number of variations on the theme are also found on trade union banners, from the miner, docker and railwayman used for the Dock,

Wharf, Riverside and General Workers' Union,[16] to the four building workers shaking hands on the Walworth branch of the National Builders', Labourers' and Construction Workers' Society.[17]

The basic form also developed offshoots, like the Trimdon Grange DMA lodge banner, where the four men shaking hands represent the four nations, England, Scotland, Ireland and Wales, or the Horden NUM banner of 'Peace and goodwill to all miners', where two pitmen shake hands over a globe with a dove of peace flying above them. While the angel and the two men shaking hands usually appear with the motto, 'All men are brethren', a variation used by North Biddick, Woodland and South Moor No. 1 lodge was the title, 'United to obtain the just reward of our labour'.

### 'TWO SIDES OF THE QUESTION'

The 1920s banners of Kimblesworth, Leasingthorne and Urpeth 'C' lodges carried a scene of a well-to-do and a poor family. The former group are well dressed, with the husband and wife walking arm-in-arm, and the husband carrying a basket of provisions. The other couple are poorly dressed, with the wife appealing to her husband for housekeeping money, and the husband displaying his empty pockets.

This visual image of the haves and have-nots, representing organized and unorganized labour, was used by other unions, like the Ipswich branch of the Transport and General Workers' Union,[18] and was also a popular Victorian moral illustration which could be used for a range of themes. It was, for instance, used on temperance banners, where comparison was made between the teetotaller's home and that of the drinker – 'The happy home of the good' and 'The drunkard's home is wretched'.[19]

### 'KNOWLEDGE IS POWER'

A woman is shown teaching a child, with unrolled scrolls inscribed with some supposed ancient script. This form of the theme is found on the banners of Dawdon, Easington and Eden, although it was more frequently used for Sunday school banners.

### 'LABOUR AND PEACE'

The design comprises two figures: a miner stands on the left of the scene, holding a lamp in his right hand and taking the hand of the female figure of Peace, standing on the right. She is usually shown as a classically dressed figure, holding a palm branch and standing by an incense-burner. Between the two figures is set up a scrolled panel decorated with the scales of Justice, set around at its base with fruit, while a dove flies above it. In the background is a pithead, and merchant ship, with a single star set in the sky. The image is found on the banners of Browney, Dawdon and Wingate lodges and Willington Mechanics (possibly the re-used banner of

The pattern-book design, 'Knowledge is Power', on the Dawdon banner.

Brancepeth A & C lodges), and was also used by other unions, including the banner of Walworth branch of the National Builders', Labourers' and Constructional Workers' Society.[20]

'THE SUNSHINE OF LIBERTY'

The socialist Sunshine of Liberty design generally showed a woman, wearing a red Phrygian cap and a long gown and draped with ribbons

Dawdon banner with
'Labour and Peace'.

of Progress, Education, Art and Science. She appears to float in the centre of the scene, and draws back the curtain of Oppression to reveal to a group an idyllic scene lit by the Sunshine of Liberty. With this design the details are not always fixed. On the Follonsby lodge banner the female figure is shown wearing a red cap and carrying a flaming torch. The 1954 Chopwell banner showed a man, dressed in red and draped with a ribbon inscribed 'He who would be free, himself must

'Sunshine of Liberty' on the Witton banner.

strike the blow', leading a group of miners to an idyllic land of Liberty, under the title, 'Gain the Co-operative Commonwealth'. The ribbon inscription is derived from Byron's 'Childe Harold's Pilgrimage' of 1812:

> Hereditary bondsmen! Know ye not
> Who would be free themselves must strike the blow?[21]

'EMANCIPATION OF LABOUR'

The principal, central figure is a woman, wearing the breastplate of Progress while carrying a garland and the flag of Emancipation of Labour. She has led the people over the mountains to a valley lit by the sunshine of the Co-operative Commonwealth.

The Clara Vale banner has one distinct modification. Instead of the

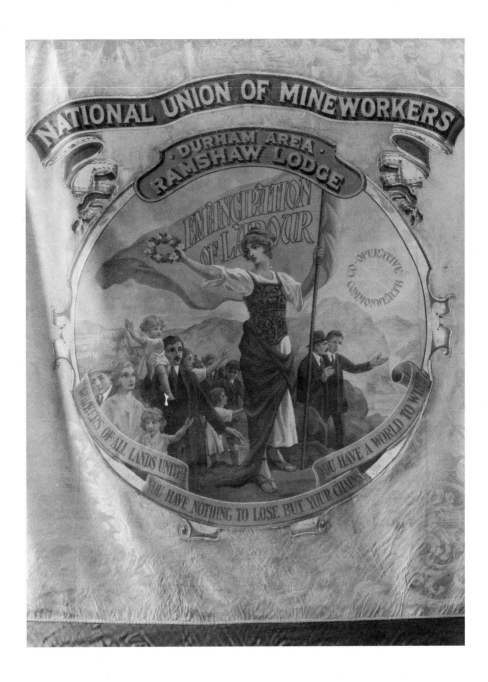

The 'Emancipation of Labour' theme on the Ramshaw banner.

Co-operative Commonwealth design, Progress leads the people to the idyllic world of fine houses with children playing on a village green, more commonly found in the Sunshine of Liberty design. The Emancipation scene is usually accompanied by a full, or shortened, quotation from the concluding lines of Marx and Engels' *Communist Manifesto*: 'Workers of the world unite! You have nothing to lose but your chains, you have a world to win.' The likely model for the

Walter Crane's cartoon of 'May Day' for the 1903 edition of *The Sun*.

Emancipation design is a cartoon created by Walter Crane for the May Day 1903 edition of *The Sun*. The figure of Progress on the banners was taken from the female figure of May Day, shown leading the masses from a city to a rural scene.

### 'GO THOU AND DO LIKEWISE'

The parable of the Good Samaritan, from chapter 10 of St Luke's gospel, appeared on banners from an early stage. One of the earliest is the Westerton banner by Hales of London, dating from around the 1870s. For some the image was symbolic, with the union coming to the aid of the man wounded by the thieves – the mine owners.

The Randolph lodge banner of 1909, produced by H. Slingsby of Nuneaton, illustrated the scene in a somewhat primitive, naïve art style, but gives a full version of the parable, with the Samaritan tending to the wounded traveller in the foreground, while the Priest and the Levite are shown moving away into the distance along the road leading down to Jericho. A fragment of the central painting of an early Deaf Hill banner also shows the Priest and Levite. The standard Tutill design, however, concentrated on the victim lying at the roadside with the Samaritan tending him. Here again there is a noticeable change. On the Westerton and Randolph banners the Samaritan is shown on the right, attending to the wounds of the man as he lies stretched out in the road. Tutill, however, moved the Samaritan to the left, showing him kneeling and supporting the victim as he gives him a drink from a

Henry Slingsby's 'Good Samaritan' in a primitive style, on the Randolph banner.

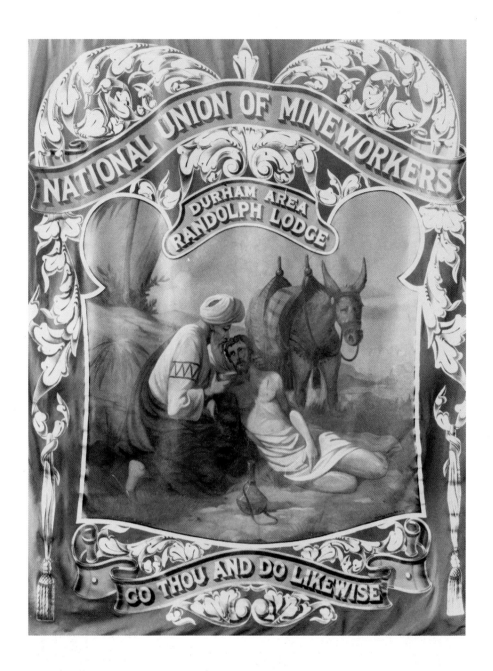

Tutill's pattern-book
'Good Samaritan' on
the Randolph banner.

bowl. The Deaf Hill banner fragment showed the Samaritan with a powerful white horse, but normally he has a donkey which is shown standing patiently behind the main characters. The donkey takes on a standardized form and is frequently shown with an elaborate Eastern saddle. Two mottoes tend to accompany the scene, either Christ's words from verse 37, used at the end of the parable, 'Go thou and do likewise', or those from St Paul's epistle to the Galatians, 6.2, 'bear ye one anothers burdens'.

## 'HE WHO WOULD BE FREE MUST STRIKE THE BLOW'

Craghead and Derwent lodges took the struggle between David and Goliath for their banner illustration. The design was chosen from the scene in verse 51 of the First Book of Samuel, chapter 17, where David, having felled the Philistine with his slingshot, stands triumphantly over the body. The illustration is usually accompanied by a version of Byron's line; 'He who would be free must strike the blow'. This design was used by other unions, like the Friendship Lodge No. 8 Skinningrove and Goodwill Lodge No. 9 Loftus banner of the Cleveland Miners' and Quarrymen's Association.

## 'SUFFER LITTLE CHILDREN TO COME UNTO ME'

The incident in Judea when Christ rebuked the disciples for not allowing the children to meet him is illustrated on two versions of the Seaham banner, using the wording from verse 14 of St Mark's gospel, chapter 10, 'Suffer little children to come unto me'. This theme was also used by Henry Slingsby for his Sunday school banners.

## 'O THOU OF LITTLE FAITH'

After the feeding of the five thousand, when Christ and the disciples were crossing the stormy sea to Genesaret, Christ walked on the water. Peter,

'Suffer little children to come unto me', on the damaged Wheatley Hill banner.

The Silksworth banner,
'O thou of little faith'.

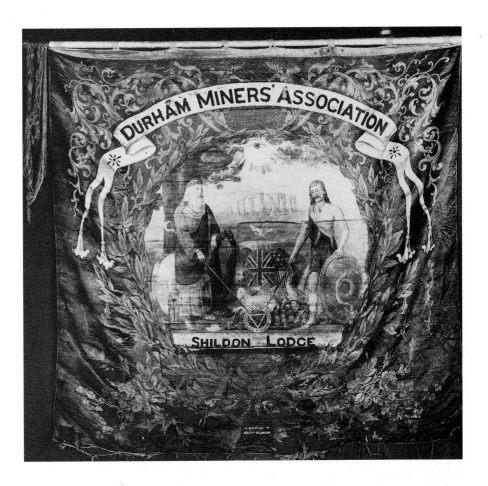

The 'Druid' banner of Shildon lodge, DMA.

following his master, began to sink, and Christ, raising him up, declared, 'O thou of little faith wherefore didst thou doubt'. This scene, and the words from Matthew 14.31, appeared on the Lambton and Monkwearmouth banners.

Perhaps the most unusual choice made by a miners' lodge from a Tutill pattern-book is the Shildon banner of the 1890s showing a Druid and an Ancient Briton. The scene is set in a clearing in broad-leaf woodland, with a henge monument in the background. The venerable Druid has a long white beard and a circle of oak leaves around his hair. He is dressed in an ankle-length gown, a cloak draped over his left shoulder, a decorated metal clasp at the right shoulder and sandals on his feet. In his right hand he holds a long staff surmounted by a sickle blade, and he is also accompanied by a star-decorated shield and a Welsh harp. The Ancient Briton is dressed in an animal skin and holds a spear in his right hand and a shield decorated with a coiled serpent in his left hand.

Both figures point with their respective staff and spear to a circle containing a downward pointing triangle, with a border inscribed

'Integritis pro rupe nobis', which may be translated as 'Integrity is our rock'. The ground between the figures is cluttered with symbols and emblems – shields decorated with the Union Jack, Stars and Stripes, a kangaroo and an elephant, a caduceus, an Angus Dei, cornucopia, hour glass and fasces. Flying above the shields is a dove, while in the sky is an all-seeing eye.

The Druids were a high-ranking caste in Celtic society, both in Britain and in Gaul, who were suppressed by the Romans in the first century AD.[22] They were the repositories of tribal knowledge and acted as teachers, but were also responsible for divination and sacrifice, which could include human victims. Classical writers associate their religious practices with the *nemetons*, clearings in oak groves. Pliny noted, in one ceremony, the cutting of mistletoe from an oak using a sickle, which may explain the sickle-headed staff in the painting. There is, however, no archaeological evidence to link Druidism with the earlier stone circles, like Stonehenge. In fact the illustration is a Victorian romanticized image of Druidism and is actually a variation on a design from Tutill's range of banners and regalia for the Order of Druids friendly society.

While the designs described above were used by Tutill in his published pattern-books, it is clear that several other banner makers were painting similar images. The 'Labour and Peace' design, for instance, was used by H. Rich, 'scenic artist', on the Grimethorpe branch banner of the Yorkshire Miners' Association.[23] Womersley & Co. Ltd of Leeds used 'All men are brethren' for Micklefield YMA, while the Sheffield firm of Cole Brothers painted the 'Good Samaritan' on the Wharncliffe–Silkstone No. 1 YMA branch banner. The banner of Paddington No. 2 branch of the NUR carried a painting by G. Kenning & Son of the graveside scene, 'We succour the widow and orphans'.[24]

# Mottoes and Quotations

Some of the early DMA banners, from the 1870s, carried doggerel verses concerning work, employers and union. Haswell banner, at the 1873 Gala, carried the lines,

> All are equal in God's sight,
> The bound, the free, the black, the white;
> He made them, all freedom gave,
> But man made the slave.

This is a modified form of the last of five verses of a song sung at the 1871 Gala by Mr W. Brown, the agent of the Staffordshire miners.

Occasionally banner mottoes were derived from Latin, like Kimblesworth's 'famam extendere factis', 'to extend fame by deeds', but manufacturers particularly favoured quotations from the Bible or from classic works of literature. Several Biblical themes have already been mentioned in relation to pattern-book images. A number of banners at the Galas of the 1870s were concerned with the subject of a fair day's wage for a fair day's work and used, either directly or with some modification, a quote from Colossians 4.1: 'Masters give unto your servants that which is just and right, knowing that ye also have a Master in Heaven.' Castle Eden carried the lines from Isaiah 3.15: 'What mean ye that ye beat my people to pieces, and grind the faces of the poor.' Psalm 41.1 appeared on both the Hedley Hill and Rough Lea banners: 'Blessed is the man that considereth the poor; the Lord will deliver him in time of trouble.' Hunwick, North Hetton and Sacriston took a quote from Matthew 7.12: 'Whatsoever ye would that men do unto you, do ye also unto them.' Elemore took 'Prove all things; hold fast that which is good', from 1 Thessalonians 5.12. East Hetton, Hobson and Marsden used the motto, 'Faithful unto death', from Revelations 20.10, either accompanying the portrait of a lodge official, or, quite frequently, with illustrations of A.J. Cook. The Haswell banner modified a quotation from Hebrews 11.4, changing it from singular to plural, 'They being dead yet speaketh'.

The lines from literature are predominantly British, like Bunyan, Burns, Byron, Goldsmith, Milton, Pope, Shakespeare and Symonds, although the American poet Walt Whitman is also quoted. Several banners included quotations from Shakespeare's works. Silksworth, for instance, took line 232 from *The First Part of the Contention (2 Henry VI)*, Act 3, scene 2: 'Thrice armed is he that hath his quarrel just.'[25] Hebburn removed a named individual (shown here in brackets) in order to use a four-line quotation from *All is True (Henry VIII)*, Act 3, scene 2, which was probably written in 1613 by Shakespeare and John Fletcher:[26]

> Be just and fear not,
> Let all the ends thou aim'st at be thy country's,
> Thy God's, and thy truths; then if thou fallest, [O Cromwell]
> Thou fallest a blessed martyr.

The lines from Burns 'The Cotter's Saturday Night', written in 1785–6 (stanza 19, lines 3–4) appeared on the Etherley banner:

> Princes and Lords are but the breath of kings
> But man is the noblest work of God.[27]

In a similar vein, Marsden lodge chose the lines from Oliver Goldsmith's *The Deserted Village* of 1770:

> Ill fares the land to hastening ills a prey;
> Where wealth accumulates, and men decay;
> Princes and lords may flourish, or may fade;

A breath can make them, as a breath has made;
But a bold peasantry, their country's pride
When once destroyed, can never be supplied.[28]

Boldon took a line from Bunyan, 'You have been so faithful and loving to us, that we shall never forget your favour towards us', to accompany the portraits of Lord Lawson, John Summerbell and William T. Wilson.

Stanza 10 of Alexander Pope's 'The Universal Prayer' was painted on the Hamsteels banner:

Teach us to feel another's woe
To heed the fault I see
That mercy I to others show
That mercy show to me.

The theme of a new and better world, and the efforts needed to achieve it, are referred to on several banners. Edmondsley chose 'Awake, arise or be forever fallen', from John Milton's pastoral drama, *Comus*. A quotation sometimes found with the Sunshine of Liberty image is from John Addington Symonds 'The days that are to be': 'These things shall be; a loftier race than 'ere the world hath known shall rise, with flame of freedom in their souls and light of knowledge in their eyes.'[29] Each version of the Chopwell 'Red' banner carried the lines, 'We take up the task eternal, and the burden and the lesson, Pioneers! O Pioneers', from Walt Whitman's poem 'Pioneers! O Pioneers', which appeared in his *Leaves of Grass* collection in 1867.[30]

CHAPTER 3

# Banners in Use

While the banner was the symbol of unionism, some coal companies, from the time of the earliest Galas, took an interest in them, perhaps as a paternalistic gesture, or as an astute political move. In June 1891 a concert was held in Waterhouses Primitive Methodist chapel Sunday school to raise funds for a new lodge banner. The event was presided over by H.H. Cochrane, the owner of New Brancepeth colliery, and he, and the directors of Pease & Partners, the owners of Waterhouses colliery, contributed to the fund.[1] In July of the following year, after a successful fund-raising effort, the new banner was unfurled by William Patterson of the DMA in the schoolroom, and this time the event's president was Thomas Greener, manager of the Peases West Collieries.[2] Similarly, in 1900, the unfurling of Browney lodge banner was attended by A.L. Steavenson, the agent for the colliery owners, Bell Bros.[3]

Increasingly the lodges tried to arrange with the manufacturer for their new banner to be available shortly before the Gala. Arrangements were made for the banner to be officially unfurled either on the evening before the Gala or on Gala morning. To give one example, Eden lodge discussed the purchase of a new banner at a meeting on 25 January 1962.[4] Information from G. Tutill Ltd was received and by the end of February it was agreed that the purchase should go ahead and the images on their old banner should be repeated. In June, having received information from Tutill's about a likely completion date, the lodge discussed the subject of who should unfurl the banner. Tony Benn was the choice, and the secretary wrote to invite him to carry out the ceremony. On receiving his acceptance, invitations were then sent out in early July to the deputies, mechanics, enginemen, other local lodges and the council chairman. On 20 July the new banner was unfurled.

A new banner was delivered to a lodge in a wooden box, known as a 'coffin'. A surviving example at Red Hill is 13 ft 1.5 in (4.03 m) long, 5.75 in (14.5 cm) wide, and the same in height, of 0.5 in (1.5 cm) planking nailed together, and fitted with a lid attached with four butt hinges. The box was normally secured with two small mortise locks. Inside, the banner

The unfurling of the 1951 Mainsforth lodge NUM banner.

would have been placed in a long, waterproof pouch, one of which still survives with the Ravensworth banner.

Banners were unfurled in lodge rooms, halls, schools, institutes, welfare grounds, a rectory garden and even near a coal depot. They were normally unfurled by men, but five instances of women carrying out this ceremony are known. In 1906 Mrs Wilson unfurled the Dean and Chapter banner at Ferryhill.[5] In 1923 Kimblesworth banner was unfurled by Mrs Blackett, the wife of the colliery manager;[6] in 1937 Shotton banner was unfurled by the village beauty queen;[7] in 1955 Sam Watson and his wife jointly unveiled the new Medomsley banner; and Mrs Attlee unfurled the Ushaw Moor banner.[8]

Frequently banners were dedicated at a religious service. The NUM (NE Area) banner, for instance, was dedicated by the Bishop of Durham, Dr David Jenkins. The Revd Martin King, during the dedication of the 1996 Trimdon Grange banner, confessed that the Church of England had often been associated with the coal owners and not with the working people. In referring to the 1810 miners' strike, when political prisoners were held under armed guard in the stables of the bishop, he expressed the Church's shame and asked the congregation 'to show the understanding and forgiveness your forebears were entitled to have received from others'.

It was general practice that men carried their lodge banner, but there are four occasions when women were banner carriers or assistants. In 1881 miners at Ushaw Moor went on strike over the dismissal of their lodge delegate by the manager employed by Henry Chaytor, who was determined to smash unionism at his pit. At the 1883 Gala the strikers brought two banners to the Racecourse, one carried by two women with the inscription, 'No Surrender'.[9] The importation of blacklegs into the pit, and a growing weariness of the strike by the DMA leaders, led to its collapse later in the year. In 1908 a violent dispute broke out at Harraton, where the women were the leading activists and frequently carried the lodge banner. On one occasion they formed a band and took the banner, and an effigy draped with a placard proclaiming 'No Surrender', to a demonstration in Chester-le-Street.[10] The women then decided to march on Fatfield, to the homes of deputies who were still working at Harraton. They refused to take a route proposed by the police, and a clash ensued in which the banner was damaged, before they eventually broke through the police line and moved into Fatfield. When it came to the July Gala, the lodge unanimously agreed that two women should carry the banner onto the Racecourse. More recently, Shotton lodge chose Frances Henderson, the daughter of the former checkweighman, to carry their banner at the 1951 Gala,[11] and two Murton miners and four canteen women brought in the lodge banner at the 1957 Gala.[12]

While the banner carried the design chosen by the lodge as its symbol as a fixed image until it became necessary to replace it, lodges were not averse to attaching posters or similar forms of message to their banner, expressing their feelings on a current subject. The banner would be displayed at two regular events – May Day, and at the Gala in July. It would also be used as a symbol and rallying point during disputes, and at occasions like the opening of aged miners homes, or at miners' funerals. They have also been carried at political events, marches and rallies.

The Gala, or 'Big Meeting', was started in 1871 at Wharton Park and was subsequently held on the Racecourse in Durham City. It was one of a series of miners' union annual gatherings in the North-East. The Northumberland miners' demonstration, or 'picnic', started in 1866 at Polly's Folly and was held at several locations in subsequent years, though from 1952 it tended to be held at Bedlington. The Cleveland miners also held a gathering at Boosebeck, near Guisborough. The Durham Gala, however, saw the greatest display of banners, with each lodge marching into Durham with its painted silk standard.

A week before the Gala, the DMA secretary would send out a notice from the union headquarters to lodge officials urging good attendance, to serve as 'an index to the interest we are taking in our personal and collective welfare', and as a clear signal to employers of the strength of this great army of miners united.[13] William Crawford wrote in 1881:

A good turn out at the Gala has an influence for good during the whole of the ensuing year. A thin bad attendance has a most damaging effect. Better to have no Gala than a one badly attended. Call Special Meetings of your men at once, and urge on them the

Banners being carried onto the Racecourse at the 1910 Gala. The leading banner may belong to the Durham Colliery Mechanics.

necessity of being at the Gala. Do not come as individuals, but as collieries following your banners and bands.[14]

As a further incentive, some lodges used the balance of their checkweigh fund to pay Gala Day attendance money to the men who went in to Durham. Brandon lodge gave 8–9*s* to each man in 1914.[15]

As the Gala was a symbol of unity among the mining workforce, those who deliberately failed to give their support were hauled over the coals. Murton lodge secretary, in 1925, minuted that 'J. Knox and M. Fahy were summoned to the committee when they apologised for working on Durham Gala day and were cautioned as to their future conduct'.[16] The Gala became a customary holiday, taken at the area union's own request, and was not included in the list of statutory paid holidays.[17]

Lodge preparations for the Gala would include booking the local colliery band, or hiring an outside band for Gala Day. Certainly in the early years the DMA provided funding towards the cost of paying bandsmen on the day. In the 1870s and 1880s this was 2*s* a head. The evening before the Gala, lots would be drawn among the lodge members for six men to carry the banner – two to carry the poles, with two men either side holding the front and back guide ropes. Two others would also be picked as reserves. The men would swap over, if necessary, on the march to the Racecourse, and on the way out.

The banner would normally be stored in a union room, institute, welfare hall or a chapel. Waterhouses lodge, for instance, whose officials were predominantly Primitive Methodists, stored their banner in the Bourne PM chapel. Hamsteels lodge kept theirs in an upper room of the local pub, at Quebec. On the morning of the Gala, at pit villages close to the city, the banner carriers, lodge officials and band would gather, sometimes, as at Sacriston, having their breakfast at the welfare hall, before the journey into Durham. Many people travelled in by trains organized by the North Eastern Railway Company, alighting at the main North Road, or Elvet, stations.[18] This was a massive logistical task for the NER, with up to fifty-six special trains being required to transport the miners and their families into the city, along with additional staff and parcel vans to take the banners and musical instruments. Once in the city, each banner would be secured to its carrying poles and the carriers would don their harness ready to receive the pole. The banner would be hoisted aloft and the rope bearers would take up their positions. Once that was in order, the lodge officials would get into position in front of the banner and the march to the Racecourse would begin, each banner preceded by its band and followed by the people of the village.

There was no specific order in which lodges progressed through the city. Order was usually influenced by the travel arrangements made by each lodge and the distance they had to cover to reach Durham. There was always great interest as to which lodge arrived in the city first and started the march.

Over the years the appearance and fashions of those who came into Durham with the banners has changed. In the 1870s Francis Addison, a draper and glover in Claypath, produced large quantities of rosettes at Gala-time for the miners, to 'rival in colour the tints of the rainbow'.[19] West Auckland men, in 1873, marched in wearing temperance and other insignia, while those from Burnhope sported white straw hats. The marshals, too, could often be distinguished by distinctive striped scarves. In the 1960s it was common practice for girls from the village to link arms and dance ahead of the banner during the procession. There was, increasingly, a carnival atmosphere, with people in fancy dress – black-and-white minstrels, lion tamers, girners etc.

For the lodges at Durham station, there was a long march through the city – down North Road, over Framwellgate Bridge, the pull up Silver Street to the Market Place, before looping round and crossing Elvet Bridge. Lodges from the north and east came into the Market Place from Claypath; others alighting at Elvet station linked into the procession by the Royal County Hotel. Banner after banner was on the march through the narrow streets which were lined with hundreds of people. The orderly movement of the procession was achieved by each group's lodge officials, and, in the early years, following a practice already used in the 1830s, stewards were appointed, who carried distinctive wands. In the 1870s, partly because some elements of the city population had feared a riotous invasion of

'Dancing in the Street'
at the 1951 Gala.

pitmen, the DMA discussed the arrangements with the police and actually paid the wages of some of the constables, while the remainder was found from the funds of the borough watch rate.[20] In later years police horsemen were employed to keep a route open through the crowds for the lodges to process. Hold-ups inevitably occurred, which gave the band and banner carriers a breather, before a drumbeat signalled imminent movement.

The visiting speakers, selected by the lodges, stayed at the Royal County Hotel in Old Elvet and as the procession passed the hotel they and the union leaders would stand on the balcony to view the proceedings. The bands and banners then marched on up Old Elvet, before the final stage, down the bank to the level plain of the Racecourse. Each lodge would then proceed with its banner to an established position at the border of the field. There the banner would be set up and tied with its guide ropes to the wooden fence. Gradually, as each lodge arrived, the border of the Racecourse became lined with banners. The banner carriers would then be paid by the lodge treasurer.

Once the banner was tied up, it became the rallying point for the men, women and children who had marched in with it. The band's musical instruments would also be left under it, and 'minders' were paid a small sum to keep an eye on things. People sat and ate their picnics in front of the banner, and it was a beacon for those who had wandered away to listen to speeches, to

Hugh Gaitskell and
Harold Wilson on the
balcony of the Royal
County Hotel at the
1958 Gala.

meet friends, or to visit the shows and pubs. Refreshment tents were set up on
the field. In the first few years of the Gala these included beer tents operated
by local publicans, but by 1874 these had been expelled, and only tea, soft
drinks and sandwich stalls were permitted by the DMA executive. Anyone
wanting something stronger had a variety of city pubs to choose from.

Around this time amusement stalls began to cluster around the margins
of the field to tempt the huge crowd – everything from shooting galleries,
boxing contests, photographic galleries and fortune-tellers to, in more
recent years, roundabouts and dodgems. James Ainsco, a member of the
Showman's Guild, who came up from Leeds every year from 1915 with a
'lucky straw' stall, described the Gala as 'the best fair in the country'.[21]
Another showman, Bob Cowie, who came to each Gala from the turn of
the century, recalled the horse-drawn caravans, the stalls lit by naptha
flares, the music of the fairground organ, the side shows and hobby horses.
The Gala was also a day for picnics and boating on the river, and for small
children – the Mothers' Union, after discussion with the DMA executive,
organized a crêche in 1937.[22]

Around 11.30 a.m. the bands would play 'Gresford', signalling the
solemn moment before the speeches from the platforms. People could
gather around and listen to reports on the state of the union from officials,
the words of the invited speakers, or simply do their own thing. At 3 p.m.

A picnic on the Racecourse at the 1937 Gala.

the Miners' Festival Service would be held in the Cathedral. In 1897 the Brass Band Association had written to John Wilson suggesting a band procession at the Gala, and Dean Kitchin had offered to assist with a cathedral service, while Bishop Westcott agreed to preach. In his monthly circular for June 1897 Wilson wrote,

> I am sure none will take umbrage at the suggestion or proposed service; but rather to do all they can to make it a success. All cannot attend, but whoever does, will be amply repaid for doing so, and I, therefore hope, that a large number will be found showing, by their presence, their appreciation of the arrangements and of the speaker. There may be (as we know there are) those who differ from the Bishop in his theological views; but whatever opinions we may hold on those matters, we are bound to admit that his Lordship is very liberal in his ideas on social questions, and very desirous to surround the home life of the people with conditions conducive to the highest comfort, and promotive of the best state of health in every aspect.[23]

The bishop was actually unable to preach on the day, Archdeacon Watkins taking his place, but he did preach at the services in 1898, 1900 and 1901.

In preparation for the Gala service, three chosen lodges, with their banners and bands, would leave the Racecourse and march back down Old Elvet, over Elvet Bridge, and up Saddler Street and Owengate to Palace Green, the broad grassed area in front of the Cathedral. Here the lodges would prepare, as the people passed in to the Cathedral to take their seats for the service. When all was ready, the great north door of the Cathedral, bearing the famous Sanctuary Knocker, would be opened and the first

Blackhall banner
entering the Cathedral
for the Miners' Service,
1939 Gala.

band would begin to play, as the banner and officials marched to the door. For the congregation inside there was an air of expectation; the music grew in intensity as the band reached the door. Then, as people looked from the dim light of the Cathedral into the daylight streaming in through the high doorway, there would suddenly appear the shape of the banner, proudly carried aloft. The band and lodge members would pass down the aisle and, as they did so, a few minutes later the next band would appear at the door ready to enter the Cathedral, and then the third band and banner.

The music played for their entrance to the Cathedral tended to be somewhat solemn and moving, like 'Abide with me'. The Dean and Chapter had actually made a grant towards the cost of bands who played at the Miners' Service in the Cathedral. In 1954, however, following discussions between the Dean and Sam Watson, it was decided that there was 'no reason why these payments should continue'.[24]

Although there was some slight variation in the form of the service over the years, it eventually came to follow a standard format. Once in place, the bands would play an introductory hymn as the clergy and choir processed down the nave and took their places. The Dean made a formal introductory welcome, followed by prayer, absolution, general thanksgiving, a hymn and the lesson. After the choir had sung the anthem, the Apostles' Creed would be followed by the main prayers. Usually the prayers, in part or whole, related to the mining industry, for example those in 1995:

> O God, our Father, we bring before thee in prayer the mining communities of our land, especially those of this region. We give thee thanks for their traditions of endurance, courage and service; we ask that thou wilt guide and guard them in the dangers and difficulties by which they are now beset; and we commend them, through all the uncertainties of change, to thy continuing care.[25]

After a hymn, the main sermon was presented, followed by a voluntary by the band, before the blessing and final hymn, during which the clergy and choir processed out. A collection would usually be taken for the Aged Miners' Homes Association. Then it was time for the bands to move. Suddenly there would be the loud beat of the bass drum, the band would break into stirring music and the three groups would march out in succession. With the service completed, there was a general exodus, as people began to make their way home.

It was a common practice that when the lodge reached its village, the band would play through the main streets, followed by the banner and those who had accompanied it. When a miner was killed in the pit, the banner would be carried, draped in black, to the funeral. It became the practice to retain the black drape, strung across the top of the banner, at the Gala. Occasionally banners would be draped in memory of departed politicians, union leaders, or other figures whom the lodge membership had respected.

# CHAPTER 4

# Banners and History

## *Banners in Use up to 1869*

The presence of banners, and the carrying of banners in procession, has a long history in the North-East. The medieval trade guilds acquired distinctive banners and held an annual procession through Durham on the Thursday after Trinity Sunday, culminating in a service in the Cathedral.[1] This practice was affected by the Civil War and was greatly reduced in form following the restoration of the monarchy in 1660, after which the role of the guilds gradually declined. In the early nineteenth century, however, it was still the practice for guilds to acquire banners and to carry them in procession. In 1818 George Allan, the Durham City MP, gave a banner to the Drapers' and Tailors' Company of the Corporation of the City.[2] Allan had been elected a member of the guild and had agreed to advance its interests. Similarly, in 1829, two other MPs, M.A. Taylor and Sir H. Hardinge, had presented the Company of Cordwainers with a new banner.[3]

It was also the practice to carry banners at mass meetings for political purposes at the beginning of the nineteenth century, if not before. In November 1819 a meeting in Newcastle to protest at the 'Peterloo Massacre' saw groups marching in organized formations, with stewards carrying distinctive wands.[4] Several flags and banners were set up at the back of the speakers' platform, one of which bore the motto, 'Order, Love and Unity'.

Of banners specifically carried by miners, there is clear evidence from the 1830s. The formation of the joint union of Northumberland and Durham miners in 1830, under the leadership of Thomas Hepburn, was followed by a strike in 1831 over the working hours of boys and the method of wage payment. During the dispute a number of mass meetings were held where it is clear that some of the new miners' lodges possessed decorated banners.

At a meeting in Jarrow, in April 1831, miners from forty-nine collieries were present, accompanied by banners said to be 'inscribed with the name of the colliery, and various mottoes'.[5] By mid-June the strike had succeeded, and boys' hours were reduced to twelve a day.

On 13 August, 10–12,000 miners met on Boldon Fell to discuss a formal address thanking the king for granting the royal assent to the Reform Bill, although much of the business concerned the development of their association. 'The men walked in procession from the different collieries, bearing flags and banners, and in one or two instances attended by bands of music. The banners were numerous and of the gayest description, nearly all being embellished with a painted design, or with a motto', and many of the banners were new, for the inscriptions apparently referred to the miners' success in the recent struggle.[6]

We do not know which specific lodges had banners at that time, or what their particular designs were like. After the collapse of the union, another union, the Miners' Association of Great Britain and Ireland, was formed in 1842. In 1844 the miners of Northumberland and Durham came out on strike over their conditions of employment. At Shadon's Hill, near Wrekenton, 35–40,000 miners attended a meeting in April with bands and banners, where, although it was felt they were 'an insulted, oppressed and degraded body of men', the time had come when they 'resolved to be free'.[7] On 29 May 800–2,000 took their banners to Tanfield Moor for another mass meeting, to maintain solidarity.[8] However, the owners hired blackleg labour, some coming from Lord Londonderry's estates in Ireland, with dragoons and infantry to guard them. There was even talk of bringing up 100 Metropolitan police to strengthen the rural force. Gradually, by eviction and starvation, the strike was broken and the association eventually fell apart.

It was not until 1863 that another attempt was made to unite the miners of the two counties. New banners appeared, and there is slightly more available detail of the designs of those in use. At a meeting at Bishop Auckland on 3 October 1863, Byers Green, Hunwick and Newfield came in with a flag, while Spennymoor, Whitworth, Page Bank and Bishop's Close marched with a large banner. At another meeting on the Batts at Bishop Auckland on 7 November the inscriptions on this banner are given. Its title was 'Spennymoor District. Northumberland and Durham Miners' Mutual Confident Association, established June 7, 1863'. Below it was a quotation from Coleridge:

> He doeth well, who doeth good,
> To those of his own brotherhood,
> He doeth better, who doth strive,
> To keep his brethren all alive.[9]

Newton Cap was also present, with a tri-coloured banner carrying some rather unusual inscriptions. At the top was the title 'Newton Cap Colliery',

William Crawford (1833–90), Durham Miners' Association general secretary, on the Cornsay banner.

followed by 'God save the Queen', 'Welcome to Great Britain', and finishing with 'Union for ever'.

General disunity, particularly among the Durham men, led the Northumberland miners to break away and form a separate union, the Northumberland Miners' Mutual Confident Association. Its first secretary was William Crawford. Crawford was born at Whiteley, in Northumberland, on 22 September 1833, the son of a miner. He started work at the local pit, but moved to various collieries for short periods. While working as a driver at Cowpen pit he was caught by tubs and seriously injured. The local surgeon proposed amputating his crushed leg, but his father refused and took him for treatment to Newcastle. The leg was saved and during his convalescence he received his first proper education. Once recovered, he returned to the colliery and worked through the grades. His administrative skills had been noted by his comrades and he was initially asked to produce a code of rules for the association and, when these were accepted, he was elected general secretary for the county. Crawford left the NMA in 1865, to be succeeded by Thomas Burt, and worked for a time as secretary for Cowpen Quay Co-operative Society and at his own business in Bedlington.

The separation of the Northumberland miners from the association, and the infamous 'Rocking Strike' at Joseph Love's collieries at Brancepeth, Willington and Sunnybrow, left unionism in Durham rudderless. Conditions of employment in the coalfield soon led to further discontent, and at Monkwearmouth colliery an important event occurred in 1869 which was to lead to the formation of a new union.

From 1866 to 1869 the wages for Monkwearmouth hewers working longwall had fallen by 46 per cent, in the broken by 33.5 per cent and at the 'A' pit by 19 per cent.[10] On average they were making 3*s* a shift. The men had agreed to try to work at the rates offered and had been bound, but soon found that they were barely making enough to survive. On 18 May the men sent a deputation to the viewer, Richard Heckles, requesting improvements in pay and working practices, including the provision of a checkweighman at bank and a definition of the quantity of stone used when laying out tubs. Heckles told them it was not possible to go back to the old rate of pay, and the men, feeling they had no option, went on strike, led by John Richardson.

Four hewers, Thomas Fenwick, James Forrest, Thomas Marshall and Robert Lackenby, were then arrested under the Masters and Servants Act for leaving work and thus breaking the provisions of their bond. The case was brought to Sunderland Police Court, the prosecution led by Mr Kidson and the defence by the radical Chartist lawyer, W.P. Roberts, 'the Pitman's Attorney'.[11] Fenwick appeared first. He said that the bond was unjust and that he would rather go to prison than labour under it. The bench considered that the bond was a valid contract, but under examination by Mr Roberts it was revealed that Fenwick could not read or write and had signed the bond with a mark. Since he could not read the bond, and the conditions had not been read over to him, Roberts considered that he was not legally bound by it. Kidson, realizing that the case could fall apart, consulted the owners, who agreed that the bond could be cancelled if the men agreed to leave their houses within a week.[12] This they agreed to do. The men met Richardson at Elliotts Yard and marched to the colliery where they handed in their lamps and colliery rules.[13] The hewers and their families then left their homes and took up residence in two marquees and a loft.[14] The remaining bound men – deputies, stonemen, shifters – proposed to leave their houses in support of the hewers. The owners realized that they could not work the pit if this happened and agreed to cancel the bond, with a fortnight's notice to be given to any man wishing to leave the colliery. However, they refused to agree to the men's request that all strikers should be reinstated. Realizing that the owners would not move on this issue, the men were forced to accept, and 240 of the 300 or so hewers were reinstated, but the strike leaders, John Richardson, W. Linney and W. Brewis, were sacked.[15] The courtroom scene of W.P. Roberts denouncing the bond was to appear on several banners of Monkwearmouth lodge.

Richardson continued the struggle for miners' unionism and presided over a meeting in a yard in Thomas Street, Monkwearmouth, on 28

The 1869 courtroom scene – 'The Cancelling of the Yearly Bond'. In 1843 W.P. Roberts had warned the miners to 'bear every outrage and indignity without retribution or remonstrance' or 'you will most assuredly be shot or sent across the sea'. In 1869 the men told him 'that they wanted to be free from the villainous and iniquitous bond'.

August, attended by delegates from Trimdon colliery, Trimdon Grange, Wingate, Heworth, Thornley, Monkwearmouth, Murton, Elemore and Houghton-le-Spring. The aim was to form a new county union, and the delegates chose Richardson to be their agent, to be sent as an agitator around the pits.[16] Fortnightly delegate meetings were held, and areas of the coalfield were chosen for Richardson to visit, to urge the miners to band together. At Thornley, on 25 September, the delegates included William Patterson of Heworth, Tommy Ramsey of Trimdon and Nicholas

Wilkinson, who had been evicted during a dispute at Trimdon Grange and was making his living selling tea.[17] On 20 November the delegates, representing 4,328 members, met at the Market Hotel in Durham and approved Richardson to be agent and secretary,[18] but on 12 February 1870 a mass meeting elected W. Crake of Monkwearmouth as the first president.[19] Membership figures fluctuated significantly during this early phase, and there were problems with unfinancial members, but the period from the 1870s to 1900 saw the appointment of a group of men who built the firm foundations of the new union.

# The Durham Miners' Association, 1869–1918

The Association was made up of lodges at each colliery, with their own president, secretary, treasurer and committee, elected by the membership half-yearly, and with a delegate to the supreme governing body of the union, the Council. The union's chief agents, the president, secretaries, and treasurer were members, and each delegate had from one to six votes, depending on their lodge membership, from 150 to 1,000. An executive committee, comprising the officials and a committee, dealt with business directed to them by the Council and also with urgent cases. The officials were elected by delegate ballot. The Association was also affiliated to the Miners' National Union, which was formed in 1863. Alexander MacDonald held the post of MNU president until his death in 1881.

In May 1870 the infant Durham Miners' Association chose William Crawford, of Northumberland, as their agent, and he became general secretary in 1871. He dominated the union, building up its strength and financial reserves, supporting arbitration and coming down heavily on unofficial strikes – his usual message to the undisciplined was 'You will get no support. Liable to punishment. Do return'. He served as secretary of the Miners' National Union from 1877 to 1890 and was corresponding secretary of the Durham Miners' Federation Board, which brought together miners, enginemen, mechanics and cokemen in 1878, as well as carrying out his duties as an MP. However, the trauma of Crawford's childhood injuries in the pit returned to affect him in later life. In 1887 his health declined, but he still continued to undertake his union work. Finally, on 30 July 1890, during the discussions at a Joint Committee meeting at the Coal Trade Hall in Newcastle, he turned to his colleague William Patterson and said, 'Well Patterson, I must go; I'm dying.' He left the meeting, took a cab to the railway station and returned home to Durham where he died at 6 a.m. the next morning.[20] His portrait appeared on the banners of Cornsay, Edmondsley, Haswell, Newfield, Ryhope and Usworth.

John Forman held the post of DMA president from 1873 until his death on 2 September 1900. Born at Allerton Burn, near Ancroft in Northumberland in 1823, he came to Durham around 1850 and worked at South Pontop, before becoming checkweighman at Grahamsley (North Roddymoor).[21] Although a quiet, reserved man, his bravery was well recorded. He had carried an injured man out of South Pontop when it flooded and he had served with the rescue teams after the explosions at Seaham (1871 and 1880), Trimdon Grange, Tudhoe, West Stanley (1882), Usworth (1885) and Elemore (1886). Forman deduced the destructive part played by coal dust in pit explosions.

William Hammond Patterson was born in 1847 at Fawdon Square, Newcastle, the son of a quarryman.[22] His stepmother sent him to work at Jesmond quarry at the age of eleven, but within the year he was taken to Heworth colliery. In 1865 a lodge was formed, with Patterson as secretary. He attended the Thornley meeting in 1869 as the Heworth delegate and served on the committee of the infant union from February 1870. In June 1870 he was appointed agent for the south-west Durham district and actively recruited with Tommy Ramsey. In 1890, following Crawford's death, he became corresponding secretary, a phase during which the union was almost crippled by the disastrous county strike of 1892. Patterson was, like Crawford, a Primitive Methodist; he was also a Radical and a close friend of Joseph Cowen, the great supporter of revolutionary and liberation movements. He died in 1896 and his portrait appeared on the Bowden Close, Burnhope, Edmondsley, Haswell and Newfield banners.

Tommy Ramsey was a leading advocate for trade unionism and had been active in Jude's union in 1844. After participating in the Thornley gathering, he was blacklisted and took on the task of spreading the union message in the colliery villages when he was appointed an agent. The white-haired old man, rattling his wooden crake and putting his case in broad dialect, intermixed with Biblical imagery, was an important and influential figure, drawing men to the DMA. The Waterhouses banner of 1892 was to show Tommy entering William Crawford's office to report, 'They are all in the union now'. Tommy's work was hazardous: he often had to sleep in hedgerows because no one dared to take him in for fear of eviction and on one occasion he was beaten by an owner's hireling and his crake was burnt. However, Tommy got another one and carried on his appointed task. At the 1872 Gala, when he saw the vast crowds gathered on the Racecourse, he declared, 'Lord now let thy servant depart in peace, for mine eyes have seen thy salvation.' Several months later he suffered a fall and died at his brother's house in Blaydon on 8 May 1873.[23] At the following Gala many banners were draped in black in honour of his memory. His portrait, with the crake, appears on the Edmondsley, Haswell and Springwell banners. Tommy gave his crake to Nicholas Wilkinson, the DMA treasurer, and it remained in the family until his son presented it to the union in 1933.[24]

The union continued to hold meetings at the Market Hotel, but as membership increased and, consequently, the number of lodge delegates,

Tommy Ramsey with his crake, on the Edmondsley (later Blackhouse) banner.

council meetings had to be held in the Town Hall in Durham. By 1873 the DMA realized that formal offices were now badly needed and, at a meeting in the Town Hall on 29 May, agreed to the construction of a new hall, with agents' houses.[25] North Road was chosen as the site, and designs in Gothic style for the new hall were produced by Thomas Oliver of Newcastle. The building work was undertaken by a Claypath contractor, Robert Robson & Sons, and was completed in June 1876.[26] It had offices for the union representatives, a large clock tower and a council chamber with platform space for around 30 and seating in the main body of the hall for 238. In 1875 Broomside and Witton lodges purchased banners showing the new hall, which at the time was incomplete.[27] The finished building also appeared on the banner of Lambton and West Thornley lodges. These latter paintings included the four statues in Sicilian marble on granite pedestals which had been set in the windows of the upper level at intervals, representing MacDonald, Crawford, Patterson and finally, in 1905, John Forman.[28]

The unveiling of the statue of William Crawford at the Miners' Hall, North Road, Durham, in 1892.

The Fabian, Sidney Webb, suggested that 'where lodges did survive in Durham before 1869, they seem to have been little more than pit clubs for benevolent purposes, rather than union branches as the term would now be understood'.[29] The association between the miners and benevolent funds, particularly of Friendly Societies, certainly predated the DMA, and the link appears to have continued well after the union's formation. The linking of the

Friendly Society regalia. Left: A member of the Grand Lodge of the Buffaloes, with sash and apron. Right: A member of the Independent Order of Oddfellows (Manchester Unity), with a sash.

new trade union with a benefit scheme covering sickness and accident had been raised at early delegate meetings. Friendly Societies had developed dramatically in the nineteenth century, and in the North-East some of the earliest were associated with trades, like the Flint Glass Makers' Benefit Society in Gateshead (1819), among the master mariners, seamen and keelmen of Sunderland, Monkwearmouth and Shields. From the 1830s they were linked to colliery relief funds.[30] After the Hartley disaster, the Northumberland and Durham Miners' Permanent Relief Fund was formed in June 1862.

The Select Society of Odd Fellows and the Ancient Free Gardeners appeared in Durham in the very early nineteenth century and were soon followed by temperance organizations. The Independent Order of Rechabites (Salford Unity), for instance, was established in 1835 and registered in 1854. Lodges, or 'tents', of the Order were being founded in County Durham by the 1840s. Many of these had a sociable function, but also provided sickness and death benefits. They are known to have had professionally made banners, and elaborate regalia. At Crook there was a 'Miners' Lodge' of the Ancient Order of Shepherds and the surviving Tutill banner of the 'Mayflower Lodge 674' Tow Law branch of the Order used the theme of 'We succour the widow and orphans'.[31] Shildon lodge of the DMA chose a Tutill pattern-book image clearly designed for the Order of Druids. The Druids, formed in 1858, also acted as a benefit society and had 78,758 members by 1875.[32]

Many of the allegorical symbols found on banners, including the pattern-book Druid banner, could also be related to aspects of another friendly

A membership certificate of the Independent Order of Rechabites (Salford Unity), with female figures and a mass of allegorical symbols.

society, namely Freemasonry. William Hutchinson, a Durham Freemason, wrote in 1775 that Freemasons had 'saved from oblivion many Druidical rites which were incorporated in the initiation to the first degree of masonry'.[33] While the square and compass, the dagger and trowel, and the laying-out string are symbols specifically orientated towards masons' work, their illustrations and regalia show elements that are more easily associated with the symbolism used by Tutill on banners, like the all-seeing eye, the sun and moon, the skull and crossbones, hour-glass, beehive, clasped hands and fouled anchor. Masons' beliefs are said to emphasize Prudence and the three cardinal virtues of Fortitude, Temperance and Justice. The three charities or graces are usually represented by them as female figures, which suggests comparison with the Friendship, Love and Truth pattern-book design. Certainly the representation of three female figures, with their distinctive attributes, are known from late eighteenth-century Freemasons' aprons.[34] The use of the term 'lodge' for both Freemasons and miners' union branches may also be suggestive, and at least two leading figures in the DMA are known to have been Freemasons – William Crawford and W.H. Patterson – both of whom rose to the rank of worshipful master. Several union lodge representatives were also members.

The banners used in the early 1870s showed a concern for good relations between owners and men, with several depictions showing the two sides shaking hands; but it was also stressed that these relations should be between equals, with a soundly based union negotiating from strength. The West Auckland banner verse indicated, too, that this was a union which also wished to emphasize its respectability: 'Let unity, peace, law

Westerton banner, with
portraits of G. Trevelyan,
Alexander MacDonald
and Lloyd Jones.

and order be our motto.' Several Biblical quotations were used to put over
the message of a fair day's wage for a fair day's work. Included in this
quest for fair dealing was the subject of payment by mineral wrought.
Black Boy banner showed two miners and an official weighing a tub, under
the title 'Justice'; Stanley lodge chose the quotation, 'A false balance is an
abomination, but a just weight is His delight'. The 1872 Mines Regulation
Act, although permitting checkweighers on site, left them in a vulnerable
position, with an owner able to rid himself of a checkweigher by
discharging all the workers, or dismissing him by Court of Summary
Jurisdiction on charges other than improper exercise of his office.[35] This
was altered by the 1887 Act, with the workers appointing and paying a
person to check both weights and the calculation of deductions.

Working practices and, particularly, industrial disputes in the county's
pits were dealt with by a system of negotiation and arbitration between the
DMA and the Durham Coal Owners' Association (formed in 1872). In
July 1872 a Joint Committee was formed, with six representatives from
both sides given wide powers to sort out disputes or to pass them on for
arbitration. Several banners showed examples of arbitration cases, with the
West Auckland banner at the 1873 Gala clearly showing the twelve men of
the Joint Committee seated around the negotiating table. The DMA chose

the respected Owenite, Lloyd Jones, to represent the union in the wage arbitration cases of 1874, 1875 and 1879. His role as arbitrator was depicted on the Westerton banner, where he is shown standing with Alexander MacDonald, holding the 1880 Employers Liability Act, and Sir George Trevelyan, who was involved in franchise reform.

By the third quarter of the nineteenth century industrial development in continental Europe and America had expanded and increasingly threatened Britain's position as the 'workshop of the world'. Towards the end of the century there were also apparent fluctuations in economic activity, both in Britain and abroad, including marked periods of depression. In the Durham coal trade wages had risen up to 1873, but the subsequent fall-off in demand for coal led to a series of wage reductions from 1874 and the adoption of a series of sliding scales from 1877 to 1889 (a practice also used to regulate the wages of other county miners' unions, Cleveland ironstone miners, Teesside blast furnacemen, and Weardale limestone quarrymen.) The reductions resulted in county coal strikes in 1879 and 1892, both of which were defeated by the owners.

Byremoor's banner at the 1872 Gala had declared,

Our masters they do tell us, that if we mean to stand,
We shall do ourselves an injury, and the trade will leave the land.
But in that we have advantage, and that you know is true;
For if the trade leaves England, we can leave it too.

As the depression bit, this became an increasingly favourable option, and the DMA and the Enginemen's Union established short-lived emigration schemes, in 1876–7 and 1897 respectively.[36] These included financial assistance for mineworkers and their families to seek new prospects in the colonies and North America – a practice also adopted by other unions, like the National Agricultural Labourers' Union and the Amalgamated Society of Carpenters and Joiners. Newspaper adverts and the arrival of American colliery agents in Britain in the late 1870s and 1880s attracted miners to the eastern states of Pennsylvania, Illinois and Kentucky. Bituminous coal and anthracite production in Pennsylvania had risen from 464,826 tons in 1840 to 11,760,000 tons in 1875, and by 1880 it formed 66 per cent of all US production, making it the nation's principal coalfield, with Illinois in second place. The new states of Minnesota, Oregon and Kansas had been established west of the Mississippi between 1858 and 1861, and by 1890 much of the interior of America was settled, with displacement and genocide wreaked upon the native Indian population. By 1881 posters were appearing in Durham offering work for miners in Kansas.[37] In Durham city, William Gray, of North Road, ran a booking office for all the principal emigrant ships which sailed to America. The emigrants who left the collieries of Durham and elsewhere and found work in the mines of America consequently increased her output and further threatened Britain's markets and the employment of *her* workers.

The union lobbied for improvements to working practices and social questions, but increasingly saw the need to be actively involved in the movement for parliamentary reform. The northern miners in the 1840s had favoured radical politics and had been leading supporters of Chartism and its demands for universal manhood suffrage, secret ballot, annual parliaments, payment of MPs and the removal of the property qualification.[38] When the Mines Regulation Bill was introduced in 1871 the miners of Lizzie lodge gave a warning on their banner: 'Pass this Bill soon, or as sure as fate if you don't pass it then we will.' In 1873 the miners and mechanics of Durham and Northumberland had demanded manhood suffrage and a redistribution of seats at a mass meeting on Newcastle Town Moor. The Woodifield banner bore the verse,

> We are resolved not to rest content,
> Until a man in parliament we have sent.

A Durham Franchise and Political Reform Association was formed in that year, with John Wilson, the rising star of the DMA, as its secretary, and numerous Liberal associations developed in mining villages, often led by lodge officials. Banners of lodges like Lambton and Westerton carried portraits of Gladstone, but the miners had favoured radicalism and were involved in many of the more contentious issues of the day. William Crawford and John Wilson, for instance, supported the Irish Land League, formed by Michael Davitt in 1879 to gain fair rents, fixed tenure and free sale. Land League branches mushroomed in County Durham and in 1881 the Durham Cokemen supported Joseph Cowen's attack on the government over its Coercion Bill and the arrest of the League's leaders, including Davitt.[40] Lloyd Jones, speaking from the balcony of the County Hotel, hoped that the 1881 Gala 'would be the commencement of the hand of good fellowship by the miners of the county of Durham to the Irish people'.[41] (This long-held concern for peace and reconciliation in Ireland presumably inspired the choice of John Hume MP as principal speaker at the 1995 Gala.)

John Wilson actually met Gladstone in 1884 as part of a joint TUC–Durham Miners' Franchise Association delegation on electoral reform.[42] With the extension of the franchise through the 1885 Reform Act, Crawford took Mid-Durham and John Wilson Houghton-le-Spring for the Liberals. It was another Liberal MP, the Quaker coal owner Sir Joseph Whitwell Pease, who nominated Crawford in 1885 and Wilson in 1890. The leaders of the DMA had worked to maintain a tightly structured and controlled union, favouring industrial peace rather than the financially damaging use of the strike weapon against the capitalists. J.W. Pease said of Crawford that he had created 'a better state of feeling between employer and employed'.[43] Crawford's death in 1890 saw no change to this policy, which was pursued by new agents, like John Wilson, John Johnson, Thomas Cann, William House, Samuel Galbraith and James Robson.

John Wilson was born in 1837 at Greatham and started work in a Weardale quarry.[44] He later found work at Ludworth, Littletown,

Thomas Cann, John
Wilson and William
House on the
Waterhouses banner.

Sherburn Hill, Broomside and Lady Seaham collieries. From 1860 he
spent some time at sea, but returned to mining and became secretary of
Sherburn Hill lodge, until it was broken by the owners. In 1864 he went
with his wife to America, but returned and formed a lodge at Haswell,
though the owners then refused to bind him. Around 1872 he was
instrumental in forming a lodge at Wheatley Hill and was elected to the
DMA council. When the colliery changed hands he was not re-employed,
and took on the job of organizer for the Miners' National Union in the
Midlands. He succeeded Nicholas Wilkinson as DMA treasurer in 1882
and rose in popularity in the union, becoming general secretary on
Patterson's death in 1895.

In 1850 John Johnson was born at Wapping, north of Newcastle.[45] From
nine years of age he worked in Northumberland pits, but moved to
Durham in 1878. He worked as a hewer at Andrews House, but in 1883
was elected to the DMA Executive Committee. He became general
treasurer in 1890, and financial secretary in 1895. Like Wilson, he was a
Primitive Methodist and a local preacher. His portrait appears on the
Blackhall and Waterhouses banners.

Thomas Henry Cann was born in Cornwall in 1868 and he started work
in the tin mines.[46] He later moved to the ironstone mines at Brotton,
Cleveland, before emigrating to the iron ore mines of Michigan.

Dangerous working practices there led to his return to Brotton. When the mine closed, he became a datal worker at Handen Hold colliery, but he later came to prominence over a case of intimidation at Castle Eden pit. Cann then joined the DMA Executive and succeeded Johnson as financial secretary. His portrait appears on a Ryhope banner.

In 1880 William House became West Auckland lodge delegate to the DMA and joined the Executive ten years later. He was vilified by extremists among the rank-and-file because of his support of moderation during the 1892 county strike.[47] However, in 1899 he became Joint Committee secretary, and in 1900 was elected union president, following John Forman's death. He appears with Johnson and Wilson on the banners of Blackhall and Waterhouses.

Samuel Galbraith, meanwhile, succeeded to the post of Joint Committee secretary. He was born in County Down in 1853, of Durham parents.[48] He started as a trapper at Trimdon Grange in 1863, but he moved around – to Tudhoe, Brancepeth 'C' pit and Browney by 1876. He began a process of self-improvement, expanding his education and joining the New Connexion Methodist chapel – virtually the company religion at Love's pits. In 1879 he became checkweighman at Browney; he joined the DMA Executive and became union treasurer. He also took a manager's ticket. In 1915 he resigned his post to become MP for Spennymoor division. He appears on the 1911 Browney banner.

James Robson was born at West Auckland in 1860 and started work at the local Harvey pit at the age of ten. He moved to Littleburn in 1871, but became checkweighman at Broompark in 1900. He later transferred to Bearpark, became a DMA agent and, on the death of Johnson, was elected Joint Committee secretary. Subsequently, he was chosen by ballot as president, following the death of House in 1917. He was over 6 ft tall and was said to have a 'considerable knowledge of the orator's art'.[49] His portrait appears on a Bearpark banner.

The late 1880s and first half of the 1890s saw major changes in the spheres of politics and trade unionism. Keir Hardie entered parliament for Mid-Lanark in 1888; the Independent Labour Party was formed in 1893; and the Miners' Federation of Great Britain broke away from the Miners' National Union in 1889, though failing to take with it Durham and Northumberland. Among its aims, the Federation sought an eight-hour day for miners, but this was opposed by John Wilson, as Durham hewers worked seven hours. Wilson, like Crawford, supported the policy of conciliation and he played a leading role in establishing Conciliation Boards in the county in 1895 and 1899. He also did not believe in the need for a separate Labour Party and remained an avowed Liberal. Increasingly, however, these policies came under attack.

In 1896 the ILP had sent Tom Taylor, their paid national organizer, to Durham;[50] and Tom Mann, a member of the Amalgamated Engineering Union and the Marxist Social Democratic Federation, travelled around the pit villages preaching socialism. Its inroads were evident, for instance, at

James Robson on the
1901 Bearpark banner.

Waterhouses, where, although the lodge officials were predominantly
Primitive Methodist and Liberal, the 100th Fabian Society had been
founded; *Fabian News* reported that 'we greatly welcome the formation of
a socialist society in a district and trade usually unfriendly to our ideas'.[51]
The clash of political beliefs was marked by the rank-and-file's choice of

Mann as a Gala speaker. At the 1901 Gala, Mann declared that 'It is no secret that he had never been at the Gala by the wish of the miner's executive' and particularly directed his attack at John Wilson.[52] At the turn of the century, at DMA council meetings, proposals to affiliate to the Labour Representation Committee had been defeated, but Cann believed there were moves to capture the union for socialism: 'personally I should be very sorry to see the union captured by the Socialists; but that is not likely to happen without a struggle.'[53] However, events moved rapidly. At the 1906 council meeting, in December, Lintz Green lodge introduced a proposal, 'To support labour candidates independent of any political party'.[54] This was supported by a majority of fifty-six. By 1907–8 fifty ILP branches had been formed around the county.

At the end of 1907 the lodges voted by 47,986 to 18,983 for the DMA to joint the MFGB, presumably aware of all that that stood for, including the Eight Hour Day, and this was carried through at the start of 1908. In 1909 the Federation affiliated to Labour. At the annual DMA council meeting in December 1909 the wording of the rules on political candidates was amended to read that they be 'run in conformity with the rules and constitution of the Labour Party'.[55] John Wilson refused to sign the Labour ticket, but continued to represent Mid-Durham as a Lib-Lab MP until his death in 1915.

The Eight Hour (Mines) Act forced the DMA leadership to negotiate an agreement with the owners on the means by which the Act should be operated in Durham. The agreement removed the limitation on the time allowed for coal drawing, and the number of shifts was to be decided by the management. The hours of hewers, stonemen, shifters etc. remained the same, while the ten hours for boys and datal men were reduced to eight. Some lodges accepted the agreement, but others objected to the three-shift arrangement and the fact that they were not consulted. A series of angry mass meetings were held, and several lodges, including Harraton, East Tanfield and Tanfield Lea, proposed that the Executive should resign. This discontent spilled over into the political field and was particularly directed at John Johnson, one of the negotiators of the agreement.

In the Lib-Lab selection of candidates to fight the Gateshead seat, Johnson had been chosen as the Labour representative over the adopted Liberal candidate, Harold Elverston. A large group of miners from South Moor, Tanfield Lea and Annfield Plain marched into Gateshead and processed round the streets urging the electorate to vote for anyone but Johnson. One of their banners was inscribed, 'We are the South Moor miners. Down with Johnson, the three-shift candidate, the miners ruination. Vote for Elverston'.[56] This action had its effect. Elverston polled 6,800 votes, followed by the Conservative candidate, with Johnson last, with 3,572 votes. John Wilson was appalled at this attack (he perhaps also knew that Johnson was ill and did not have long to live) and rebuked the perpetrators in his newsletter. Disturbances had also broken out at South Hetton, Murton and Horden, but eventually all returned to work.

Miners with a banner inscribed 'We are the South Moor miners. Down with Johnson, the three-shift candidate, the miners ruination. Vote for Elverston', attempting to influence the Gateshead electorate, 1910.

In 1910 George Harvey wrote an article in *The Socialist* asking, 'Does Dr. John Wilson MP serve the working class'.[57] This was picked up with interest by the lodges; Washington Glebe, for instance, purchased fifty copies of his pamphlet.[58] Wilson subsequently took Harvey to court over certain comments made in the article. Although he won the case, it was a hollow victory, with Harvey gaining popular support. Harvey was born in 1885 at Beamish. He studied at Ruskin College, Oxford, became a member of the Socialist Labour Party and in 1913 became checkweighman at Follonsby (Wardley).

Jack Lawson, who had started work at Boldon colliery, and, like Harvey, studied at Ruskin College before becoming checkweighman at Alma in 1910, was actively involved in the campaign to achieve a miners' minimum wage agreement, with W.P. Richardson and Joe Batey. Lawson later recalled,

> The need was very great, for I knew good men who sometimes got less than a pound for a week of coal hewing. I wrote a pamphlet, and came into conflict with one of the older miners officials who didn't believe in it, but I got cheered by conferences and great crowds – who agreed with me but did not believe we would ever get a minimum wage.[59]

From October 1911 the question of a minimum wage had been discussed by the MFGB, leading to a strike at the beginning of March 1912. A Minimum Wage Bill was introduced on 19 March, which eventually led to a decision to ballot the members on a return to work pending the settlement of district rates by joint boards under the new Act, which had received the Royal Assent on 26 March. This ballot was attacked in an open letter to Durham miners signed by Jack Lawson, Andrew Temple (Twizell lodge), H. Bainbridge (Shield Row) and W.P. Richardson (Usworth). They declared that 'A very prominent feature is that the Prime Minister, backed up by the capitalist press and our leader John Wilson MP are doing their level best . . . to prejudice the issue and to secure a majority for resumption of work. . . . Our policy must be one of no surrender until we know, and have laid down in plain figures, what we are going to work for. Vote against resumption.'[60]

In the county, support for the Labour Party at this time varied. In 1914 Arthur Henderson sent William Holmes as an organizer to North-West Durham, where, although the LRC was weak, ILP and Women's Labour League branches had been formed.[61] However, in Wilson's constituency of Mid-Durham, the ILP noted that attempts to form Labour organizations there were looked on with suspicion by the local lodges:

> Things that have been said in the past by some of our more enthusiastic friends have led to the miners imagining that any move that is being made is one that is in opposition to the sitting member, and it will take a good deal of plodding work on the part of the new organisation to overcome this prejudice.[62]

Wilson's popularity is shown in the number of banners which carried his portrait. He is frequently shown seated and in a pose probably based on a photograph which appeared in his history of the union, published in 1907.[63] In 1910 Durham University awarded him the honorary degree of Doctor of Civil Law.[64] This honour was also recorded on the banners of Dean and Chapter, Whitworth Park and Witton lodges, showing him in his doctoral gown. The gown is still preserved by the NUM (NE Area.) However, in 1915 Wilson died, and change became inevitable.

Seven months after Wilson's death the union moved into a new, larger hall, as membership and union business had increased. At the time of the 1871 Gala, membership had been around 4–5,000; the following year it was 31,000; and by 1914 it was 141,947 (120,881 full and 21,066 half members). The richly furnished, Edwardian Baroque-style hall was designed by H.T. Gradon, and completed by his assistant, E. Rutherford, when Gradon fell ill. A site was chosen at Red Hill, near the main railway line, and the work was begun in February 1914 by C. Groves of Chester-le-Street. The completed building was opened on 23 October 1915.[65] The great council chamber was fitted with oak seats and desks providing accommodation for nearly 400 delegates. The headquarters became a popular image on banners, like those of Esh Winning and Springwell. The old hall was sold in 1916, along with the agents' houses at 13 and 14 North Road, and 54–56 Crossgate.[66] The statues were taken from the windows of the old hall and set up at the side of the drive to the new building.

Springwell lodge banner with a view of the Miners' Hall, Red Hill.

After Wilson's death, additional agents were installed and, as James Larkin had advised at the 1914 Gala, 'If they were going to have an independent Labour Party, for God's sake let it be independent and not connected with the flabby, vindictive Liberal Party',[67] these new appointments clearly represented the party political changes of the DMA. These appointments included W.P. Richardson, who had opposed Wilson over the minimum wage. He was born at Usworth in 1873 and worked at the local pit, where his father was killed in the 1885 explosion, becoming lodge secretary in 1898.[68] Another was Joseph Batey, who was born in 1867 at Killingworth, Northumberland. He moved to South Shields, where, as a socialist, he became involved in local politics and was elected president of the St Hilda lodge, becoming checkweighman in 1897.[69] He joined the DMA Executive in 1901 and became an agent in 1915.

## The Interwar Period

The First World War influenced the choice of only a small number of banner paintings following the armistice. There was no attempt in them to glorify war, in fact a moral, Christian view was taken, emphasizing a desire for the end of all war and violence, giving highest praise to those

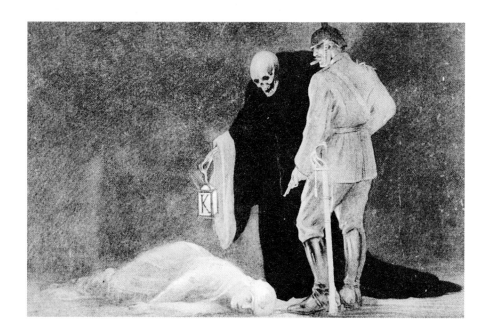

A propaganda postcard on the shooting of Nurse Cavell. German 'Kultur' says 'Well done' to her executioner.

who attempted to relieve the suffering in those years of carnage and remembering those who had paid the ultimate price.

Lumley Sixth pit lodge took an anti-war theme for its new banner, derived from Isaiah 2.4: 'they shall beat their swords into ploughshares, and their spears into sickles; nation shall not lift sword against nation, neither shall they learn war anymore.' The lodge expanded on the theme by adding a further motto, 'Time shall come when war shall cease, then union shall prevail', while the reverse followed with the image of the lion lying down with the lamb. Bowburn banner carried a portrait of Edith Louisa Cavell. She had studied medical treatment techniques in Germany and at the London Hospital, before becoming matron at the École Belge d'Infirmières Diplomées in 1907.[70] On the German occupation of Belgium, she was arrested for helping allied soldiers to escape across the Dutch border and was executed by firing squad on 12 October 1915. In 1919 her body was taken and reburied at Norwich Cathedral. Sacriston purchased a Tutill banner with a detailed illustration of a military hospital ward, showing a doctor dressed in khaki uniform visiting a patient, accompanied by a Queen Alexandra's nursing sister. The scene carries the motto, 'Be not weary in well doing'.

Three banners carried paintings of war memorials. Elemore banner showed the Easington Lane clock tower memorial, built on a site given by the Hon. F. Bowes Lyon in front of the village school.[71] It was designed by Jonathan Coxon, architect to the Lambton, Hetton & Joicey Coal Company; the firm paid for the erection of the tower, while the miners contributed to the purchase of the clock. The memorial plaques, bearing

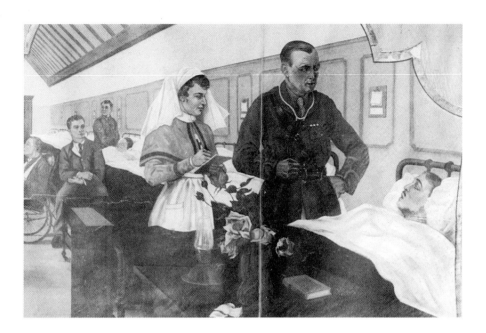

A military hospital ward
on the Sacriston banner.

the names of 151 local men who died in the war, were unveiled by Lord
Joicey on 27 August 1921. Murton banner, unfurled in 1925, showed the
cenotaph raised by the miners and officials of the colliery, recording 215
names. The white granite memorial was later to receive the names of 74
victims of the Second World War. The banner of Tursdale lodge, also of
1925, displayed the local aged miners' homes, laid out in a crescent, with
a war memorial in the form of a soldier set on a granite block bearing
plaques recording 41 dead.

The soldiers who returned were promised a 'fit country for heroes to
live in' and, though there was little sign of this, there was a deeply held
desire for a better world. This was expressed in a variety of pictorial and
literary forms on Durham banners, where oppression is cast aside to reveal
a rural idyll of pleasant houses and gardens, with children playing in the
sunshine. The pattern-book 'Emancipation of labour' also saw the people
being directed by 'Progress' to a new world, the 'Economic
Commonwealth'. Adventure, Pelton Fell and Witton lodges took as their
motto a quote from Symonds: 'These things shall be; A loftier race than
e'er the world hath known shall rise, with flame of freedom in their souls
and light of knowledge in their eyes.' Craghead and Derwent lodge
banners carried the Biblical image of David standing over the body of
Goliath, where the small figure of Labour has dealt the death blow to the
giant of Capitalism.

Capitalism was often depicted as the evil beast. Walter Crane used the
theme in a cartoon, 'Socialist reconstruction versus capitalist constriction',
produced for the May Day 1909 issue of *Justice*. The female figure of

May Day, standing over the earth and raising aloft the torch of Socialism, is shown throttling the snake of Capitalism which has bound itself around the peoples of the globe. The Tutill banner of the Dock, Wharf, Riverside and General Workers' Union of Great Britain and Ireland (Export Branch) followed a similar theme, in which a man wrestles with a serpent on a storm-girt crag, with the mottoes, 'We will fight and may die but we shall never surrender' and 'This is a holy war and we shall not cease until all destitution, prostitution and exploitation is swept away'.[72] Perhaps these designs reached their most powerful and dramatic climax in an Ashington banner from Northumberland, where a line of injured miners are marching from a burning colliery, carrying the coffin of a dead brother. Near the pithead is the brooding menace of the dragon of 'Profit and Private Ownership', but rising up from the flames is a male figure ready to hurl the spear of 'State Control' that would destroy the monster.[73] The image of the workers achieving victory over the old order in the Russian Revolution began to attract a number of Durham miners to Communism. Certainly by 1919 the *Durham Chronicle* could report that Bolshevik literature, and revolutionary leaflets, were distributed broadcast.[74]

Three years after the Russian Revolution, the Communist Party of Great Britain was formed. It became affiliated to the Communist International and was required to infiltrate and take over trade union and Labour Party branches, with the aim of ultimately achieving a socialist revolution. The executive of the Labour Party were aware of the Communists aims, and attempts at CP affiliation to the Labour Party were blocked at party conferences from 1921. Vigorous attacks were made on Communist activity by Labour and MFGB leaders, with a similar response from DMA officials. Three lodges, however, all in the northern part of Durham, towards the Tyne – Chopwell, Follonsby (Wardley) and Bewicke Main – chose banner designs which were the most obviously socialist and Communist in character. The area around Chopwell had a reputation for militancy going back to the early nineteenth century, particularly among the forgemen at Crossleys iron works at Winlaton. The village grew up in the 1890s, around the pit which supplied the fuel for the blast furnaces of the Consett Iron Company. From the 1920s the socialist influence can be seen in the naming of the parallel rows of Marx and Lenin terraces, with the neighbouring E.D. Morel and Owen terraces.

James Stephenson, secretary of Rowlands Gill lodge and chairman of the Durham District Committee of the National Miners' Minority Movement, said, 'there are two ways of making a Communist; one is reading Karl Marx and the other is being kicked around by the employers. Consett Iron Company made far more Communists than ever Karl Marx made.'[75] A small group of left-wing militants were active in Chopwell and district before the First World War, and a Socialist Sunday school (associated with the Labour Church movement founded by John Trevor in the 1890s) had been formed,[76] but the anti-war stance taken by them was not popular in the village and their numbers declined. This was reversed with the postwar problems in the coal industry. Best known of the group was the Lawther family. Will Lawther was born at Choppinton, Northumberland, in 1889 and moved with his parents to Chopwell, where he started work at the pit. By 1909 he was secretary of the Chopwell ILP branch and later moved to South View, Highfield, when he became checkweighman at Victoria Garesfield colliery. He was not a member of the Communist Party, but had studied at the Central Labour College from 1911–12, where classes were Marxist orientated. He was a member of the Durham Miners' Forward Movement and one of the leaders of the National Left Wing Movement, which aimed at creating a more militant socialist Labour Party. Lawther was a close friend of John MacLean, the great teacher of Marxist economics, a leading revolutionary figure of Red Clydeside and one of the honorary presidents of the First All-Russian Congress of Soviets, alongside Lenin, Trotsky and Liebknecht.[77]

Steve Lawther, born in 1896, lived in Marx Terrace, Chopwell, and had been a local lodge official before taking up the position of rent collector for Blaydon Urban District Council. By 1927 he was secretary of Chopwell, Spen and District Labour Representation Committee, with brother Will as chairman. Steve's younger brother, Andrew, born in 1905, lived at 23 Trent Street, Chopwell, and worked as a miner. Other left-wingers included Vipond Hardy, an atheist, born in 1870, who lived in Severn Street, Chopwell; Robert Curry, of Blyth Street, Chopwell, who had studied at Ruskin College and was described as 'one of the most active Communists in the district';[77] Edward Wilson, of Glenburn Terrace in Rowlands Gill; and William Jobling of Chopwell. Jobling was active during the 1926 strike and in 1934 debated at Hetton-le-Hole on the subject, 'That the policy of the Russian Communist Party, known as Bolshevism, would, if applied to Britain, be beneficial to the workers'. He died later in Spain.

In 1924 Chopwell lodge purchased a banner from Tutills which carried three portraits – a central painting of Keir Hardie, flanked by those of Marx and Lenin. Accompanying the portraits were the badges of the Labour Party and the Communist Party, and a motto taken from a Walt Whitman poem:

> We take up the task eternal, and the burden and the lesson,
> Pioneers! O Pioneers!

The banner was unfurled on 25 July, the eve of the Gala, apparently by James Larkin (1876–1947). Larkin worked for the National Union of Dock Labourers in his home town of Liverpool, before being sent as a militant organizer to the Dublin docks, where he was involved in the 1912 Lock-Out. He spoke at the 1914 Gala, making an undisguised attack on John Wilson and the Liberal Party. Soon afterwards he went to America and was active in the trade union and syndicalist movements, for which he spent some time in prison, before being sent back to Ireland. During the

The Chopwell 'Red' banner, with (left to right) Jack, Will and Steve Lawther, John Gilliland, Ned Wilson, John Stevenson and Eddie Lawther

year that he came to Chopwell he was also involved in the formation of the Communist International-approved Workers' Union of Ireland.

The choice of banner design was not unanimously accepted, and when it was unfurled some women threw stones at it.[79] The next day, Gala Day, as it was being carried to the station, there was a further attack, in which stones and soot were thrown. On reaching the Racecourse at Durham, it was set up in a prominent position near one of the platforms. There had been a threat to burn it while it was in Durham, but George Lansbury, commenting on the banner, urged understanding: 'The only enemies of the working class today', he said, were 'ignorance and prejudice'. On 23 August 1924 the banner was again unfurled, this time by A.J. Cook.[80]

The Follonsby banner bore a central portrait of Lenin, with surrounding portraits of A.J. Cook, James Connolly, Keir Hardie and George Harvey. With Lenin were the Communist symbols of the Red Star and the Hammer and Sickle, set in laurel wreaths on either side of a rising sun. The banner also carried the verse,

> Come join in the only battle
> wherein no man can fail;
> where whoso falleth and dieth,
> yet his deeds shall still prevail.

The Follonsby (Wardley)
'Red' banner, with
portraits of Lenin, James
Connolly, Keir Hardie,
A.J. Cook and George
Harvey.

James Connolly, born in Edinburgh in 1868, was chosen for inclusion on
the banner because he was a syndicalist, socialist theorist and Marxist.[81]
He became Belfast organizer of the Irish Transport and General Workers'
Union in 1911, after a spell in America, and was associated with the Irish
Citizens Army, formed during the Dublin Lock-Out. Increasingly he
moved towards nationalism and when the First World War broke out he

The 1924 Bewicke Main 'Red' banner, with portraits of Ramsay MacDonald, Keir Hardie, Lenin, Ben Oliver and A.J. Cook.

discussed armed insurrection with the Irish Republican Brotherhood. He joined the IRB's secret army council in February 1916 and stood on the steps of the General Post Office in Dublin when Pearse declared an Irish Republic and the start of the Easter Rising. During the ensuing battle Connolly was wounded in the ankle and, when the rising was crushed, he was taken, court-marshalled and, on 12 May, executed by firing squad, strapped in a chair. George Harvey, who had attacked the policies of John Wilson, was a socialist thinker, pamphleteer and militant trade unionist, who acquired the sobriquet of 'Wardley's Lenin'.

The village of Bewicke Main lay close to the River Team and the pit, sunk in 1868. Long and Short Row formed the north side, with High Row on the west, two short streets called Cross Row in the middle, and the pit on the east side. South of High Row were the only public buildings, a stone-built school, a corrugated iron Primitive Methodist chapel and an institute. The lodge banner carried a central portrait of Ramsay MacDonald, with flanking portraits of Keir Hardie, Lenin, Ben Oliver and A.J. Cook. Ben Oliver started work at Birtley iron works, but moved to the Pelaw Main collieries, and in 1915 became checkweighman of Ouston 'E' lodge. He served on the Chester-le-Street Board of Guardians, but was expelled by the government with other members for their support of miners and their families during the 1926 strike. He became chairman of the Rural District Council and in 1928 was elected to Durham County Council with a 1,207 majority.[82]

During the short boom at the end of the war, the MFGB pursued demands for 30 per cent wage increases, a six-hour day and nationalization of the mines, with joint worker-state control. The government offered only an additional shilling a day, plus an inquiry into the industry, to which the miners' response was to vote by an overwhelming majority for strike action – Durham by 76,024 to 16,248. This, however, was postponed when the Federation was persuaded by the government to participate in the 1919 Sankey Royal Commission inquiry. The two-stage Sankey investigation concluded that the miners' claims on wages, hours and nationalization were justified. The government then deceived the miners by appearing to accept the findings, leading to the strike being called off, before making changes to all but the fundamental question of nationalization.

There was no follow-up action, apart from a 'Mines for the Nation' propaganda campaign (a Mainsforth banner carried this slogan) and a 'Datum Line' strike in October–November 1920 on wage claims. A far more serious event occurred at the end of March 1921 when the government deregulated the mines and returned them to the coal owners. The owners offered dramatically reduced wages for increased output, while the Federation called for a National Wages Board and national pool. The stoppage of underground pumps and the support of their colleagues in the Triple Alliance – with the Transport Workers' Federation and the railwaymen – were the miners' principal levers, but at a private meeting in the House of Commons, the MFGB secretary, Frank Hodges, was said to have made certain comments which were taken to indicate his willingness to accept temporary district settlements, which excluded the question of a national pool. Lloyd George used this, calling on the miners to negotiate on the basis of this new situation. Hodges denied using the words attributed to him and reaffirmed their demands, whereupon the TWF and NUR called off their support on 'Black Friday', 15 April. The offer by Lloyd George to provide a subvention in support of wages, and then his threat to withdraw it, led to the MFGB leaders sueing for peace, even though the districts had just voted to stay out (Durham by a 49,247 majority). A national wage agreement was accepted in July 1921 and it was not long before wages began to fall.

In 1922 the Lloyd George coalition was succeeded by a short-lived Conservative administration under Bonar Law and his successor, Stanley Baldwin, which collapsed over tariff reform. It was replaced in January 1924 by the first, minority Labour government, led by Ramsay MacDonald, with the left largely excluded. Philip Snowden was appointed Chancellor of the Exchequer, with Arthur Henderson at the Home Office, Emanuel Shinwell as Minister of Mines and Attlee as MacDonald's parliamentary private secretary. Frank Hodges gave up the secretaryship of the MFGB, expecting a cabinet position, only to receive a junior minister's post. He was succeeded by the syndicalist agent of the South Wales Miners' Federation, A.J. Cook.[83] Changes also occurred at Red Hill in 1924 when Thomas Cann died. W.P. Richardson moved to the post of general secretary. He had been chairman of the Durham Miners' Forward Movement from 1914. In 1915 he became a DMA agent, and joined the executive of the MFGB in 1917, later becoming its treasurer.

James Gilliland became an agent. He was born at West Rainton and worked in the Peases West district of Crook.[84] He served as checkweighman at Lintz Green from 1897 until 1907 when he was elected parliamentary agent for the Chester-le-Street division. As a result of the 1909 Osborne Judgement, he moved to Ouston 'E' as checkweighman, before his transfer to Red Hill. His portrait is shown on a Hamsteels banner. John Edmund Swan was born in 1877 and brought up at Dipton.[85] He started work as a farm hand, but changed to mining, becoming checkweighman at East Howle in 1904 and subsequently at Dipton Delight in 1912. He studied at Ruskin College and served on the DMA Executive from 1909. In 1918 he took the Barnard Castle seat, only to lose it at the 1922 General Election. When Joseph Batey was elected to Spennymoor, Swan's nomination for the post of financial secretary was not initially accepted, but after complaints by lodges like Washington Glebe, he was nominated and chosen for the post.[86] Swan's portrait appeared on the Hobson banner.

Another agent was Peter Lee. Born in 1864 at Duff Heap Row, Fivehouses, Trimdon Grange, he started work as a pony driver at Littletown, aged ten.[87] Between 1879 and 1886 he worked at fifteen Durham collieries. He briefly emigrated to America, returned to Durham pits and spent 1896–7 mining in South Africa, before coming back again to Durham. In 1902 he became checkweighman at Wheatley Hill and his portrait appears on two of the lodge banners. He served on the parish council, Easington Rural District Council and, in 1909, Durham County Council. In 1919 he became a DMA agent. His portrait also appears on the banners of Elemore and South Hetton.

Ramsay MacDonald chose Jack Lawson as Financial Secretary to the War Office in the Labour government. He started work at Boldon colliery, but dramatically changed his habits from gambling to Methodism, reading extensively and becoming involved in lodge debates.[88] In 1904 he joined the ILP. With the help of his parents and Canon Moore Ede he went to Ruskin College in 1907–8, but returned to the pit. In 1910 he became checkweighman at Alma and in 1912 was involved in the Minimum Wage debate with John Wilson. Seven years later he was returned as MP for Chester-le-Street division.

The MacDonald government recognized Soviet Russia, but a Communist incident in Britain – the mishandling of the Campbell sedition case – led to the government's collapse. J.R. Campbell had been arrested for publishing an 'Appeal to Soldiers' in the Communist journal *Workers*

The portrait of Peter Lee
on the Wheatley Hill
banner.

*Weekly*, urging them not to use their weapons in a class war against fellow workers. It turned out that Campbell had a good war record and was only the acting editor. When the case was withdrawn, the government was defeated on an opposition vote for an inquiry and MacDonald dissolved parliament. The Zinoviev Letter, purporting to be from the president of the Communist International to McManus, the CPGB representative on the executive of the Third International, urging the formation of Red Army units in the British Party, as part of the developments towards revolution, destroyed Labour's chances in the subsequent general election. The letter had actually been forged by Sidney Reilly, an agent of the British Secret Service.[89]

Baldwin formed a new government and accepted a return to the Gold Standard, as a means of restoring prestige and economic stability. In fact it worsened the country's ability to export, particularly her staple products, like coal, in an increasingly competitive market. The owners' solution, at the end of June 1925, was to cut wages and increase hours, while ensuring to themselves guaranteed profits. The MFGB reacted by seeking support from the TUC General Council, which they got, including an agreement by the road, rail and docks unions not to move coal supplies if the owners threatened a lock-out. This had the desired effect. The owners withdrew their notices and Baldwin agreed to provide a subsidy up to 1 May while another inquiry into the state of the industry was carried out. This was accepted on Friday 31 July 1925.

'Red Friday' was seen by some as a victory for the Left, but by others as simply an armistice. In a newspaper article, Hensley Henson, the Bishop of Durham, had referred to the economic and moral consequences of a strike, and Dean Welldon had adversely commented on the actions of trade unions. At the Gala, on 25 July 1925, a banner inscribed 'To hell with bishops and deans, we demand a living wage' was displayed on the Racecourse and Ramsay MacDonald attacked the bishop's interference in the coal dispute.[90] During the proceedings, Dean Welldon was making his way to the platform to give a pre-arranged address on temperance, once the speeches had concluded. Certain elements in the crowd, however, hustled him towards the river, aiming to throw him in. Police quickly moved in, a motor launch was hailed and the dean was extricated unhurt.

The TUC, during this phase, made no significant preparations in the event of a breakdown in negotiations until 27 April 1926. The government, on the other hand, moved quickly to prepare plans for troop deployments and the stationing of warships, while giving active support to regional counter-strike groups and the Organisation for the Maintenance of Supplies.

The Royal Commission under Sir Herbert Samuel recommended nationalization of royalties, restructuring of the industry, but also reductions in wages. A.J. Cook's slogan, 'Not a penny off the pay, not a second on the day', marked deadlock between the two sides. As April ended, the owners' notice expired and the government invoked the

Emergency Powers Act, although they agreed to private negotiations, though this was quickly dropped when NATSOPA members refused to print a virulent condemnation of the strike in a *Daily Mail* leader article. On 4 May the General Strike started.

Under the government's emergency plan, Sir Kingsley Wood was appointed as Civil Commissioner for the Northern District, with an emergency administration based in St Mary's Place, Newcastle. The response of the miners was the formation of Councils of Action to organize the area and ensure effective picketing. This was described as 'a practical experiment in Bolshevism'.[91] Thirteen councils were active in Durham by May 1926.[92] Miners at the Consett Iron Co. collieries of Chopwell, Derwent, Langley Park, Medomsley and Westwood had been locked out since June 1925 and it was the Council of Action in the Chopwell area that organized mass picketing and issued permits for the transport of foodstuffs, while also transmitting propaganda through a newsheet, *The Northern Light*, produced by Steve Lawther from a council house he shared as an office with the local sanitary inspector. George Lumley, a member of the Stanley Communist Party, compared their local Council of Action to a Soviet and said that they 'got an immediate working class dictatorship in their own locality'.[93] When the police arrived at Chopwell they were told by the pickets, 'There is no government here today. We are carrying on.'[94] Flying squads were organized to break up the picketing and a new police division was created in the area, under Supt Davis of the North Riding constabulary. Cuthbert Headlam, Conservative MP for Barnard Castle, noted in his diary that the Chief Constable, even with Yorkshire reinforcements, had insufficient men to cover all the pit villages: 'If the strike goes on his job will be one of the greatest difficulty.'[95]

During picketing, Will Lawther and Henry Bolton, the chairman of Blaydon UDC, were arrested trying to prevent a food wagon under police escort moving from Winlaton Mill without a Council of Action permit. They were tried at Gateshead, found guilty under the Emergency Powers Act and fined. Both men refused to pay and were sentenced to two months' imprisonment. Demonstrators outside the court were dispersed by police, while Lawther and Bolton were taken to Durham gaol under heavy guard. They were released on 29 June and returned home to a hero's welcome.

Edward Fairbridge recalled the Council of Action office in Stanley – the Council's committee and local leaders were watched by police and public meetings were attended by police note-takers.[96] Two officers had been present at meetings at Catchgate and Tanfield Lea, where speakers included Ralph Jobling, of New Kyo Council of Action, and John Jeffery, chairman of Tanfield UDC. Both were later arrested. Jobling was accused of saying that his friends in the army and navy had reported a good many of their number would follow the Red Flag when the opportunity arrived. He was sentenced to three months' imprisonment. Jeffrey was released when it emerged the police had memorized his speech and written it up later.

While the General Strike remained solid in the pit villages, the TUC was desperate for a solution to the crisis and, without any form of guarantee, accepted the personal solution proposed by Herbert Samuel. This included reorganization of the industry, a reduction in the basic rate of pay and a 7.5 hour day. Samuel had no government backing, but through the influence of moderates like J.H. Thomas of the NUR and Arthur Pugh of the Iron and Steelworkers' Union, the General Council accepted Samuel's suggestions and met Baldwin to call off the General Strike.

Not surprisingly there was great bitterness at this betrayal. Councillor Pearson of Whitburn said that 'The TUC had left the miners to be crucified'.[97] Baldwin then removed the veil of impartiality by taking the side of the owners, introducing legislation to increase the miners' hours to eight. The MFGB refused to accept the changes to wages and hours and the miners were left to fight on.

While soup kitchens were set up in most mining communities, the provision of relief in the Chester-le-Street area had major repercussions. The local Board of Guardians had fifty-nine members, thirty-nine of them union officials or miners. On 6 May an emergency committee was established, which co-opted other Labour representatives and effectively took over. On 3 June they agreed to make full payments to single men on strike who were financial members of the DMA, which was considered an illegal act – a single man had to be starving to be eligible for aid. The government reacted on 30 August when the Ministry of Health removed the Guardians under the Chester-le-Street (Default) Order 1926 and appointed their own officials under N.B. Batterbury.[98] Batterbury immediately had police placed at offices to deter single men from seeking relief. Over 5,000 miners marched to the Board's offices in support of the old Guardians, carrying the red banner of Birtley Communist Party and another inscribed, 'We want bread. To hell with the Ministry'.[99]

The government's decision to reduce relief was roundly attacked as a measure to break the miners' will. A.J. Cook spoke of the effect on wives and children and declared, 'Baldwin, may your conscience worry you to the grave for your act.'[100] The new Chester-le-Street Guardians cut the relief to the miners' wives from 12s to 8s, as it was felt that it was helping to maintain the striker. The response, in October, was a mass march of women, with miners' bands and banners, to the Guardians' offices. They were prevented from entering by ranks of police, though a deputation was allowed to enter. They left with the offer of an inquiry, but a small group of the crowd rushed the gate and broke through, only to be ejected by police reinforcements. As the crowd was moving away, a bandsman, James Slater, was knocked down and killed by a coal wagon carrying police. At his funeral, the cortège was accompanied by the banners of Ouston 'E', Urpeth, Bewicke Main and Black House lodges and the flags of Birtley Labour Party and Communist Party.[101]

The Communist Party in County Durham expanded at this time, their number raising the party's national membership to 10,730 in October, its peak figure. At Chopwell, membership rose from 1, at the beginning of May, to 200 by August, and in the Fatfield area 230 new members were recruited in July–August.[102] This was, in part, attributable to the missionary work of men like Robin Page Arnot, a member of the Central Executive Committee of the CPGB from 1924, and William Brain, the CP Midlands organizer, though some of the party's popularity seems to have been short-lived.

Leading Communists, like Harry Pollitt, Shapurji Saklatvala, Tom Mann (former chairman of the British bureaux of the Red International of Labour Unions until he became president of the National Minority Movement in 1924) and Willie Gallacher (leader of the shop stewards in the Clydeside dockers' strike of 1916), were brought to Durham to stir up and maintain the unity of purpose.[103] Gallacher had not long been out of prison, having been arrested with many of the CP leaders in October 1925.

The Gala in Durham was cancelled, because of the dispute, but an unofficial Gala was held at Burnhope on 17 July, organized in about five days by Jim Hobbs, the local lodge secretary. Around 35,000 attended, with 50 lodge banners. The lodge also pulled off a coup by bringing A.J. Cook to speak, accompanied by Will Lawther, Ebby Edwards and the Revd Dunnico, the Consett MP. Cook, already hoarse, spoke for ninety minutes, stating their case, declaring how 'Their opponents said that there was too much coal, so they must work longer and produce more', but that it was 'Better to fill all their gaols and workhouses than to fill any more of their cemeteries with longer hours'.[104]

From July, however, men gradually started to return to work under heavy police guard. As three workers were returned to their homes in Silksworth by police, they cordoned off the street and secured the surrounding side streets by baton charging anyone in the way. Councillor Martin of Chester-le-Street condemned their actions: 'It is my candid opinion that we are just about reaching a state in this county where a second Prussia is existing.'[105] Efforts by police to move blacklegs to their homes in Esh Winning led to a disturbance, during which a red flag was waved and a banner displayed, inscribed on one side, 'Cowards, traitors, blacklegs', and on the other, 'United we stand. Good old Cook'.[106] Two lodge officials were arrested, and at other incidents, lodge officials from Thrislington, Hamsteels and Thornley were taken.

As the strike dragged on, destitution drove increasing numbers to return to work. A.J. Cook played a prominent role, with his visits and speeches, in maintaining the strikers' morale, and there was also increased Communist activity; however, political involvement in the dispute also led to the creation of breakaway non-political unions.[107]

There had been meetings in Newcastle and at Esh Winning, leading to the formation of a Northumberland and Durham Miners' (Non-Political) Union, though the constitution of the coal owners' association did not

Hamsterley Colliery Comic Band at the Burnhope Gala during the 1926 strike.

permit them to negotiate with the union as it did not represent the majority of the miners. The number of the union's branches rose to thirty-seven in 1927, and by the beginning of 1928 seventeen were added, with another nine in the process of formation.[108] By January 1928 George Spencer was taking non-political miners to work a new district at Harworth, in Nottinghamshire.[109] Frank Hodges, the former MFGB secretary and secretary of the International Miners' Federation (IMF) in 1925, gave his support to longer hours and the non-political unionists and was rewarded by the Conservative government with a position on the Northern Electricity Board. The IMF reacted by forcing his resignation from the Federation in June 1927, and at the Gala in July banners carrying his portrait were covered over.[110]

Through Stalin's influence, the Communist Party's attitude to the Labour Party changed dramatically in 1928.[111] At the Ninth Plenum of the Comintern in February it was decided that the Labour Party was no more than another bourgeois capitalist party which had failed the workers and should not be supported by Communists. This decision split the British members into those, like Harry Pollitt of the Boilermakers' Union, who accepted the Comintern view, and those like Gallacher, who still believed the defeat of capitalism could only be achieved by affiliation to, and eventual takeover of, the Labour Party.

The change from the 'United Front' approach of the Communist Party to one of sectarianism, 'Class against class', had an impact in the Durham coalfield, where conditions after the strike got worse. As a means of recovering lost markets, the coal owners began to export coal at dramatically reduced prices.[112] To enable this practice of undercutting to be carried on, hours were increased (hewers from 6.5 hours in 1921 to 7 hours 50 minutes in 1927) and operating costs were reduced by cutting wages.

At the District Board meeting on wages at the beginning of 1928, the 'independent' chairman, Sir William Plender, took the side of the owners and reduced the minimum percentage to basis wages (then at 89) to 65, and the subsistence wage from 6s 8½d to 6s 6½d. Consequently hewers' wages would be reduced by about 1s 2d per shift. Several collieries immediately reacted by restricting output, principally led by the putters at Horden, Ryhope, Harton, Shotton and Thrislington. The Communist Party saw this as an ideal opportunity to become involved in the dispute, to develop it and to destabilize the existing union leadership. James Robson, the DMA president, was aware of their activities in the coalfield and had said at the unfurling of the Twizell lodge banner in 1927, 'so far as the Communist party are concerned, the fact was plain that members of that party sought election to miners' councils or executive committees not to obey the orders of those who elected them, but to obey the orders of Moscow.'[113]

The Durham Miners' Minority Movement and the Communist Party began the attack by issuing inflammatory strike bulletins. In one issue they announced,

> You have been waiting for Jim Robson and Co to sound the Call to Action. They will not do it Comrades. They have lined themselves up with our enemies. What are you going to do about it? Will you meekly submit because the Leaders have failed? No!! A thousand times No!! Be MEN!! Refuse any longer to descend the Pits for wages which mean Semi-Starvation.[114]

A series of mass meetings were also organized at Horden, Chester-le-Street, Ferryhill, Felling, Blaydon, South Shields and Herrington Burn, where Sam Cotterill of Townley (secretary of the Durham Miners' Minority Movement), James Ancrum of Felling, Alec White of Morrison lodge and twenty-five others were elected to meet the DMA leaders and to urge action. The meeting, at Red Hill, was acrimonious and the representatives left, aiming to carry out more widespread local stoppages. Within the month, however, most of the strikers had agreed to go back. A Communist news-sheet, *Durham Woman*, issued by the Durham Women's United Front Campaign Committee on 16 April, declared, 'It was only the action of the Red Hill officials that got the men back to work. The Unity of the workers was broken by the leaders.'[115]

Pollitt put forward the Comintern view at a meeting in Horden on 15 July 1928, believing that 'thousands of men and women (are) fed up to the teeth with the treacherous policy pursued by the Labour leadership at the present time, and who will welcome the opportunity of sending to

Parliament the representatives of a party whose business it will be, all the time, to rally the workers, both politically and industrially, in a common fight against our class enemies'.[116]

At the Gala in July the speakers chosen by the lodges included Maxton, along with Emmanuel Shinwell and David Kirkwood, another Clydeside shop-steward, deported under the Defence of the Realm Act in 1916 and involved in the 1919 40-hour week strike on the Clyde with Gallacher and Shinwell. Also on the platform was Shapurji Saklatvala, the Communist member of the North Battersea Labour Party, returned as MP in the November 1922 and 1924 general elections. Unlike Gallacher, Saklatvala supported the new thesis. From the platforms, Kirkwood and Saklatvala attacked the discussions between prominent industrialists and leading figures in the TUC, the Mond–Turner talks, which sought to achieve peace in industry, Saklatvala referring to them as 'a damnation for the working classes'.[117] Trouble erupted when Saklatvala announced, from Platform 2, that Scottish miners' delegates had come to the Gala, and that he hoped they would speak to the Durham miners. When the official speeches were concluded, members of the Labour League of Ex-Servicemen, wearing uniforms, took over the platform and were joined by the Communist Lanarkshire miners' secretary, Willie Allan. They then sang 'The Red Flag', but left when Peter Lee (a fist-fighter of some repute) threatened to throw them off personally. Peter Lee later warned the Durham miners of the disunity caused by Communist and Minority Movement activity in Scotland, and of what might happen in Durham: 'They stand for change by civil war and destruction, we for change through the ballot box and reconstruction to bring in the new social order.'[118]

Nationally, the new line had a serious effect on the membership of the CPGB. In Durham, a Communist group was formed at West Cornforth in 1929, and the Seaham and Dawdon party had 120 members in the same year.[119] Movements for closer ties with the Soviet Union were also fostered. Will Lawther became chairman of the British National Committee of the Friends of Soviet Russia, while Victoria Garesfield and Chopwell lodges urged the formation of an Anglo-Russian Miners' Committee, but the DMA executive consistently voted it out of order.[120]

For the majority of miners, however, the Labour Party was seen as their best hope for a better world, and when the Communist Party chose Harry Pollitt to oppose Ramsay MacDonald for the Seaham seat at the general election in May 1929, Pollitt took 1,541 votes to MacDonald's 35,615.[121] MacDonald's popularity is evinced in the number of banners which carried his portrait, like those of Bewicke Main, Brandon, Langley Park, Littleburn and Tursdale lodges, and probably others.

Will Lawther, who had been elected to the Labour Party National Executive in 1922, took Barnard Castle at the 1929 election. He became a DMA agent in 1935. Communist-supported disturbances, however, continued into 1929 with an outbreak at Dawdon over proposed reductions in piece rates.[122] Lodge officials opposed their involvement: 'They are appealing for funds and using the same at their own discretion for feeding etc., for the sole purpose of furthering their political aims and objects.'[123] This included appealing to the Workers' International Relief (or Mezhrabkom), an organization founded initially as a charity, but known to the Home Office as a subversive organization which devoted itself to propaganda disguised as relief.[124]

A.J. Cook also opposed the 'new line' policy and attacked the Party in a speech in Dawdon Miners' hall in May: 'There is a deliberate campaign being conducted with the object of disintegrating this organisation, destroying the Miners' Federation, and defeating the return of the Labour Government. . . . Your dispute has suffered considerably by the interference of an organisation that is discredited wherever it has interfered during the last three months.'[125] The dispute was eventually concluded through arbitration by the Ministry of Mines. A.J. Cook died on 2 November 1932 from overwork and cancer. James Robson summarily commented, 'No doubt his impatience of the general conditions under which thousands of miners were living and working led him into extreme methods of thinking and acting. Upon this rock many capable and useful men have floundered. A little experience would have tempered and increased the value of those services, and there is no doubt that Cook was getting that when he died.'[126] However, there clearly was a great rapport between Cook and many people in the mining communities of Durham, which is reflected in the number of banners which bear his portrait. Robson, too, was suffering the strain of overwork; he suffered a physical breakdown in 1931 and died in 1934.

In County Durham at this time, the impact of the depression was there for all to see. Wages per man shift in 1931 had risen 28 per cent above the 1914 rate, but the cost of living had risen by 47 per cent.[127] A range of schemes appeared to alleviate the destitution, most of which only scraped the surface of the problem. There were initial aid projects, basically charitable giving, ranging from the Mansion House Fund to southern towns and counties adopting a depressed colliery village. Other schemes involved the relocation of people from the distressed areas, like the government's Canadian harvester scheme which shipped 8,449 miners from the areas in 1928, theoretically to cut corn in the prairies, though they largely found themselves in competition with native workers.[128] The Child Emigration Society transported children from Durham, Lanchester, Teesdale and Hartlepool workhouses to farm schools in Australia,[129] where Kingsley Fairbridge's imperialist aim was to create new empire builders,[130] and the United Service Employment Scheme transferred boys, girls and married couples to the south as domestic servants.[131] Back-to-the-land projects were also tried, with allotments and pig-poultry units. In 1934 there were 15,731 participants in County Durham,[132] with 13 units and planned expansion to 51.[133]

People responded to these years of hardship. In 1921 the unemployed became organized, with the formation of the National Unemployed

Workers' Committee Movement – a broad-church organization, but with the leadership dominated by Communists. One of the early successes occurred during a dispute at Marsden in 1925, when unmarried miners, refused assistance by the Guardians, occupied the Laygate Lane workhouse, supported by contingents from Whitburn and South Shields, until outdoor relief was paid.[134] The DMA leadership, like the TUC, was highly suspicious of the movement because of the Communist presence. In February 1929 W.P. Richardson refused a NUWM request for assistance to marchers passing though Durham, seeing it as a futile gesture: 'our unemployed are suffering sufficiently without imposing further useless suffering on them . . . by marching to London to meet a Government who have nothing to offer the mining community.'[135]

The Wall Street Crash of October 1929 had heralded the beginnings of this world depression. In Britain, the May Report to the MacDonald government advised deflationary policies, including cutting public expenditure, which included unemployment benefit. The TUC strongly opposed the cuts and the government became irrevocably split. On 24 August MacDonald resigned, but was persuaded by the king to lead a National government, forming a New Labour Party. The split was disastrous for the Labour Party and at the election in October the National Party had a majority of 497. Among those Labour MPs who lost their seats were Will Lawther at Barnard Castle and John Herriotts at Sedgefield. Herriotts had held the post of checkweighman at Binchester, Windlestone and Fishburn and had been a county councillor from 1907 to 1910, before he took Sedgefield. His portrait appears on two Chilton banners. MacDonald's control, however, became increasingly weakened and, when the Liberals left the government in 1932, the National Party was essentially Conservative controlled.

MacDonald's action was seen as a great betrayal and it aroused considerable bitterness in Durham. At the 1932 Gala it was noted that several banners 'had quite new faces, and it was learned that these had, until the last election borne portraits of Mr MacDonald which had been absolutely erased'.[136] MacDonald's portrait on the Brandon banner was replaced with a view of Durham Cathedral;[137] Littleburn covered the portrait with a boating scene; white paint was used on the Bewicke Main banner; and Langley Park lodge had a white sheet sewn over his face on their banner.

Measures were quickly taken to tighten up on the provision of unemployment benefit. The Boards of Guardians had been replaced by Public Assistance Committees in 1929, but the Durham PAC was removed in 1932 and replaced by government appointees because it had suspended the Means Test and was generally paying out maximum benefit. In 1933 demonstrators, with banners inscribed 'Down with the Means Test', had protested outside the Durham PAC office, but were baton charged by the police, leaving several injured.[138] A new Unemployment Bill proposed to develop means testing, tighten up on payments and establish Unemployment Assistance Boards to administer transitional payments, with the recipient requested to attend instructional training camps. A national Hunger March was held to oppose the Bill, with the North-East contingent receiving financial support from a number of lodges, including Follonsby, Harraton, Heworth, Marsden and Mainsforth.[139] The Bill was described as a step in the same direction as Fascism, but became law in June.[140] The 'labour' or 'slave' camps were established at Redcar, Marsden and in Hamsterley forest, west Durham, and were run on semi-military lines. At the same time other deputations met PACs requesting that they give full assistance to any who refused to go to the camps, that they create work schemes and give extra winter relief. It is clear that lodges like Ravensworth, Eppleton and Ryhope were supporting the NUWM deputations to the PACs.[141]

In January 1935 the establishment of Unemployment Assistance Boards, to deal with transitional payments, and a new Means Test, under part 2 of the Unemployment Act 1934, came into effect. It was roundly attacked by the DMA. At a meeting of 175 lodge delegates, representing 122,000 miners, at Red Hill in March, a resolution was unanimously carried calling for its removal and urging the government to find employment for all workers, or state maintenance until work could be found.[142] Ryhope lodge called it 'a further step in the degradation of the moral standard of our people'.[143]

A number of protest marches to UAB offices were held. A planned march to the Durham PAC in April 1935 had been a low-key affair, probably because a previous march had been attacked – 'the marchers were driven down Gilesgate and blood was flying in all directions.'[144] Billy Todd, a Communist representative at Dean and Chapter colliery (known as 'the Slaughter-house' because of its accident record) took part in one of the unemployment marches and during a skirmish was beaten across the head with a police truncheon. He suffered headaches for several years afterwards and when he died in 1946 many felt that the blow had ultimately killed him. Through the efforts of another Communist lodge official, his portrait was painted on the lodge banner.

Proposals to cut transitional payments and make the Means Test permanent led to the last Hunger March, in 1936, including a contingent marching with a banner inscribed 'Durham March Against Starvation'.[145] Around the same time the Jarrow Crusade set off for London to seek support for 'The Town that was Murdered', accompanied by their MP, Ellen Wilkinson. Some concessions were achieved.

These struggles against the Act, and the 'slave camps', were linked to increasing concerns over the development of Fascism in Britain, following the models in Germany and Italy. Oswald Mosley founded the British Union of Fascists in October 1932 and quickly began recruiting in the North-East. BUF offices were established at Clayton Street, Newcastle, and in Claypath, Durham City. At the same time close links were being forged between certain businessmen, like Lord Londonderry, and the Nazi leadership in Germany.[146]

Dean and Chapter
banner with the portrait
of Billy Todd.

The DMA moved quickly to play a leading role in opposing the evil of
Fascism, standing alongside the NUWM, the Communist Party and the
majority of the population of County Durham. Anti-fascist meetings were
organized by the lodges. J.M. Stephenson, the secretary of Blaydon Burn
lodge, spoke of the impact of Nazism in Germany and warned his
audience of Hitler's Nuremberg speeches which threatened territorial
expansion.[147] Sam Watson told a meeting of Dawdon lodge that 'Fascism
can rest assured that in the struggle for democracy and democratic rights
we shall not be found wanting'.[148] As the civil war unfolded in Spain, the
Communist Party on Wearside began recruiting for the International
Brigades, and several unemployed, like Frank Graham, Nixon Powell and
Bobby Quaid (the Olympic bantamweight champion of 1935–6), joined
the British Battalion.

Twenty-five men from Durham and Northumberland were killed in
Spain.[149] Clifford Lawther wrote to his brother Will, 'It is wonderful to
think that there were many besides myself who were leaving our nearest
and dearest to fight against the greatest danger that working-class
solidarity has had to face. . . . I am going up the line to give my life, if
necessary.'[150] Harry Pollitt, searching the Spanish hospital wards, later
wrote to Will that his younger brother had been killed at Jarama on
27 February 1937. Wilf Jobling, a Communist from Chopwell, also died at
Jarama, and William Tattam, another Communist, from Dawdon, fell
during fighting on the Madrid front.

The British government appears to have followed a policy of nonintervention in the civil war, but the DMA supported the Republic. The Executive sent a message of congratulations to Captain J.H. Still of Swalwell and the crew of the *Hamsterley*, who broke through the Fascist blockade to bring supplies to Bilbao.[151] Boldon lodge also urged the government to send the Royal Navy to pick up refugees following the shooting of Asturian miners and their families by the Fascists.[152] The MFGB organized a levy of its members, and two homes for the orphans were provided in northern Spain, opened by Will Lawther.[153] Some Basque child refugees were also brought to Durham, to St Mary's Home at Tudhoe.

Following the military involvement of Italy and Germany in support of Franco, the central European situation rapidly declined. Hitler's seizure of control in Germany was followed by the occupation of Austria in March 1938 and the Sudetenland, an area of Czechoslovakia with a minority German population, in September. The DMA, who had been keen supporters of the League of Nations' peace efforts, became increasingly alarmed at the government's policy of appeasement and the Council subsequently agreed to provide aid to Czechs made homeless by the occupation.[154] The Executive also sent a strongly worded resolution to the German ambassador in London registering their 'horror and indignation' over the treatment of the Jews, following the November 1938 pogrom of *Kristallnacht*: 'We feel that the Government of a nation guilty of these practices places itself outside the ambit of civilised people.'[155]

# *War and Nationalization*

When Chamberlain resigned on 10 May 1940 – the day that Germany began *Sichelschnitt* (sweep of a scythe), the invasion of the Low Countries and on into France – a coalition government was formed, headed by Churchill. Included in the War Cabinet were the leader and deputy leader of the Labour Party, Clement Attlee and Arthur Greenwood. Herbert Morrison, leader of London County Council, became Minister of Supply, and in 1940, Home Secretary. Ernest Bevin, of the TGWU, went to the Ministry of Labour and National Service and Hugh Dalton, MP for Bishop Auckland, to the Ministry of Economic Warfare. The 1942 reshuffle brought Stafford Cripps back from Moscow, initially to the post of Lord Privy Seal, and later as Minister of Aircraft Production, while Hugh Dalton moved to the Board of Trade.

In 1945 war ended in Europe and in the Far East. In the same year the National Union of Mineworkers was formed and Will Lawther, the president of the MFGB since the start of the war, became its new president. Arthur Horner, the Communist checkweighman of Mardy lodge and president of the South Wales Miners' Federation from 1936, was elected NUM secretary in 1946. In Durham Lawther's new posting led to

Heworth banner
showing Emmanuel
Shinwell handing a
copy of the Coal
Industry Nationalisation
Act to Lord Hindley.

the appointment of new agents, but only one, Jack Joyce, the financial secretary, was to appear on a banner, that of his local lodge, Ushaw Moor.

The National Government was dissolved in 1945 and the July General Election brought Attlee and the Labour Party to power. In a war-devastated country, the new government introduced its programme for the establishment of a welfare state, including Aneurin Bevan's creation of the National Health Service in 1948, and for nationalization. On the nationalization of the coal industry, Bevan spoke at the 1946 Gala of the end of a black era and the beginning of a new dawn, declaring that 'Young miners need never fear unemployment again or suffer victimisation at the hands of vicious colliery owners'.[156] When Vesting Day came in January 1947, ceremonies occurred throughout the county, but Whitburn lodge refused to attend because of the composition of the new NCB.[157]

Manny Shinwell, who had taken Seaham Harbour from Ramsay MacDonald in 1935, was appointed Minister of Fuel and Power. Heworth lodge banner displayed the scene of Shinwell handing over a copy of the Coal Mines Nationalization Act to Lord Hindley, chairman of the

Northern Division of the NCB, an event which must have raised eyebrows given Hindley's connections to Powell-Duffryn, the largest privatized coal combine in Britain. A Fabian Society inquiry among miners found them supportive of the principle of nationalization, but critical of the new setup: 'Too many of the old brigade, and too many superfluous officials.'[158]

On 26 April 1949 the NCB received its coat of arms, with the motto 'E tenebris lux' (Light out of darkness). This was displayed on the banner of Craghead lodge, with its own motto of 'Independence, Liberty and Co-operation'. Nationalization was represented on banners both naturalistically and symbolically. Eppleton's banner, for instance, simply showed a view of the colliery under the title, 'Nationalisation 1947', while Greenside banner had an NCB flag flying from the pithead, with the motto, 'For the people, by the people'. Beamish Air later showed the changes which had been achieved in the pits developed from private ownership to nationalization – 'The March of Progress'.

Other banner designs used symbolism to illustrate the great change. Harton lodge decided on a scene where a couple with their child have passed through the gate of 'nationalization' and are looking across a cornfield to the sunshine of 'security'. It follows the 'Sunshine of Liberty' pattern-book tradition and was a theme also used by the Ashington Federation in Northumberland, where the family group (with the man clearly dressed and equipped as a miner) look to the sunshine of nationalization rising over a colliery.[159] Fishburn had another image of passing through the gate of nationalization, with an angel of trade unionism providing a miner with the key. The end of private ownership also saw a re-emergence of the 'destruction of the evil monster' theme. Crook Drift Hole in the Wall lodge showed a female figure, with the shield of Justice and Equality, and a drawn sword, standing by the slain wolf of Capitalism, while a miner, who has broken his chains, sets his foot over the beast's neck. Boldon's banner showed a miner standing over the body of the dragon of Tyranny and taking the hand of the female figure of Trust. Tanfield Lea, like Acton Hall branch in Yorkshire, chose the dramatic image of a female figure driving a chariot through the sky, with the motto, 'Hail the Dawn', the dawn of a new era.

Shinwell's planning failures and the bad winter of 1947, however, resulted in a coal shortage, which seriously affected economic production and created increased levels of unemployment.[160] It also dramatically ate into US and Canadian loans provided after the end of Lend-Lease to enable Britain to reconstruct her industrial base, though this was stemmed by budgetary measures. As a stimulus to increased coal output, Tutill's offered a production bannerette, to be competed for each year.[161]

The crisis led to a leadership challenge from Cripps and, although Attlee stood his ground, Cripps came out of it with the Ministry of Economic Affairs. Harold Wilson took over his position at the Board of Trade, while Hugh Gaitskell replaced Shinwell at the Ministry of Fuel and Power. Further changes occurred in November 1947 when Dalton, the

Harton and Westoe lodge banner, with a family passing through the gates of 'Nationalisation' to a new world of 'Security'.

Chancellor of the Exchequer, gave away details of his budget to the press and was forced to resign. Cripps took over his office and moved to expand exports, while fostering, domestically, a policy of restraint and austerity. This policy, along with the major injection of aid under the Marshall Plan, greatly improved the situation, as did the 30 per cent devaluation of the pound, as a result of external pressures, in August 1949.

The return of Labour in the 1950 General Election was affected domestically by two damaging events. First, the split between Gaitskell (who had succeeded Cripps as Chancellor of the Exchequer) and Bevan over budgetary measures (influenced by the rearmament programme associated with the Korean War), including proposed health service charges, led to the resignation of Bevan and Wilson. Secondly, a balance

Fishburn banner, with the angel of 'Trade Unionism' giving a miner the keys to the gate of 'Economic Emancipation'.

of trade deficit brought on the 1951 election and a long period of Conservative rule, initially by Churchill, followed by Anthony Eden (1955–7), Harold Macmillian, who resigned in October 1963 principally because of the Profumo scandal, and, briefly Sir Alec Douglas-Home.

It was during this period, when Labour was in opposition, that the majority of Attlee banners appeared in Durham. They began at East Hetton and Byremoor in 1951 and continued after 1955, when Gaitskell succeeded Attlee as party leader, with the 1957 Sacriston banner. Also during this period, other Labour figures appeared on Durham banners – Dalton, on the 1954 Randolph banner, and Cripps, on the 1957 Middridge Drift banner, with Bevin and Jack Lawson (Lord Lawson of Beamish).

The Bevanite splinter group, which also included Michael Foot, Richard Crossland, Ian Mikado and Harold Wilson, created a disunity in the party which assisted in keeping Labour from office. Will Lawther, the NUM

Crook Drift banner,
showing the death of
the wolf of 'Capitalism'.

president, who had supported Attlee, had become increasingly disillusioned with the far left and the Soviet system and became one of the Bevanites' leading opponents. He was never chosen for inclusion on a Durham banner, while the Communist, Arthur Horner, was to appear on the banners of Craghead and West Auckland.

In Durham, the right-winger, Sam Watson, a close friend of Attlee,[162] gave his support to Gaitskell. Watson was born in 1898 at Donkin's Row, Boldon colliery, the third of six children.[163] At fourteen years of age he started at the local pit and by 1927 was secretary of both the lodge and

Boldon lodge banner, with its theme of nationalization, the end of tyranny.

Clement Attlee at the unfurling of the 1951 East Hetton banner.

Boldon ILP. He studied in his spare time and before his appointment as agent, following the death of Peter Lee in 1935, had won two literary prizes – one for an essay on the political and economic significance of the Tolpuddle Martyrs, and the second, the Sir Arthur Markham memorial prize from Sheffield University, for an essay on machine mining. During his secretaryship of the lodge he published studies on the Unemployment and Health Insurance Acts and on his DMA appointment became treasurer and unemployment officer. He served on the NUM National Executive and became chairman of the Labour Party. Because of his anti-Communist stance, Watson developed links with the American administration and became actively involved in trying to split the left.[164] Watson was certainly influential in persuading Bevan to change his mind over opposing H-bomb construction, and was accepted by Gaitskell as a member of the shadow cabinet. However, for a period of seven years from 1953 Bevan was not chosen to speak at the Gala and his portrait only began to appear on banners after his death in 1960, for example, Kibblesworth (1961). Gaitskell appeared on the 1961 East Hetton and 1962 Lambton banners in the latter stages of his leadership, just before his sudden death in January 1963.

The Cold War influenced attitudes in Durham. When Arthur Horner came to Chopwell in 1954 to unfurl a new banner, which copied the earlier 'Red' banner, he compared his base at Mardy, South Wales, to Chopwell and said, 'Both were "Little Moscows"', but qualified it by adding 'but that was because the people refused to be bullied in the bad old days'.[165] In the following year Ivan Rossochinsky, president of the Central Committee of the Soviet Union of Mineworkers, led a team on a ten-day fact-finding tour of the North-East, looking at aspects of life in the Durham coalfield, including pithead baths and aged miners' homes. During their visit to Chopwell, Len Hawkshaw, chairman of the local lodge, presented the visitors with the 1924 banner.[166] While this gift may have been presented in recognition of the support given to the people of Chopwell from the Donbas miners in 1926 and as a symbol of solidarity among miners, Hawkshaw clearly indicated in a later comment that the old image had changed: 'Chopwell is certainly not a "Little Moscow", and we are all sick and tired of the nickname. We are Socialists, but we are certainly not Communists.'[167]

Rossochinsky also attended the 1955 Gala, with Alexi Korchunor, a face worker, and Nikolai Serbinovich, a combine operator, and they presented a bannerette to Sam Watson.[168] Soviet visitors were also guests of Dean and Chapter lodge in the same year, and at the 1956 Gala their lodge banner was draped with a red bannerette inscribed 'Fraternal greetings to the miners of Durham from the miners of the Soviet Union'. There was, however, by the 1950s a more clear understanding of the dictatorship of the Communist Party, its all-pervading influence on society and the loss of personal freedoms by Soviet citizens. In Communist-controlled Poland, for instance, poor living conditions, taxation, mixed with a degree of liberalization, including the release of political prisoners, led to an uprising in Poznan, centred around the Zispo motor factory, in 1956, when workers marched with banners calling for 'Bread and Freedom'.[169] As events were unfurling, Sam Watson, in his eve of Gala message, said,

The portrait of Hugh Gaitskell on the 1963 East Hetton banner. This damaged image has been restored using photographic and computer-enhancing techniques.

Here in this island of much tolerance, justice and freedom, we owe it to the brave working men and women of Poznan to say a prayer for their safety and to proclaim our faith with them in the dignity and decency of ordinary people and to send to them from our Gala – the greatest demonstration of free people in the world – our hope that they will be spared the brutalities and injustices that were perpetrated on thousands of Russian workers who dared to protest against dictatorship under the leadership of Stalin.[170]

The rising was crushed, with 53 killed and around 300 wounded.

Many of the banners carried to the Galas at this time bore images related to social questions, which were less overtly political, such as the provision of aged miners' homes, medical care and welfare facilities. The colliery house was a tied cottage, with the tenant liable to eviction during industrial disputes or when he became incapable of work through age or debility. In 1896 Joseph Hopper, a miner and lay preacher from the Wrekenton area, held a meeting in a Newcastle café, where the Durham Aged Mineworkers' Homes Association was formed. The movement started with a series of colonies, at Haswell Moor, Shotton, Shincliffe Bank Top and Houghhall, in the period 1899–1908. The Association then turned to the provision of single-storey cottages within the pit villages. The 1920s was the peak period of cottage building, and their significance to the miners is apparent in the number of homes displayed on banners, for example, Washington Glebe, Sherburn Hill, Ryhope and Tursdale.

Improvements to the lives of miners and their families were made by the Miners' Welfare Commission, which, in 1952, became the Coal Industry Social Welfare Organisation (CISWO). Conishead Priory was opened as a rehabilitation centre in 1930.[171] The frontage of Conishead became the most popular structural scene on Durham banners. Only Bowburn broke the mould, with a fine aerial view of the Priory. The Commission also acquired The Hermitage at Chester-le-Street in 1943 for conversion to another rehabilitation centre.[172] It was refurbished and opened on 24 June 1944, with facilities for patients suffering from limb injuries, and appears on the banners of Vane Tempest and Witton lodges. In 1961 a CISWO facility, the Sam Watson Rest Home, was opened at Boldon Crofts, Richmond, North Yorkshire, to provide fortnightly breaks for the wives of NCB employees and female NCB staff in the Durham Division.[173] The frontage of the home is depicted on the banners of Langley Park (later East Hetton) and NACODS. Little else of the welfare scheme found its way onto Durham banners, with only Brandon choosing to show the pavilion and green of its recreation ground.

The dangers of mining were frequently recalled at the Galas, with banners draped in black denoting a fatality at the colliery during the year. At the 1948 Gala Sam Watson recited Joseph Skipsey's 'The Caller', reminding his audience, if they needed reminding, of the hazards:

Conishead Priory on the Leasingthorne banner. Between 1930 and 1969 the centre received 72,164 admissions. It was sold in 1971.

The Hermitage, near Chester-le-Street, on the Witton lodge banner.

Get up the caller cries, get up
And in the dead of night,
To win the bairns their bite and sup,
I rise a weary wight.

The East Hetton
(formerly Langley Park)
banner at the 1995
Gala, showing the Sam
Watson Rest Home.

My flannel dudden donned thrice o'er,
My bairns are kissed, and then,
I, with a whistle, opt the door,
I might not close again.[174]

The picture of the miner going out to work and not returning appeared on
the Monkwearmouth lodge banner, with its 'The Last Good Morning'
scene, and in sculptural form on the memorials to the Tudhoe and Trimdon
Grange explosions. A number of lodges, like West Stanley, chose to

The West Stanley
banner, with the image
of the explosion and
'The Unknown Miner'.

remember these dangers and to recall their own particular catastrophes on
their banners. The 1949 Whitworth Park banner displayed a painting of
the miners' memorial in Durham Cathedral.[175] The idea for a memorial
came in an anonymous letter to the Dean of Durham in the summer of
1946. The letter was shown to Sam Watson and, after some discussion, the
idea was widely approved.[176] On 28 September, part of a seventeenth-
century fireplace from Ramside Hall, which had been given as a gift to the
Cathedral by the Pemberton family, was chosen as the basis for the
memorial. Additional woodwork was inserted by the Cathedral carpenters
and after considering possible inscriptions, the Chapter, on 26 October,
approved the words, 'Remember before God the Durham Miners who
have given their lives in the pits of this county and those who work in
darkness and danger in those pits today', with the accompanying lines
from Job 28.4: 'He breaketh open a shaft away from where men sojourn.
They are forgotten of the foot that passeth by.'[177] The completed memorial
was set against the wall of the south aisle and was dedicated by Bishop
Alwyn Williams in February 1947.[178]

Whitworth Park banner showing the Miners' Memorial in Durham Cathedral.

In 1953 a memorial garden was also created at Red Hill, and it is shown on the banners of Burnhope and New Herrington. Following the explosion at Easington colliery in 1951, the Yugoslav miners sent a wreath which was laid at the mass grave.[179] Attached to the wreath was a Yugoslav pennant. The Yugoslav government also arranged holidays in their country for the widows and orphans. The pennant was later taken from the wreath and secured to the lodge banner and has been carried by Easington lodge ever since. The 1954 Crookhall banner, under the motto of 'Dignity through Labour', showed a modern miner, but in the background were scenes of the horrors of a pit disaster – miners caught in the blast of a firedamp ignition, the hands of a miner sticking out from the debris of a roof fall and the scene of a 'penitent' attempting to fire a pocket of gas.

East Tanfield, in 1955, chose to remember a Welsh pit disaster on its new banner, showing a colliery band in front of Durham Cathedral, with the title 'Gresford. Lest we forget'. Gresford colliery, in Clwyd, was operated by United Westminster and Wrexham Collieries Ltd.[180] On 22 September 1934 an explosion occurred in the Dennis section of the Main seam, killing 261. The subsequent inquiry failed to reach a positive conclusion as to the seat and cause of the firedamp ignition, but exposed a catastrophic list of failures and shortcomings at the pit, with a demoralized management, inadequate ventilation, a lack of suitable arrangements for the withdrawal of workmen and absence of measures for the suppression of coal dust. The assistant surveyor confessed that he had not taken air measurements for two months prior to the explosion in the Dennis section and had, with the collusion of the manager, added imaginary measurements to the colliery books after the disaster. A five-man rescue team sent into one of the districts without a lifeline or backup was caught by gas, killing three and raising the final death toll to 265. This was the second most disastrous event to occur at a Welsh colliery since the 1913 explosion at Senghenydd, where 439 were killed, and the third highest disaster toll at a British pit – the 1910 explosion at Pretoria pit, Hulton colliery, in Lancashire took 344 lives.

Following the disaster, Robert Saint composed a piece of music entitled 'Gresford', which he conducted at the Galas up to his death in 1950. It has been the hymn tune of the Durham miners ever since. At the 1956 Gala one reporter wrote, 'Five bands assembled near Platform 1 and on the stroke of noon, more than 5,000 people stood up, the men with bared heads, while the bands played Bob Saint's hymn.'[181]

## The Coalfield that was Murdered

In July 1950 Hetton Lyons colliery closed with the loss of 430 jobs. At the Gala, the banner carried a notice, 'The NCB has closed our colliery – Y'.[182] In 1942 UK deep-mined coal output stood at 206.9 million tonnes. This figure fell as the war ran to its conclusion and only began to rise again after 1946 as the process of reconstruction got underway. The industry reached a deep-mined peak in 1954 of 217 million tonnes, but the trend after that was one of decline. This was influenced by the expansion of the market for other sources of energy. The development of oilfields in the Middle East offered a major alternative to coal. From the 1950s oil began to increase its share of the market which rose rapidly in the 1960s. Natural gas was located on the UK Continental Shelf in 1965 and began to be exploited in 1967; and in 1956 Calder Hall nuclear station was built in Cumbria.

As the demand for oil increased, the government's 'National Plan' and 'Fuel Policy' White Paper suggested that by 1970 coal requirements would be unlikely to exceed 170–80 million tons. Consequently coal production was extensively cut, with a massive pit closure programme carried out in Durham.

The bulk of the collieries listed in the following table (fifty of them) were closed during the Wilson administration of October 1964 to June 1970 (including Thornley, near the end of Labour's office, in January 1970). Nationally the heaviest toll was in 1968–9, with fifty-four closures and four mergers. The Lambton lodge secretary, A. Garland, recalled that when the pit was threatened with closure in 1965 the miners and their supporters marched to Seaham with their banner draped in black, to confront Lord Robens:

The great Lord eventually came, and he got out of his car, along with his police escort, and confronted us Lodge officials. We presented

| | | | |
|---|---|---|---|
| South Garesfield | Feb. 1960 | Witton | Jan. 1966 |
| Garesfield | Jul. 1960 | Lumley Sixth | Jan. 1966 |
| Ushaw Moor | Aug. 1960 | Dean & Chapter | Jan. 1966 |
| Malton | Jul. 1961 | North Tees | Jan. 1966 |
| Barlow Townley | Oct. 1961 | Clara Vale | Feb. 1966 |
| Westerton Drift | Oct. 1961 | Beamish Mary | Mar. 1966 |
| Ravensworth Shop | Feb. 1962 | Barcus Close | Apr. 1966 |
| Esperley Lane | Feb. 1962 | Greenside | Jul. 1966 |
| Randolph | Feb. 1962 | Waterhouses | Aug. 1966 |
| Victoria Garesfield | Jul. 1962 | Middridge | Aug. 1966 |
| Tanfield Lea | Aug. 1962 | Chopwell | Nov. 1966 |
| Eldon Drift | Oct. 1962 | Ryhope | Nov. 1966 |
| Wingate Grange | Oct. 1962 | Deaf Hill | Feb. 1967 |
| Beamish Second | Nov. 1962 | Thrislington | Mar. 1967 |
| Addison | Feb. 1963 | Bowburn | Jul. 1967 |
| Fenhall Drift | May 1963 | Brancepeth | Jul. 1967 |
| Heworth | June 1963 | Standrop Field House | Jul. 1967 |
| High Marley Hill | June 1963 | West Auckland | Jul. 1967 |
| Stargate | June 1963 | Chester South Moor | Oct. 1967 |
| Roddymoor | Aug. 1963 | Kimblesworth | Nov. 1967 |
| Lanchester Townley | Aug. 1963 | Byermoor | Feb. 1968 |
| Crookhall | Nov. 1963 | Hamsterley | Feb. 1968 |
| South Pelaw | Jan. 1964 | Ravensworth Park | Feb. 1968 |
| Haggs Lane | Jan. 1964 | Trimdon Grange | Feb. 1968 |
| Watergate | Aug. 1964 | Handen Hold | Mar. 1968 |
| Phoenix Drift | Aug. 1964 | Brandon Pit House | Mar. 1968 |
| Derwent | Nov. 1964 | Emma | Apr. 1968 |
| Hole in the Wall | Nov. 1964 | Wheatley Hill | May 1968 |
| East Tanfield | Jan. 1965 | Stanley Cottage | May 1968 |
| Pelton | Feb. 1965 | Brusselton | May 1968 |
| Lambton 'D' | Feb. 1965 | Esh Winning | June 1968 |
| Stanley Burn | Feb. 1965 | Whitburn | June 1968 |
| Tudhoe Mill | Feb. 1965 | Washington 'F' | June 1968 |
| Harraton | May 1965 | Burnopfield | Aug. 1968 |
| Sherburn Hill | Aug. 1965 | Mainsforth | Dec. 1968 |
| New Shildon | Aug. 1965 | Craghead | Apr. 1969 |
| Bradley Drift | Sep. 1965 | Tudhoe Park | May 1969 |
| West Thornley | Nov. 1965 | Harton | Jul. 1969 |

Closure dates of the Durham collieries.

him with a resolution from our Lodge, also a set of proposals to make our pit a paying concern. He took them, and said he would study them. All this time good humoured back-chat was going on, and a little chap was very enthusiastic and waving his fist shouted "Howay the lads", the battle cry of our two famous football teams, Newcastle

Hetton Lyons banner, 1950, and the question 'The NCB has closed our colliery Y?'

and Sunderland. This seemed to upset Robens, and he menacingly went toward him, and showed completely his lack of self control, and our members repeatedly pointed to our banner blowing slightly in the wind, to the symbolic phrase, and shouted to him 'Oh ye of little faith, why dost thee doubt'. But our protests were in vain, and the pit eventually closed on Feb. 28th. 1965.[183]

Miners increasingly saw themselves as 'gypsies', moved around the county or to other coalfields as the government followed short-term policies, and new trends, while sterilizing that fuel supply (i.e. coal) upon which they could rely. At the 1969 Gala, Roy Mason, the Minister for Fuel and Power, said that the worst of the closures was over and that 'the miners had given a lead unparalleled in British history and a loyalty of unbelievable dimensions to the Labour Government'.[184] Joe Gormley, who became president of the NUM in 1971, conceded that the union made little attempt to oppose the closures, for no one wished to threaten the position of Labour and have a Tory government returned.[185] However, while Mason spoke of a need for large quantities of coal 'as far ahead as we can see', he warned that coal would have to compete with other fuels. On the same platform, Lawrence Daly, the NUM general secretary, replied by warning

George Brown unfurling the Horden banner, with its portrait of Harold Wilson, in 1966.

Mason that the government had become 'perilously dependent upon fuels such as oil'.

Subsequent closures were not so numerous but continued the decline – six during Heath's government of 1970 to February 1974 (Silksworth, Washington Glebe, Shotton, Medomsley, Morrison Busty and Fishburn) and seven under Wilson and Callaghan, from 1974 to March 1979 (Elemore, Whitworth Park, Usworth, Kibblesworth, Langley Park, Metal Bridge and Adventure). This slow-down followed the 1972 and 1974 miners' strikes and the realization of the danger about which Lawrence Daly had warned – the Yom Kippur war and the rapid rise in the cost of oil. These events forced an energy review, which led to the upgrading of coal, with the 1974 'Plan for Coal'. Production was increasingly linked to the planned massive expansion of liquid steel capacity by the British Steel Corporation in the early 1970s, with particular emphasis placed on Teesside.[186] BSC's proposed programme included new furnaces and a Basic Oxygen Steel plant at Redcar, with two associated dry-charge coke oven batteries, capable of taking particular ranks of Durham coal. Consequently, production in the Durham coalfield was directed to mining metallurgical grade coking coals.

Unfortunately, this programme was quickly followed by an international recession, with a fall in demand for steel, while the country's manufacturing base also went into decline. BSC consequently introduced a policy of retrenchment, cut development at Redcar, closed Consett in 1980 and moved to import cheaper coking coals. This included the conversion of the Redcar coke ovens from dry to wet charging, making them suitable for imported coals, which had a serious impact on the Durham collieries which were working to supply Redcar. A search for other markets became increasingly desperate, and although some coal still went to BSC, by the late 1970s output was directed to power station use. Collieries were also shut down. In the period from 1979, when Margaret Thatcher took office, to 1983, Hylton, Eden, Houghton, Boldon, Marley Hill and East Hetton were closed. In December 1981 Joe Gormley retired and was succeeded by Arthur Scargill, with over 70 per cent of the vote. Joe's portrait appeared on the South Hetton banner.

Arthur Scargill began his mining experience at Wooley colliery, near Barnsley, at the age of fifteen. At twenty-seven he became branch delegate and became a full-time official in 1972, as Yorkshire area compensation secretary, during which time he was involved with the Lofthouse and Houghton Main disaster inquiries. On becoming NUM president, Scargill was faced with the Thatcher government's plans for further pit closures, spearheaded by the new NCB chairman, Ian MacGregor. Years of pit closures had reduced the available reservoirs which could take miners coming from closed pits, and more and more men were being made redundant. The closures also meant that miners' sons had no source of employment to which to look. In Easington district 190 male school leavers had found work with the NCB in 1974; in 1980 the figure was 153; in 1983 6. This raised the spectre that 'if coal mining in the District declines even further than it has already, there will be no future for the communities in the area'.[187]

In late 1983 the NCB refused to discuss wage improvements until the closure programme was carried through. The NUM reacted by voting for an overtime ban, which was followed, in March 1984, by the proposed closure of Corton Wood colliery in Yorkshire. This triggered a strike, which quickly spread to the other areas, including Durham.

The strike was for the right to work and to maintain the communities which were so heavily dependent on coal. The threat of pit closure was a threat to the whole community and it was the members of the mining communities – the miners, their families and their supporters – who stood up against the destroyers. Women played a major part in maintaining the strike, organizing the Support Groups, standing on the picket line, running the canteens and speaking out at marches and rallies around the country. Many support groups in the North-East coalfield produced their own banners, carried like miners' banners at demonstrations.

However, the full force of the state was ranged against them. Miners' families were hit by the government withholding tax refunds to strikers; sweeping deductions were taken from the supplementary benefit being paid to strikers' families. A challenge to these deductions at the High Court failed on 22 January 1985. On the picket line unarmed strikers were faced with massed ranks of police in riot gear, armed with shields and batons, mounted police and dogs. Police flooded into the mining areas and there was widespread abuse of civil liberties.[188] The government also directed the intelligence services to carry out a 'dirty war' against the miners.[189] Stella Rimmington, head of the F2 section of MI5's counter-subversion branch, controlled the campaign against the NUM. MI5 used British Telecom's telephone tapping unit to listen in on communications between the national and area offices of the union and the lodges. Just as in 1844 when Durham's Chief Constable, James Wemyss, had a spy attending miners' meetings, and in the 1930s, when the police had an informer on the executive of the NUWM, so in 1984–5 a 'deep throat' had been planted in the upper levels of the NUM. Elements of the press and media were also recruited by the service, or fed stories, to smear the miners generally and the union leadership in particular. GCHQ Cheltenham, the Combined Signals Organization Station at Morwenstow, Cornwall, and the US National Security Agency also illegally hacked into the European and Soviet banking systems to trace contributions to the NUM and also the movement of the union's funds following the appointment of sequestrators by the High Court on 25 October 1984 to seize its assets.

Mass picketing of collieries, cokeworks, like Orgreave, and power stations continued. Attempts at negotiation were made on several occasions, though largely stalling over the demand for pit closures. On 23 January 1985 Peter Walker, the Energy Secretary, refused an appeal from the leaders of the Welsh Churches for an inquiry into the industry, on the same day that Ian MacGregor thwarted moves by Peter Heathfield, NUM general secretary, for informal negotiations. Pit closures were the only option. Attempts by the TUC to end the strike also failed in February, but on 3 March the NUM Special Delegate Conference voted by ninety-eight to ninety-one for a return to work without a settlement.

On 5 March most of the miners on strike returned to work. At Monkwearmouth, the miners, with a band and their banner of 'The last good morning / We seek compensation', accompanied by women and children, marched from the welfare hall to the pit. As they neared the gates, twenty police blocked their way. 'They gave no clear indication of what they wanted the march to do. They just started to push the 1,000 or so people back.'[190] In the ensuing melée the police tried to take the instruments off the band; they hauled down the banner, ripping it across the motto 'In God is all our trust', and arrested six people, including Bob Clay MP.

The strike and its aftermath saw a range of new banners appearing in various coalfields. The military-style standard, with battle honours, was used by the Nottinghamshire strikers to record the twenty-six lodges which remained loyal to the NUM. Others used more traditional banner layouts. The 1989 Chippenham banner for Gascoigne Wood branch (Yorkshire NUM) shows pickets being beaten by police cavalry: 'Our spirits were bruised, but never broken.' Within the central panel of the Stillingfleet (Yorkshire NUM) banner, produced by Turtle & Pearce in 1987, is an illustration of a striker at Orgreave, stripped to the waist and bleeding from a head wound, being force-marched by four riot police, with the motto, 'Come dungeons dark and gallows grim'. Bolsover carried a picture of Arthur Scargill being arrested at Orgreave on 30 May 1984. The Stillingfleet and Bolsover banner images were derived from 'News Line' photographs published in book form in 1985, which also served as a source for banner designs in Durham.

In 1988 the DMA, the Northumberland Miners' Association, the Durham and Northumberland Mechanics' Associations and the Durham Winding Enginemen's Association joined to form the NUM (NE Area). Their new banner was dedicated by the Rt Revd David Jenkins, Bishop of Durham, at Red Hill on 6 December 1991. The leading side emphasized the amalgamation of the unions of the two counties, with illustrations of the Tyne Bridge and Durham Cathedral alongside clasped hands. Portraits of the founding fathers of North-East mining unionism, Thomas Hepburn and Martin Jude, flanked the main scene of bands and banners processing from the Miners' Hall at Red Hill. The reverse side took up the theme of the great struggle, showing pickets with banners of 'Coal not Dole' and 'Victory to the Miners' and baton-wielding police, alongside a pithead, flying the NCB flag, and a derelict pit wheel. Below the main scene was a view of two men working underground. The picket and police scene was a modification of the 'News Line' photograph of an incident at Kellingley colliery.[191] Later, a motto, 'Our Fight is For the Right to Work', was added.

Murton banner carried a painting of the colliery, showing the pithead and Koepe winder, with a motto indicating the lodge philosophy of 'Production for use, not for profit'. The reverse bore a central portrait of Thomas Hepburn, with his words: 'The time will come when the golden chain which binds the tyrants together will be shattered, when men will be properly organised, when coal owners will only be like ordinary men, and

Murton lodge post-1984–5 strike banner, with the portrait of Thomas Hepburn.

Westoe lodge banner with images of the 1984–5 strike, 'Eternal Vigilance is the Price of Freedom'.

will have to sigh for the days gone by.' These words, recorded by Fynes, were spoken after the 1832 strike had been broken.[192] Blacklisted and destitute, Hepburn accepted work at Felling colliery on condition that he should never again have anything to do with unionism, though he retained the dream that in time things would change. Four vignettes concerning the 1984–5 strike accompanied the portrait, showing banner carriers, a canteen scene, a police cavalryman batoning a striker and an imprisoned miner.

Westoe lodge banner took the theme 'Agitate, Educate, Liberate' for its new banner. The 'Educate' image showed a miner, with blackened face and wearing a vest and pit helmet, holding his young daughter in one arm and an open book in the other. The 'Liberate' scene carried a subtitle, 'The Enemy Within', a phrase used by Thatcher when referring to the miners during a speech to the backbench 1922 Committee on 19 July 1984. The image used was of a man breaking his chains, harking back to Marx and Engels' final words from the *Communist Manifesto*. 'Agitate' was directly related to the strike, showing police cavalry bearing down on the lines of unarmed strikers during the second battle of Orgreave on 18 June 1984. Westoe miners had been present during that violent assault. Tursdale Mechanics also showed a police cavalryman, though the artist changed the perceived gender roles of the other figures, showing a man holding a baby, while a woman raises her hand to protect him from the police baton. Arthur Scargill's portrait, not surprisingly, appears on several Yorkshire area banners, but only appears once in Durham, on the Monkwearmouth banner, alongside Thomas Hepburn and A.J. Cook.

Tursdale Mechanics'
banner, with imagery of
the strike, by Barry
Ormsby.

The seizure of assets had particularly aggrieved the Durham NUM, because not only had the union lost control of its finances, but also its money was then invested against its will in apartheid South Africa. At the 1985 NUM conference, Durham had a motion passed to support and recognize the South African National Union of Mineworkers. They also actively supported the demands for the release of political prisoners, and particularly Nelson Mandela. Vane Tempest lodge, with its banner, had been present at the 1988 Nelson Mandela Freedom March from Glasgow to London. Black South African miners visited Durham, and David Guy, the area president, saw at first hand conditions at Matla colliery and in the Alexandria township, near Johannesburg, in 1991. Demonstrations were held in Sunderland, Seaham Harbour and Teesport against the importation of South African coal. Teesport was picketed when the *MV Ave* brought in 17,000 tonnes of apartheid coal, while the importation of such coal into Seaham caused great resentment.[193]

The Conservative government's overriding interest in market forces and privatization ultimately (or deliberately) led to the removal of markets from one of Europe's most efficient, technologically advanced and unsubsidized deep-mined coal industries. In 1986 the gas industry was privatized *en bloc* by Peter Walker, while moves towards the electricity sell-off began under Cecil Parkinson in 1987 and were completed by John Wakeham. The electricity industry had major contracts with British Coal until 1993. In December 1990 the twelve electricity distributors, the Regional Electricity Companies, were sold, and this was followed in March 1991 by the generators, National Power and PowerGen, with the government retaining a 40 per cent holding. Nuclear Electric was retained in government hands. The nuclear industry was ring-fenced with a maximum 20 per cent share in the electricity market and also received around £1,300 million per year from a levy on electricity generated from fossil fuels, such as coal and oil.

The distribution companies feared the dominant position of the generation duopoly and when the EC Council of Ministers, in March 1991, removed an earlier restriction on the use of gas for power station burn, the distributors moved to establish their own interests in new gas-fired stations – the so-called 'dash for gas'. Northern Electric, for instance, took out a 15 per cent holding in Teesside Power Ltd., with its 1,700 megawatt Enron gas-fired station at Teesside. However, these plants had been established at high capital cost, with the fuel purchased from British Gas at high prices. The 'sweetheart deals' arranged between the RECs and the companies operating the new plants gave them an additional source of unregulated income, while securing the electricity on fifteen-year purchase contracts, giving these projects a guaranteed price and return on investment with little risk.[194] This policy cut out competition from coal-fired stations for fifteen years. It also meant a higher price for the customer – coal-fired stations in 1991 were producing electricity at 2.2p per kilowatt hour (kWh) (or 2.7p per kWh when fitted with flue-gas desulphurization equipment) compared with 2.9p per kWh from the gas-turbine stations, at British Gas tariffs.[195]

British coal production was also trying to compete against foreign subsidized industries – in 1990 Belgium paid a subsidy of £55.19 per tonne, Germany £39.23 and France £10.99.[196] In 1993 coal production in the USA received a $700 million subsidy, and further subsidies were provided for the South American and South African industries. Surprisingly, also, from 1979 the NCB (and subsequently British Coal) invested around £20 million in Capricorn Coal Management in Australia (10.5 per cent of the company's costs) to supply coking coal to the UK, thereby undercutting British operations.[197]

New deep-water facilities were constructed at Immingham to receive foreign coal, but no attempt was made by the government to take measures against them under EC anti-dumping legislation. Consequently South American coal was shipped to the North-East. In May 1992, for instance, the *Nordic Trader* arrived at the port of Sunderland with 15,000 tonnes of Venezualan coal, while Columbian coal entered at Seaham Harbour.[198] John Major had personally supported Columbian coal exports to Britain during a visit in June 1992, even though around 890 of the 1,280 mines there employed child labour.[199]

In 1988 Cecil Parkinson told the Tory party conference that the coal industry would be privatized. For potential buyers, only the highly profitable super-pits would be considered, while the remaining pits in the British Coal empire were seen as dead weight to be discarded. The government's advisers, merchant bankers N.M. Rothschild, proposed this course of action in 1991, recommending that the number of UK pits should be cut to twelve. *The Times* discovered that 'while the bank was reviewing the coal industry for the government, it was advising its four REC clients to invest in ten gas generating projects. These account for 41 per cent of the new gas-fired generating capacity now under construction', which was 'largely responsible for the collapse of demand for coal'.[200]

Short-term expediency was the rule. Pits making a loss were to be killed off, even though a pit might be making a loss because it was in a development stage, driving to a new seam which, when flowing, would bring the pit into profit again. Closing pits with viable reserves not only destroyed the livelihoods of the miners and their families (with all the knock-on consequences for all those others reliant on the industry), it also wiped out a power source for present and future generations.

The Hawthorn-Eppleton-Murton combine was reorganized and Hawthorn was closed in 1983. Bearpark ceased production in 1984. On 30 September 1985 Eppleton was closed, with 403 men made redundant, and the others transferred to Murton. A break-even figure of 6,060 tonnes per day was proposed by the NCB for the combine, although the Board only aimed to work 6,000 tonnes, guaranteeing a loss.[201] No precise figures seem to have been calculated for this reorganization and job cuts, the Area Industrial Relations Officer declaring, 'The precise cost savings from centralisation at Murton will emerge from experience'.[202]

Herrington and Sacriston closed in November 1985, followed in February 1986 by Horden, where massive investment had been made to expand output to supply the Redcar steel works. In the 1970s coal extraction in the Zone 6 development area was subdivided between Easington, working the Low Main (J), and Horden, taking High Main (E) and Yard (G). During the drivage into E, and against all advice, the management opened the faulted E80 area, rather than work the rich 4 ft 10 in– 5 ft 5 in bulk reserves.[203] This area developed water problems, which stopped production and threatened the long-life Easington reserves. This sabotage sterilized areas of profitable reserves, leading to the pit's closure.

In June 1990 British Coal, increasingly aware of the effects of electricity privatization on its markets, produced a report on the possible closure of twenty pits.[204] This was submitted to the Secretary of State for Energy, but was rejected by Margaret Thatcher. However, in the North-East, the appointment of a new area director in the summer of 1991 witnessed an aggressive style of management. On 25 July Dawdon, a former 'super-pit', was closed, affecting 570 jobs, 313 of the men accepting transfers. On 13 August the closure of Murton was proposed. Although the NUM national engineer advised that if four of the fourteen faces were shut down the pit could work normally until November 1992, while new development work could be pushed through, development work stopped on 11 September. The workforce agreed to fight the closure by going through the pit review procedure, but, as Christmas approached, British Coal threatened to reduce redundancy payments if the closure was opposed. The threat succeeded. Work on the cavity filling of a roof fall at the E78b face was suddenly stopped on 7 November, and production ceased on 29 November.[205]

The Queen's Speech of 6 May 1992 announced the government's plans to introduce a bill to privatize the coal industry. British Coal was also clearly aware that the threat from gas would result in a declining role for coal in power generation and there was an increasing momentum to reduce capacity. Operations at Easington, Vane Tempest, Wearmouth and Westoe, consequently, came under very close scrutiny as part of a national review.

During the summer of 1992 a number of incidents indicated that the major pit closures recommended by Rothschilds were about to happen. Malcolm Edwards, British Coal's commercial director, resigned over the government's energy policy and the impact it would have on coal. A leaked letter from Tim Eggar to the Transport Minister, Roger Freeman, of 27 July, indicated that thirty pits were in line for closure by British Coal.[206] This would involve the loss of around 25,000 jobs. This figure of thirty pits was repeated by Arthur Scargill on 17 September, when he revealed the contents of a letter from Tim Sainsbury, at the DTI, to Michael Portillo, the Chief Secretary to the Treasury.[207] The list included Vane Tempest, which employed 936 men and had achieved a profit of £2.3

million by producing 830,000 tonnes of coal in 1991, and Easington, where 1,394 men had raised 1.4 million tonnes in the same year.

On 13 October Neil Clarke, chairman of British Coal, announced a modified list of thirty-one pit closures, with the loss of around 31,000 jobs. Only nineteen UK pits would survive. Of the thirty-one, twenty-seven, including Easington, Vane Tempest and Westoe, would close completely, while Wearmouth and three others would be mothballed. The decision was confirmed, the same day, by the President of the Board of Trade, Michael Heseltine.

The immediate sterilization of such a huge part of the nation's strategic fuel reserves, and the impact this would have on the mining communities during a recession, when national unemployment levels stood at 2,843,000 (with an unemployment level in the North-East of 11.5 per cent), struck at the national consciousness. The figure of 30,000 mining job losses did not take into account those supplying and servicing the industry who would be affected. This would raise the jobless total to around 78,900, while the expected Exchequer costs of closure was considered to be at least £1.3 billion in 1993–4, around £0.6 billion in 1994–5, with declining expenditure in subsequent years.[208] No attempt had been made by British Coal to carry out the cuts in a structured manner, negotiated with all concerned and with resources built into the proposals to cushion the serious impact the cuts were bound to make. In fact British Coal did not consult at all with the unions over the cuts, as they should have done under UK and EC law. Furthermore, it failed to appraise the Department of Employment adequately of the proposed massive job cuts. Gillian Shepherd, the Secretary of State for Employment, it turned out, 'had little if any role in the discussions'.[209] No advanced planning was therefore possible to minimize the impact, and Heseltine confirmed that 'No consideration of the employment consequences of the policy relating to pit closures could be allowed to interfere with the decision about whether to shut down the coal-producing capacity'.[210]

The national outcry (but particularly the fear of a backbench revolt) forced Heseltine, on 19 October, to announce that ten pits considered unviable by British Coal, including Vane Tempest, should close, following a statutory consultation period. A moratorium was announced for the other twenty-one, with a proposed wide-ranging review to assess the prospects for alternative markets.[211] On hearing Heseltine's statement, Tony Benn MP commented on the closure programme: 'It is a political act, long prepared by the Government, to rig the market, to close the pits and to punish the National Union of Mineworkers.'[212]

British Coal withdrew the closure notices and agreed to a statutory ninety-day consultation period. They gave assurances that the consultations would be fair and open-minded, but considered that unless there was a radical transformation of the energy market the pits would be closed. During the ninety days, the fabric of the pits was to be maintained, no redundancy notices were to be issued, except to volunteers, and redundancy payments were to be based on earnings up to 13 October. The remaining twenty-one pits were to stay open until early 1993.

On 21 October, during a debate on an opposition motion in the Commons, Heseltine informed the House that the review would be carried out by the Pittsburg mining firm, J.T. Boyd, with other consultants to look at the broader markets. The consultation process started on 30 October.

At the same time, the NUM and NACODS sought a judicial review in the High Court on the decision to close the ten collieries without resorting to the Modified Colliery Review Procedure, British Coal's decision to cease production at the ten pits, the failure of Heseltine to require British Coal to consult with the unions and his decision not to include the ten pits in the review of the other twenty-one. Lord Justice Glidewell, on 21 December, found these decisions either to be unlawful, or, in the failure to include the ten pits in the review, irrational, and ordered that British Coal should not make a decision on closing the ten pits 'until a procedure substantially to the same effect as the Modified Colliery Review Procedure, including some form of independent scrutiny, had been followed in relation to each of the collieries'.[213] On 23 December Heseltine announced that Boyd's would also examine the ten pits.

Meanwhile, on 21 October a massive demonstration by around 200,000 miners, their families and supporters, including contingents from the North-East with their lodge banners, was held in Hyde Park to protest at the closures. Two days later, 23 October saw the last shift worked at Vane Tempest and the pit was retained on a 'care and maintenance' basis during the ninety-day consultation period.[214] At Easington (which had previously shared pumping costs with Vane Tempest and was left to shoulder the full burden) the Bishop of Durham and the Roman Catholic auxiliary bishop of Hexham and Newcastle led prayers at the pit gates, with miners, teachers, schoolchildren and the majority of the population of the village, for the salvation of their pit.[215]

The ninety-day consultation period arrangement was soon exposed as a sham – the pits were closed and the miners paid to stay at home. British Coal then used the inducement of a sliding scale of redundancy payments to get them to leave – more if they left quickly, less if they waited the ninety days.[216] On 9 January there was a mass march through Seaham in support of the Vane Tempest miners, and a group of local women, members of Women Against Pit Closures, started a vigil.

In January the House of Commons Employment Select Committee and the Trade and Industry Committee published their reports. Boyd's report on the twenty-one pits appeared on 22 January, and the report on the ten on 15 March. Boyd's, who were not considered to be either independent or impartial by the unions, estimated the reserves at the Durham collieries at: Vane Tempest, 6 million tonnes; Easington, 8.4 million tonnes; Westoe, 22.9 million tonnes; and Wearmouth, 56.2 million tonnes.[217] On their figures Wearmouth alone had a life expectancy of 35.1 years.

On 25 March 1993 Heseltine introduced a White Paper, 'The Prospects for Coal – Conclusions of the Government's Coal Review', which proposed the closure of eighteen collieries.[218] Twelve of these, including Vane Tempest, would close completely, while six, among which were Easington and Westoe, would be mothballed. It claimed that Wearmouth would be reprieved. The closed pits would be offered for sale, but later in the month, as British Coal finally agreed contracts with National Power and PowerGen, it became clear that their coal needs would decline, from 40 million tonnes in the first year, to 30 million tonnes in each of the four following years, and that British Coal would have to look elsewhere for markets, or cut its production.

At Easington it was decided not to take the colliery through the pit review procedure; rather they would maximize their redundancy payments and see if a private buyer would take over the pit. Two faces were left in production, with J23 put into care and maintenance. On 7 May production stopped at Easington and Westoe, and on 4 June Vane Tempest closed.[219] A further stage of the pull-out occurred in July when British Coal announced the closure of its North-East headquarters.

British Coal then began the process of offering the surviving pits to private operators. When R.J. Budge moved to offer tenders for Easington, British Coal began asset-stripping at the pit.[220] Budge pulled out, apparently over the charges that would be laid on the company for the increasing pumping costs. On 26 October British Coal switched off the underground pumps and the pit flooded. With no bids for Westoe, British Coal announced its demolition on 25 November.

Wearmouth had been visited by Ian MacGregor, the then new chairman of the NCB, in 1983. He said that it was 'a model pit, profitable and efficient. It represents the future of the mining industry'.[221] Since the summer of 1982 a drilling ship, the Geocore, had put down a series of test boreholes and discovered that the Yard G1 and G2 seams had come together to form a 2.3 m thick seam, covering an area of 25 square kilometres.[222] It was described as a 'Klondyke' and £17.5 million was invested to develop it. After a four-year drivage the seam was reached. Powerful, top of the range equipment, including four Joy 12 Continuous Miners and a 700 hp Eickhoff double-ended ranging drum shearer, was installed in early 1992, and work started on the first 250 m long retreat face in November. Bill Fairbairn, the colliery manager, declared, 'We've now got the reserves, investment and equipment to make Wearmouth a highly profitable business. We're on the threshold of an exciting new era.'[223] In March 1993 the GG1 face was producing 5,100 tonnes per week, a pit record. On 24 November 1993 British Coal declared it had failed to find a market for the coal and that the pit would close.[224] Again, the sliding scale of redundancy payments was offered, and the 640 workers voted to go. The last salvage shift finished on 8 July and although the pit closed on 10 December, Caledonian Mining, R.J. Budge and Sherburn Stone Co. were prepared to tender for the pit.[225] Sherburn Stone pulled out first and, as British Coal began asset-stripping, Budge pulled out, followed by Caledonian, apparently over pumping costs.[226]

All the collieries were demolished and the sites quickly cleared, leaving blank spaces at the heart of each community. The whole process seemed like indecent haste; principal centres of employment were killed off and bulldozed so that there could be no chance of their being revived. However, on Saturday 9 July 1994 the call went out to march into Durham for the 110th Gala: 'Let us demonstrate by our presence at this great event that although they have destroyed our industry they cannot destroy our traditions.'[227] The streets were choked with thousands of people, bands playing and banners blowing in the breeze, a potent reminder of the importance of coal and the miners in the history of Durham, and the nation.

# CHAPTER 5

# Catalogue of Banners

(Where dimensions are given in the banner description, length is given first, followed by height. The location of the surviving banners is given, but, for various reasons, some may change. Where a banner has been transferred, to one or more lodges, its location is given with the last lodge to use it.)

## *Durham Miners' Association/National Union of Mineworkers Area Banners*

ADDISON

The Stella Coal Co. colliery was sunk in 1864,[1] and was ultimately linked underground with their operations at Stargate, Greenside, Clara Vale and the Emma pit at Ryton. Manpower levels remained stable through the 1930s and '40s at 475, but by 1950 it was 386 and it fell to 145 by 1960. The colliery was closed in February 1963.

In 1873 the banner showed a school scene, with an overworked child and an eager pupil, with the text below:

> The miner's boys would have to go to school,
> The Mines' Inspection Bill says so,
> To learn to read, and write, and spell,
> This parents you must know.

On the reverse side was an arbitration scene, with 'In friendship we have met to discuss labour's laws. Let reason be our guide, whilst justice is our motto [or cause]'.[2]

ADELAIDE (SHILDON BANK TOP)

The Jane pit was operated by Joseph Pease & Partners from 1830 to 1889, working the Busty and Harvey.[3] It was subsequently controlled by the West Durham Wallsend Coal Co. up to 1925.

The lodge carried a banner to a manhood suffrage demonstration at Bishop Auckland on 17 May 1873,[4] and at the Gala in June 1873 the banner was decorated with a beehive and the words, 'We will recover our rights', on one side, and the Good Samaritan on the other.[5]

ADVENTURE

Sinking started *c*. 1815, but water halted the project and it was not until *c*. 1821–2 that it restarted.[5] Drawing began in 1823, initially from the Hutton and by the 1870s from the Low Main. The Londonderry family carried on mining operations up to 1896, but the workings were later re-opened by Messrs Cooks in 1912–13. This was a drift mine, initially to the Main seam in 1916, using bord and pillar, but in the 1930s it was worked under the name of Rainton Coal Co. Ltd.[6] After nationalization arc-wall cutting was employed in 1951. In 1959 the Maudlin was worked out and mining continued extracting remaining Main and Low Main coal. The pit was wet and, with declining reserves, was officially closed on 21 July 1978.

A DMA banner, probably of the 1920s, carries a central illustration showing a female figure holding a torch and draped with bands of Art, Science, Education and Progress, drawing back the cover of Oppression to reveal to four figures an idyllic scene of houses, people and children playing: 'These things shall be: a loftier race than e'er the world hath known shall rise / with fame of freedom in their souls and light of knowledge in their eyes.' The other side has a central panel containing three roundel portraits of Joseph Ritson, James Robson and John Adair. It was produced by Tutill and is blue with a red border.
*Location*: Private owner.

A new banner was unfurled at Rainton working men's club by T.C. Cook, the colliery manager, in 1951.[8] No details were recorded of the designs, but it may have been the DMA South Hetton banner (q.v.), with 'Emancipation of Labour' on one side and aged miners' homes on the other.

The lodge later acquired the 1956 South Hetton banner (q.v.).
*Location*: Holy Trinity church, South Hetton.

ALLERDENE

Mining was taking place in the area in the eighteenth century, and probably for centuries before. Allerdene, or Ravensworth Shop (q.v.), was in use with a pumping engine in 1844 and, along with the Betty and Street pits, comprised Team colliery.[9] It was worked by Messrs Perkins &

Partners, later using the name Pelaw Main Coal Co.[10] The Yard was abandoned in 1930,[11] and the Low Main in 1938.[12] The pit closed in 1962.

Both sides of the DMA banner bore the motto, 'Unity is Strength'. One side was illustrated with the bundle of sticks fable,[13] while the other showed workmen, with the message, 'United to obtain the just rewards of their labour'. It was blue and light green damask silk, with a red border. This banner was at the 1947 Gala.[14]

## ALMA AND TWIZELL

*See* Twizell.

## ANDREWS HOUSE

Some mining had taken place near Andrews House farm and on Fortune Hill, but both pits were disused by 1856.[15] The main pit was sunk in 1843 by John Bowes & Partners, immediately south of Marley Hill colliery. In the 1890s the Main seam was worked.[16] The pit closed in 1931.

A late nineteenth-century DMA banner showed, on one side, two men, one in a suit, the other in a frock coat and carrying a walking stick, standing either side of Justice. From her feet ran a ribbon inscribed 'In thy dealings with all men be impartial and just for the peace of society depends on justice'. The reverse concentrated on the sick and poor: a sickbed scene on a panel was supported by two angels, with a third flying above and blowing a trumpet. Below this panel is a smaller sickbed scene and a widow and orphans image, accompanied by the mottoes, 'Blessed is he that considereth the poor' and 'Whoso stoppeth his ears at the cry of the poor, he shall cry himself but shall not be heard'. The banner was later transferred to Hamsteels lodge (q.v.). It is purple and yellow damask silk, with a red border, now damaged. The lower border and main ground below the roundel are missing, and its present dimensions are 11 ft 2 in × 8 ft (340 × 244 cm).

## AUCKLAND PARK

Bolckow, Vaughan & Co. took over and renamed the former Black Boy colliery (q.v.) between 1856 and 1897. There were two shafts – North and South. In the 1890s the Harvey and Brockwell were worked, with the coal washed on site and coked in beehive ovens for metallurgical use. The firm was taken over by Dorman, Long & Co. in 1929. Manpower in 1930 totalled 47, rising to 318 in 1940. It closed in 1948.

The lodge carried a banner to a manhood suffrage demonstration at Bishop Auckland on 17 May 1873, but no account is given of its design.[17]

A banner, certainly in use in 1910,[18] carried a roundel bearing a representation of Justice, holding scales and seated on a pedestal. Flanking it were angels, one beside a grieving widow and orphan, while the other assisted a poor man. At the foot of the scene was a lamb lying beside a lion, with the motto, 'Amicitia Amor et Veritas'.

The Byers Green No. 2 lodge banner, with portraits of John Johnson, William House, Samuel Galbraith and Thomas Cann, around the central painting of John Wilson.

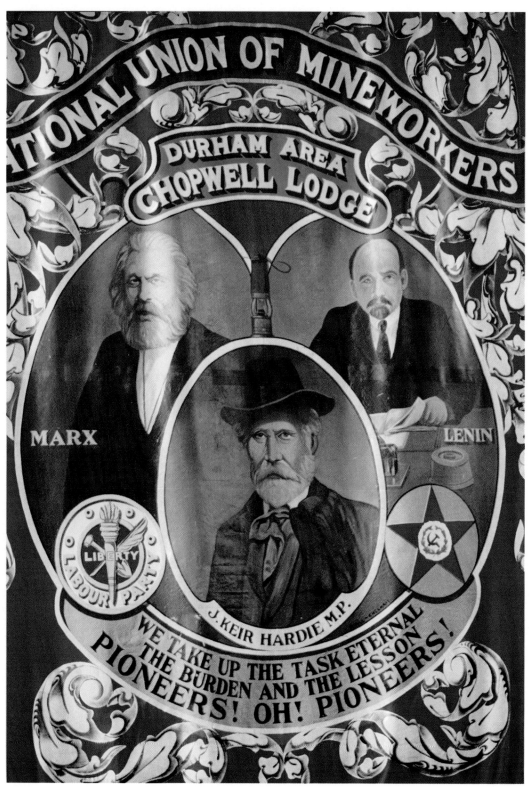

The 1954 Chopwell 'Red' banner, with portraits of Keir Hardie, Marx and Lenin.

The Tutill pattern-book 'Labour and Peace' on the Clare Vale banner.

A Roman soldier and a miner on the banner of Fenhall Drift, near Lanchester.

Houghton lodge banner, on the theme of injury and compensation.

A detailed illustration of the Seaham Miners' Hall.

The Byron Terrace aged miners' homes on the Seaham banner. The homes were opened in 1915 and 1924.

Tursdale banner, showing Keir Hardie, Ramsay MacDonald and Philip Snowden, Chancellor of the Exchequer in the 1924 and 1929 Labour governments.

West Thornley banner, by Slingsby & Son of Nuneaton, showing the North Road Miners' Hall.

Whitworth Park banner and the price of coal.

The 1937 Durham County Enginemen's, Boiler Minders' and Firemen's Association banner, with portraits of W.H. Lambton, W.B. Charlton and George Peart.

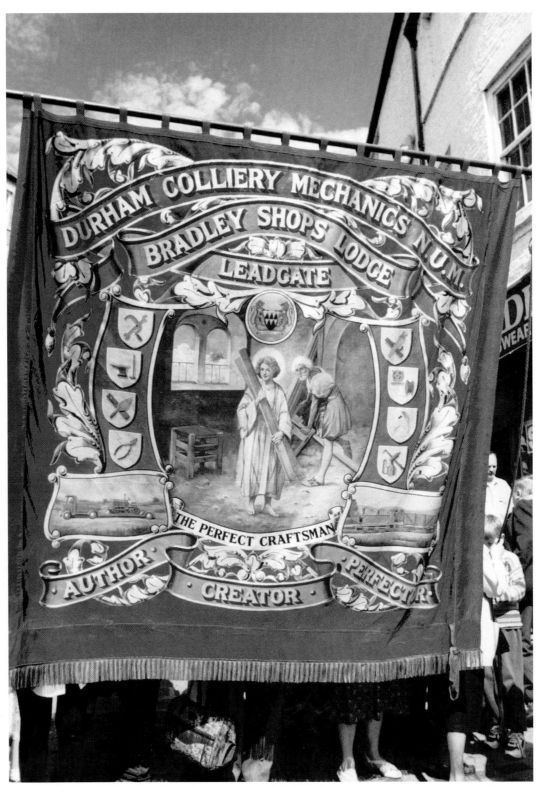

Bradley shops mechanics' banner, showing Christ as 'The Perfect Craftsman'.

BEAMISH

There had been mining operations here since at least 1763, with Morton Davidson's winning. Beamish Air pit was sunk in 1849. James Joicey sank the Mary in 1883 and the James shaft in 1885. Joicey also worked Beamish Second (*see* Chophill) and the Busty in the 1880s. Work on the Shield Row and Hutton at the James stopped in 1911, and at the Brockwell in 1926, but all three restarted in 1929. The Coppy shaft was sunk further north in 1942. Mary then served as the main coal winding shaft.[19] Major underground reconstruction was carried out in 1951 and skip loading was introduced in 1954–5. Mining ceased in March 1966.

The Beamish Air damask silk banner at the 1947 Gala carried the Tutill pattern-book designs of 'Both sides of the question' and the Good Samaritan, 'Go thou and do likewise'.[20] The first Beamish Air NUM banner, from Tutill's City Road works, showed a miner and an Australian shaking hands in front of a female figure with flags. The figures were surrounded by shields, a lion, kangaroo and a globe, with the words, 'The grip of brotherhood the world o'er'. It was red and gold damask silk, with a yellow border.

This was replaced in 1959 by the NUM No. 5 Area NCB banner which shows on the obverse, 'The March of Progress', with a colliery, two pitheads and a smoking chimney at the end of a field, with the description, 'Beamish under private enterprise'. The reverse side, also entitled 'The March of Progress', shows buildings and forecourt, representing 'Beamish under nationalisation'. It was produced by Tutill at Chesham (no. 659) and is red with a blue border.
*Location*: Derwentside District Council, Civic Centre, Consett.

BEARPARK

The Bearpark Coal Co. began sinking Bearpark Brancepeth colliery in 1872, with a shaft to the Hutton, followed by the No. 2 shaft to the Brockwell in 1874.[21] Coking using beehives started in 1877, though these were later replaced by Simon Carves retort ovens.[22] The site washery closed in 1961, and Victoria coal was sent to Morrison Busty washery, and Tilley to Brandon Pit House. Skip loading was introduced in 1962. By 1982–3 there were 500 men raising 152,000 tonnes from the thin Tilley and Harvey seams using multi-jib cutter loaders. The pit closed on 6 April 1984.

The lodge probably purchased a banner in 1874 or 1875. A new banner was unfurled on the recreation ground in 1897 by B. Dunn.[23] It had portraits of John Wilson MP and Matthew Fowler MP on one side and a 'We succour the widow and orphans' scene on the other.

A new damask silk banner from Tutill's City Road works was unfurled on 3 July 1901, which carried a full-length portrait of James Robson.[24]

The 1926 DMA banner carried a large roundel full-length portrait of 'Mr Kingston' on the obverse and an 'All Men are Brethren' pattern-book design on the reverse. The banner has the Tutill City Road mark, stitched into a damask silk field of cream and blue, bordered with pale red silk, finished with a yellow and blue fringe. It measures 8 ft 8 in by 7 ft 11 in (264 × 241 cm) and has Tutill brass discs.

*Location*: The office of Gerry Steinberg MP, Claypath, Durham City.

A portrait of William Kingston, seated at a desk, was shown on the subsequent banner, which was in use by 1938. The reverse showed the 'Unity is Strength' theme.

The replacement 1951 NUM banner was unveiled by Ald. Kingston on the eve of the Gala.[25] It shows on one side, in a roundel, the bundle of sticks fable, with 'Unity is Strength' at the base of the scene. The other side, with similar union scroll and title, has a depiction of the 'Bearpark Aged Miners' Homes'. It was produced by Tutill at Chesham and is a light red and yellow damask silk, with a blue border.

*Location*: On loan from NUM (NE Area) to Durham Heritage Centre, St Mary-le-Bow Church, Durham City.

Both designs were repeated on the final lodge banner, unfurled by Will Paynter on 19 July 1963. It is red with a blue border.

*Location*: St Edmund's Church, Bearpark.

## BEWICKE MAIN

Mining is recorded in the early nineteenth century, with a wagonway and self-acting incline constructed in 1809–10.[26] A later pit was sunk in 1868 by Perkins & Partners, who operated Birtley iron works and the associated collieries of Ouston, Ravensworth and Urpeth.[27] The company name changed in 1906 to the Owners of Pelaw Main Collieries Ltd, and in 1926 to Pelaw Main Collieries Ltd, but at Bewicke Main the working out of the Six Quarter in 1931, and the Low Main and Hutton in 1932, led to the pit's closure by 1933.[28]

The banner in use in 1873 showed a view of the colliery, an iron steamship, an engine crossing a viaduct on the local wagonway and a picture of Birtley iron works, with the motto, 'Success to the coal and iron trade by land and sea'. The reverse side showed a master and workman shaking hands: 'He that oppresseth the poor reproacheth the Master.'[29] It was painted by William Gowdy for Bainbridges of Newcastle and was blue with a red border. It measured 9 ft × 8 ft (274 × 244 cm).

In 1901 a new banner was unfurled by T.H. Cann,[30] though the illustrations are unknown.

The 1924 banner shows a central portrait of the Rt Hon. J. Ramsey MacDonald, in a roundel, flanked by portraits of J. Keir Hardie MP, Lenin, Mr Ben Oliver and Mr A.J. Cook, with scenes of a pithead and a miner's lamp. It carries the painted mark of G. Tutill, London, and the motto, 'The Mines for the People', at the base of the illustration. The reverse shows a female figure, draped with the ribbon of 'Trade Unions', leading six miners to the 'Dawn of a new era', with an idyllic scene of good-quality houses and children playing. Below the scene is a ribbon inscribed, 'We work for the health of the people and demand a living wage'. The portrait of MacDonald was later covered with white paint, but subsequently exposed during restoration. The painted section has been carefully cut out and reset on new silk, though retaining the Tutill brass discs and tapes. It is light blue with a red border and measures 8 ft 8 in × 8 ft (263 × 244 cm). *Location*: Kibblesworth County Junior and Infant School.

BINCHESTER

Binchester was sunk in 1872 by the West Hartlepool Harbour & Rail Co., and subsequently by the Hunwick & Newfield Coal Co. It was then sold to Bolckow, Vaughan & Co., certainly by the 1880s, and was linked underground with Westerton (q.v.). In the 1890s the Harvey and Brockwell were worked.[31] A new ventilating shaft was sunk at Merrington Lane in 1906,[32] but the pit closed in 1908. The Vinovia shaft is currently used for water pumping.

The ribbon from a banner of 'Durham Miners' Association Binchester Lodge' survives.
*Location*: Binchester Community Centre.

A banner, thought to be from Binchester, was sold at Sedgefield car-boot sale in September 1995.[33] The current owner is unknown.

BLACK BOY

Mining was carried out here from 1830 by Nicholas Wood & Co. and into the 1850s under the title Black Boy Coal Co.[34] There were three Black Boy pits: Old Black Boy colliery, north of Auckland Park, the Machine pit, to the south, and the Gurney, near Coundon Grange. By 1860 Black Boy is recorded as being under the control of the executors of J. Backhouse.[35] It was later acquired by Bolckow, Vaughan, certainly by 1884, and the Machine pit was renamed Auckland Park colliery (q.v.). In the 1890s mining concentrated on the Main and Five Quarter.[36] The pit closed in December 1924, but restarted, only to be closed again in May 1928. It was absorbed by Dorman, Long in 1929, but closed in 1939.

In 1872 the lodge banner was at the Bishop Auckland manhood suffrage demonstration in May,[73] and at the Gala the banner showed a couple of miners and an official weighing a tub, with the title 'Justice'. The reverse bore the verse,

> Miners throughout the land,
> Join in one social band;
> If you would happy be,
> Free from all slavery,
> Banish all knavery,
> And free yourselves.[38]

## BLACKHALL

Horden Collieries Ltd leased the site in 1901 and started sinking the upcast and downcast shafts in October 1909 through water-bearing strata. The work was completed by 1913.[39] Work was initially by bord and pillar in the Low Main and Hutton, but longwall was introduced in 1947. The pit was reorganized in 1956, by introducing skip loading to maintain output levels. In the 1960s power-loading and supports were introduced, with an Anderton shearer in 1962. By then the Main, Low Main and Hutton were being worked, with the principal output going to ICI. However, in the 1960s water was becoming a serious problem, and in 1979 2,300 gallons a minute were being pumped at the shaft. This resulted in shorter faces being worked, and output increasingly concentrated on Low Main for Redcar steel works. Water eventually forced closure on 16 April 1981.

A banner was purchased in 1920.[40] The obverse illustration shows a prominent portrait of John Wilson, with smaller representations of John Johnson and William House. The reverse shows a miner and owner flanking a central panel as part of a 'Friendship, Love and Truth' pattern-book design. The banner was produced at Tutill's City Road works and is a light blue silk; the border, which was originally red, is now missing, and the banner now measures 7 ft 10 in × 7 ft 6 in (239 × 229 cm). It still retains its Tutill brass discs and was last used at the 1935 Gala.[41]
*Location*: Red Hill.

A new DMA banner, by G. Tutill, was acquired in 1936 and unfurled by T. Anson, the lodge chairman, in the Welfare Park on the evening of 24 July.[42] On the front were three linked portraits within a central roundel, showing 'A.J. Cook' (top), 'Peter Lee' (bottom left) and 'Keir Hardie' (bottom right); the reverse carried the motto, 'United we stand, divided we fall'. It was blue, red and yellow.

The NUM banner was unfurled on 15 July 1955 by Emmanuel Shinwell.[42] It showed three linked circular portrait panels of A.J. Cook, E. Shinwell and J. Keir Hardie. The reverse showed the figures of Friendship, Love and Truth. It was purple silk with a red border.

This banner was replaced by a second-hand banner from Craghead (q.v.), certainly by 1977,[43] which showed the reversed image of Durham Cathedral on one side and Earl Attlee, Aneurin Bevan and Arthur Horner on the other.
*Location*: Red Hill

The last NUM Blackhall banner was produced by Turtle & Pearce (no. 779) and carries three roundel portraits, of A.J. Cook, Keir Hardie and Aneurin Bevan, on a brown shield. The reverse carries a small portrait of 'T. Hepburn 1830', over a shield of three scenes: at the top left, a pithead with pit ponies in a field; at the top right, people relaxing at the seaside; and in the background, a cliff on which are standing statues of the founding fathers of the DMA (which now stand outside Red Hill). The lower scene shows men playing bowls and is entitled 'Leisure through

modernisation'. It measures 7 ft 9 in × 6 ft 10 in (236 × 208 cm) and is red with a yellow border. Although the colliery officially closed in 1981, salvage work was being undertaken during that year, and the banner was carried into Durham for the Gala.[44]
*Location*: Blackhall Colliery Miners' Welfare Hall.

BLACK HOUSE

Black House 'H', or Wash House pit, near Birtley, formed part of the Pelaw Main Collieries group, with Urpeth 'C', Bewicke Main 'D', Ouston 'E' and the Betty and Shop pits at Ravensworth. It opened in 1913, but in 1930 a French syndicate acquired a controlling interest in Pelaw Main Collieries,[45] and when the Townley was abandoned, the pit closed in May 1932.

Black House acquired the Ouston banner (q.v.), with its portraits of Whiteley, Robson, Cook, Gilliland and Cann.
*Location*: Beamish (1984-10-2).

In 1926 the lodge acquired the Edmondsley Elam banner (q.v.) and simply attached its own name over Edmondsley. The banner was used until the pit closed.
*Location*: Beamish (1984-10-5).

BLACK PRINCE

The colliery, near Dans Castle, Tow Law, was sunk in 1846 by Charles Attwood, the founder of the Weardale Iron Co., near the Royal George pit. It had extensive batteries of coke ovens, extending towards Inkerman (q.v.). In the 1890s 640 hands worked the Ballarat, Five Quarter, Top and Main coal.[46] The Victoria pit operated on Tow Law Fell between *c.* 1858 and 1921, and was linked to the main site by tramway.[47] A new drift was driven to the Five Quarter in 1906, with capital outlay on a new hauler and washery.[48] The pit closed in 1933.

The banner at the 1872 and 1873 Galas showed a master and workman standing either side of a shield, and shaking hands, with the emblems of 'Peace, Plenty and Friendship' and the verse,

> Success to the trade
> Both by sea and by land
> Out of the interest that's made,
> The workman should have his demands

and 'A fair day's wage for a fair day's work'. The reverse showed the bundle of sticks fable, with the motto, 'United we stand, divided we fall'.[49]

A banner was unfurled on 22 September 1894, but there is no record of its design.[50]

The earliest surviving DMA banner carries a sickbed scene on the obverse, 'Help in time of need', and the 'Friendship, Love and Truth' image on the reverse. The banner is blue and grey damask silk with a red border and measures 8 ft 9 in × 6 ft 8 in (267 × 203 cm).

*Location*: Beamish (1984-10-1).

This was replaced in the 1920s by one showing the bundle of sticks fable, with 'Unity is Strength' at the bottom of the border, and on the reverse a miner coming to comfort a widow and child at a grave: 'We succour the widows and orphans.' This was produced at Tutill's City Road works and is a blue and light green damask silk, with a red border, finished with a blue fringe. It measures 8 ft 6 in × 7 ft 10 in (259 × 239 cm) and was later transferred to Hedleyhope lodge (q.v.).

## BLAYDON MAIN

Mining had taken place here in the seventeenth – early eighteenth century, but new workings were undertaken in 1837, possibly by G.H. Ramsay.[51] It was then purchased, in 1884, by the Stella Coal Co. which worked the Hazard, Speculation and Mary pits.[52] In 1908 the operations were purchased by Priestman Collieries Ltd. The coal was shipped from Tyne Dock and there were associated coke ovens at Derwenthaugh. Mining ceased in March 1921.

The banner at the 1873 Gala showed Labour and Capital exchanging their commodities, with the figure of Justice exclaiming to Capital, 'Put more in the scale'.[53] Below the picture was the motto, 'United we stand, divided we fall'. The reverse showed a hewer at work, with a putter pushing a tub, inscribed 'Manhood Suffrage', to a pony driver with the line, 'The working man is the pride and stay of the country'.

## BOLDON

The pit was sunk by the Harton Coal Co. in 1866–9. An explosion at the No. 8 surface boiler killed two in 1884. The Bensham and Hutton seams were worked in the 1890s.[54] In 1949 the surface operations were reconstructed, and in the 1950s Anderton disc shearers were introduced on longwall retreating faces. In 1961 the workforce totalled 1,240 men, but by October the NCB was planning a rundown of the pit. In February 1981 the Board announced its closure. When the men struck, demanding test borings be carried out to search for more coal, a survey was undertaken, but insufficient reserves were apparently located. The last shift, at the G.03 face, was on 24 June 1982.

The banner at the 1872 Gala carried an arbitration scene on one side, with the figure of Justice standing between a group of masters and men. The reverse showed clasped hands, a rose, shamrock and thistle, with the line, 'Masters, do to your servants that which is just and equal, knowing that you also have a Master in heaven'. [55] It was blue silk.

A green and yellow damask silk banner used in the 1920s showed the frontage of Boldon Colliery Miners' Hall of 1891 in a roundel. On the

reverse was a wheatsheaf in a field, with a spade and sickle by it. Across the sheaf was a pink scroll inscribed, 'Each for all, all for each'. The painted section was subsequently cut from the banner which is now 4 ft 10 in × 4 ft 10 in (58 × 58 cm).
*Location*: Red Hill.

It was replaced in 1947 by a socialist NUM banner showing a miner, draped with a ribbon marked 'Tyrannicide', standing over the dragon of Tyranny, and holding the hand of the female figure of Trust. Behind them is a large wheel inscribed '1946 Evolution, 1947 Nationalisation', and the motto 'Forward with Socialism'. On the reverse is shown a handshake over a globe, with the words, 'Workers of the world unite for peace and progress'.[56] This design is comparable with a damask banner of North Walbottle branch of the Northumberland NUM, with the motto, 'Unity is Strength'.

A new banner was unfurled in 1957 by Ernest Fernyhough, MP for Jarrow, in the Miners' Hall on the eve of the Gala. The NUM banner bears three linked roundels carrying the portraits of Lord Lawson, John Summerbell and William T. Wilson. Accompanying them is the quotation, 'You have been so faithful and loving to us that / we shall never forget your favour towards us. Bunyan'. On the other side are depictions of aged miners' homes at Downhill, '1900–1949' and Hedworth, '1914'. It was produced by Tutill at Chesham (no. 657) and is red silk, with a yellow border and red fringe. It measures 6 ft 10 in × 7 ft 8 in (208 × 234 cm).
*Location*: Red Hill.

The lodge later acquired the Tudhoe Mill Drift banner (q.v.). This NUM banner is illustrated with a painting of 'The Big Meeting', showing crowds on the Racecourse, with banners lining the fence. A red V-shaped label painted across the sky is an addition and is inscribed 'Unity is strength', surmounted by a DMA shield. The reverse carries a central yellow plaque decorated with a blue DMA 1869 shield. In the lower segment of the illustration was added a note that it was 'Presented by the Tudhoe Miners Lodge / To the Boldon Miners Lodge 1977'. A further note records that it was 'Restored and repainted for the 100th. Durham Big Meeting'. This banner is blue with a red border and measures 7 ft 4 in × 7 ft 10 in (224 × 239 cm).
*Location*: The Shack, North Road Social Club, Boldon Colliery.

BOWBURN

There were two collieries. The earliest was held initially by William Hedley, and later by West Hartlepool Harbour and Railway Co. The later Bell Bros colliery was sunk using the piling method by E. Johnson & Sons in 1906 to relieve heavy haulage at their Tursdale pit.[57] The operation was taken over by Dorman, Long in 1923. A new screening plant and washery were installed in 1932.[58] Tursdale coal was drawn via a drift through the goaf to Bowburn shaft in the 1930s, and the old shaft, used for ventilation, was converted for coal drawing and man-riding.[59] Manpower in 1930 stood at 639, but rose to 2,358 by 1940 and remained relatively stable, falling slightly to 2,102 by 1960. The pit was closed in July 1967.

The earliest known banner carried a depiction of Edith Cavell, painted by Marrington, the local colliery painter, which must have been used on or after 1915.

*Location*: The banner was held by Mr J. Hutchinson, Gilesgate, Durham.

A Tutill damask DMA banner carried a roundel painting of Emancipation of Labour.

The banner at the 1947 Gala carried an image with the motto, 'You have nothing to lose but your chains' on one side and 'United to obtain the just reward of our labour' on the other.[60]

The 1959 banner was unfurled by Christopher Mayhew MP on 17 July.[61] It shows, on one side, a distance shot of the Racecourse on Gala day, with the motto, 'Workers of all lands unite', and an aerial view of Conishead Priory on the reverse. At the 1967 Gala a notice was attached to the banner inscribed, 'Going on the dole next week'.[62] The banner was transferred to COSA (q.v.), probably after 1969.[63]

## BOWDEN CLOSE

Test borings located the Brockwell in 1839, and the Norwich pit was operated by Joseph Pease & Partners, later Pease & Partners Ltd.[64] It closed in June 1930 with the loss of 1,200 jobs.[65]

A banner at the 1873 Gala, described as Boldon Close, which may be Bowden Close, carried a full-length portrait of Thomas Ramsey, 'The Pioneer of the Western District', along with portraits of William Crawford, Nicholas Wilkinson, John Foreman and William Patterson.[66] The accompanying motto read 'We deem those men the grandest, most noble, and good, who plan and win our victories, and shed not a drop of blood'.

The banner at the 1893 Gala illustrated the value of cooperation.[67]

A new banner was unfurled on 27 June 1914 by James Robson.[68] The obverse showed the aged miners' homes at Crook, while the reverse carried the pictorial representation of 'Unity is Strength'. The banner measured 11 ft × 10 ft 6 in (335 × 320 cm).

## BRANCEPETH

Brancepeth 'A' pit was sunk around 1840, by the Northern Coal Mining Co., and worked subsequently by Straker & Love. The 'B' pit, at Oakenshaw (q.v.), followed in 1855, and the 'C' pit in 1865. Output was principally from the Hutton, Seggar, Jet, Three Quarter, Ballarat, Harvey and Brockwell. Coal was coked on site, with 420 ovens in 1852, rising to 1,700 in 1894.[69] An explosion at the 'A' pit on 13 April 1896 killed twenty.[70] By-product recovery was undertaken at the site in 1902 with the installation of 120 Semet Solvay ovens. Manpower figures fell in each decade, from 2,653 in 1930 to 1,529 in 1960. The pit closed in July 1967.

Brancepeth (formerly Roddymoor) banner, with the Peter Lee Memorial Reservoir.

The banner at the 1872 and 1873 Galas showed an arbitration court, with two men arguing, and the message (variously recorded), 'the life of the Union [or 'the allied union'] causeth the death of the bond, and freedom is sweet to the working man [or 'to all workmen']'.[71] The reverse carried a portrait of Alexander MacDonald and the line, 'Behold how pleasant it is for brethren to dwell together in love and unity'.

An indistinct photograph taken on 22 July 1908, of the lodge banner at the unveiling of a memorial to Brancepeth 'A' miner, Thomas Barton, 'the

Willington Hero', shows a large central roundel, with a right profile portrait in a circle at the base, while the upper, split segment contains two figures, the left seated and the right bearded.[72] Conceivably they may be William Crawford and Alexander MacDonald.

Another DMA banner, of uncertain date, had a central roundel of a graveside scene: 'We succour the widows and orphans.' This was a damask silk banner, grey and red, with a yellow border.

On 27 July 1923 J.E. Swan unfurled a Tutill banner, which probably had an illustration of the local aged miners' homes.[73] It was certainly at the 1947 Gala. Also in 1923 there were negotiations concerning the sale of the old banner to the 'A' pit lodge, with the proceeds going to the Willington aged miners' homes fund.

The NUM banner showed the frontage of 'Conishead Priory Convalescent Home'.[74] The reverse was probably an illustration of 'Brancepeth Colliery Aged Miners' Homes'.[75]

After seeking prices from Tutill in August 1962, the lodge acquired the 1954 Roddymoor banner.[76] It was renamed, 'Durham Area / Brancepeth Miners', and unfurled by L.W. Robson and W. Bourne at Willington on 19 July 1963.[77] The large central roundel shows the Racecourse on Gala day, with the Cathedral and Castle in the background. At the base of the scene is the title, 'The Big Meeting'. The reverse side, with similar titles, shows an aerial view of Burnhope reservoir in a roundel, with the base title, 'Peter Lee's Memorial Burnhope Reservoir'. The banner was produced by Tutill at Chesham and is an orange and red damask silk with a green border. It measures 7 ft 8.5 in × 7 ft 7.5 in (235 × 232 cm).
*Location*: Beamish (1971-152).

BRANDON

This was initially a landsale pit operated by John Shaw from *c*. 1836. Straker & Love sank the 'A' shaft in 1856, and the 'C' pit to the Busty in 1860. Further sinking at the 'New Side' was carried out in 1884 to extend the Busty workings. As the Busty and Brockwell neared exhaustion, a new shaft was sunk at Brandon Pit House in 1924 to take the outlying Busty, with a second shaft in 1931. Reconstruction work in 1927 included a new heapstead, while the site's beehive coke ovens were demolished.[78] As the 'C' pit reserves declined, Pit House was developed, with underground conveyers in 1948–9, a joint washery in 1957 and the replacement of cage winding by drift conveyor in 1960. Pit House was closed on 15 March 1968.

The banner at the 1873 Gala showed a man waving a flag on the summit of a black hill.[79] Three others were shown climbing up, and one man had rolled to the bottom and was being assisted by a friend. Below the scene was the motto, 'Nil Desperandum'. The reverse side showed three girls, the one in the centre on a pedestal, with the words, 'How pleasant it is for brethren to dwell together'.

Brandon lodge banner, with the welfare ground pavilion. The banner is now in Canada.

A new banner was purchased in 1874.[80] It carried portraits of MacDonald, Burt and Crawford. On the reverse was a 'picture illustrating the great improvement which has been effected during the past few years in the social and physical condition of the miners'.

The banner used at the 1893 Gala showed portraits of Ald. Fowler of Durham City and Mr Whitley, the lodge secretary.[81]

In the 1920s the lodge purchased a banner bearing a panel with two roundels containing the portraits of Thomas Carr on the left, and Ramsay

MacDonald on the right. Discussions were held on the removal of MacDonald's portrait on 26 May 1932, and his portrait was overpainted with an illustration of the west end of Durham Cathedral.

In 1949 a new banner was acquired, and unfurled by Sam Watson, accompanied by Dr Hugh Dalton MP, on 9 July.[82] It was crimson and gold, with a central roundel showing the 1946 Victory Gala, designed by Walter Lishman, art master of Durham Johnson School, and based on a photograph taken by Charles Hodgson from Pelaw Heights.

The 1963 NUM banner again shows the Racecourse on Gala day, while the reverse shows the pavilion of the local welfare ground. It was unfurled by Michael Foot. The banner was produced by Tutill at Chesham (no. 363) and is red silk with a yellow border.

*Location*: The banner was presented to Steve Magnaca, the Mayor of Brandon, Manitoba, Canada, by Brandon lodge, following the closure of Brandon Pit House in 1968.[83] Mayor Magnaca subsequently presented it to Brandon and District Labour Council. There are proposals to house the banner in the Brandon University Archive.

## BROOMSIDE

Broomside (the Lady Adelaide) was sunk to the Hutton in 1835 for Lord Londonderry, with the coal shipped from Sunderland and Seaham Harbour.[84] In the 1870s and 1880s it was worked under the name of Broomside Coal Co., but closed due to exhaustion in 1890.[85]

The banner at the 1872 Gala showed a man holding a pair of scales, 'Masters give unto your servants' etc. The reverse carried a representation of Peace holding a laurel wreath.[86]

The 1873 Gala banner showed, on one side, underground and surface scenes, and on the other, an arbitration case.[87]

A new banner was displayed at the 1875 Gala, showing the Miners' Hall in North Road, Durham.[88]

## BROWNEY

The colliery was sunk in 1871–3 by Bell Bros, with three shafts. Most coal in the 1890s was taken from the Brockwell, Busty and Hutton.[89] The firm was taken over by Dorman, Long & Co. Ltd in 1923. Manpower in 1930 was 625. The pit closed in July 1938 because of flooding.

The 1873 Gala banner showed a miner and sinker, with a central portrait of William Crawford, and the verse,

> We pierce the ancient strata,
> Nature's geologic roll,
> Till we reach God's hidden treasure,
> The world-wide famous coal.[90]

The 1911 Browney lodge banner.

The reverse showed two miners, and a further verse:

> Through geologic records,
> Great nature's printed scroll,
> We work the famed black diamond,
> The heat sustaining coal.

In July 1900 a new banner was unfurled.[91] One side carried a portrait of Ald. Sam Galbraith, the former lodge checkweighman, while the reverse bore an illustration of 'Liberty, Truth and Justice'. The banner was designed by R. Hodge of South Shields.

On 17 July 1911 a new banner was unfurled at Browney colliery institute by John Wilson.[92] On the obverse were portraits of Ald. S. Galbraith, M. Eddy (secretary), W. Walton (compensation secretary) and R. Haley (treasurer). On the reverse was 'Labour and Peace'.

Another DMA banner shows a miner and Britannia standing in front of Justice. The miner, who is wearing a MFGB belt, holds a scroll inscribed 'Mines owned by the nation for the nation. Loyalty, endeavour, good citizenship', while Britannia holds a scroll with the message, 'Humane conditions, higher standards of living, adequate compensation, safety measures etc'. The scene is entitled 'A fair exchange'. The reverse again shows Justice, with a seated mother and two children, two women and a seated figure with a book and cross, positioned around a lyre and incense burner. The ground is strewn with fruit and in the sky is an all-seeing eye. The banner is blue with a red border and measures 8 ft 11 in × 7 ft 9 in (272 × 236 cm).
*Location*: Beamish (1984-10-3).

## BRUSSELTON

A pit was sunk in 1834 and there was some mining in the latter half of the nineteenth century. Another colliery was sunk between 1897 and 1920, but was replaced by the Ladysmith colliery, to the south of Backsandsides farm, by 1939.[93] Also, between 1920 and 1939 a new Brusselton colliery was sunk further east. After 1947 the Haggs Lane drift worked Main coal, but in 1959 the Beaumont seam was flooded. By 1967 the Harvey No. 1 seam was declining in quality, and geological problems occurred in the Busty, leaving only the Harvey No. 2. The colliery closed on 7 June 1968.

The DMA banner showed a shoulder-length portrait of Peter Lee, though the 'Brusselton Lodge' label at the top of the roundel portrait had been repainted, suggesting a reused banner.[94]

The NUM banner has a large central roundel showing the standing figure of 'Mr C.R. Attlee MP'. The reverse shows Durham Cathedral, with the motto, 'Unity is Strength'. It was unfurled on West Auckland village green by Attlee on 15 July 1955,[95] and was used up until closure in 1968. It was produced by Tutill at Chesham and is gold and orange damask silk with an orange border, measuring 7 ft 9 in × 7 ft 4 in (236 × 224 cm).
*Location*: Red Hill.

## BURNHOPE

The Fortune (or Sykes) pit was sunk in 1845 by Thomas Hedley Bros. In 1868 the Annie, Fell and Jaw Blades were sunk, although Jaw Blades only operated for three years. The pits passed to Messrs Sowerby & Fletcher and were then sold to Utrick Ritson in 1881. He worked the Annie, Fell, Fortune, Rabbit Warren and Ralph drifts until around 1934. Burnhope was then mined by Halmshaw & Partners, but by the end of the decade it was under the control of Bearpark Coal & Coke Co. Ltd, with a linking aerial flight to Bearpark by 1942. Burnhope closed in 1949.

The 1873 Gala banner carried portraits of Crawford, MacDonald and Patterson, and a boy holding a placard inscribed 'The Mines Regulation Bill, 1872. Ten hours from bank to bank'.[96] Below these images was the verse,

> This bill has passed, and it does say,
> The boys to have ten hours a day;
> But in this bill it does say more,
> Though I have not time to
> Tell you all.

The reverse side showed a child leading a lion and a lamb, with the verse,

> We have met again, my dear friends,
> Hand and heart we have joined,
> For our rights we mean to fight,
> But as our flag waves in the air,
> The capitalist he begins to stare,
> And does cry out, 'I do declare,
> I'm afraid the union's off for fair.

A new banner was acquired in 1924.[97] A Tutill damask silk banner, possibly the 1924 banner, showed a version of the 'Friendship, Love and Truth' pattern-book design, in a form similar to that used at Harraton.

In 1947 the banner at the Gala carried the images of 'Emancipation of labour' and 'United we stand, divided we fall'.[98]

This was replaced in 1959 by a banner unfurled by J.W. Ainsley, MP for NW Durham, at Burnhope Miners' Hall.[99] The obverse showed Durham Cathedral, with the Miners' Hall and Memorial Gardens at Red Hill on the reverse. It was red silk with a blue border.

## BURNOPFIELD (HOBSON)

The pit was operated from 1849 by John Bowes & Partners Ltd. In the 1890s Main and Busty were worked, with an annual output of 140,000 tons.[100] Manpower figures rose from 394 in 1930 to 669 in 1940, but were reduced in the 1960s, until the exhaustion of the Tilley forced closure on 9 August 1968.

The Burnopfield banner carried at the 1872 Gala showed a master and workman shaking hands, 'Unity is strength', with the Good Samaritan on the reverse: 'Labour is honourable, we seek its reward. A fair day's wage for a fair day's work; why not have it? Heart and hand united we stand.'[101] It was blue, with a red and green border.

The NUM Hobson banner bears the 'Emancipation of Labour' scene on one side, and portraits of 'A.J. Cook. Faithful unto death', and 'J.E. Swan. Agent DMA.' on the other. The banner was produced by Tutill at Chesham and measures 8 ft 9 in × 8 ft 3 in (267 × 251 cm). It is dark purple with a red border. This banner was at the 1946 Gala.[102] The Cook and Swan design was probably repeated on a banner of 1958.
*Location*: Beamish (1978-934-1).

## BUTTERKNOWLE

In the early 1960s, miners at a private venture at Low Butterknowle broke into old workings and discovered two bronze cauldrons, and two repaired skillets, dated to the fifteenth century. These items are now in Bowes Museum (Acc. 1964. 958–961).

William Prattman became involved in mining at Butterknowle in the 1820s and 1830s, though attempts to sink a second shaft, the Diamond, led to his bankruptcy. The operations were transferred to trustees, and as the market improved the Diamond pit was restarted. In the 1880s the Butterknowle Coal Co. also operated Marsfield drift, Quarry and Slacks pits, with Moor Hill added in 1885. Claims for subsidence damage in the High Court Chancery Division (Bishop Auckland Industrial Co-operative Flour and Provision Society Ltd v. The Butterknowle Colliery Co. Ltd) forced the pit's closure in 1906.[103]

On one side of the surviving banner is a ribbon inscribed 'Union is Strength', over a roundel showing a version of the bundle of sticks fable, with a man attempting to break the bundle over his knee and a boy triumphantly holding a broken stick. At the right is a man in a black frock coat, apparently John Wilson. The reverse carried the label of 'Butterknowle Collieries' over a roundel showing six men seated at a table, entitled 'Conciliation'. It is red and blue damask silk, with a yellow border, and was produced at Tutill's City Road works.
*Location*: Beamish (1986.132).

## BYERMOOR

Mining had been carried out here in the eighteenth century by the Claverings, but by the 1860s the principal operations were undertaken by John Bowes & Partners Ltd. In the 1890s the Busty and Brockwell were mined.[104] The Brass Thill was abandoned in 1938.[105] The pit closed in 1968.

The 1872 Gala banner showed 'Two marrows changing', with one well-dressed miner (wearing boots, socks, trousers, linen underclothing and flannel jacket) about to descend, while another, in red waistcoat, is ready to ascend.[106] On the other side was the verse,

> Success to every union,
> And every one that's true;
> Now we're bound together,
> Let's try what we can do.
> Our masters they do tell us,
> That if we mean to stand,
> We shall do ourselves an injury,
> And the trade will leave the land.
> But in that we have advantage,
> And that you know is true;
> For if the trade leaves England,
> We can leave it too.

The banner at the 1873 Gala showed a master reading a document to a number of workmen.[107] On the reverse was the verse used on the 1872 banner.

The NUM banner carried a small portrait of Attlee set over a view of the Houses of Parliament, with the motto, 'Organisation the key to economic freedom'.[108] The reverse showed the Hermitage, 'Building your association firmly and strong', accompanied by small illustrations of safety lamps, an anvil and a pit head. This Tutill banner was blue and silver damask silk, with a red border. It was later transferred to Vane Tempest lodge (q.v.).

## BYERS GREEN

The Durham County Coal Co. leased royalties at Byers Green, and the sinking of the Michael pit took place in 1840. This was completed, after flooding, in 1845. Other shafts were sunk in 1859 and 1873.[109] It was then taken over by the West Hartlepool Harbour & Railway Co., who sold it to Bolckow, Vaughan & Co. *c.* 1877. Work in the 1890s concentrated on the Busty and Brockwell.[110] It temporarily closed in April 1927, but was amalgamated with Newfield, and finally closed in June 1931.

The lodge purchased a banner from W. Elam of Bethnal Green on 3 May 1873.[111] The obverse showed a widow with three orphans leaving a church and being met by an angel who crowned the woman with a laurel wreath. This was accompanied by the motto, 'Protect the widows and orphans'. The reverse showed several workmen belonging to different crafts – a miner, coke drawer, blacksmith, joiner, mason and labourer – standing above a scene of 'Peace', represented by a lion and lamb, with the motto, 'It is well for brothers to dwell in unity'. The banner was blue silk, with a red border.

The banner used in the 1920s has a central roundel with 'No. 2 Lodge Byers Green' on the border. The obverse shows a row of aged miners'

homes, with four portraits, entitled 'Aged Miners' Homes and Aged Miners', while the reverse shows portraits of Johnson, House, Galbraith and Cann around the central portrait of John Wilson. It is orange and yellow damask silk with a red border.
*Location*: High Street Methodist Church, Byers Green.

## CARTERTHORNE

This colliery was operated by Henry Chaytor of Witton Castle in the 1870s. In 1885 Carterthorne was worked by Hodgson and Simpson, but it passed to Carterthorne Colliery Owners in 1886. In 1891 Chaytor proposed restarting the colliery.

New Carterthorne colliery was held on a yearly tenancy from the Earl of Strathmore, on the terms of an agreement of 1887 for a fourteen-year lease which was never executed. Due to the case, Walton v. Dowdeswell, in the High Court Chancery Division, the receiver operated the colliery and it was put up for sale in 1895.[112] It restarted, but closed again in October 1925.

The 1873 Gala banner showed a widow and orphan appealing to a colliery owner for compensation.[113]

## CASTLE EDEN

The pit was sunk in 1840–2 and had several owners. In 1856 Messrs Cook & Co. were the operators, and by 1879 it had been taken over by the Castle Eden Coal Co.[114] Water was a major problem, though some control was achieved by 1881, allowing increased coal production.[115] It soon closed, however, though there were suggested plans for reopening in 1885.[116] Castle Eden Coal Co. Ltd do appear to have restarted it, though the pit was again flooded in 1893. It was purchased by Horden Collieries Ltd in 1900 and was pumped out, though it was not a productive unit.

The banner at the 1872 and 1873 Galas showed two boys embracing each other, and the scriptural inscription, 'What mean ye that ye beat my people to pieces, and grind the faces of the poor'. The reverse showed a master and workman shaking hands.[117]

## CHESTER MOOR

The pit, also called Chester South Moor, was initially worked by Sowerby, Phillips & Co., and in the 1880s by Thiedemann & Wallis. A new sinking took place in 1889.[118] Later (certainly in 1889) it was worked by Priestman Collieries Ltd. The workforce figures rose from 403 in 1930 to over 700 in the period 1940–60. In 1959 the Brass Thill was being worked, but the pit closed in 1967.

A new banner was unfurled by G. Robson, the lodge president, on the morning of Gala day 27 July 1929.[119]

The local aged miners' homes were shown on the 1947 banner, with the lines, 'These things shall be, a loftier race than ere the world has seen shall rise, with flame of freedom in their souls, and light of knowledge in their eyes', on the reverse.[120]

A later NUM banner, of the 1950s, shows the Hermitage, 'Chester-le-Street / Rehabilitation Centre', on one side, and a 'Sunshine of Liberty' design on the other. It was certainly in use in 1962,[122] and was later transferred to Monkwearmouth (q.v.).

CHILTON

The sinking was carried out in 1872 by H. Stobart & Co. Ltd, but by 1879 it was in the possession of the South Durham Coal Co.[123] The Five Quarter, Harvey and Brockwell were worked. Water was a serious problem, though the installation of new pumping engines by 1881 enabled coal production to expand.[124] The lease was, however, allowed to expire, and the landowner, Lord Eldon, came into possession of the pit around 1884.[125] In 1887 it was dismantled, but in 1893 Bolckow, Vaughan & Co. acquired the lease. The Five Quarter and Main were tubbed off, and a new shaft sunk to the Brockwell. In 1924 it was taken over by Pease & Partners, but closed in 1930, only to be reopened by Dorman, Long & Co. in 1934 to work Main and Five Quarter.[126] Some of their output, with coal from Leasingthorne, was coked at Chilton. Operations were merged with Dean and Chapter in 1960, but the pit closed on 15 January 1966.

A DMA banner produced around the 1920s carries a central roundel on the obverse, divided into three, and containing portraits of J. Herriotts, A.J. Cook and J. Keir Hardie. The reverse carries the bundle of sticks image. The main ground is a purple and red damask silk with a light blue border, and was produced by Tutill at the City Road works. It measures 7 ft 8 in × 7 ft 2 in (234 × 218 cm). This banner was at the 1947 Gala.
*Location*: Beamish (1964-1079).

The obverse design is repeated on the 1961 banner, while the other side shows a local scene with the banner being carried in procession. The scene is surmounted by the Labour Party emblem of crossed quill pen, spade and torch of Liberty. The banner is blue silk with a red border, measuring 7 ft 8 in × 6 ft 7 in (234 × 201 cm), and was produced by Tutill at Chesham (no. 661).
*Location*: Chilton Junior School.

CHOPHILL

This is another name for Beamish Second pit.

The 1872 Gala banner bore a beehive and the words 'Unity', 'Love', 'Faith' and 'Justice'.[127] The banner was green with a gold fringe.

The banner at the 1947 Gala showed aged miners' homes on one side and a portrait on the other.[128]

## CHOPWELL

Mining was carried out at the Maria (*c.* 1795), Taylor (1798), Conclusion (1799) and North pits (1800) by George Silvertop of Minsteracres.[129] Later operations were carried out by the Marquis of Bute, certainly from 1860,[130] until mining rights were secured by the Consett Iron Co. in 1891. Three shafts were sunk, in 1894, 1898 and 1909, and mining was by longwall, with Blacketts conveyors. A day-hole drift at Whittonstall was driven to the Tilley in 1907. In 1913 Chopwell's output was *c.* 3,000 tons per day.[131] No. 2 shaft closed after the 1926 strike. Production declined from 1933. In the 1950s drifting was expanded, with the East Townley and the reopening of the Whittonstall drift, which had become derelict by 1940.[132] No. 3 pit closed in 1959, and No. 1 in 1960. Mining by drift continued until November 1966.

The 1873 Gala banner showed Justice holding the scales at equal balance between master and man, with the words, 'Masters, give unto your servants that which is equal and just, knowing that ye also have a master in heaven'.[133] Other messages included, 'An unjust weight is an abomination to the Lord, but a just weight is His delight' and 'The labourer is worthy of his hire'. The reverse side showed a beehive and Justice.

The 1907 banner carried portraits of J. Keir Hardie, J.W. Taylor and Frank McKay, with a view of the colliery: 'Labour is the source of all wealth.' The reverse showed a view of the North Road Miners' Hall.

The 'Red' banner was introduced in July 1924[134] and the basic design was repeated on new banners in 1935 and 1954. The design on the 1954 banner had a large roundel containing a central portrait of Keir Hardie, flanked by Marx and Lenin, with the badge of the Labour Party and the Red Star with hammer and sickle. At the base was a motto, 'We take up the task eternal, the burden and the lesson, Pioneers! Oh! Pioneers'. The reverse side showed a male figure, dressed in red and draped with ribbons, inscribed 'He who would be free / Himself must strike the blow', revealing to a group of miners an idyllic scene of houses, children playing and the red flag of Liberty. The advice given to the miners is 'Gain the Co-operative / Commonwealth'.

The 1924 banner was unfurled by Jim Larkin on 25 July,[135] and again on 23 August by A.J. Cook.[136] It was later torn above the roundel painting.

The 1935 damask banner was replaced in 1954, and in 1955 presented to a Soviet fact-finding delegation led by Ivan Rossochinsky, president of the central committee of the Soviet mineworkers.[137] The banner was displayed in the Palace of Culture at Kotchegarka colliery, Gorlovka, in the Donbas, East Ukraine, before touring other mining areas of the country.[138]

*Location*: Said to be in Moscow, but precise location not confirmed.

The 1954 banner was unfurled by Arthur Horner, general secretary of the NUM, on Friday 16 July, before the Gala, at Chopwell football

ground.[139] The banner was produced by Tutill at Chesham and is red silk with a blue border. It measures 6 ft 8 in × 7 ft 10 in (203 × 239 cm).
*Location*: Red Hill.

CLARA VALE

This Stella Coal Co. colliery was sunk in 1890–3 to the Brockwell.[140] The company also operated Stargate (1800), Emma (1845), Addison (1864) and Blaydon Main (1884). In 1897 the first turbine-driven fan, by Parsons, was installed.[141] In 1951 the Five Quarter, Tilley, Ruler, Stone Coal and Brockwell were worked. Manpower had remained stable in the 1930s and '40s at 980, but numbers fell sharply from 800 in 1950 to 590 in 1960. Clara Vale closed in 1966.

The banner at the 1947 Gala displayed the pattern-book images of 'Labour and Peace', and 'Emancipation of Labour'.[142] It was a damask silk type.

The lodge purchased a new, NUM, banner in 1954 repeating the designs.[143] The silk carries the mark of G. Tutill, 83 City Road, London, while the main roundel scene is marked 'Tutill–Chesham'. It is blue and cream damask silk, with a renewed red border. It measures 8 ft × 7 ft (244 × 213 cm).
*Location*: Clara Vale Community Centre.

COLD KNOTT

The pit comprised two shafts, either side of Mown Meadow Road, and was operating in 1857.[144] By 1897 it had largely been replaced by Harperley colliery, centred around Cabin House. This became linked by tub-line to Craig Lea pit by 1921. Cold Knott closed in December 1924.

The 1873 Gala banner showed three local lodge officials, Joseph Lauder (secretary), William Martin (chairman) and Thomas Allison (treasurer), with the verse,

> Then let us pass our time in peace,
> The little time we stay:
> Nor let our acts of friendship cease,
> Till life shall pass away.

The reverse side carried portraits of Crawford, Ramsay, Patterson and Wilkinson, and the verse, 'Truth and justice is our standard; / Peace and order is our motto'.[145]

COPT HILL

Although there is a Copt Hill at Houghton-le-Spring, the precise location of this colliery is unclear.

The banner carried onto the Racecourse in 1893 showed, on one side, the message, 'Masters do unto your servants that which is just'.[146]

## CORNSAY

Cornsay was sunk in 1868 and was worked by Ferens & Love. Mining was principally by drifts – High, Low, Colepike (near Hollinside Terrace, Lanchester), Ford (Throstlenest Plantation), Chapelflat, Ragpath and Ravenbush. Water was a major problem and the Ford drift was drowned in 1885. A major programme of water-drift construction, at Margery Flatts farm and Low Mill in 1891, succeeded in draining much of the royalty. The firm also operated three Belgian continuous kilns, producing bricks and sanitary pipes.[147] The colliery workforce totalled 300 in 1930, but lack of trade forced a temporary closure in 1938. By 1950 manpower had fallen to 47, and the pit closed in September 1953.

The banner at the 1872 Gala showed the three Graces, with the title 'Truth'.[148] This was also carried at the April 1873 manhood suffrage demonstration in Newcastle. The 'Truth' side also carried the title 'Messrs. Ferens and Love's Workmen, Cornsay Colliery'.[149] The reverse showed a master and workman shaking hands, with the inscription, 'Three cheers for the Durham Miners' Association' and 'United we stand, divided we fall'.

For the Gala in June 1873 the lodge had acquired a new banner. One side showed men turning a wheel and the lines,

> Altogether boys, we'll make the wheel go round
> For we know by our union great benefit can be found.

The other side carried a widow and orphan scene:

> Let us help them all we can.
> Our glorious union deny it who can,
> Defence, the right of the working man.[150]

This was replaced, after 1896, by a red silk banner with blue border, from Tutill's City Road works, showing two standing figures on the obverse, with the motto, 'Do unto others as ye would they should do unto you'. The reverse carries a portrait of William Crawford: 'He is dead but his spirit lives on in the quenchless devotion we feel.' It measures 9 ft 7 in × 8 ft 5 in (292 × 257 cm).
*Location*: Beamish (1984-10-4).

A later DMA banner, of damask silk, carried, on the obverse, the seated figure of John Wilson, with a widow and orphan scene on the reverse.[151]

A DMA banner was unfurled on 18 July 1939.[152] The obverse bore portraits of A.J. Cook and Peter Lee, with Conishead Priory on the reverse. This was carried at the 1947 Gala.

A Cornsay colliery lodge banner is known to have been transferred to Derwent lodge (q.v.) in 1961.

## COXHOE AND QUARRINGTON HILL

Operations in this area were carried out by William Hedley from 1832. The Engine pit was sunk in 1836.[153] Subsequently mining was undertaken by Messrs James Morrison & Co., who owned Ferryhill iron works and Thrislington colliery.[154]

The 1872 Gala banner showed a man, in a billycock hat and white collar, marching to work. The reverse showed a well-stocked co-operative store, and the line, 'Masters, give unto your servants that which is equal and just'.[155]

A small banner was displayed at the 1873 Gala. On one side a thin pony was shown attempting to pull a tub, encouraged by a driver, 'Come up, Bobby, ten hours a day', and on the other was a strong pony, with the driver exclaiming, 'Who Bobby, who Bobby, eight hours a day'.[156]

## CRAGHEAD

William Hedley and, later, Thomas Hedley & Bros, sank the William pit in 1839, the Thomas to draw Main coal in 1841, the Fortune (Sykes) at Burnhope in 1845, the George in 1854 and the Oswald, to the Hutton, in 1878.[157] Two new shafts were later sunk, the Edward in 1909 to the Hutton (and reworked to the Brockwell in 1919–20) and the downcast Busty, sunk in 1916–18. Thomas Hedley & Bros Ltd amalgamated with South Moor Collieries Ltd. Following nationalization the pit underwent major reorganization, including electrification, in 1955–8. In 1963 output fell below target, and the introduction of a coal shearer into the Busty in 1966 extracted the remaining reserves, leaving only thin Harvey and Brockwell. Work ceased on 11 April 1969.

A Tutill banner was unfurled by John Johnson in 1909, but there is no record of its illustrations.[158]

A DMA banner carried a depiction of David standing triumphant over the body of Goliath, with the message, 'He that would be free must strike the first blow'.[159] The reverse side showed a miner in jacket and pit hoggers, holding a cap and safety lamp.[160] At his feet was probably a wheatsheaf, with a globe in the sky. The lower border of the scene was inscribed 'Comrades in every clime'. It was carried at the 1947 Gala.

The NUM banner in use by 1954, carried, on the obverse, the NCB arms, 'E tenebris Lux', and the motto 'Independence, Liberty, Co-operation'.[161] The reverse bore the title 'Nationalisation, Unionism, Modernism' and illustrated the theme, 'Modern homes and modern collieries', with a pithead, modern houses and a family group, painted within a roundel. It was a yellow and red damask silk, with a yellow border.

A new banner was unfurled by George Brown on 20 July 1962. It carries, on one side, a reversed scene of the Cathedral, entitled 'Durham', with a series of scrolls on 'Liberty', 'Security', 'Safety', 'Consultation', 'Education' and 'Recreation'. On the other side are three linked roundels

The 'Three Men of Merit', Attlee, Bevan and Horner, on the Craghead banner.

carrying portraits of Clement Attlee, Aneurin Bevan and Arthur Horner – the 'Three Men of Merit' – set against the background of a colliery scene and miner's lamp. It was produced by Tutill at Chesham (no. 762) and is yellow with a dark blue border. It measures 8 ft × 8 ft 10 in (244 × 269 cm). This banner was certainly present at the 1976 Gala,[162] but was transferred to Blackhall (q.v.), and was present at the 1977 Gala.[163]

## CROOK COLLIERY

This pit was in operation after 1856[164] and by 1879 was worked by Messrs Chapman and Morson.[165] It was disused by 1897.

The 1873 Gala banner showed an arbitration scene and the message, 'We will do our utmost to uphold the cause of unity and freedom'.[166] The reverse side showed Justice, with the motto, 'Truth will prevail'.

## CROOK DRIFT

The drift, known as the Hole in the Wall colliery, was operated by the Craggs family (W. Craggs, as managing director, and his children, Ernest, Alan, Harold and Flora.) Test borings were carried out in 1936, quickly followed by driving the drift. By 1939 it employed 102.[167] In 1958–9 the Hutton and Victoria were worked. It closed in 1964.

The NUM banner carries a plaque inscribed 'Durham Area / Crook Drift Lodge / Hole in the Wall Colliery'. A central roundel painting shows a backdrop of a colliery scene, with two figures in the foreground. On the

left is a female figure with breastplate, carrying an unsheathed sword and the shield of Justice and Equality. On the right is a miner breaking his chains. His right foot is set on a crude depiction of the dead wolf of Capitalism. At the base of the scene is the title 'The triumph of labour'. The reverse shows a female figure, draped with a ribbon of 'trade unionism', handing to a standing miner the key of the gate of 'Organisation', set in an arch inscribed 'Economic Emancipation'. The banner was produced by Tutill at the City Road works and is red and silver damask silk, with a green border. It measures 7 ft 10 in × 6 ft 11 in (239 × 211 cm) and was in use by 1948.
*Location*: Wear Valley Council, Crook.

### CROOKHALL

This was a Consett Iron Co. colliery. The site was originally worked by Latterday Saint pit, which was operating in 1857, and had expanded by 1896, but was disused by 1921.[168] It was replaced by the Victory, sunk between 1921 and 1926. Associated with it were the Woodside Winning and Humber Hill Winning. In 1947 the Brockwell and Busty were worked, and by 1959 the Brockwell and Townley. The main working closed in 1963. Woodside drift was closed in 1964, but small-scale work was proposed in 1965 under the Crookhall Coal Co. of A. Marr, R. Knowles and G. Hodgson.[169]

A banner of Victory and Humber Hill lodge was present at a demonstration at Consett on 29 July 1926, but no details are recorded of its designs.[170]

The banner used in the 1930s and 1940s carries the 'Emancipation of Labour' image on one side and Conishead Priory on the other. It is damask silk, blue and yellow, with a red silk border, and measures 11 ft 5 in × 10 ft 2 in (348 × 310 cm).
*Location*: Red Hill.

A new banner was designed by Frank Burden, a local man, and unfurled on 16 July 1954 by Norman Nattrass, Director of Labour to the Durham Division NCB.[171] On one side was 'Britain's Basic Industry', while the reverse showed 'Dignity Through Labour', with a modern miner surrounded by illustrations of different events associated with the Durham coalfield. It was red, with a blue border.

Another NUM banner carried a picture of 'Conishead Priory convalescent home for Durham mine workers'.[172]

### DAWDON

Lord Londonderry sank two shafts, the Castlereagh (19 March 1900 – 10 September 1907) and the Theresa (17 April 1900 – 5 October 1907).[173] The sinking was carried out using a freezing process, by Messrs Gebhardt and Koenig, and aimed to take undersea reserves beyond the reach of Londonderry's Seaham pit. Major reconstruction and development work was carried out in 1953, 1957 and in the 1960s, with the replacement of steam winding by two tower-mounted multi-rope friction drum winders, the installation of underground diesel locos and power-loading with coal ploughs. In 1969 Roy Mason, Minister of Fuel and Power, described Dawdon as 'a jewel in the crown of the British coal industry, and . . . a classic example of what can be achieved'.[174] By the 1970s production concentrated on the High Main and Yard – in 1974 1,742 underground workers were raising 1,579,000 tons annually. However, offshore borings in 1975–6 revealed two anticlinal dome-shaped structures affecting undersea reserves, and in 1986 water problems forced the abandonment of tunnelling work at the Zone 29 sea drift, leading to the pit's closure on 25 July 1991.

The 1933 banner was unfurled by Councillor R. Lawson at the local Miners' Hall.[175] It carried a large roundel image of 'Labour and Peace'. The reverse showed a woman, seated at a table, teaching a child that 'Knowledge is Power'. It was red and yellow silk.

The 1952 NUM banner repeated the 'Labour and Peace' / 'Knowledge is Power' designs. The silk was produced at Tutill's City Road works and is a red and blue damask, with a yellow border, and red and blue fringe. It measures 7 ft 6 in × 6 ft 8 in (229 × 203 cm).
*Location*: Red Hill.

A new banner was purchased in 1980 from Tutill's Chesham works (no. 278.) It repeated the 'Knowledge is Power' image. It is red with a yellow border.
*Location*: Dawdon Welfare Hall.

## DEAF HILL

The Nos 1 and 2 shafts were sunk in 1877 by the Trimdon Coal Co.[176] The pit was later laid in, but reopened by Trimdon Coal Co. in 1885.[177] The explosion of Nos 3 and 4 surface boilers in 1889 killed one.[178] The No. 3 shaft was sunk in 1891. The workings were flooded in 1919.[179] The Nos 1 and 2 shafts became the principal operations, No. 1 for coal drawing and downcast, and No. 2 for man-riding and upcast. In 1944 the Hutton seam was closed and 160 workers transferred to Blackhall. Surface operations were combined with Wingate in 1955, with a rail link. Reconstruction work in 1964 included a new loading facility for lorry transport to Billingham, removing the need for the rail link.[180] The exhaustion of economic reserves led to closure on 24 February 1967.

Part of the central panel of the 1892 banner, produced by Bainbridges of Newcastle, survives. On one side are three figures, thought to be A.G. Taylor (?), Teddy O'Neil and Peter Lee, standing in a room and facing a person, or persons, now missing. The reverse shows part of a Good Samaritan scene, comprising the legs of the wounded man, a fine white horse and the Priest and Levite walking away into the distance. Following the purchase of a new banner, the 1892 banner was raffled and eventually came into the hands of the O'Neil family.
*Location*: Private owner.

The DMA banner from the 1930s has a roundel painting of Conishead Priory on the obverse and a Good Samaritan scene on the reverse. It is a gold and blue damask silk with a red border, and was at the 1946 Gala.[181]
*Location*: Deaf Hill Welfare Hall.

A replacement banner was purchased around the 1950s, repeating the designs of the previous banner. It is also a gold and blue damask silk, with a red border and gold fringe, and measures 9 ft × 8 ft 4 in (274 × 254 cm).
*Location*: Red Hill.

## DEAN AND CHAPTER

Bolckow, Vaughan & Co. began work on the Nos 1 and 2 shafts in 1902, which were completed in 1904.[182] The pit was taken over by Dorman, Long & Co. Ltd in 1929. Following nationalization it was amalgamated with Leasingthorne in 1950, and Chilton in 1962. By the late 1950s Top and Bottom Busty and Harvey were worked using jib cutters on longwall faces, and raised by skip-winder from 1956. The pit closed in 1966.

The first banner of Dean and Chapter lodge was unfurled by John Wilson, in front of the institute, in 1906. It was illustrated with a view of the colliery.[183]

A second banner was purchased in 1915 and unfurled by T. Cann, again outside the institute.[184] The banner carried a large roundel portrait of John Wilson wearing his Doctor of Civil Law robes. The reverse had an illustration of 'Unity is Strength'.

This was replaced in 1930 by a banner which may have shown Keir Hardie, George Lansbury and Ramsay MacDonald on one side, and the Dean Bank aged miners' homes, 'For humanity's sake', on the other.[185]

The first NUM banner was acquired in 1946.[186] The main roundel carried a portrait of William Todd, with side wings around the roundel bearing the names of E. Shinwell, Dr Hugh Dalton, W. Whiteley, J.J. Lawson, J.E. Granville, C.E. Grey, J.R. Leslie, S. Lavers, Ellen Wilkinson, W.R. Blyton and J.D. Murray. The reverse showed the traditional view of Durham Cathedral.

The 1955 banner was unfurled by Sam Watson at Ferryhill Market Place. It shows a European (dressed in brown suit and tie) persuading an Asian (in brown trousers, blue-grey top and Mao-type cap) to shake hands with a Negro (in white outfit with rolled-up sleeves), with the motto, 'Fellowship is life, Fellowship for all'. The reverse shows Durham Cathedral. It was produced by Tutill at Chesham and is red with a blue border.
*Location*: Ferryhill Town Hall.
*See also* 'Associated foreign pennants, banners and bannerettes' (pp. 264–5).

## DERWENT

The colliery, at Medomsley, the property of E. Richardson, was sunk *c*. 1853, and worked by the Derwent Iron Co., subsequently Consett Iron Co.[187] In the 1890s mining concentrated on the Busty, worked by 450 men and boys.[188] Manpower levels fell in each decade, from 1,094 in 1930 to 324 in 1960. The pit closed in November 1964.

The banner displayed at the 1873 Gala showed a joint committee in counsel: 'The workmen of Derwent Colliery wish to settle all disputes by arbitration.'[189] The reverse showed a night school, with a master and three boys. One boy is alert, representing the eight-hour system, another has his eyes half closed, ten hours, and the third is asleep, twelve hours.

The lodge is known to have had a DMA banner carrying a shoulder-length portrait of Peter Lee.[190]

Another DMA banner, of yellow and green damask silk with a red border, showed a scene of David standing triumphant over the body of Goliath, with the motto, 'He who would be free must strike the first blow'.[191] The reverse probably followed the theme, 'All men are brethren'. This was at the 1947 Gala.

Derwent acquired the Cornsay colliery banner in 1961 (q.v.).

EASINGTON

Mining operations began in 1899, but the sinking was only completed by using the freezing process in 1910.[192] Three shafts were used, the North (946 fath.), South (250 fath.) and West (250 fath., for ventilation.) Initially output was by bord and pillar, later longwall was introduced, and power loading in 1950. An explosion on 29 May 1951 killed eighty-one.[193] Major development work was carried out in 1958 and 1975–81, with skip winding and increased bunkerage with merry-go-round trains. Mining concentrated on the High Main, Main, Yard and Low Main. Although it had an estimated 8.4 million tonnes of reserves, British Coal included Easington in the list of thirty-one pits to be closed, announced by Heseltine on 13 October 1992.[194] From 19 October it was included in the moratorium on the closure of twenty-one of those pits. On 15 April 1993 the demoralized miners voted not to enter the pit into the Modified Pit Review Procedure. Production ceased on 7 May, with the mothballing of the J23 face. A possible purchase by R.J. Budge fell through, principally over pumping costs, and on 26 October pumping was stopped by British Coal. Demolition quickly followed in 1994.

A banner was destroyed by fire in the Miners' Hall, *c.* 1928.

The 1932 banner was unfurled by Peter Lee at the Welfare Ground on 16 July. It carried portraits of Robert Smillie and Keir Hardie, with a pithead scene, on one side; and Easington Welfare Hall on the reverse.[195]

In 1959 the lodge purchased a new banner from Tutill's Chesham works, repeating the previous banner illustrations. It is red with a blue border and measures 7 ft 10 in × 9 ft (239 × 274 cm). This banner was last used at the 1977 Gala.[196]

*Location*: Easington Welfare Hall.

A new banner was ordered in 1977 from Tutill's, and unfurled in 1978. It bears a central roundel, split into two, with portraits of Lawrence Daly and Tommy Hepburn. Between the two paintings is a colliery scene and a pit lamp

with two tokens, inscribed 12 and 1977. The reverse side shows a central roundel depiction of the Easington disaster memorial: 'We remember'. It is red with a green border, and measures 8 ft 6 in × 7 ft 1 in (208 × 216 cm).
*Location*: Easington Welfare Hall.
*See also* 'Associated foreign pennants, banners and bannerettes' (p. 267).

### EAST HETTON (KELLOE)

The North pit was sunk in 1836 by the East Hetton Coal Co.,[197] with further sinking in 1856.[198] By 1873 the Five Quarter had been worked out, and in 1880 the pit was sold to Walter Scott Ltd and linked underground with Trimdon Grange. In 1887 the Main was finished, and in the 1890s work concentrated on the Low Main, Hutton and Harvey.[199] An inundation on 6 May 1897 killed ten.[200] By the early 1930s all coal was mechanically cut, and a dry-cleaning plant was erected in 1933. From 1935 to 1946 the pit was operated by East Hetton Collieries Ltd. In 1959 power-loading was introduced, and a new winder was installed at the South shaft. However, test borings revealed over 100 million gallons of water in Thornley Tilley goaf, threatening the development of the Busty reserves.[201] Consequently the pit closed in July 1983.

The banner at the 1873 Gala showed a widow and orphan at a tomb, 'In memory of a deceased brother miner'.[202] The tomb was covered in flowers, and an angel was depicted descending with a wreath. The reverse carried a Good Samaritan scene.

The 1932 DMA banner was unfurled by Joshua Ritson on 16 July. It carried a large roundel portrait of A.J. Cook, 'Faithful unto death', on one side and a roundel scene of the Good Samaritan, 'Go thou and do likewise', on the other.[203]

A new banner was unfurled on 20 July 1951 by Clement Attlee.[204] The obverse carried a large roundel portrait of Attlee, standing, with the motto underneath, 'Forward to Freedom'. The reverse bore a Good Samaritan scene, 'Go Thou and Do Likewise'. It was red, purple and green, with a yellow border.

The 1963 banner was unfurled by Alf Hesler, NUM Durham Area general secretary, who had worked at the pit since leaving school in 1919. It was produced by Tutill at Chesham (no. 363) and bears a shoulder-length portrait of the 'Rt Hon Hugh Gaitskell, MP, PC' within a large roundel. The reverse carries a Good Samaritan scene, 'Go thou and do likewise'. This banner was used certainly up until the 1977 Gala.[205] It is yellow with a blue border and measures 6 ft 9 in × 7 ft 7 in (206 × 231 cm).
*Location*: Cassop County Junior and Infant School.

In 1977 the lodge acquired the Langley Park lodge banner showing 'The County Hall' and 'The Sam Watson Rest Home'. This was produced by Tutill at Chesham (no. 763), and is red with a green border. It measures 7 ft 4 in × 6 ft 10 in (224 × 208 cm).
*Location*: St Paul's Methodist Church, Kelloe.

## EAST TANFIELD

The pit was sunk in 1844 by James Joicey with two shafts, the Busty and Brockwell. In the 1890s 390 men and boys worked here, producing an annual output of 170,772 tons.[206] It was purchased by the East Tanfield Colliery Co. Ltd in 1917, but passed to the South Derwent Coal Co. Ltd in 1929 after a year's closure.[207] Manpower then rose to 899 in 1940, but slowly fell to 520 in 1960. The pit closed in January 1965.

The first banner was purchased in 1940. On one side, within a roundel, was a central signpost dividing the scene into the 'Past', showing drab colliery rows, and 'Future', with neat, tree-lined streets and Labour Hall, with the title 'Progress'. The other side carried a portrait of A.J. Cook. The banner was torn at the 1954 Gala.

The 1955 banner, designed by Mrs Florence M. Cook, was unfurled by Arthur Horner, at Stanley, on 15 July.[208] On one side was the portrait of A.J. Cook and on the other a painting of a band about to enter Durham Cathedral. It also carried the words, 'Gresford. Lest we forget'. This was transferred to Whitworth Park (q.v.) in 1966.

## EDEN

Eden colliery was sunk in 1844 by E. Richardson, but taken over by the Derwent Iron Co., subsequently Consett Iron Co., with output principally being sent to the iron works.[209] The main workings started just after the First World War, including a series of drifts – the Hutton (opposite St Ive's Church), the Main, Castle, Water Level (by Newhouse Burn), Collierley and Deacon. From 1962, workers at South Medomsley were gradually assimilated with Eden. From September 1962 Collierley drift was finished, along with surface operations at Deacon drift. In 1976 work on the Harvey ceased, and efforts were concentrated on the Busty, with 298 men. It remained a hand-filled pit, but declining reserves forced closure on 18 July 1980, with the loss of 180 jobs, though 65 were transferred to Marley Hill and Sacriston.[210]

The only surviving DMA banner carries, on one side, the 'Amicitia Amor et Veritas' image, while the other shows a mother teaching her child, with the motto, 'Knowledge is Power'. This banner was produced by Tutill at the City Road works and is a pale blue silk with a red border and blue and red fringe. It measures 10 ft 10 in × 9 ft 10 in (330 × 300 cm). It is possible that this may be the banner, of unrecorded design, reported in the press as having been unfurled on 20 August 1921.[211]
*Location*: Red Hill.

The subsequent NUM banner followed the 'Amicitia Amor et Veritas' design, with updated illustrations of miners supporting the central sickbed scene. They are shown wearing helmets with cap lamps and holding windy picks. There are also some minor alterations to the positioning of the shields of England, Scotland, Ireland and Wales, normally found with this pattern-book design. The reverse also continued the 'Knowledge is Power' theme, though the illustration has no title plate. Again there are alterations to the layout of the scene and the positioning of the figures. The 8 ft 8 in × 7 ft 8 in (264 × 234 cm) banner is red silk with a green border and carries a maker's label attached to the top border, 'George Tutill Ltd., 9 Higham Road, Chesham, Bucks'. The upper part of the painting is now torn.

*Location*: Red Hill.

On 22 February 1962 the lodge agreed 'That a replica of our present banner be purchased'.[212] The banner was unfurled by A. Wedgwood Benn on 20 July 1962 and carried the 'Amicitia Amor et Veritas' design on the obverse and the 'Knowledge is Power' image (though not named) on the reverse. It was produced by Tutill at Chesham and is red with a green border. The banner is 7 ft 8 in × 9 ft (234 × 274 cm). It was carried into the Cathedral service in 1980 for its last Gala.

*Location*: St Ive's Church, Leadgate.

## EDMONDSLEY

The pit was worked, certainly from the 1850s, by Samuel Tyzack & Co.[213] and was called West Edmondsley, later Edmondsley colliery Wellington pit. By the 1890s it was operated under the title Edmondsley Coal Co. The Hutton and Busty were worked, with about a third of the output coked.[214] The pit closed in 1921.

The banner of Edmondsley and the Byron colliery at the 1873 Gala was produced by W. Elam at Bethnal Green, London[215] and shows William Crawford and William Patterson standing either side of a seated Joseph Cowen, who is holding a copy of the Mines Regulation Bill. The accompanying motto reads 'Masters and men should unite and this would keep the trade alright; Compensation would then take its flight if all were found in union'. On the other side is a portrait of Tommy Ramsey with the words, 'Awake, arise or be forever fallen'. The scene is accompanied by the lines, 'Our motto is the greatest amount of happiness for the greatest number of individuals with the least injury to any', and 'Wealth gotten by vanity shall be diminished, but that gathereth by labour shall increase'. It is red, with cream top and bottom strips, and measures 11 ft 8 in × 10 ft (356 × 305 cm). This banner was transferred to Black House colliery (q.v.) in 1925–6.

A new banner was unfurled on 21 July 1905 by J. Watson, the colliery manager.[216] The obverse showed Gladstone in a central position, with portraits in the lower corners of Mr MacDonald and William Crawford. The reverse side carried a portrait of 'Old Tom Ramsey'.

## ELDON

The North pit was begun in 1829, to work the Main coal, and in 1840 a New Winning was put into the seam. Shafts were also sunk to the Harvey and the Brockwell, probably around the 1860s, and the John Henry to the

Hutton in 1890. The John Henry was known as Old Eldon colliery by 1897.[217] The colliery was worked by the South Durham Coal Co., who also worked South Durham colliery (q.v.), but in 1903 the operation was taken over by Pease & Partners Ltd.[218] Confusingly, South Durham was named Eldon colliery at some stage between 1897 and 1920. Eldon Old colliery closed in 1931, and Eldon was disused by 1939.

The lodge attended a manhood suffrage demonstration at Bishop Auckland in 1873, apparently with a banner.[220]

A DMA banner, of around 1915, shows a portrait of 'The late John Wilson Esq. DCL, MP.' on the obverse, with two miners shaking hands before an angel, shown holding a ribbon inscribed 'Unity is Strength', on the reverse. This light blue silk banner with a red border was produced at Tutill's City Road works. It measures 9 ft 3 in × 8 ft 6 in (282 × 259 cm). *Location*: Beamish (1984-10-6).

ELDON DRIFT

The drift, in Eldon Hope Plantation, worked from 1934 until October 1962.

A Tutill banner from the Chesham works was unfurled at Coundon Grange by Sid Lavers, chairman of the Northern Clubs Federation Brewery and former MP for Barnard Castle, on 20 July 1956. On one side are portraits of A.J. Cook, Keir Hardie and James Callaghan, with the motto, 'Unity is Strength – They gave us Unity'. The other side shows 'Red Hill and Memorial Gardens, Durham'. It is dark green with a yellow border and measures 5 ft 11 in × 7 ft 8 in (180 × 234 cm). *Location*: Beamish (1984-10-7).

ELEMORE

Two shafts were sunk by the Hetton Coal Co. in 1825–7 – the Isabella (upcast) and George/Lady (downcast, divided into two by bratticing).[220] An explosion on 2 December 1886 killed twenty-eight.[221] The pit was incorporated into Lambton & Hetton Collieries Ltd in 1896, and Lambton, Hetton & Joicey Collieries Ltd in 1924. After nationalization Elemore became linked underground to a central drawing shaft at Hawthorn (sunk 1952–8) and formed a combine with Murton and Eppleton. In the 1960s a new working area in the south Busty was cut off by a washout, dramatically reducing the face room, forcing eventual closure on 1 February 1974.[222]

The 1873 Gala banner showed a well-dressed mother and her son with the texts, 'Ten hours bank to bank' and 'Prove all things; hold fast that which is good'.[223]

A new banner was unfurled by Councillor T. Dickinson before leaving for the 1939 Gala. [224] One side carries the inscription, 'Easington Lane War Memorial', over a roundel with an illustration of the memorial and clock. The reverse carries portraits of Peter Lee and George Lansbury. It is blue and silver damask, with a broad red border.[225] The bottom corners have been repaired in purple, and there are purple rosettes round the brass discs. It was at the 1965 Gala.

*Location*: Hung in the Railway Tavern, Shincliffe; transferred for exhibition, in the late 1970s/early 1980s, to Laurel Avenue school, Gilesgate, and subsequently removed to Beamish (1993-119).

The NUM banner was acquired from Sherburn Hill (q.v.) and shows aged miners' homes on one side, and the frontage of Conishead Priory on the other.

*Location*: Methodist Church, Union Street, Hetton-le-Hole.

## ELVET

The main colliery was sunk in 1823 by the Crawford family, though there had been mining in the area from the eighteenth century.[226] The operation expanded with the sinking of the South Engine pit in 1858, and the Hutton was worked. Declining reserves led to pillar extraction, causing subsidence and house damage, leading to a court case, the costs of which resulted in the company's collapse in 1908.[227] The main shaft is now within Durham University Science Site, marked by a fossil tree stump, and there is a water-level near Prebend's Bridge[228] and probably another in Pimlico, exposed in April 1997.

The banner at the 1873 Gala showed the bundle of sticks fable and 'Unity is strength' on one side and a widow and orphan scene on the reverse, with the gravestone inscribed, 'In memory of a brother deceased'.[229] Accompanying this scene is an angel, descending with a wreath.

## EPPLETON

The colliery, with Hetton Lyons and Elemore, was originally owned by the Hetton Coal Co. It was sunk in 1825–33,[230] with the Jane (to the Busty) and the Caroline (to the Main, as a man-riding shaft). The Lindsay (or New) shaft was added in 1870–4. The pit was later incorporated by Joicey in the Lambton & Hetton Coal Co., and subsequently Lambton, Hetton & Joicey Collieries Ltd. Arc wall cutting, with American loading machinery, was in use in the 1940s. An explosion on 6 July 1951 killed nine.[231] In the 1950s Eppleton was linked to a new drawing shaft at Hawthorn[232] and closed in 1986 following a merger with Murton.

A banner for Hetton Lodge (Eppleton colliery) was purchased *c.* 1909.[233]

A new banner for this lodge was unfurled in 1925.[234] The obverse carried portraits of Joshua Ritson MP and Joseph Robson, The reverse showed miners leaving work, 'United to obtain the just reward of our labour'.

The first NUM banner showed Emmanuel Shinwell on one side and a view of the colliery on the other, with the title 'Nationalisation 1947' and the motto 'Security'.[235]

The Eppleton banner at the 1967 Gala.

On the closure of Leasingthorne (q.v.) in 1967, their NUM banner was transferred to Eppleton. It shows aged miners' homes on one side and Conishead Priory, with the motto, 'Health is Strength', on the other.[236]
*Location*: Leaholme and District Working Men's Club.

Eppleton received the Silksworth (former Ryhope) banner (q.v.), when the pit closed in 1973.
*Location*: Red Hill.

The 1981 banner, of red silk with a yellow border, was produced by Turtle & Pearce (no. 9.81.) It carries, on one side, a split roundel showing Hetton Hall and an engine, with the wording on a scroll below it, '1822–1912 / The oldest working locomotive in the world'. On the other side is a view of the Jane shaft. The banner measures 7 ft × 8 ft 5 in (213 × 256 cm) and retains an attached maker's address tag on the left

guide tie. It was dedicated 27 June 1982 at All Saints', Eppleton, and taken to the Gala on 10 July.
*Location*: All Saints' Church, Eppleton.

### ESH HILL TOP

The 'take' was originally between Millgate Cottages and Low Esh, and was worked for Ushaw College by R. Halliday, on a lease from Sir Walter Smythe, certainly in the 1880s. This working provided fuel for college domestic use, and in the 1890s Hutton was worked by drift.[237] Around 1900 it was sub-leased to Sir S.A. Sadler, with an agreement to supply the college with coal and coke.[238] At the same time the pit was linked by aerial flight to Sadler's Malton colliery. In 1913 two miners were gassed.[239] Malton closed in 1961.

The lodge is said to have acquired a Harton & Westoe banner.[240]

### ESH WINNING

Joseph Pease began a shaft north of the Priest Beck in 1859, but water problems delayed completion until 1865–6.[241] Drift mining was also carried on. By 1919 reserves of Main coal were declining, and work concentrated on Five Quarter, Hutton, Ballarat and Brockwell. The colliery was closed from 1930 to 1942. Plans were considered at this time to transform the site into a main drawing shaft, linking the pit with the allied workings at Waterhouses and Ushaw Moor, but this was never carried through.[242] In 1962 the Ragpath drift was closed, though the Esh shaft was retained for travelling, but the exhaustion of the Tilley and the unsatisfactory position of the longwall face in the North Drift Top Busty affected operations. By 1968 the pit employed 230, hand hewing, and producing 1,400 tons per week. Financial losses led to the pit's closure on 28 June 1968.[243]

The 1894 banner showed portraits of A. MacDonald, William Crawford and Ernest Jones (the father of Atherley Jones, MP for NW Durham) on the obverse and the Good Samaritan on the reverse, with the motto, 'Bear ye one anothers burden'.[244]

The post-First World War banner showed a seated portrait of Ernest Hull, a sapper killed in June 1917 at Ypres. The reverse may have shown the local aged miners' homes.

The NUM banner shows Red Hill on the obverse and a miner and owner shaking hands in front of an angel on the reverse. This Tutill City Road banner measures 7 ft 9 in × 7 ft (236 × 213 cm) and is purple and red damask silk, with a turquoise border.
*Location*: Beamish (1984-10-8).

### ETHERLEY

Henry Stobart & Co. were working Main coal at the Phoenix pit, Old Etherley, certainly in the 1840s. They also had two Etherley shafts – the

George, at Escomb, and the Jane, close to Witton Park iron works. The Jane ceased operations between 1887 and 1897,[245] while the George fell into disuse between 1897 and 1920. The Jane was restarted, operating until 1925.[246]

The 1873 Gala banner showed a cottage interior, where a woman, with a baby sleeping on her lap, is reading the Bible to her husband. The scene was accompanied by the lines, 'Princes and Lords are but the breath of kings, / but man is the noblest work of God'.[247] On the reverse was a portrait of MacDonald with the Mines Regulation Bill; on the left is a tired miner going to work at 5 a.m. and, on the right, a healthy miner going to the pit at 7 a.m.

## EVENWOOD AND TEES HETTON

These pits lay to the west and east, respectively, of Evenwood village. Evenwood colliery was sunk in 1834–5, but in 1836 was sold to the Durham County Coal Co., and later to the Northern Coal Co., until its financial collapse in the 1840s. In 1869 it was the property of Armstrong & Co., but passed to Messrs Charlton,[248] and then to the Tees Hetton Coal Co. Ltd for the period 1883–91. The laying in of Tees Hetton was discussed in 1884, but it seems to have restarted.[249] Evenwood then passed to the North Bitchburn Coal Co.[250] The collieries closed in 1895.

The 1873 Gala banner showed an arbitration scene on one side, with the words,

> The hands of the thousands are clasped,
> Employer and employed meet as brother with brother;
> Miners are gathering from east and from west,
> Union and liberty in their behest.

On the reverse was a symbol of Justice, with the motto, 'United to protect our interests, and not combined to injure'.[251]

## FELLING

The High Main was opened out by Charles Brandling in 1779,[252] and was mined until 1811, though the Low Main had been started in 1810. Two shafts were used, the John and William. An explosion on 25 May 1812 killed ninety-one,[253] with a further twenty-two on 24 December 1813 and six on 23 October 1821. In the 1850s the seams were worked by Messrs Carr, Potts & Co.[254] It was purchased in 1883 by John Bowes & Partners. The Low Main continued to be worked into the 1890s, with the Maudlin and Hutton.[255] The pit closed in 1931.

The banner in use in 1873 carried a bundle of sticks scene, with the motto, 'United we stand, divided we fall'. On the reverse was a view of the colliery. It was red with a blue border.[256]

Fenhall Drift banner,
with a detailed painting
of Lanchester Church.

## FENHALL DRIFT

The drift was driven in 1954 to work the Townley seam, but only operated for nine years as reserves were high in sulphur and not considered marketable. The lodge was formed in 1956. Production ceased on 10 May 1963.[257]

The NUM banner was purchased in 1960 and unfurled by the local vicar, the Revd W.E. Wright, but not displayed at the Gala until 1961.[258] The illustrations were designed by Ernie Reay and George Thomas, lodge members. They show the south front of Lanchester church, with the motto, 'Strength stands the test', and, below it, 'Lanchester'. On the other side is a panel divided into two, showing a Roman soldier, 'C 1st AD', and a miner, 'C 20th AD'. It was produced by Tutill at Chesham (no. 659 and measures 5 ft 9 in × 6 ft 11 in (175 × 211 cm). It is red with a blue border. This banner was transferred to Thrislington (q.v.), and later to Harton and Westoe lodge (q.v.), certainly by 1973.

## FISHBURN

Two shafts, No. 1 (south) and No. 2 (north), were sunk in 1910–13 by H. Stobart & Co. using the Bourgii cementation process. Robey winders were used, with four Bowstock self-firing boilers. Coal was wound from the Low Harvey at the No. 1 downcast, while the No. 2, to the Harvey, was used for man-riding. Coking was carried out on-site, and in 1919

Fishburn banner, with
portraits of Keir Hardie,
A.J. Cook and George
Lansbury.

comprised fifty duplex ovens, with a by-product plant. In 1934 a Baum washery was built. Mining concentrated on the Harvey, Top Busty and Brockwell, principally using advancing longwall, with machine-cut, hand-filled faces, although Joy loaders were used in some bord and pillar Brockwell.[259] In 1954 the W-D Becker Underjet cokeworks came into operation, and major development at the colliery was carried out in 1956, when the shafts were deepened and their function reversed. 'Nip-out' conditions were noted in the South Winning in 1970; the Harvey was exhausted, and geological problems in the Busty and Brockwell led to closure on 1 December 1973.[260]

The first NUM banner, present at the Gala in 1951 (and probably in 1947), carried a moulded panel bearing three roundels containing portraits of J. Keir Hardie, A.J. Cook and G. Lansbury, with a colliery scene in the background. On the other side was the angel of 'Trade unionism', handing to a miner the key to the gate of 'Organisation', set in an arch inscribed 'Economic emancipation'. Beyond the gate was an idyllic garden scene, with the motto, 'The cause of labour is the hope of the world'.

The design was repeated on the 1959 banner from Tutill's Chesham works (no. 359), unfurled by Will Paynter, NUM general secretary. It is blue with a red border and measures 7 ft 6 in × 6 ft 10 in (229 × 208 cm). It was subsequently transferred to New Herrington (q.v.).

## FOLLONSBY (WARDLEY)

Wardley colliery was sunk in 1855 (later known as the Nos 2 & 3 shafts) by John Bowes & Partners. In the 1890s the Maudlin and Hutton were worked south of the Tyne,[261] but the pit closed in 1911. The main Follonsby (Wardley No. 1) shaft was sunk in 1911–12. It was closed in the early years of the Second World War, but reopened in 1942.[262] In 1948 proposals were introduced for combining with Usworth (q.v.), though this was not achieved until 1958, with a new linking underground loco road and the installation of a 1960 h.p. Ward Leonard winder at the No. 1 shaft, replacing the 700 h.p. geared A.C. parallel drum winder.[263] In 1969 further reorganization was carried out, with Usworth used for man-riding and Wardley for coal drawing. Output was concentrated at Usworth in the Harvey and Busty.[264] Operations at the combine ceased on 8 August 1974.

The DMA banner carried a central portrait of Lenin, flanked by James Connolly, Keir Hardie, A.J. Cook and George Harvey.

The banner at the 1947 Gala carried portraits of Keir Hardie, A. Joyce and Smith on one side, and the theme, 'The world for the workers', on the other.[265]

The 1962 NUM banner carries portraits of Keir Hardie and the lodge officials Anthony Joyce and E. Justice on one side. The reverse carries a 'Sunshine of Liberty' image. Under the scene is the title, 'The world for the workers'. The banner was produced by Tutill at Chesham (no. 1162) and is red with a blue border. It measures 7 ft 6 in × 8 ft 5 in (229 × 256 cm).

*Location*: Council chamber, Gateshead Civic Centre. The banner was presented by D. Hopper and unfurled by the mayor, Joe Hattam, in 1988.[266]

FRAMWELLGATE MOOR

The pit was sunk by the Northern Mining Co. in 1838–41, with one shaft.[267] Following the company's collapse, it was worked by W. Hunter & Partners and Thompson & Green, but came under the control of Lord Londonderry in 1859.[268] It was either sold by Londonderry, or operated by him as a subsidiary, under the title Framwellgate Coal Co. in 1878 (later Framwellgate Coal & Coke Co. Ltd). The company worked the Hutton, but by the early 1870s it was nearing exhaustion and the Harvey was opened out. In 1908 Durham Main and Caterhouse (or Cathouse), associated with Framwellgate Old pit, were abandoned because of geological problems.[269] Harvey coal continued to be sold in 1923,[270] but the site was put up for sale on 21 April 1925 and the pit was demolished in the same year.[271]

The 1873 Gala banner showed Capital and Labour, 'Benevolence with prudence unite to relieve the distress'. On the reverse was a cottage interior on a Sunday, with a wife reading to her pitman husband.[272]

A subsequent DMA banner carries a central circular panel showing a female figure surrounded by five other figures, the panel supported by two angels, above which is an angel blowing a trumpet. Below the panel is a small Good Samaritan scene, with the motto 'Go thou and do likewise'. The reverse shows a large Good Samaritan scene, 'Bear ye one anothers burdens'. The banner is red and purple damask silk with a yellow border, but is seriously damaged. It measures 5 ft 4 in × 6ft 8 in (163 × 203 cm). *Location*: Beamish (1984-10-9).

GORDON HOUSE

The first colliery was sunk between 1856 and 1879 on Cockfield Fell and worked by W.H. Hedley & Co., based at Norwood.[273] By 1921 it had largely been replaced by a new colliery to the south, which closed in the 1940s.

A DMA banner showed two angels flanking the bust of William Crawford, set in a laurel wreath.[274]

GRAHAMSLEY

This is another name for North Roddymoor, near Billy Row, where Joseph Pease sank the Lucy pit in 1846. This had become a fan shaft by 1921.

The 1873 Gala banner showed a representation of the Wood Memorial Hall in Newcastle, and the words, 'Do unto all men as ye would they should do unto you' and 'An injury to one is an insult to all'. The reverse carried a widow and orphan scene:

> The tyrant's chains are only strong
> Whilst slaves submit to wear them,
> No power can bind them on the throng
> Determined not to bind them.

The banner was blue, white and red silk, with a gold fringe.[275]

## GREENHEAD

Initial mining was for iron ore to feed the Tow Law furnaces in the 1840s, though coal extraction was subsequently associated with Low Beechburn colliery.[276] There were no surface features in 1856, and in 1897 the operation was small, with a series of drifts.[277] All had gone by 1921.

The 1873 Gala banner showed a Lion and Lamb scene, with the couplet, 'Knowledge applied with truth and grace, / Will elevate the human race'. The reverse side carried a portrait of George Woodhall, the lodge secretary, and the lines, 'Let's greet him as the best, and help him all we can / The brightest gem in nature's crown is an honest working man'.[278]

## GREENSIDE

There had been mining at Greenside by R. Simpson in the 1880s, but the main pit was sunk in 1902 and worked by the Stella Coal Co.[279] In 1947 the Brockwell was worked, and in the 1950s, the Tilley. Manpower levels remained stable in the 1930s and '40s at 1,035, but declined rapidly from 990 in 1950 to 520 in 1960 as seams were abandoned (Victoria 1951; Crow 1952; Top Busty Q1 1953; Three Quarter R, Bottom Busty Q2 and Brockwell S in 1956). The threat of rising water, following the closure of Clara Vale, led to its closure in July 1966.[280]

The NUM banner was purchased in 1950 and showed a pithead with the NCB flag flying. At the base of the scene were the words, 'Greenside Pit / For the people, by the people'. The reverse side showed 'The Hermitage, Chester-le-Street Rehabilitation Centre' with the motto, 'Many can help one, where one cannot help many'.

The banner was damaged by the weather, and replaced with a banner bearing similar designs, by Tutill at Chesham (no. 1057). It was unfurled by Bob Woof, MP for Blaydon, in Greenside County School yard, on 21 June 1958.[281] It is red with a blue border and measures 7 ft 9 in × 7 ft 2 in (236 × 218 cm).
*Location*: Greenside and District Social Club.

## HAMSTEELS

The colliery was sunk in 1868 by Joseph Johnson, the owner of Durham Brewery, and T.M. Reay, later known as 'The Owners of Hamsteels Collieries', with the Taylor and Busty pits. The Brockwell and Busty were initially worked, with drifting to the Harvey in 1890.[282] There was a series of drifts – Clifford, West Harvey and Hall Harvey, near Wilks Hill – which were worked from the 1890s into the 1920s but were disused by 1939. They were linked to Hamsteels by aerial cable. The colliery was taken over by Sir S.A. Sadler in 1932, but closed in 1958.

A new banner was used at the 1874 Gala. On one side was the Good Samaritan, and the text,

> Teach me to feel another's woe
> To heed the fault I See,
> That mercy I to others show
> That mercy show to me

The reverse showed a widow and two orphans at a graveside, with 'a suitable motto'.[283]

On 5 December 1894 the lodge agreed to purchase a new silk banner, similar in size to their previous banner, but in the following January asked, 'can the figures in the centre be woven instead of painted'. No details are given of the design, but it was unfurled on 15 June 1895.[284]

At an uncertain date the lodge acquired the Tutill banner of Andrews House lodge (q.v.), which was illustrated with themes of justice, and care of the poor, widows and orphans.
*Location*: Beamish (1984-10-10.)

The NUM banner carried a large panel bearing three linked roundels containing the portraits of J. Gilliland, Peter Lee and A.J. Cook.

## HAMSTERLEY

A drift was driven in 1864 by Dr H.W. Watson at Croniwell, to work the Top Busty, Three Quarter and Brockwell. A drift was driven in 1884, which located the Busty seam. The John shaft was sunk in 1908, using underhanging tubbing, and was worked by the Hamsterley Coal Co.[285] Manpower slowly declined from 379 in 1930 to 260 in 1950 and 225 in 1960. By 1963 reduced output from the Park Row Tilley threatened closure,[286] but in 1965 reserves were located in the redundant Derwent colliery area.[287] Eventual exhaustion of reserves led to closure on 2 February 1968, with the men transferred to Marley Hill and Elm Park Drift.[288]

At the 1873 manhood suffrage demonstration in Newcastle, a reporter noted Hamsterley and Milkwell Burn collieries with one banner. On one side it showed a master holding a copy of the Master and Servants' Act, with a miner pointing with his pick to an all-seeing eye as a reminder that 'Liberty and Justice' are due to all. It also carried the motto, 'Numquam dormio'. The other side showed a pit boy of 1850 and another of 1873.[289]

The lodge acquired the South Moor NUM No. 2 lodge banner (q.v.). This carries a large roundel showing a winged Faith raising up a male figure representing Labour. To the right of the scene is blind Justice,

The Hamsterley banner, with the theme of 'Progress' in mining.

carrying a sword and scales. The other side shows an old miner with a lamp and pick, and he points to a modern miner, wearing a pit helmet and carrying a pneumatic pick: 'Now it depends on you.' Under the scene is the title, 'Progress'. The main silk ground was produced at Tutill's City Road works, but the painting was done at Chesham.
*Location*: Derwentside District Council, Civic Centre, Consett.

## HANDEN HOLD

This pit formed part of West Pelton colliery (q.v.), with the Alma pit at Grange Villa. Two shafts were sunk in 1857–60, and it was worked by James Joicey, ultimately forming part of the Lambton, Hetton and Joicey collieries empire. New shafts were sunk in 1898–1901 to the Busty, with a drift to the High Main in 1915. Batteries of coke ovens were constructed in 1948–52, to work the Tilley and Brockwell, with a surface washery added in 1953–6.[290] Exhaustion of reserves led to closure in March 1968.

The 1938 banner carries a split roundel bearing the portraits of Robert Smillie and Keir Hardie. Between the panels are flowers, a safety lamp, pick, shovel and token. Above the roundel is the misspelt title, 'Handon Hold Lodge'. The reverse side carries a wheatsheaf and the motto, 'Each for all, All for each'. The banner was produced by Tutill's City Road works and is 8 ft 10 in × 8 ft (269 × 244 cm). It is a red and pale orange damask silk, with a turquoise border, and red and yellow fringe.
*Location*: Red Hill.

This was replaced by the NUM banner showing a portrait of Aneurin

Bevan, 'Loyalty and Endurance'[291] and the wheatsheaf with 'Each for All, All for Each'. This was used until 1968 and was transferred to Murton (q.v.) in 1971.

HARRATON

There was mining at Harraton in the seventeenth century, and workings were carried on by the Lambton family certainly from the early eighteenth century until their sale to Joicey in 1896. The Big and Billy shafts were near Nova Scotia, giving the colliery the nickname 'Cotia'. The Maudlin and Hutton were mined, with an output of about 940 tons per day. In 1913 about 700 men and boys worked the Hutton by bord and pillar.[292] Haulage reorganization was carried through in 1947–50.[293] Productivity declined in the late 1950s, and even with the introduction of a coal plough with armoured face conveyor in 1962, roof conditions were a serious problem, and the pit closed in 1965.

The banner at the 1873 Gala carried portraits of Bruce and MacDonald: 'Honour is due to whom honour belongeth; long live Bruce and MacDonald for the sake of the miners of the United Kingdom.' The reverse showed an arbitration board, 'the rich and poor meet together, but God is the maker of them all'.[294] It was blue and red.

The NUM banner bears an eliptical portrait of Keir Hardie,[295] with the reverse panel showing three female figures representing 'Friendship, Love and Truth', similar to that used at Burnhope (q.v.). It was produced by Tutill at Chesham and was in use by 1962. It is blue silk with a red border. *Location*: Harraton & District Community Centre. Installed to commemorate the service of H. Wilkins, lodge secretary, 1941–60.

HARTON

The pit was sunk in 1841–44 to the Bensham seam by Harton Coal Co. (Blackett, Wood, Anderson and Philipson) as a downcast to St Hilda colliery (q.v.), with an outlying shaft at Westoe (q.v.) in 1909–11.[296] The company also sank a shaft to work the Bent House Farm reserves in 1895, taking the coal to Cookson's Quay staithes.[297] Manpower figures for Harton fell from 2,007 in 1930 to 1,101 in 1940. In 1957–8 reconstruction work was carried out, including a new heapstead, and work at the shaft bottom. In the 1960s work concentrated on the Brass Thill,[298] but financial problems led to its being closed in July 1969.

The banner paraded in April 1873 showed a master and worker.[299]

The banner used in 1893 bore a central portrait of Gladstone, accompanied by John Wilson and William Crawford.[300]

The NUM Harton, later Harton and Westoe, banner, from Tutill's City Road works, carries the portraits of K. Hardie, A.J. Cook and C. Attlee, 'Stalwarts of Justice', on the obverse, while the reverse shows a family passing through the gate of a cornfield, representing Nationalization, and viewing the bright future of 'Security' – 'Our Heritage'. It measures

BANNERS OF THE DURHAM COALFIELD

8 ft 9 in × 8 ft 10 in (267 × 269 cm) and is light green and blue damask silk with a red border.
*Location*: Beamish (1974-187).

The lodge acquired the Fenhall Drift banner (q.v.), which had been passed on to Thrislington. It showed Lanchester church on one side and a split panel on the other, with illustrations of a Roman soldier, 'C 1st AD', and a miner, 'C 20th AD'.
*Location*: Derwentside District Council, Civic Centre, Consett.

## HASWELL

Exploratory work through the magnesian limestone was carried out in 1811, and the Engine pit was sunk in 1831.[301] This was followed by the Little pit in 1833 and operated by the Haswell, Shotton & Easington Coal Co. to work the Five Quarter, Main, Low Main and Hutton.[302] Coal was first won on 11 March 1835 and shipped from Seaham on 2 July 1835.[303] There was an explosion in the Meadows Flat of the Little pit on 28 September 1844, killing ninety-five.[304] The pit was closed and dismantled in 1896–7.[305] The North pit was later opened by Horden Collieries Ltd in 1900–4.[306]

The lodge purchased a banner probably in 1872, and certainly before April 1873. It showed the Good Samaritan on one side, 'Go and do likewise', while the other showed MacDonald, Crawford, Burt and Pritchard giving thanks to Mr Bruce, the Home Secretary, for passing the Mines Regulation Bill:

> All are equal in God's sight,
> The bound, the free, the black, the white;
> He made them, all freedom gave,
> But man made the slave.[307]

It was blue with a red border and yellow fringe.

The 1893 banner shows, on one side, Tommy Ramsey standing, holding his crake, accompanied by the seated figures of Alexander MacDonald and William Crawford: 'they being dead yet speaketh.' On the other side are the seated figures of William Patterson, John Foreman, John Wilson and John Johnson (?): 'But to act that each tomorrow finds us further than today.' It is dark blue with a red border and gold fringe.
*Location*: Durham Cathedral, south transept.

## HEBBURN

Sinking began in 1792, with the 'A' pit to work the Main seam.[308] It was operated by a number of owners, including Messrs Easton, Anderson & Partners around 1857–60, Tyne Coal Co. in the 1880s, and Wallsend & Hebburn Coal Co. Ltd in the 1890s. In 1884 the heapstead was destroyed by fire. At that time the 'A' pit served as a downcast, and men were raised at the 'C' shaft. The Low Main and Beaumont were abandoned in the first two decades of this century, followed by the Five Quarter, Six Quarter, Hutton and the Yard, leading to closure in 1932.

The 1873 Gala banner showed the British Lion: 'We came in earnest.' The reverse showed Justice standing between an owner and miner: 'Be just and fear not; let all the ends thou aim'st at be thy country's, thy God's, and thy truth's; then if thou fallest, thou fallest a blessed martyr.'[309] It was dark blue with a red fringe and was painted by W. Gowdy for Bainbridge of Newcastle.

## HEDLEY HILL

Charles Attwood's Weardale Iron Co. operated a colliery here in the upper Deerness valley (with a linked drift at Hedley Hill Fell.) Output was converted to coke in beehive ovens for use at the company's iron works at Tow Law. The company was sold to Sir C. Furness & Co. in 1899 and renamed Weardale Iron & Coal Co. The pit was closed from 1904 to 1906 and on reopening the coke ovens were not lit.[310] The colliery closed in 1929 and again in 1940, but small-scale mining restarted, with between twenty-two and twenty-six men. It finally closed in 1966.

The banner at the 1873 Gala carried a poor-quality portrait of James Fowler, mayor of Durham, wearing his chain of office, with the words, 'Blessed is the man that considereth the poor; the Lord will deliver him in the time of trouble'. The reverse showed two miners, one creeping out of a hole in the dark: 'We get our bread at the peril of our lives. Our skin is black like the oven, because of the labour we perform.'[311]

## HEDLEYHOPE

Test borings were carried out in 1836, and the Edward pit was sunk by Joseph Pease.[312] In the early 1880s it was worked by the Hedley Hope Coal Co., with East Hedleyhope, but in 1887 it was operated by Sir Bernhard Samuelson & Co., to supply fuel for his iron works at Newport, Middlesbrough.[313] In 1923 the firm was amalgamated with Dorman Long and the pit operated under the title 'Hedleyhope Coal Co.' From 1936 it was worked by Bearpark Coal & Coke Co., until closure in 1945.

The 1873 Gala banner carried an unspecified portrait and the verse,

> Sons of labour, toiling millions,
> Wealth creators in all lands,
> Claim your share of nature's blessings,
> And the produce of your hands.

The reverse bore the bundle of sticks fable, with 'Unity is Strength'.[314] This seems to have been a joint banner with Sunniside.

A banner in use in 1953 showed two pit ponies and may have been acquired from another lodge.[315]

The NUM banner carried a large roundel scene of the Good Samaritan, probably with the bundle of sticks fable on the other side. It was certainly present at the 1958 Gala.[316]

Hedleyhope lodge later acquired the redundant Black Prince lodge banner and simply attached a ribbon marked 'Hedleyhope' over the title scroll. The obverse shows the bundle of sticks fable, within a roundel, and 'Unity is strength' at the bottom of the border. The reverse has a roundel scene of a miner coming to comfort a widow and child at a grave: 'We succour the widows and orphans.'

*Location*: In 1984 the banner was temporarily hung in the Lady Chapel of St Paul's Church, Waterhouses.[317] During restoration work the ribbon was removed and the original name was revealed. The banner was later returned to Red Hill.

## HETTON

The sinking of Hetton pit by Mr Mowbray in 1818 was stopped by quicksand.[318] A successful working was carried out in 1821–2 by the Hetton Coal Co., with two shafts, the Minor and Blossom, and the Lyon's Winning in 1857.[319] There were explosions on 29 January 1836, with twenty killed, and on 24 February 1845, with twenty-nine killed. A boiler explosion on 26 December 1860 saw twenty-two killed.[320] The company was taken over by Messrs Joicey & Co. in 1911 and reformed as the Lambton & Hetton Coal Co. Ltd. It was consolidated as Lambton, Hetton & Joicey Coal Co. Ltd in 1923. The pit closed in 1950.

The Hetton collieries banner at the 1872 and 1873 Galas showed a master and workman standing either side of a shield and shaking hands. In the background was a colliery scene. On the reverse was an emblem of Justice, with the mottoes, 'Masters act with justice to your servants, knowing also that you have a master in Heaven', 'Servants be diligent and honour your masters' and 'Unity is Strength'.[321] The banner was painted by W. Gowdy for Bainbridge of Newcastle, measured 11 ft × 10 ft (335 × 305 cm) and was described as either blue or green.

A later DMA banner had a roundel scene showing two miners in pit hoggers shaking hands. Between, and just behind the two figures, was an angel. It was certainly in use in 1932.

A later DMA banner of 'Hetton Lyons lodge Hetton-le-Hole' showed, on one side, a roundel scene of a standing miner with a pick over his left shoulder and a female figure at a gate. The reverse carried a 'Sunshine of Liberty' image.

## HEWORTH

Mining was carried out in the mid-eighteenth century (in 1758 it was known as 'Mr Blackett's colliery'),[322] and in the nineteenth century shafts were sunk in 1819, 1876 and *c.* 1890. Owners of Heworth colliery, or the Heworth Coal Co., operated these shafts, the John, Ada and

Fanny, with the coal shipped from Tyne Staithes at Pelaw. Mining ceased in 1963.

The banner used at the 1872 Gala showed a workman presenting a petition to the pit owner for 'A fair day's work for a fair day's pay'. The reverse depicted a workman and master shaking hands, with the line, 'We miners of Durham do meet and unite to keep good on union and seek our just right'.[323]

The banner used at the 1893 Gala carried the beehive symbol of industry.[324]

A new banner was unfurled on 16 July 1904 by Peter Curran, the Labour candidate.[325] The principal illustration was a portrait of John Wilson.

By 1911 the Heworth banner carried a portrait of John Johnson,[326] though he may have been depicted on the 1904 banner with John Wilson.

The NUM banner has a large roundel scene of Emmanuel Shinwell presenting a copy of the Coal Industry Nationalisation Act to Lord Hindley. At the top of the roundel is the message 'Justice, Service, Security', with the base title 'Coal Industry Nationalisation Act, 1946'. In the background are the initials NCB. The reverse side shows a portrait of 'James Keir Hardie MP'. It measures 8 ft 7 in × 8 ft 2 in (262 × 249 cm) and is light blue with a yellow border.
*Location*: Beamish (1984-10-32).

HOBSON

*See* Burnopfield.

HORDEN

Three shafts, the North, South and East, were sunk in 1900–8 by Horden Collieries Ltd using the cementation process through Permian limestone – the North (downcast) to the Hutton, the South (downcast) to the Low Main, and the East (upcast) to the Hutton.[327] North and South were used for coal drawing, and the East as a man-rider. In 1919 man-riding cars were introduced and in the 1920s surface developments included the building of a Baum washery and dry-cleaning plant (updated in 1955 and 1960). Output fell during 1940–5 because of shortages of labour and materials. After nationalization, power-loading was introduced, principally by arc shearers, with chain and belt conveyors. An explosion at the NE 5 district plough face of the Low Main, on 23 March 1953, killed one and injured two.[328] Major reconstruction work took place in 1966–7, with skip winding at the North shaft and stone and material winding by mine car at the South.[329] In the 1970s coal extraction in the Zone 6 development area was from the High Main (E) and Yard (G).[330] Water problems and a rock fall in 1985 seriously affected operations.[331] Proposed closure went to appeal, but was approved on 30 January 1986,[332] and the pit closed in February 1986.

The portrait of
Emmanuel Shinwell on
the Horden NUM
banner.

The banner used in the 1920s showed a miner offering a petition to Justice of 'Mines owned by the Nation for the Nation. Loyalty, Endeavour, Good Citizenship etc. etc'. Britannia, at the other side of Justice, holds a scroll whose wording offers 'Humane conditions, higher standard of living, adequate compensation and safety measures etc., housing improvements'. At the base of the roundel scene was the title, 'A fair exchange'.

A damask silk banner, presumably old and superseded, was repainted and used in the 1920s or 1930s. The top scroll was inscribed 'Horden Colliery Rag Time Band', while the central roundel was overpainted with the motto, 'Help those who / cannot help / Themselves'.

A Tutill damask silk banner of the 1930s or '40s had a before and after scene – 'as it is', and 'as it should be', the latter showing a group of boys walking towards a large school or college.

The 1952 NUM banner has a highly decorated upper section with three roundel portraits of A.J. Cook, Peter Lee and Robert Smillie. Below them, the main panel shows a young miner standing astride a colliery heapstead with the motto, 'The courage of youth can safeguard the future'. The reverse side shows two miners, dressed in sleeveless shirts and pit hoggers, with helmets and cap lamps, shaking hands across a globe: 'Peace and Goodwill to all Miners.' Above them, in a beam of light, is a dove carrying an olive branch. It is green silk with a red border and a gold fringe.
*Location*: Red Hill.

The second NUM banner was unfurled by George Brown at Horden colliery welfare football ground on 15 July 1966.[333] On one side is a large roundel portrait of 'Harold Wilson MP / Prime Minister', with Emmanuel Shinwell, the Easington MP, on the other. The banner was painted by Pauline Tait at Sharp Studios, Hitchin. It measures 6 ft 7 in × 7 ft 10 in (200 × 239 cm) and is green silk, with a red border and green fringe.
*Location*: Red Hill.

The 1981 NUM banner was unfurled on the evening of the Gala at a ceremony attended by Neil Kinnock MP (then shadow spokesman on education.) It carries a shield panel depicting two miners shaking hands, one in shirt and trousers with knee pads, holding a lamp, the other in boiler suit and helmet, standing by a heap of coal. In the background is a colliery scene, and the motto reads, 'Our future we build from the past'. On the other side is an illustration of 'St Mary's church / Miners Cathedral'. The banner was produced by Turtle & Pearce (no. 6.81) and is red with a yellow border.
*Location*: Horden Welfare Hall.

HOUGHTON

This pit was sunk in 1827–31 to the Hutton by the Earl of Durham, with an upcast in 1865.[334] There were explosions on 1 September 1827, killing seven, 11 November 1850, killing twenty-seven, and 3 June 1885, with twelve dead. Main and Hutton were being worked in the 1870s, but there was extensive faulting. It was taken over by Joicey in 1896. In 1905 the Hutton was worked out, but Houghton Meadows (which was worked by Londonderry until 1896)[335] was reopened, and worked from 1936 to 25 March 1960.[336] The Five Quarter was finished in 1952, followed by the Maudlin and Low Main in 1964. Work then concentrated on the Busty, using shearer power-loading, but eventually, with only high sulphur Harvey remaining, the pit was closed on 26 September 1981.

The banner at the 1872 and 1873 Galas showed an arbitration scene on one side and, on the reverse, a man urging a group of miners to be true to the union: 'Our motto is and ever shall be, the protection of our industry.'[337] The banner was produced by W. Whaites of Manchester and had a blue border with yellow fringe.

A new banner, of unknown appearance, was purchased in 1910.

This was replaced on 22 July 1923 by a new G. Tutill banner. On one side was a portrait of Thomas Husband, the late lodge secretary and, on the other, the Newtown aged miners' homes.[338]

A new Houghton-le-Spring lodge banner was unveiled by James Robson on 21 July 1932.[339] It was designed by Miss Vera Nichols of Houghton-le-Spring and showed a symbolic design of a sunrise on the sea.

Another DMA banner, produced at Tutill's City Road works, carries the bundle of sticks fable on one side and a medical scene on the other. The latter is shown in a split roundel, with three injured miners in a waiting room and a miner, with his arm in a sling, seeing a doctor. The scene is entitled 'Compensation Day', with the motto, 'Organisation is Security'. It is 8 ft 9 in × 8 ft (267 × 244 cm), of cream and blue damask silk, with an orange border and purple and yellow-green fringe. One of the Tutill brass disks survives.

*Location*: Red Hill.

The 1957 NUM banner, formerly belonging to Westerton (q.v.), carried the Latin motto, 'E Tenebris Lux' over 'Durham Area / Houghton Lodge'. The central panel showed a miner and an apprentice, both dressed in overalls, with helmets and pit lamps, standing in front of a table, on which was laid a book, ruler, ink bottle and pen, compass and set-square. In the background was a pithead. The reverse showed a Gala scene, with bands and banners crossing Elvet bridge on their way to the Racecourse.[340]

*Location*: Destroyed by fire, Houghton Comrades Club.


HUNWICK

The colliery was sunk in 1854 and was worked by the Hunwick & Newfield Coal Co., until it was taken over by Bolckow, Vaughan & Co. in the 1870s.[341] An explosion in the Victoria killed a putter in 1912.[342] Closure took place in 1940.

The banner in use in 1873 showed Labour and Capital, with three men on each side, and two in the centre shaking hands: 'Come let us reason together.' The reverse bore a scene of a hand holding scales, and the words 'A just weight is His delight' above a picture of Christ pointing to a cherub holding a scroll inscribed 'Whatsoever ye would that men do unto you, do ye also unto them'. The illustration also bore Christ's command, 'See that ye love one another'.[343]

## HYLTON

The Wearmouth Coal Co. sank the pit in 1897–1900.[344] It had three shafts, the East and West for drawing and the South as an upcast shaft. Ventilation was by 25 ft Waddle fan.[345] Development of the Brass Thill and Hutton was undertaken in 1970–1, but adverse geological conditions reduced the workable area to a thin area of Harvey, while attempts to develop the Yard encountered a serious washout. The pit was closed on 13 July 1979.[346]

The lodge banner, dating from around 1915, carries a portrait of Keir Hardie on one side and the 'Friendship, Love and Truth' image on the other, with the motto, 'By industry we flourish, united in truth and justice'. It is red and purple-blue damask silk, produced by Tutill at 83 City Road, and measuring 8 ft 10 in in length, but is now fragile.
*Location*: Red Hill.

The first NUM banner, dating from sometime between 1945 and 1957, carries a shoulder-length portrait of Keir Hardie, wearing a black hat, cravat and cape and holding a pipe. On the reverse is a pattern-book 'Friendship, Love and Truth' design. It is a red and grey-blue damask silk from Tutill's City Road works, with a yellow border, and measures 8 ft 7 in × 8 ft 1 in (262 × 246 cm).
*Location*: Sunderland Museum & Art Gallery (TWCMS: P26).

The 1960 NUM banner carries a panel showing a line of semi-detached aged miners' homes, with the motto, 'Friendship, Love, Truth', at the base. The reverse shows Hylton Castle, with the motto, 'Unity is Strength'.[347] Repairs to the banner fittings by Messrs Fattorini, a Birmingham firm, are referred to in the lodge minutes of October 1960.
*Location*: Castle View County Secondary Modern School, Sunderland.

## INKERMAN

There was a small-scale operation here in 1858, with further sinking in 1873.[348] From 1886 Inkerman was operated by J.G. Wild, formerly manager for the Hedley Hope Coal Co., but the site seems to have been disused by 1897.[349] Black Prince cokeyard extended towards Inkerman, but as this was cleared away, the Inkerman Drift, operated by the Inkerman Colliery Co. Ltd, was opened up in the 1930s.[350] It probably closed in the 1940s.

The banner at the 1872 Gala was a white material without elaborate decoration. It bore clasped hands and the line, 'You miners throughout the land, we pray unite in heart and hand'.[351]

The 1873 Gala banner bore a full-length portrait of Tommy Ramsey on one side and representations of Capital and Labour on the other, with the verse,

> By clinging closely together, no foe can assail,
> Our banner must triumph, our cause will prevail;
> Come and join us! come join us, no time for delay,
> Wait not till tomorrow, no time like today.[352]

## IVESTON

Sinking was carried out in 1839 by Black, Reay & Co.,[353] but by 1857 the pit was operated by Jonathan Richardson & Partners.[354] It was subsequently taken over by the Consett Iron Co., certainly by 1884, and worked until 1892. Small landsale operations continued, through a bequest of the coal royalty by the Clavering family to the local people. Bogglehole drift was worked by the Harpers from 1890 to 1902, and Neashams drift operated around 1915.[355]

The banner in use in 1873 showed a number of miners toiling up a long flight of steps to the summit of a broad landscape: 'By justice and perseverance we elevate our position.' The reverse bore illustrations of the advantages of arbitration and unionism.[356]

## KIBBLESWORTH

The pit was sunk in 1842 and by the 1850s was worked by John Bowes & Partners, using the Robert shaft. The Glamis pit was sunk in 1935 and linked to the Robert. A new drift was driven in 1965–6, with belt conveyor, to eliminate the use of shaft winding,[357] and a further drivage connected the colliery with Ravensworth Ann (q.v.) in April 1973.[358] The 301-rank coking coals were, however, in increasingly thin seams, and the pit was closed on 4 October 1974, with the loss of 622 jobs.[359]

The banner in use in 1873 showed a master and worker shaking hands, with the motto, 'An honest man is the noblest work of God', and the verse,

> Let's greet him as the best,
> And help him all we can.
> That brightest gem in nature's crown.
> Is an honest working man.

On the reverse was a shamrock, rose and thistle, with the mottoes, 'Union is strength' and 'May God defend the right'. It was blue with a red border.[360]

The 1934 banner shows two miners shaking hands in front of an angel with a ribbon inscribed 'Unity is strength'. The reverse shows the frontage of Conishead Priory. It is a red and grey-blue damask silk with a red border. It measures 7 ft 11 in × 7 ft (241 × 213 cm) and still retains a black drape.

*Location*: Red Hill.

The 1961 NUM banner was produced by Tutill at Chesham (no. 261).[361] It carries a large roundel portrait of 'Aneurin Bevan / Unity is Strength' on the obverse, and 'Conishead Convalescent Home for Durham Mineworkers' on the reverse. It measures 7 ft 8 in × 9 ft (234 × 274 cm) and is red with a blue border.
*Location*: Kibblesworth Working Men's Club.

KIMBLESWORTH

Sinking by the Charlaw & Sacriston Coal Co. began in 1873, and three shafts were completed – the Old and Busty as drawing shafts and a third, sunk in 1894–5, for pumping. On 16 August 1885 three men were killed in a shaft accident. Drift mining was also employed, and in 1913 work concentrated on the Brass Thill, Hutton and Busty.[362] Seams were gradually worked out – the Low Main and Brass Thill in 1953, the Harvey in 1954, Hutton in 1958, Main 1961, High Main 1965 and Five Quarter and Busty in 1967. In 1965 it was listed as a 'C' pit with limited life expectancy and was closed on 4 November 1967.[363]

A damask silk banner was unfurled in 1923 by Mrs Blackett, the wife of the colliery manager, and Mrs Bradford.[364] On one side were roundel portraits of J. Ritson MP, J. Lawson MP, R. Hodgson (lodge chairman) and W. Gray (lodge secretary). The reverse showed the pattern-book 'Two sides of the question' design. The banner was badly damaged by wind at the 1947 Gala, and the portrait roundels were cut out. The surviving roundel showing 'Mr W Gray Secy.' is 2 ft 1 in (63.5 cm) in diameter.
*Location*: Mr Dougray, Bowburn.

A replacement was purchased in 1948.[365] It bore the National Union of Mineworkers title on a scroll over a roundel showing the three Graces, accompanied by a number of symbols, a sickbed scene, and the Latin inscription 'Famam extendere factis' around a Durham City shield.[366] The reverse shows clasped hands over a globe: 'Workers of the world unite.' It measures 8 ft 7 in × 8 ft 2 in (262 × 249 cm) and is red with a green border. At the 1948 Gala, the new banner was accompanied by Councillor T. Sharp, the ex-pitman's boxing champion.
*Location*: Beamish (1984-10-11).

Probably after 1960 the lodge acquired the Ushaw Moor banner (q.v.) showing Jack Joyce and Red Hill. The Ushaw Moor title was overpainted, but was restored in 1995.
*Location*: D. Williams, Ushaw Moor. Formerly displayed in Durham Town Hall.

LAMBTON

Two shafts were operated by the Earl of Durham, the Lady Anne as an upcast and the 'D' (sunk in 1831) as a downcast. The latter was originally known as Bourn Moor colliery 'D' pit and had associated coke-ovens and a washery dolly. Further ventilation was supplied by an old shaft, the

William Henry, on the east bank of Break Neck Gill.[367] In 1896 it was purchased by Joicey. In 1913 the Five Quarter, Maudlin and Low Main were worked. In 1963 Lambton absorbed 200 miners when the Meadows pit at Houghton closed.[368] On 26 January 1965 Dr W. Reid, NCB divisional chairman, announced that the 2 ft 4 in seams were uneconomic, and Lambton D closed in February 1965.[369] Land reclamation in 1995 and subsequent archaeological excavation have uncovered important remains of preserved timber wagonways, along with evidence of possible coal-handling platforms and other structures, thought to date to the 1780s.

At the 1872 Gala, Lambton had a small banner inscribed 'Union is Strength' and 'Knowledge is Power'.[370]

The banner at the 1883 Gala bore designs drawn by two workmen at the pit. The obverse carried the message, 'Masters, do act with justice to your servants', with the scene of a widow appealing to a colliery owner for compensation, 'We claim compensation for loss of life'. The reverse showed an emblem of manhood suffrage: 'With unity, firmness and perseverance, we will obtain our rights.'[371]

An 1890s DMA banner had the main top ribbon attached to two cameo panels bearing the names 'Storey' and 'Ramsay', but with the portraits painted out. The central panel shows Gladstone standing at the dispatch box in the Commons, pointing. The reverse carries cameo portraits of 'Wilson' and 'MacDonald' over a central rectangular panel containing a portrait of Robert Burns in a laurel-leaf surround, and a view of his birthplace. Both sides carry a monogram of interwoven letters L and C. This banner was produced by 'S.M. Peacock, Banner Manufacturer, S. Shields'. It is 10 ft × 9 ft (305 × 274 cm) and is dark blue.
*Location*: Beamish (1962-270).

A subsequent blue and light green damask silk DMA banner, with a red border, carries a portrait of Gladstone at the dispatch box on one side and view of the Miners' Hall in North Road, Durham, on the reverse. It measures 10 ft × 7 ft 8 in (305 × 243 cm) and is post-1905.
*Location*: Beamish (1962-271).

A banner used in the early decades of the twentieth century carried a portrait of Frank Hodges, though this was later blackened out, probably in 1927.[372]

Lambton later acquired the Lumley Winning lodge banner (q.v.). This may be the one unfurled by James Gilliland, in the Miners' Hall, Fencehouses, on 13 July 1935.[373] It carries an 'All men are brethren' scene on the obverse and, on the reverse, a sickbed scene, 'Bear ye one anothers burdens'. It is red and cream damask silk, with a dark blue border, and measures 9 ft 10 in × 9 ft 5 in (300 × 287 cm).
*Location*n: Beamish (1962-272).

This banner was subsequently replaced by one carrying a shoulder-length portrait of A.J. Cook.[374] The reverse shows the biblical scene of Christ walking on the sea, with the words, 'Oh thou of little faith wherefore didst thou doubt'. This was produced by Tutill at the City Road

works. The banner was repaired several times, but was badly torn at the 1961 Gala. The bottom section of the border is now missing, and the remainder of the banner measures 8 ft 10 in × 8 ft 2 in (269 × 249 cm). It is blue and yellow damask silk with a red border.
*Location*: Beamish (1962-273).

The 1963 banner was unfurled by Gaitskell on 20 July at Fencehouses. On the obverse were portraits of Hugh Gaitskell and Ald. M. Doyle, Lambton lodge chairman for thirty-two years, and on the reverse a repeat of the New Testament scene. The pit closed in 1965 and about 120 men were transferred to Silksworth. The banner went to Red Hill, but was subsequently sent to Silksworth (q.v.) where the portraits were overpainted, much to the discontent of the Lambton lodge officials.

LANGLEY PARK

This was a Consett Iron Co. colliery, with three shafts sunk between 1873 and 1875, and later outliers at Kaysburn in 1889 and Hill Top in 1904, enabling an expansion of mining from the initial operations in the Busty and Hutton to the Brockwell and Brass Thill.[375] Output was largely converted to coke in the beehive ovens for the Consett works, although these were seriously damaged when an underlying roadway between the No. 1 shaft and the Hill Top shaft collapsed in 1904.[376] They were replaced with Otto ovens. The Brass Thill was exhausted in 1914. In the 1930s efforts to expand output led to development of the Five Quarter and Victoria, followed in the 1940s by the Main and Harvey. Gradually seams were worked out – Five Quarter in 1952, Busty in 1955 and Brockwell in 1963. Final operations concentrated on the Harvey and Victoria, but with the abandonment of the Victoria in April 1975, the pit closed on 31 October 1975.

On 11 July 1884 there were proposals to purchase a banner,[377] and a concert was held to raise funds, but the lodge minute-book gives no further details.

A DMA banner of the 1920s showed three men seated at a table, one of whom was Ramsay MacDonald. At the 1932 Gala, MacDonald's face was covered by a sheet.[378]

An NUM banner carries a scene of an idyllic tree-lined street with houses and gardens, 'Our Aim'. Above the scene is a roundel portrait of Joseph Robertshaw (lodge chairman 1924–54) which was added after the banner was displayed at the 1954 Gala.[379] The reverse shows the frontage of 'The Hermitage Rehabilitation centre for Durham mineworkers'. The banner is 7 ft 10 in × 6 ft 9 in (239 × 208 cm) and is red with a green border and yellow fringe.
*Location*: Langley Park Community Centre.

The subsequent 1963 banner was unfurled by Sam Watson on 19 July.[380] It is red silk, with a green border, and shows the frontage of the 'Sam Watson Rest Home', with County Hall on the reverse. It was carried to the last Gala in 1975[381] and was transferred to East Hetton lodge (q.v.) in 1977.

## LEASINGTHORNE

Messrs King, Mearse & Campion signed an agreement to work coal in the township in 1836. It then passed to a series of owners – James Reid in 1841, Andrew Spottiswoode *c.* 1845, Messrs Backhouse & Co., Nicholas Wood & Co. by 1856 and Bolckow, Vaughan & Co. by the 1870s.[382] They worked the Five Quarter and Main in the 1890s.[383] The company was absorbed by Dorman Long in 1929. Following nationalization the pit was merged with Dean and Chapter (q.v.) in 1950. It was closed in October 1967.

The lodge attended the manhood suffrage demonstration at Bishop Auckland in 1873, apparently with a banner.

John Wilson unfurled a new banner on 18 May 1912. It carried a central roundel showing, seated in the foreground, John Wilson in his Doctor of Civil Law robes, and standing behind him, Mr Bradlaugh and Mr Crawford.[384]

A new banner was unfurled in 1928.[385] On the front was the aged miners' homes at Coundon and on the reverse the pattern-book 'Two sides of the question' design.

The 1950 NUM banner shows the local aged miners' homes on one side and Conishead Priory on the other, with the motto, 'Health is strength'. The banner is 6 ft 9 in × 6 ft 4 in (206 × 193 cm), of blue and gold damask silk, with a yellow border and yellow and blue fringe. The silk was made at Tutill's City Road works, but the painting was added at Chesham. There is a Chesham address label attached to the top of the banner. The banner was transferred to Eppleton (q.v.) after the closure of the Leasingthorne pit in 1967.

## LINTZ

The Lintz and Anna pits were sunk by the Lintz Colliery Co. (Messrs McLean and Prior) in 1855, and continued by McLean until *c.* 1885, when it was laid in.[387] The pit restarted in 1889 under John Shield, to work Main, Busty, Three Quarter and Brockwell. Around 1899 it passed to the South Garesfield Colliery Co. and it closed in 1929.

The 1873 Gala banner showed a school scene with an alert pupil, representing the eight-hour system, a sleepy boy, ten hours, and a sleeping boy, twelve hours. The reverse showed a master and workman shaking hands, with the words, 'United and combined to protect and not to injure'.[387]

## LITTLEBURN

North Brancepeth Coal Co. sank the Engineer shaft in 1870 to the Busty, followed by the Merchant to the Brockwell in 1871.[388] It was linked underground with their Ironmaster pit at Broompark (sunk in 1870). The Merchant was idle from 1881 to 1893, with coal drawn at the Busty shaft, until a new stone drift was driven to link the two. In 1931 the company went into liquidation, but the pit was reopened on a smaller scale by the Bearpark Coal & Coke Co. Ltd to work the Busty.[389] Flooding from the River Browney led to closure in December 1950.

In 1909 a banner was unfurled by John Wilson at North Brancepeth School.[390] On one side was the standing figure of Wilson, while the reverse showed Justice standing between an owner and worker, with the motto, 'Be just and fear not'.[391] It was produced by Messrs Riley & Co. of Leeds and was *c*. 8 ft × 7 ft (242 × 213 cm).

A DMA banner of the 1920s has a central roundel portrait of Ramsey MacDonald, accompanied by an all-seeing eye, an angel, Britannia, a woman and child and several figures, including a Red Indian. Under the roundel is the wording, 'Spectemur Agendo', with a wheatsheaf, beehive, fruit and a ribbon scroll inscribed 'Love, Friendship and Truth'. The reverse carries a Good Samaritan scene, with the motto, 'Bear ye one anothers burdens'. MacDonald's portrait was subsequently painted over with a boating scene on a river. It is blue silk with a red border, by 'G. Tutill – London'. The banner is damaged and measures 9 ft 7 in × 8 ft 3 in (293 × 253 cm).
*Location*: Red Hill.

The designs on the 1930 banner are not recorded, but they may have been the Good Samaritan, 'Bear ye one anothers burden', and 'Love, Friendship, Truth', which are known to have been on a Littleburn banner at the 1946 Gala.[392]

A top pole with fragments of red ground and blue border is from an unidentifiable Littleburn banner. It is 10 ft 1 in (308 cm) long.
*Location*: Red Hill.

LIZZIE

This is probably the Lizzie pit at South Pontop. Lizzie was sunk in 1861 by the Ritsons to work the Five Quarter and Brass Thill.[393] In 1866–7 a second shaft, the Willie, was sunk to the Hutton. Work on the Shield Row in 1877, the Little Hutton in 1892 and additional sources kept the pit going until closure in 1927.

The banner at the 1872 and 1873 Galas showed a conference between legislators and workmen concerning the Mines Regulation Bill. In front of a group of workmen stood MacDonald holding a scroll bearing the title of the bill. The workmen demand, 'Pass this bill soon, or, as sure as fate, if you don't pass it, then we will'. The legislators' comment is 'Never mind these miners, let them wait a little longer for the bill'. The scene on the reverse was entitled 'Arbitration' and showed an employer coming down stairs to a workman who asks,

> Deal freedom's sacred treasures light [or free] as air,
> Till slave and despot be but things that were.

This green banner was produced by Elam of London.[394]

## LUMLEY AND COCKEN HALL

A series of pits were worked at Lumley, certainly from the 1790s, including the George (where explosions killed thirteen on 9 October 1819 and fourteen on 25 October 1824), the West, First, Second, Third, Sixth, Seventh and Eighth. The Second was sunk in stages and by 1872 was at the Harvey level, at 76 fathoms. A downcast was at the Forrest pit. The Sixth was idle for much of the first half of the nineteenth century, but restarted in 1864. By 1896 only the Sixth pit was working. The Third pit was transformed into Lumley New Winning in 1910 and worked alongside the Sixth (q.v.).

There was early evidence for coal mining in the Cocken area. Opencasting in 1986 exposed old workings and two shovels, a sledge runner, cracket and pair of clogs.[395] Winding and pumping engines were removed from Cocken and Brasside collieries to the Earl of Durham's Philadelphia engineering works, and the sites were cleared. There were plans by the Finchale Coal Co. to work a drift at Cocken Ford in 1939.[397]

The joint banner of these workings carried at the 1872 and 1873 Galas bore the text, 'Behold, how good and pleasant a thing it is for brethren to dwell together in unity'. The reverse had images of Justice and Truth. It cost £18.[398]

## LUMLEY SIXTH

Lumley Sixth was worked by Lord Joicey, ultimately forming part of Lambton, Hetton & Joicey Collieries Ltd. An inundation on 18 September 1946 killed one. The pit closed in 1966.

The 1929 banner bore a central roundel scene of a child sitting on the back of a lion, lying beside a lamb, with flowers and fruit strewn across the ground: 'The Reign of Peace'. The reverse showed four ancient smiths working at an anvil, in a rural setting, beating swords into ploughshares, with the Biblical quotation from Isaiah 2.4

The 1960 banner, with repeat designs, was unfurled by Lord Lawson of Beamish at the colliery on 15 July.[399] It was blue with yellow border. Following closure in 1966, it was transferred to Morrison Busty (q.v.).

## LUMLEY WINNING

The first banner was unfurled by J. Gilliland on 6 June 1914. On one side was a portrait of T.H. Richardson, checkweighman and lodge secretary, and on the other, a sickbed scene, 'Bear ye one anothers burden'.

A second banner, probably of the 1920s, repeats the sickbed scene and motto. The other side shows two miners shaking hands in front of an angel who carries a ribbon inscribed 'All men are brethren'. The damask banner was produced at Tutill's City Road works and was later transferred to Lambton lodge (q.v.).

MAINSFORTH

The colliery was initially worked from 1872 until around 1876, but was then laid in. It was restarted by the Carlton Iron Co. in 1904, with new plant and coal cutters by 1906.[400] This company was absorbed by Dorman, Long & Co. in 1923. Output concentrated on the Harvey, Busty and Brockwell, followed by the Hutton and, in the 1950s, by the Main (with a new loco drift). The 1963 manpower profile indicated serious financial losses, and work was directed to the Main, Low Main and Top Busty. Pumping was stopped at Dean and Chapter in 1967, and the water ran to Chilton and Leasingthorne.[401] In September 1967 water flooded the Low Main at Mainsforth.[402] The pit was consequently closed on 3 December 1968.[403]

A post-1915 DMA banner bears a painting of the colliery, with the title, 'Mines for the Nation'. The reverse carries a small standing figure of Tommy Ramsey set over a painting of Red Hill, with the mottoes, 'Remember the past' and 'Courage for the present'. It measures 8 ft 9 in × 8 ft (267 × 244 cm) and is blue with a red border.
*Location*: Beamish (1969-238).

A later DMA banner carried a rectangular panel showing the semi-detached aged miners' homes of 'Peace Haven' at Ferryhill.[404]

The 1951 NUM banner was unfurled by J. Slater MP, in the Welfare Hall, Ferryhill Station, on 20 July.[405] It carries, on one side, the 'Peace Haven' design in a square panel, while the reverse bears a painting of 'Conishead Priory convalescent home for Durham mine workers'. It was at Spennymoor Miners' Gala day in 1958.[406] It was produced by Tutill at Chesham and is blue with a red border. The banner measures 6 ft 10 in × 7 ft 9 in (208 × 236 cm).
*Location*: Red Hill.

MARLEY HILL

Initial workings were carried out at North Bank colliery in the late eighteenth century by the Grand Allies, but the main Lodge shaft was sunk in 1840–1 by John Bowes & Partners Ltd. In the 1890s the Busty and Brockwell were worked, with two thirds of the output coked on site.[407] In 1955 a new man-riding West shaft was sunk. Output continued from the Busty and Brockwell, using pneumatic picks in bord and pillar extraction, and the Harvey and Tilley with Reisshakenhobel ploughs onto armoured face conveyors.[408] Around the same time Clockburn drift was developed, linked to Marley Hill, enabling output to be sent direct to Derwenthaugh cokeworks. A rundown began in 1981 as adverse geological conditions affected production.[409] Declining reserves led to closure on 3 March 1983.[410]

The 1873 Gala banner bore a representation of Justice and a widow and orphan scene: 'Masters give unto servants that which is just and due, knowing also that ye have a master in Heaven.'[411] It was blue silk with a red and green fringe.

The Mainsforth banner, with a view of the aged miners' homes at Ferryhill, 'Peace Heaven', at the 1949 Gala.

The banner at the 1893 Gala carried depictions of Brotherhood and Justice.[412]

The banner seen at the 1946 Gala depicted some aspect of the welfare scheme.[413]

The NUM banner bears a central panel showing a widow and orphans at a grave, accompanied by three angels, and the message, 'We support the widow and orphans'. It also carries the words,

> Then let us pass our lives in peace
> the little time we stay
> nor let our acts of friendship cease
> till life shall pass away.

The reverse shows a 'Durham Gala' Racecourse scene. The banner was produced by Tutill at Chesham and is dark blue with a red border. It measures 6 ft 10 in × 7 ft 10 in (208 × 239 cm).
*Location*: Red Hill.

## MARSDEN

Whitburn colliery was sunk in 1874–81 by the Harton Coal Co., using the Kind-Chaudron process.[414] They then acquired the coal royalty of Marsden. Some undersea work was carried on to work the Bensham. In 1953 rope haulage was replaced by battery loco, and shaft sinking was carried through with a new winding system in 1958–9. By 1962 the pit was thoroughly mechanized, with two disc shearers and two ploughs. Financial losses in 1967 and geological problems led to closure on 31 May 1968.

The DMA banner of 1900 carries a portrait of John Thompson (1859–1926), the checkweighman and lodge secretary, set in a laurel wreath, above a view of Marsden Rock, with the title, 'Firm as a rock we stand'. The reverse side shows a figure in a frock coat, holding papers and standing at a table, probably W.S. Robson, the local Liberal MP.[415] This was accompanied by the motto, 'Labour is the source of all wealth'. When the banner was replaced, the central painting was cut out, framed and hung for a time in the lodge office. The roundel is 163 cm in diameter.
*Location*: Beamish (1984-10-31).

The 1921 damask silk banner also carried a portrait of Thompson, with the inscription,

> Faithful unto death
> Ill fares the land to hastening ills a pray
> where wealth accumulates and men decay.[416]

The reverse side carried a depiction of Marsden Rock: 'Firm as a rock'. A banner, possibly this one, was at the 1934 Gala, showing the rock in a moulded panel.[417]

The NUM banner carries the same picture of Marsden Rock, but with the wording, 'Firm as a rock we stand'. The reverse design comprises a magnet attracting iron, set over the letters DMA on a purple shield. It is accompanied by the motto, 'Drawn together in unity', on overlaid scrolls. It was produced by Tutill at Chesham, on light blue and gold damask silk from the City Road works, with red border. It measures 7 ft 8 in × 7 ft 11 in (264 × 241 cm).
*Location*: Red Hill.

## MEDOMSLEY

The colliery was sunk in 1839 by Edward Richardson & Co., but was taken over in the 1850s by Consett Iron Co. and known as the Busty, after the principal seam worked in the late nineteenth century. Output in the 1890s was coked in waste-heat ovens. In 1898 the Isabella shaft was sunk.[418] Between 1896 and 1921 drifts were driven to the Main and Hutton. Medomsley shaft was closed, and Elm Park drift was driven in 1962. Output from thin seams was won using windy picks and coked at Derwenthaugh, principally for use at Consett.[419] By 1970 the Busty was nearing exhaustion, and Three Quarter reserves were opened out.[420] The pit closed on 6 October 1972.[421]

In 1955 Sam Watson referred to a banner which was torn in bad weather.[422]

The 1955 banner was unfurled by Sam Watson and his wife at Pont Hall, Leadgate.[423] It carried portraits of J. Gilliland, Peter Lee and A.J. Cook, within a panel.

## MERRINGTON

The Spennymoor pit was operating in the 1850s,[425] close to Whitworth colliery, but was disused by 1897. Mining restarted, but operations finally ceased in June 1927.

The Rock, or North Close colliery, was sunk in 1887 and worked with about twenty-four hands, producing household coal for the local market. The shaft collapsed in 1911, but seems to have been restored, and by 1919 was renamed Merrington Park colliery.

A Tutill City Road banner of damask silk carried a central roundel divided into two.[426] On the left, a well-dressed boy, with his cap and satchel of books, is entering a secondary school, while in the right-hand panel another boy is heading for work at the pit. The message accompanying the two scenes is 'What is good for the rich man's child should be within the reach of the worker's child'.

## MIDDLE BEECHBURN

This pit was worked by the Middle Beechburn Coal & Coke Co. It closed in 1894.

The 1874 Gala banner bore scenes of Capital and Labour, and Peace and Friendship on one side and a pastoral scene with the motto, 'As water is to the trees, so is labour to commerce'.[426]

### MIDDRIDGE DRIFT

Mining at Middridge had been carried on by the Weardale Iron & Coal Co., with the Eden (1872) and Charles (1874) pits. A drift was worked from *c.* 1954 until 1966.

The post-1950 NUM banner carries three linked roundel portraits of Sir Stafford Cripps, Ernest Bevin and Lord Lawson of Beamish, with the words, 'Unity is Strength'. On the reverse is a fine picture of a pit pony in a field: 'Lest we forget'. This banner was at the 1962 Gala.[427] It is 6 ft 8 in × 7 ft 8 in (203 × 234 cm), of purple silk with a red border. *Location*: Red Hill.

### MILKWELL BURN AND BROAD OAK

The colliery lay in woodland at Milkwell Burn, close to Broad Oak farm and south-west of Chopwell. It was sunk between 1856 and 1898, but in an area of earlier workings. There were still buildings on the site in 1919, but greatly reduced in extent.

The obverse of the banner at the 1873 Gala showed two images. In one, a mother is shaking a boy and asking, 'John, wake up; are you not going to the night-school?' The boy replies, 'No, mother. I am so tired and sleepy. I have been in the pit 14 hours today'. The other image is of a boy with books and slate under his arm, with his mother asking, 'John, where are you going to?' John replies, 'I am going to school. I have only been in the pit eight hours today'. The reverse showed the cap of Liberty being held over the scales of Justice, while a pitman and owner are shown weighing coal.[428]

### MONKWEARMOUTH (OR WEARMOUTH)

The 'A' and 'B' shafts were sunk by Messrs Thompson, Pemberton & Co. in 1826, reaching the Maudlin in 1835 and the Hutton in 1846.[429] In 1847 the enterprise was sold to Messrs Bell & Co.[430] and in the 1880s worked under the title Wearmouth Coal Co. The 'C' pit was sunk in 1906. In the first half of the 1960s the surface and underground works were reconstructed, with a tower-mounted friction drum winder over a new 'D' shaft, to work undersea reserves. Work then concentrated on the Yard, Maudlin and Low Main. In 1992 it was estimated, by the American mining firm, J.T. Boyd, to have 56.2 million tonnes of reserves, with an expected life of 35.1 years.[431] On 13 October 1992 it was included in the closure list announced by Heseltine. Subsequently, it was one of ten included in a moratorium on 19 October. The pit was closed in December 1993 with the loss of 670 jobs, but was then offered to private enterprise.

The Nottinghamshire firms, R.J. Budge and Caledonian Mining, put in bids for the pit. Budge withdrew in March 1994 following removal of equipment from the site by British Coal. Caledonian Mining finally pulled out at the end of March, apparently because of pumping costs, the chlorine content of the coal and the threat to local markets from Ellington colliery, though these reasons were bitterly attacked by the unions. Actual operations finally ceased on 8 July 1994 at the Yard GG5 face. The colliery was demolished and the site used for the new Sunderland football stadium.

In 1873 the lodge had a blue banner with red border, inscribed 'Do justice, love mercy, walk humbly with God'.[432]

The lodge later chose the courtroom scene concerning Mr Roberts and the cancelling of the bond, with the title, 'In God is all our trust'.

The 1921 DMA damask silk banner, from Tutill's City Road works, again showed the courtroom scene, with the title, 'The Cancelling of the Yearly Bond by Mr Roberts in 1869', and the message, 'Come let us reason together'. The reverse carried a split design showing a miner leaving home to go to work, 'The last good morning', and his widow seeking aid, 'We claim compensation'.

This was replaced by one with a similar design, which was unfurled by Joshua Ritson in March 1931.[433]

These designs were repeated on a Tutill banner of around 1950, painted at Chesham, using silk woven at the City Road works. It is a creamy-gold and blue damask silk, with a red border, and measures 8 ft 1 in × 8 ft 2 in (246 × 248 cm).
*Location*: Red Hill.

Probably around 1967 the lodge acquired the 1954 Chester Moor banner (q.v.) showing the Hermitage on one side and a Sunshine of Liberty design on the other, with the verse,

> These things shall be;
> a loftier race than e'er the world hath known shall rise,
> with flame of freedom in their souls,
> and light of knowledge in their eyes.

The banner was produced by Tutill at Chesham and is blue silk with an orange border. It measures 8 ft × 9 ft (244 × 274 cm).
*Location*: Red Hill.

This was replaced by a banner showing the courtroom scene, with the 'Last good morning / We claim compensation' design on the reverse. The banner is by Turtle & Pearce Ltd (no. 1079) and is green with a red border. It measures 7 ft 7 in × 6 ft 9 in (232 × 206 cm). It was badly damaged in an incident during the march back to work at the conclusion of the 1984–5 strike, but was repaired and was present at the 1985 Scottish Miners' Gala.[434]
*Location*: Red Hill.

The succeeding NUM banner was purchased in 1986 and was unfurled by Arthur Scargill at the Miners' Welfare, Thompson Road,

Monkwearmouth banner with the theme of the miner leaving home never to return alive and the widow seeking assistance, 'In God is all our trust'.

Southwick, just before the Gala.[435] The banner was produced by Red Wedge, of Brighton, and has a central eliptical panel with portraits of 'Cook, Hepburn, Scargill'. Hanging on chains below it is a plaque with the words, 'As in the past, we fight for the future'. The other side carries the traditional court scene, with an inscription at the base, 'Come let us reason together'. It is turquoise silk with a red border.

*Location*: Bill Etherington MP, Parliamentary office, House of Commons.

The Monkwearmouth banner, with portraits of Thomas Hepburn, A.J. Cook and Arthur Scargill.

## MORRISON

The Morrison North and South shafts were sunk by Thomas Hedley & Bros in 1869, and they became associated with the Louisa Old and New and William shafts. They were controlled from 1925 by Holmside & South Moor Collieries Ltd. An explosion on 22 August 1947 killed nineteen instantly, with three others dying later in the year.[436] The pit was merged with South Moor in the 1950s. The South pit was closed in 1961, and the North in 1964.

The NUM banner carries portraits of A.J. Cook and T. Hepburn, with the motto, 'He who would be free himself must strike the blow'. The reverse side shows Conishead Priory. It is red with a blue border and measures 7 ft 10 in × 7 ft 4 in (239 × 224 cm).
*Location*: Beamish (1983-129).

The 1956 banner was unfurled by W. Stones, MP for Consett, at New Kyo Miners' Hall. It carried portraits of Cook and Hepburn, while the reverse showed 'Red Hill and Memorial Gardens'.

## MORRISON BUSTY

The sinking, by Holmside & South Moor Collieries Ltd, of the West (upcast) and East (downcast) shafts, was carried out in 1923–5.[437] The 1926 strike delayed coal drawing until 1928. In the 1940s the pit worked the Townley, Busty and Brockwell, and a German plough was introduced in 1947. In 1956 the Louisa workings were linked to Morrison Busty and this development work was followed by a reorganization in 1959–60, with the electrification of the winder, introduction of skips and the building of a new washery. Louisa coal was wrought by pneumatic picks, principally from the Low Main, Brass Thill and Hutton. The Harvey, Top and Bottom Busty and Bottom Brockwell were worked at Morrison Busty by pneumatic picks on longwall faces. The Louisa section was closed on 8 February 1964. Declining reserves in the principal seam, the Busty, and faulting in the Harvey forced the pits closure on 5 October 1973.[438]

The 1920s banner carried the messages, 'United to retain the just reward of our labour' and 'Unity is Strength'.

A later DMA banner carried large roundel portrait of A.J. Cook. In 1955 an A.J. Cook banner carried the message, 'Agitate, Educate, Organise'.

The 1966 NUM banner was acquired from Lumley Sixth pit (q.v.), showing 'The Reign of Peace' and the smiths beating swords into ploughshares. It was carried into the Cathedral for the Gala service in 1971.[439]

*Location*: Annfield Plain Central Methodist Church. Destroyed by fire in an arson attack on the church, 10 March 1993.[440]

## MURTON

South Hetton Coal Co. (Col. Braddyll & Partners) sank three shafts – the East, Middle (Polka) and West (or New pit) between 1838 and 1843 to work the Hutton.[441] An explosion on 15 August 1848 killed fourteen.[442] A Koepe winding plant was set up at the West pit in 1922. A further explosion on 26 June 1942 killed thirteen[443] The pit was linked in 1959 to a new main drawing shaft at Hawthorn (sunk 1952–8) and was merged with South Hetton in 1983 and Eppleton in 1986. Work concentrated on the C seam, High Main and Harvey, using chainless haulage in-web shearers. Roof collapses close to areas previously worked and increasing costs led to closure on 29 November 1991.[444]

The banner at the 1872 and 1873 Galas showed a miner with a pick and lamp and an owner, with the lines, 'Masters give unto your servants that which is just and equal, knowing that ye also have a Master in heaven' and 'Manhood suffrage we demand'. The reverse showed a widow at a graveside, with an angel, and the line, 'Oppress not the fatherless or the widow'.[445]

The 1884 banner showed John Wilson presenting a petition to Gladstone, with MacDonald, Crawford and Lloyd Jones present.[446]

The 1925 DMA banner carries portraits of Ramsey MacDonald, James Robson, James Gray and Ald. Rees Williams (the lodge president), with a depiction of the war memorial and aged miners' homes on the reverse.[447] It is a purple and gold damask silk, with a yellow border, and was produced by G. Tutill at the City Road works.

*Location*: Murton Welfare Hall.

The 1955 NUM banner was unfurled by Lord Lawson of Beamish on 15 July. It shows a miner, holding a book inscribed 'Knowledge is Power' and standing over the Houses of Parliament. The scene is accompanied by the motto, 'The future is "In your hands"'. The reverse side shows Conishead Priory. The banner is red silk, with a blue border, and measures 6 ft 7 in × 7 ft 8 in (200 × 235 cm).
*Location*: Red Hill.

Murton then received the Aneurin Bevan/Wheatsheaf banner from Handen Hold (q.v.) in 1971.
*Location*: Murton Welfare Hall.

A later NUM banner, by Turtle & Pearce (No. 678), repeated the 1955 design of the miner standing over Parliament. The reverse shows the central figure of a miner holding up a bannerette inscribed 'NUM Unity is Strength'. Flanking him are bannerettes inscribed, 'A Secure Future' and 'Health and Safety'. The banner is red with a blue border and measures 7 ft 6 in × 6 ft 5 in (229 × 196 cm).
*Location*: Murton Welfare Hall.

The Murton NUM North East Area banner carries a painting of the colliery with the message, 'Production for Use / Not for Profit'. The scene is flanked by smaller cameos of the local 'Cenotaph', 'Colliery Inn', 'Murton Welfare Hall' and the 'Aged Miners' Homes'. The reverse side bears a large portrait of 'Thomas Hepburn Pioneer of Mining Trade Unions', with text below:

> The time will come when the
> golden chain which binds the
> tyrants together will be snapped, when
> owners will only be like ordinary men , and will
> have to sigh for the days gone by.
> Thomas Hepburn 1832.

Around the portrait are four smaller scenes – a miner behind bars, 'Victimised'; a baton-wielding police cavalryman bearing down on a protester, 'State Violence'; miners carrying their previous banner, 'Forward'; and a canteen scene, 'Support Groups'. The banner was produced by Chippenham Design and is red with a blue border. It was in use by 1992.
*Location*: Murton Welfare Hall.

NETTLESWORTH

There was a colliery here by 1856, worked by Messrs Jonasshon & Co., but by the 1880s Nettlesworth was operated by Elliott & Hunter.[448] It was disused by 1896 and replaced by workings near the Black Burn, south of Nettlesworth Hall. The site was probably disused by 1920. By the 1930s the West, Pump and Railway drifts had been driven. Nettlesworth Dene drift operated from 1945 until exhaustion of reserves led to closure on 27 September 1974.[449]

The 1873 Gala banner showed a checkweighman saying to a young miner, 'Wait a little longer and I will free you'. Adjoining this scene was a depiction of a master and miner, with a girl appealing to the master 'not to take all from our fathers; give him a fair share of that he laboured hard for'. Near the girl was a boy facing a bishop, whose mitre was engraved '£16,000 a year', with the appeal, 'It is you that rob us of our bread, Beware our Saviour is on the other side'. The bishop pointed to the master saying, 'Leave something more for me'. These scenes were accompanied by the mottoes, 'He that oppresseth the poor to increase his riches shall surely come to want' and 'The days of serfdom are fast dying out'. The reverse side showed Christ turning the tradesmen out of the temple: 'My house shall be called a house of prayer; but ye have made it a den of thieves.'[450]

## NEW BRANCEPETH (SLEETBURN)

Some small-scale activity was underway in the 1850s near Scouts House farm, but the main sinking was at the site of Sleetburn farm, for Brodie Cochrane, in 1856–8.[451] Three shafts were used. New Brancepeth Coal Co. was absorbed by Weardale Steel, Coal & Coke Co. Ltd in 1933. Veins of witherite and barytes were also worked, and the pit had a washing and milling plant by 1911. Barytes was used in the manufacture of white paint, for bleaching flannel and shoddy cloth and in asbestos goods. Witherite was used in the preparation of barium compounds and in treating wallpaper and linoleum. Coal reserves were gradually exhausted – the Busty and Ballarat in 1934, Brockwell in 1944 and Tilley in 1952. By 1952 output was 400 tons per week, and the pit was closed in June 1953.[452]

The 1872 Gala banner showed two miners standing in front of a colliery, and above the scene it read 'United we stand, divided we fall'. On the reverse was the emblem of Justice: 'Masters, do unto your servants as ye would that they should do unto you.'[453]

The banner used in the 1930s showed Conishead Priory and the 'Emancipation of Labour'.

The banner seen at the 1946 Gala carried a painting of the Miners' Hall at Red Hill.[454] The reverse was probably the bundle of sticks fable, in a rectangular format.[455]

## NEWFIELD

The Robson and Burnett pits were sunk c. 1840, and worked by John Robson & Partners (Newfield Coal Co.), with output transported to West Hartlepool docks by rail.[456] By the 1870s it was operated by Bolckow, Vaughan & Co.,[457] and in the 1890s the Busty was worked, with drifting to the Beaumont and Harvey.[458] It was later amalgamated with Byers Green.

The company was absorbed by Dorman, Long & Co. Ltd in 1929, but continued to be operated after nationalization by Dorman, Long (Steel) Ltd from 1954 to 1959. Newfield drift closed in March 1963.

The banner at the 1874 Gala showed Alexander MacDonald MP holding a tablet inscribed 'The Mines Regulation Bill' and standing beside a weeping widow and orphans. The reverse showed an arbitration scene: 'Behold how good it is for brethren to dwell together in harmony.'[459]

A post-1896 damask silk banner shows W.H. Patterson, A. MacDonald and W. Crawford, seated, with the message, 'Gone but not forgotten'. The reverse carries a pattern-book 'Amicitia Amor et Veritas' design, with the motto, 'We unite to assist each other'. The banner was produced by Tutill at the City Road works and has brass tie discs. It measures 10 ft × 8 ft 10 in (305 × 269 cm).
*Location*: Beamish (1984-10-12).

NEW HERRINGTON

*See also* Philadelphia.

Mining began in the Philadelphia–New Herrington area in the eighteenth century with the Margaret (Peggy) pit, followed in 1816 by the Dorothea (Dolly). The workings were bought in 1819 by the Earl of Durham. By the early 1870s the Dolly worked Five Quarter and Maudlin and the Peggy worked Hutton, Five Quarter and Main. Further development took place in 1874, with the sinking of the Lady Beatrice (or New pit) with two shafts.[460] Output reached 1,600 tonnes per day at the end of the nineteenth century, and machinery was introduced to maintain high levels. On 3 June 1885 twenty-three workers were drowned in the Peggy. The Peggy closed in the 1930s, but was retained for ventilation. The Dolly closed in 1958. Reconstruction work took place in the mid-1950s, with power loading and skip winding.[461] New Herrington closed in November 1985.

The DMA banner of around 1932 carries an 'Emancipation of Labour' pattern-book design, with the motto, 'Workers of all lands unite! You have nothing to lose but your chains, You have a world to win'. The reverse shows the frontage of Conishead Priory. The banner is turquoise-blue silk with a red border, measures 7 ft 11 in × 6 ft 8 in (241 × 203 cm) and has the painted label, 'G Tutill London'.
*Location*: Red Hill.

The 1955 NUM banner shows 'Men of the People', with linked roundel portraits of A.J. Cook, Peter Lee and J. Keir Hardie set against the background of a colliery scene and miner's lamp. The reverse carries the motto, 'For Peace and Freedom', and a painting of 'Miners' Hall and Memorial Garden, Red Hill, Durham'. This banner, produced by Tutill at Chesham, was noted at the 1956 Gala.[462]
*Location*: Red Hill.

The lodge then acquired the Fishburn banner (q.v.). This carries portraits of J. Keir Hardie, A.J. Cook and G. Lansbury on the front, and 'The Cause of Labour is the Hope of the World' on the back.
*Location*: Fishburn Working Men's Club.

### NEW SHILDON

Shildon colliery was operated by the Shildon Coal Co. Ltd, who worked the Busty and Brockwell in the 1890s.[463] Shildon Lodge colliery closed in June 1928.[464] New Shildon closed in August 1965.

The lodge attended a manhood suffrage demonstration at Bishop Auckland in 1873, apparently with a banner.[465]

The NUM banner carried a portrait of Hugh Dalton MP. This was later transferred to Whitworth Park (q.v.).

### NEWTON CAP

The colliery was sunk in 1859 and was worked by W.C. Stobart & Co., sometimes under the name of Toronto colliery, and in the 1880s by Henry Stobart & Co.[466] By 1894 the Harvey, Constantine, Five Quarter and Brockwell seams had been located. It was closed in the late 1920s or 1930s, but was reopened by the North Bitchburn Fireclay Co. Ltd in 1937 and reached a manpower peak of 119 in 1950. The pit closed in 1967.

The 1873 banner design was devised by an old miner, drawn up by George Coxon, another miner, and painted in Newcastle.[467] It was unfurled at Newton Cap Hotel on 15 February. The obverse showed scenes of unorganized and organized miners. In the first, an owner, with a box of gold, stood at one end of a balance, outweighing an emaciated miner, watched by other miners – 'Unorganised and Plentiful Labour'. The miner asked, 'Let me have fair', but the owner replied, 'You must yield. You see I am too heavy for you'. In the next scene, 'Labour Scarce', the miners had pulled down their end of the balance, 'We have you now'. The owner replied, 'A truce. Let us meet and try to come to terms'. In a third scene, the miners' agent and employers' chairman are set at either end of an equal balance, 'Arbitration', with the line, 'We agree to settle our differences in future by this means, And let Justice hold the balance. Hurrah for Justice!' The reverse theme was 'Justice leading to home-comfort and happiness, is the true object aimed at by all intelligent unionists'. There were three scenes: blindfolded Justice holding her scales; in the centre, 'A happy home: the result of organisation and arbitration', with a miner and his family at dinner, seated in a comfortable parlour with a prominent bookcase; while the third scene showed a miner and employer meeting, 'Henceforward let strife cease between us, and our joint aim be the true happiness of all'. The banner was double silk, 11 ft × 10 ft (335 × 305 cm).

### NORTH BIDDICK

A pit was working in the eighteenth century, with an 80 fathom shaft. On 18 January 1743 miners holed into an old drift. Gas in the goaf was ignited, killing seventeen. Again on 6 December 1773 gas was fired, killing nineteen men and boys.[468] In the 1880s it was worked by Sir George Elliott.

A DMA damask silk banner carries the bundle of sticks fable, with the old man holding a scroll inscribed 'Unity is Strength'. A ribbon over the illustration bears the motto, 'United to obtain the just reward of our labour'. The reverse shows the 'Unity is Strength' image, with two miners shaking hands in front of an angel. The banner was produced at Tutill's City Road works and has been repaired in the past. It measures 9 ft 10 in × 9 ft 2 in (300 × 280 cm).
*Location*: Beamish (1984-10-13).

## NORTH BITCHBURN

Sinking took place in 1840 to work the Brockwell.[469] It was operated initially by Henry Stobart & Co, in the 1880s by the North Bitchburn Coal Co. Ltd, and from 1934 by the North Bitchburn Fireclay Co. Ltd. The workforce of 202 in 1930 dropped to 150 in 1940 and fell to 44 by 1960. The pit closed in 1966.

The obverse of the 1873 Gala banner showed a board of conciliation and the motto, 'Unity and Harmony', with a widow at a graveside on the reverse.[470]

## NORTH BRANCEPETH COLLIERIES

These comprised Littleburn and Broompark collieries. The North Brancepeth Coal Co. went into liquidation in 1931.

The banner at the 1873 Gala showed several miners turning a wheel, with the verse,

> We miners of England have all begun the scheme,
> To put our shoulders to the wheel and work the great machine;
> We have tried single handed, and found it would not do at all,
> But now we have united, and tyranny must fall

The reverse showed the first committee of masters and men that met at Newcastle, 'Unity is our motto'.[471]

## NORTH HETTON COLLIERIES

These comprised the Hazard and Moorsley pits. The company became a subsidiary of the Hetton Coal Co. and was taken over by Joicey in 1911.

The 1873 Gala banner bore the Good Samaritan on one side, with the line, 'Do unto all men as you would that all men should do unto you'. The reverse showed MacDonald addressing a crowd of miners who are waving their caps.[472]

A later DMA banner, in use probably around the 1920s, carried a central panel containing three roundels bearing portraits of an unidentified figure, Jack Adair and James Robson.

## NORWOOD

Although there had been mining in the area in the eighteenth century,[473] a colliery was leased to the Earl of Strathmore in 1807. A series of partnerships then followed, until a lease was secured by the Durham County Coal Co. in the 1830s, and later by the Northern Coal Co., until its collapse in the 1840s. By 1869 the operation, along with Thrushwood, was run by the Norwood Coal Co. (Miles Bruce, John Todd, Michael Brown and John Hedley), but it was put up for sale in 1898.[474] It was reopened in 1900 by Dunston & Swalwell Garesfield Colliery Co.[475] and mining continued until 1931.

A banner was unfurled in 1874.[476] On one side was the Lion and Lamb, with the words 'May the rose and the thistle long flourish and twine round the sprig of shillelagh and shamrock so green'. The reverse showed the colliery owners, E. Charlton, M. Bruce and M. Brown, with the overman, W. Pearson, talking with four old men from the colliery, Messrs Dinsdale, Wilkinson, Bell and Longstaffe.

## OAKENSHAW

The Brancepeth 'B' pit was sunk by Straker & Love in 1855. It closed in 1967.

The banner displayed at the 1872 Gala, and present in 1873, showed two horses pulling tubs on a tramway. The driver of a willing horse holds a placard inscribed 'Eight Hours'. The other, with an unwilling horse, has an attached placard inscribed 'Twelve hours'. The reverse carried a design of 'Friendship', with the motto, 'Hitherto we have been foes; henceforth we will be friends'.[477]

## OLD DURHAM

The pit was sunk in 1849 to work the Low Main and Hutton, and closed around 1893.[478]

The banner at the 1872 and 1873 Galas carried the emblem of 'Excelsior' on the obverse, and the Lion and the Lamb on the reverse.[479]

## OLD ETHERLEY

This was an H. Stobart & Co. colliery. *See* Etherley.

The 1873 Gala banner depicted Capital and Labour, with a colliery scene in the background and the line, 'Do unto others as ye would others do unto you'. The reverse showed the figure of Justice.[480]

This banner, or one with a repeated design, was at the 1893 Gala.[481]

## OUSTON

There was mining here in the early nineteenth century by Messrs Hunt, Perkins & Co. On 3 November 1817 one person was killed and three badly burnt in an explosion.[482] The shafts comprised the 'A', 'B', 'C', and 'E' pits, with Ouston Winning. Later the principal operator was E.M. Perkins, owners of Birtley iron works, and the Ouston and Urpeth pits, working under the title of Owners of Pelaw Main Collieries Ltd from 1926. The 'B' worked from 1824 until 1875. Air compressing and electric power plants were erected at Ouston 'E' in 1914.[483] Ouston and Ouston Winning lodges were united on 20 May 1916.[484] By 1928 three seams were worked by 1,200 men and boys at the 'E' pit.[485] A new winding engine was installed in the same year. The 'E' merged with the 'C' pit in 1957. The site was closed in January 1959.

The banner carried to the 1897 Gala was marked 'On Strike Against Non-Unionists'.[486]

A banner, probably of the 1920s, carries portraits of A.J. Cook, W. Whiteley, T.H. Cann, J. Robson and J. Gilliland on one side and Durham Cathedral on the other. It carries the mark 'G. Tutill London' and is blue with a red border. It measures 9 ft 6 in × 8 ft 3 in (290 × 251 cm). This was later transferred to Black House lodge (q.v.).

The subsequent DMA banner had a roundel scene of 'Conishead Priory Convalescent Home for Durham Mine Workers'.[487] This was transferred to Tudhoe in 1962 (q.v.).

## PAGEBANK

The colliery, also known as South Brancepeth, was sunk *c.* 1855, with the pit divided by bratticing into three shafts – two as downcast and one as upcast. A fire in the shaft on 30 September 1858 killed ten.[488] At this time the pit was owned by the West Hartlepool Dock & Railway Co., but certainly by 1879 it was operated by Bell Bros, who were taken over by Dorman, Long & Co. in 1923. The working out of the Busty and Brockwell led to closure in July 1931.[489]

The banner of South Brancepeth displayed at the 1872 and 1873 Galas showed clasped hands over a beehive:

> People throughout the land
> Join in one social band,
> And save yourselves.

The reverse advised, 'Let your watchword be justice and liberty'. The illustration included a globe, a rose, shamrock and thistle, with the additional line, 'Toil unwearied to save yourselves'.[490]

The 1884 banner carried the figures of Bradlaugh, holding the pensions list, Crawford, with arbitration, and Burt, with the Employers' Liability Bill.[491] The reverse scene referred to royalty rents, with an owner taking 10*d* per ton for no effort, and a miner receiving 1*s* per ton for hard labour.

A fragment of banner painting, conceivably part of the above banner, shows a white bearded miner, wearing cap, scarf, jacket and hoggers, and carrying a pick over his right shoulder. Restored and framed, it now measures 2 ft 6.25 in × 4 ft 7.25 in (77 × 141 cm).

*Location*: Beamish (1965-9). Donated by Spennymoor UDC.

The banner of around 1910 carries a similar message – 'Let your watchword be justice and liberty'. Around the border of the large central roundel is the message, 'People throughout the land join in one social band and save yourselves'. The scene shows a top-hatted owner and a miner carrying a pick over his shoulder. The owner holds a scroll inscribed 'Land owner's coal rent ten pence per ton. To workmen for hewing coal one shilling per ton tax on labour'. In the lower part of the roundel, below the figures, are the inscriptions, 'One colliery on my estate returns me £10,000 per year without risk of life or capital' and 'The same colliery returns to me £60 per year for labour and risk to life and limb every day'. The reverse carries a portrait of John Wilson in Doctor of Civil Law robes. The banner was later transferred to Whitworth Park (q.v.).

PELAW MAIN

This colliery was operated by the Perkins family (of Birtley Iron Co.) along with Bewicke Main, Ouston and Urpeth. The company name changed to Owners of Pelaw Main Collieries Ltd in 1906, and Pelaw Main Collieries Ltd in 1926. The firm came under the control of a French syndicate, which collapsed following the German occupation of Paris in 1940.

The 1873 Gala banner carried an arbitration scene, 'Let brotherly love prevail'. The reverse showed lords and commoners petitioning Edward I to stop the importation of coal in 1306, with the motto, 'Knowledge is power'.[492]

PELTON

Pelton colliery was sunk by Messrs Kingscote & Co., but was later operated by James Reid & Partners, Messrs Swabey & Co. and Messrs W.C. Curteis & Co. (up to 1860).[493] In 1866 the pit was operated by a company with W.J. Hutchinson as managing partner. At this time the Hutton was worked, and the Busty had started in 1865. An explosion in the Busty on 31 October 1866 killed twenty-four.[494] By the 1880s the pit was in the hands of Lord Dunsoney & Partners[495] and in 1901 was controlled by the Owners of Pelton Colliery Ltd. It was closed in 1928 and placed in the hands of the Receiver. A possible sale to Arthur Kellett & Son fell through, and the site was dismantled.[496] Mining was restarted in 1929 by M.H. Kellett,[497] possibly under the name of Mid Durham Coal Co., who operated Pelton Fell in 1932. In that year three men were killed in a cage accident.[498] The colliery finally closed in February 1965.

The banner carried to the Galas of 1872 and 1873 showed, on one side, what was said to be a somewhat unrealistic representation of a hewer, sitting on a cracket, ripping coal, with a large horse apparently about to draw tubs. The reverse showed the interior of a cottage, with the miner handing his wages to his wife. The banner also bore the motto, 'United we stand, Divided we fall'.[499]

The NUM banner shows a female figure pulling back the cover of 'Oppression' to reveal to a group of miners and a woman an idyllic scene of a pleasant house and garden. The reverse shows a sickbed scene, 'Help and sympathy in time of sickness'. Only the ribbon and panel now survive, measuring 7 ft 7 in × 6 ft 2 in (231 × 188 cm).
*Location*: Beamish (1984-10-14).

## PENSHER

The site was leased by Sir George Elliott from 1864 to 1879, and was then taken by the Earl of Durham. The 'D' pit was sunk in 1931.[500]

The banner at the 1872 and 1873 Galas carried representations relating to education and the short-time movement, with a school scene of eager and tired pupils. The reverse carried the bundle of sticks image.[501]

## PHILADELPHIA

*See also* New Herrington.

The 1872 Gala banner carried an arbitration scene, with two figures (including Mr Morton, agent to the Earl of Durham), seated at a table, with a group of workers standing at the opposite side. The reverse showed a master and worker shaking hands. The banner was produced by W. Whaite, of Manchester, and cost £22 14s.[502]

A later DMA Tutill banner carries the portrait of A.J. Cook, Peter Lee and J. Keir Hardie. The reverse shows a version of the 'Friendship, Love and Truth' design. The banner measures 8 ft 10 in × 8 ft 2 in (269 × 249 cm) and is blue with a red border.
*Location*: Beamish (1984-10-15).

## PITTINGTON

The pits comprised the Buddle, Adolphus, Londonderry and Lady Seaham, which were operated by Lord Londonderry.[503] The Buddle closed between 1856 and 1897. The operation was worked by North Hetton Coal Co. The Londonderry/Adolphus closed in 1891, and the Lady Seaham was not restarted after the 1912 strike.

The 1873 Gala banner bore emblems of Peace and Plenty.[504]

## PONTOP

A number of pits were worked at Pontop and its surroundings, including the Spring pits, the Hive, the Bog and the North pit, near Bantling Castle.[505] Pontop South colliery was just west of Annfield Plain, with the Moor pit near Harelaw, the Staple at West Kyo and Pontop Pea pit southwest of Whiteley Head. The Success pit, at Pontop Pike, was an air shaft in the late nineteenth century, but was operated in the 1930s by R. Southern of Hamsterley House, Dipton.[506] In the 1880s John Bowes & Partners were also working at Pontop.

The 1873 Gala banner showed MacDonald, in the centre of a group of miners, and the verse,

Our great race accomplished, has been won by tedious fight,
  Weary months and years of effort have from darkness brought the light.

The reverse showed a meeting of the joint committee of mineworkers and men.

Oh men of dauntless daring, go arm you for the fight.
Stand up for the wrongs of millions, do battle for the right;
Who do their duty bravely despite of passing ill,
Through life's rugged journey as men of wisdom will.[507]

### RAINTON AND LETCH COLLIERIES

This collective title covers Londonderry's Rainton collieries of Adventure (q.v.), Resolution (1816–19), Nicholson (1817), Plane (1817) and Meadows (1821–4) pits; the Letch, or Alexandrina (1823–4), was near Moorsley.

The banner at the 1873 Gala carried a widow and orphan scene on one side, 'We succour the widows and befriend the fatherless', and on the reverse, an arbitration scene. The latter was accompanied by the lines,

Masters, give unto your servants that which is just and equal, knowing that ye also have a master in heaven. Servants in all things obey your masters according to the flesh, not with eye service as men pleasers, but singleness of heart, fearing God.[508]

### RAMSHAW

A colliery was operated from 1807 by the Earl of Strathmore, and in the 1830s there were four shafts, A–D. The Ramshaw Coal Co. Ltd were mining here from 1942. Operations ceased in October 1959.

The NUM banner carries an 'Emancipation of Labour' pattern-book design on one side and the traditional view of Durham Cathedral on the other. The banner is red silk, with a blue border, and was produced at Tutill's City Road works. It has brass discs at the bottom corners of the silk for blue ties and measures 8 ft 8 in × 8 ft (264 × 244 cm).
*Location*: Red Hill.

### RANDOLPH

This North Bitchburn Coal Co. pit was sunk in 1893 near the Wigglesworth fault. In 1889 the Brockwell was ventilated by a 30-ft

Waddle fan. Coal was raised in double-decker cages, and was processed by jigging screen, with a Luhrig washer, before coking in eighty-six Coppee ovens.[509] Around 1927 it became part of Pease & Partners mining operations, but passed to the Randolph Coal Co. Ltd in 1933. Following nationalization, a new drift was driven to the Hutton in 1953. The pit was closed in February 1962.

A DMA banner was unfurled by Arthur Henderson MP on 12 June 1909. It carries a large panel with a detailed perspective view of the colliery, cokeyard and rail track, with the title at the base, 'Randolph Lodge Evenwood'. Randolph had Koppers waste heat ovens. The painted scene includes the 1906 0–4–0 saddle tank *Mostyn*, in front of the oven-quenching bench, pulling loaded North Bitchburn Coal Co. Ltd five-plank open wagons. The reverse shows an expanded Good Samaritan scene, with mottoes of 'Universal brotherhood' and 'Help in Time of Need'. The banner was produced by H. Slingsby of Nuneaton and is turquoise-blue silk with a red border. The silk ground is now incomplete, but is 11 ft (335 cm) long.
*Location*: Red Hill.

The 1954 NUM banner carries small circular portraits of 'C. Attlee' and 'H. Dalton', over a panel showing the colliery, with the first-aid station in the foreground. At the base is the inscription 'Randolph Colliery'. The reverse shows a Good Samaritan scene, with the motto, 'Go thou and do likewise'. The banner is blue silk, with a red border, and was produced by Tutill at Chesham (no. 754.) It measures 7 ft 11 in × 9 ft 1.5 in (241 × 278 cm).
*Location*: Red Hill.


RAVENSWORTH

Mining was undertaken in the eighteenth century. On 10 June 1757 fifteen men and boys were gassed.[510] E.M. Perkins (subsequently Owners of Pelaw Main Collieries Ltd, 1906, and, in 1926, Pelaw Main Collieries Ltd) operated the Betty and Shop pits (Team colliery) from the 1850s. In 1930 they added Ravensworth Ann, and in 1936 Ravensworth Park drift. Ann's Metal and High Main seams closed in 1960, and work concentrated on the Tilley using ploughs. Ravensworth Shop, or Allerdene (q.v.), closed in February 1962, and in 1968 coal drawing was transferred to Ravensworth Park. The Ann was linked underground to Kibblesworth in April 1973 and most of the surface operations at the former site closed.

The 1873 Gala banner carried representations of the Lion and Lamb and 'Knowledge is Power'. One side carried the mottoes, 'Labour and capital combined, bless and elevate mankind', 'Success to the trade in coal' and 'Justice to each and love to all'. Below, was a figure of Justice, flanked by a man holding a ball and a miner with a safety lamp. At the base were the lines,

Let's hold fast the profession of our faith without wavering, not forsaking the assembling of ourselves together, as the manner of some is, and let's consider one another, and provoke into love and good works.[511]

The banner was blue with a white fringe.

A later DMA banner, which was certainly at the 1947 Gala, carried a traditional view of the west end of Durham Cathedral in a rectangular panel, with Conishead Priory on the reverse.[512]

The 1949 NUM banner, produced by Tutill at Chesham, bears a shield panel showing 'The Hermitage, Chester-le-Street, Rehabilitation Centre'. The reverse has a view of 'Conishead Priory Convalescent Home for Durham Mineworkers'. It is a red and pale orange damask silk, with a blue border, and measures 8 ft 7 in × 8 ft 6 in (262 × 257 cm).
*Location*: Red Hill.

A subsequent NUM banner carries a painting of Conishead Priory Convalescent Home for Durham Mineworkers on one side and a view of the Racecourse on Gala Day, 'The Big Meeting', on the other. Produced by Tutill at Chesham, it is blue with a red border and measures 6 ft 7 in × 7 ft 9 in (200 × 236 cm).
*Location*: Gateshead Central Library, Prince Consort Road, Gateshead.

RODDYMOOR

The area had good seams of Main, Five Quarter, Ballarat and Yard, and a pit was sunk by Joseph Pease in the 1840s to work the Main.[513] There are references to leases in 1851 and 1873.[514] Manpower levels in the first half of the twentieth century were over 1,000 and reached a peak of 1,055 in 1940. After nationalization the operation was merged with Wooley in 1951. The pit closed in August 1963.

The banner at the 1873 Gala carried portraits of Joseph Cowen, Joseph Fowler and Joseph Laverick, with the verse,

> Such men are gems of priceless worth,
> The real saviours of the earth;
> They bring reforms and show the way,
> To better things – a brighter day;
> Where shall we find through history's page,
> Three brighter names grace any age.

The other side showed a miner standing near a colliery, with the verse,

> Give me the pick and the men that can use it;
> They turn the black coal into bright shining gold;
> What would our futures have been, lads, without it,
> When the lands lay all bare and the north winds blow cold.[515]

A subsequent DMA banner carried a Good Samaritan scene, with the motto, 'Go thou and do likewise', on one side and 'We succour the widow and orphan' on the other.[516]

The 1954 NUM banner shows the 'Big Meeting' on one side and Burnhope reservoir on the other. This was transferred to Brancepeth lodge (q.v.) in 1963.

## ROUGH LEA

A colliery was sunk in 1858 by Henry Stobart & Co.[517] and later operated under the title of the North Bitchburn Coal Co. Ltd. It closed in 1926, but reopened as a Pease & Partners subsidiary until *c.* 1931.

The 1873 Gala banner carried portraits of Home Secretary Bruce, with MacDonald and Crawford. The reverse bore the forty-first Psalm: 'The lord will deliver him in the time of trouble.'[518]

The 1890 banner[519] carries the title 'Durham Miners Association Rough Lea Lodge' on a blue ribbon, over a large roundel showing a child holding stalks of corn, sitting on the back of a lion and feeding a garlanded lamb. The sky is painted with a loop of cloud around sunlight illuminating a heart and hand design. Within the scene is a scroll bearing the motto, 'Peace and Friendship'. The reverse carries a large roundel with a Good Samaritan scene; the inscriptions around the border read 'Bear ye one another's burdens' and 'Blessed is he that considereth the poor'. It is red silk with a blue border and measures 9 ft 9 in × 7ft 10 in (297 × 239 cm). *Location*: New Hunwick Methodist Church.

The 1890 Rough Lea banner. After restoration, the banner was dedicated by Arthur Scargill and blessed by the Revd Paul Blanch at New Hunwick Methodist Chapel, on 16 May 1994.

RYHOPE

Sinkings were carried out in the 1840s, with further development in 1905. By 1913 the Maudlin, Low Main, Hutton and Harvey were worked.[520] In 1933 the vertical winding engine was replaced by a 500 h.p. electric Frazer & Chalmers engine.[521] This was superseded by a tower-mounted multi-rope friction drum winder in 1956. Mining in the 1950s concentrated on the Five Quarter, Low Main, Harvey and Busty.[522] Output per man shift reached 26 cwt in 1960, but in 1963 the Harvey and Busty were stopped and work concentrated on the Five Quarter. Financial losses forced closure on 26 November 1966.[523]

The banner carried at the 1873 Gala bore portraits of H.A. Bruce (the Home Secretary), MacDonald, Burt and Crawford, and the inscription, 'The Mines Regulation Bill, passed August 10, 1872. Arbitration, by which we got our boys 9 hours per day.'[524]

A later DMA banner carried a large portrait of Gladstone, while the reverse probably also showed Gladstone, in a circular panel, with four accompanying portraits.

In 1925 a new banner was unfurled by Peter Lee.[525] On one side was a portrait of Ramsey MacDonald, accompanied by Sam Wraith, Robert Richardson MP, Tom Cann and Keir Hardie. The reverse carried a sickbed scene with the motto, 'Bear ye one anothers burden'.

Another DMA banner carried a central portrait of A.J. Cook, with accompanying portraits of Joseph Fee, George Lumley, John Trotter, Robert Richardson, Sam Wraith and J. Keir Hardie. The reverse carried the theme, 'Bear ye one anothers burden'.[526]

The 1950 NUM banner showed a miner with his wife and two children greeting a soldier, sailor and airman, with the message, 'Unity in Peace, In War'.[527] The reverse showed Conishead Priory.

The 1964 banner was unfurled by Harold Wilson, on 17 July. It shows aged miners' homes, 'Pioneers of the Movement / Haven of Rest', on one side and Conishead Priory on the other. It was at the 1966 Gala, but was then transferred to Silksworth lodge (q.v.). In 1973 it was transferred to Eppleton (q.v.). Of red silk with a broad blue border, it was produced by Tutill at Chesham (no. 264) and measures 7 ft 10 in × 8 ft 10 in (239 × 269 cm).

SACRISTON

The Victory pit was sunk in 1839, with a downcast to the Five Quarter and an upcast to the Main.[528] The Main was worked out in 1881, and the Five Quarter in 1884. Sacriston and the Witton pit (q.v.) were linked at the Busty level in 1882. The Shield Row drift was driven in 1900. An inundation on 16 November 1903 drowned three miners.[529] Shield Row closed in the 1940s. By the 1950s and '60s efforts were concentrated on the Brockwell and Victoria. The prime coking coal of the Victoria was 20 in thick, and hewn with pneumatic picks on longwall faces. Output was coked at Derwenthaugh for foundry use. Following the 1984–5 strike, declining reserves, geological problems and the men's request to cease mining were given as the reasons for closure, although the threatened loss of full redundancy benefits must have been an influencing factor on the men's request.[530] Production, including the use of ponies, stopped on 15 November 1985 and closure was completed on 28 December.[531]

The banner at the 1872 and 1873 Galas showed a beehive on one side, surmounted by 'Education and Co-operation'.[532] Below the illustration were the words, 'Do ye unto all men as ye would they should do unto you'. The reverse showed men trying to turn a wheel, with their leader proclaiming, 'All together, boys, we will make the wheel go round, / For we know that by our union great benefit will be found'.

In 1919 the lodge purchased a banner showing John Wilson, seated, and W. House, standing at the left. The reverse carries a detailed illustration of an army hospital ward. The ward is a long, panelled room, lit by pitched roof lights, with a line of beds and a table in the foreground, on which is a vase of flowers, a book and an oil lamp. The main part of the scene shows a doctor, dressed in khaki uniform, talking to a patient in bed, while a Queen Alexandra's nursing sister takes notes. Behind this is another patient in bed and several others sitting or standing around, dressed in 'blues'. One of the wounded, a corporal, with an arm in a sling, is sitting in a wheelchair, and a nurse stands by him. Below the scene is the motto, 'Be not weary in well doing'. Both banner scenes carry the painted mark of 'G. Tutill London'. The main ground is a pale blue fabric, with a light purple strip added at the base and the subsequent addition of red bordering. It measures 8 ft 9 in × 7 ft 6 in (267 × 229 cm).
*Location*: Chester-le-Street Civic Centre.

The 1931 DMA banner was unfurled by James Gilliland at the Workmen's Club grounds and carries a rectangular panel with portraits of Robert Smillie and Lord Sankey on one side and Conishead Priory on the other.[533] While there are no manufacturer's details, the style of the paintings suggests that they were produced by Tutill, but the decorated surrounding ground seems out of place. The banner is light blue silk, with repairs at the top and bottom using light purple fabric, while the border is pale orange. There is a faded blue braid surrounding the painted panel on both sides. It measures 8 ft 9 in × 7 ft 8 in (267 × 234 cm).
*Location*: Sacriston Community Centre.

The first NUM banner was unfurled by Sam Watson at the local cricket field on 19 July 1957.[534] It was produced by Tutill at Chesham and carries a standing figure of 'Earl Attlee KG, OM, CH' on one side and a traditional view of the west end of Durham Cathedral on the other. The banner is red with a blue border and measures 7 ft 6 in × 8 ft 9 in (229 × 276 cm).
*Location*: Sacriston Community Centre.

A new banner was unfurled by Tom Callan on 8 July 1983.[535] On one side it carries small portraits of 'Thomas Hepburn 1831', 'William

Crawford 1869–70' and 'Sam Watson 1936–63', around an illuminated miner's lamp, with the words, 'Aye a hundred years are gainin mair / And brighter burns the beam'. The reverse shows a painting of the colliery. The banner was produced by Turtle & Pearce (no. 5/83) and is red with a yellow border. It measures 7 ft × 8 ft 5 in (213 × 256 cm).
*Location*: Sacriston Community Centre.
*See also* Witton Lodge, Sacriston.

SEAHAM

Sinking was carried out in 1845–9 and the first coal was drawn in 1852. The operation was owned by Lord Londonderry, with the Nos 1 and 2 shafts at Seaham, and the No. 3 at Seaton; the group was known as the Nicky Nack.[536] Explosions killed 26 on 25 October 1871 and 164 on 8 September 1880.[537] In 1958–63 the pit was modernized, with skip winding at the No. 1 shaft, an electric winder at No. 2 and a new coal preparation plant. Mining concentrated on the Five Quarter (E), Maudlin (H) and Low Main (J) using trepan and drum shearers. The pit was merged with Vane Tempest (q.v.) on 11 July 1983, and mining concentrated on the C seam reserves, with trunk conveying to the Seaham skip winder. Within the combine, Seaham undertook surface preparation ready for power station use.

The 1873 Gala banner showed a Joint Committee, 'We want a fair day's wage for a fair day's work'. The reverse showed the exterior of a colliery, 'Do you think it would pay well?', 'Oh yes; 100 per cent'.[538]

A banner at the 1921 Gala was a damask form carrying three portraits in a large central roundel.[539]

The earliest surviving DMA banner has the 'Seaham Single Aged Miners' Homes' on the obverse and the New Testament scene, 'Suffer the little children to come unto me', on the reverse. A single men's hostel was opened at Seaham in January 1929 and the banner may be from around this date. It is blue and light green damask silk, with a red border, and was produced at Tutill's City Road works.
*Location*: Christ Church, New Seaham.

The 1949 NUM banner carries a large roundel picture of a curving row of aged miners' homes, with the caption at the base, 'Aged Miners' Homes. Byron Terrace, Seaham'. The reverse shows a detailed illustration of the local Miners' Hall, 'The meeting place of Seaham miners'. The banner is orange and red damask silk, with a turquoise border, and was produced by Tutill at Chesham. It measures 7 ft 4.5 in × 7 ft 6 in (225 × 229 cm).
*Location*: Red Hill.

The NUM Durham Area banner carries a central roundel showing lodge officials marching with a band and banner along a street, past the Independent Methodist Church. The reverse side repeats the 'Suffer little children to come unto me' scene. It was produced by Tutill at Chesham and is blue silk with a red border.
*Location*: Lodge/Christ Church, New Seaham.

## SHERBURN

Boring, and probably the first shaft, was completed in 1828 by the Earl of Durham and the Lady Durham shaft was added in 1873. Sherburn collieries were transferred to Messrs Samuelson & Co., operators of the Newport Ironworks, Middlesbrough, in January 1914.[540] Samuelson worked the Low Main at the Lady Durham. Sherburn closed in 1921.

Sherburn lodge carried a banner inscribed 'Let's not be weary in well doing; for in due season we shall reap, if we faint not' at the 1872 Gala.[541]

## SHERBURN HILL

Two shafts, the North and West, were sunk in 1830 and 1835 by the Earl of Durham to work the Hutton.[542] It was purchased by Samuelson in 1914 and worked Low Main, Main and Busty.[543] It was absorbed by Dorman Long in 1923. Surface drifting took place in 1951, serving as a downcast with the West shaft, while the North shaft was the upcast. There were four other shafts within the 'take', providing additional ventilation. The 1964 Manpower Profile indicated that geological problems would affect its economic position, though output per man shift increased to 23 cwt, working Five Quarter, Harvey and Busty.[544] Sixty-five men were subsequently transferred to east coast pits, and the colliery closed in August 1965.

The Tutill damask silk banner at the 1939 Gala showed Conishead Priory[545] on one side and the aged miners' homes, 'Eventide', on the other.[546]

An NUM banner was purchased in 1953 and showed, on one side, the local aged miners' homes.[547] At the 1962 Gala it is clear that the other side carried a roundel painting of Conishead Priory.[548] The banner was present at the 1965 Gala,[549] but was later transferred to Elemore lodge (q.v.).

## SHERBURN HOUSE

The pit was sunk by the Earl of Durham in 1840 to the Hutton. Washed coal was coked at the Lady Durham pit. Like Sherburn and Sherburn Hill, it was transferred to Samuelson in 1914, with sinking to the Busty. It closed in 1940.

A new banner was unfurled by William Whiteley on May Day 1929.[550] On one side was a portrait of William Kelly, lodge secretary and checkweighman, and on the other, 'Emancipation of Labour'. The banner was produced by Tutill and was red with a blue border. A DMA banner at the 1939 Gala., which may have been the same one, showed a seated male figure.[551]

## SHILDON

The Engine pit was sunk in 1830, with a further sinking in 1831 by R. Surtees to work thin coal.[552] The pit was locally known as Dabble Duck. It was later worked by Bolckow, Vaughan & Co., who sank the

Furnace shaft in 1864.[553] In 1908 200 men and boys were employed, though the seams were said to be thin and unprofitable.[554] It closed in 1937. New Shildon colliery, sunk in 1949, closed in August 1965.

The 1872 Gala banner had no pictorial embellishments, but simply bore the name of the lodge, the date of its formation and the mottoes, 'We are lovers of liberty' and 'Long live our union'.[555] The only other known detail was that it was green.

The subsequent banner is highly elaborate, with a scene showing a Druid and Ancient Briton, accompanied by shields, a lion and lamb, all-seeing eye, hour glass, cross, fasces and cornucopia, with Stonehenge in the background. The reverse shows a sickbed scene, with an elaborately dressed visitor. The banner was produced at Tutill's City Road works and is yellow and green damask silk, with an orange border, now fragmentary. It measures 7 ft 3 in × 7 ft 1 in (221 × 216 cm).
*Location*: Beamish (1984-10-16).

SHINCLIFFE

The pit, at Shincliffe Bank Top, or High Shincliffe, was sunk in 1837 by Bell & Co. An explosion on 17 December 1840 injured five.[556] In the 1860s the pit was worked by Joseph Love & Partners, but it closed in 1875.[557]

The 1873 Gala banner carried portraits of MacDonald, Crawford and Bruce, with the motto, 'The diligent hand shall bear rule'. The reverse showed two men pushing a wheel, while a third pushed the other way, 'Pulling against the stream'.[558]

SHOTTON

The Engine and South pits were sunk in 1840–4 and worked by the Haswell, Shotton & Easington Coal & Coke Co. Ltd. They were abandoned in 1876–7. It was reopened by Horden Collieries Ltd in 1901, with two shafts, the North and South. The Three Quarter was worked out by 1913, though the Main, Low Main, Hutton, Harvey and Busty continued to be worked.[559] Peak production was in the 1920s, with half a million tons annual output, but losses in production in the 1950s led to the replacement of endless rope haulage by diesel loco and the introduction of mine cars to improve the situation. The cokeyard closed in 1958.[560] By 1971 the miners were cutting Yard and High Main coal. The product was blended for sale, but with declining reserves in the Yard seam, the pit was closed on 1 September 1972.[561]

The 1872 Gala banner carried a shield inscribed 'Little does the miner good and little do they get. Stand firm to one another and we'll be better yet'. The reverse showed a master and well-dressed workman.[562]

At the 1873 Gala the banner carried figures of Truth and Justice on one side, and, on the other, two angels dispensing food to the poor, with the command, 'Go and do likewise'.[563]

A new banner was unfurled on 23 July 1937 at the local Miners' Welfare ground.[564] It shows the blacksmith and carpenter scene, with an angel carrying the message, 'Unity is Strength'. The reverse shows 'Conishead Priory, Restore to health and vigour'. The banner was produced by Tutill at the City Road works and is pale blue with a red border. It measures 8 ft 9 in × 8 ft (267 × 244 cm).
*Location*: Beamish (1984-10-17).

The 1956 NUM banner repeated the design of the two workmen, with the angel holding a long ribbon inscribed 'Unity is strength / Liberty / Egalte (*sic*) / Freedom / Unite'. The reverse also repeats the Conishead Priory painting. It is blue silk, with a replacement red border, and was produced by Tutill at Chesham. It measures 6 ft 3 in × 7 ft 6 in (190 × 229 cm). The banner was renovated and repainted by Dawson Brenen in 1983, and again repainted by W. Hudson in 1994.
*Location*: Parish Council meeting room, Shotton.

SILKSWORTH

The Nos 1 and 2 shafts were sunk in 1869–73[565] and were operated by Lord Londonderry. It was acquired by Lambton & Hetton Collieries Ltd in 1920. The pit underwent reconstruction in 1948–58, with electric skip winding and reinforced concrete headgear.[566] In 1970 the Hutton was exhausted, and miners were transferred to the Harvey. Deteriorating geological conditions led to closure on 6 November 1971.

In 1892 the lodge asked Bainbridge, of Newcastle, for an estimate for a blue silk banner with gold fringe.[567] Bainbridge sent three blue silk samples ('Best', second, and third), and offered a choice of three mottoes – 'Quit ye like men, be strong' (St Paul), 'Act – act in the living present! / Heart within, and God o'er head' (Longfellow), and 'Conquer we shall, but we must first contend' (Cowley). The banner, with unspecified design, was unfurled on 8 July 1893.

On 17 July 1909 a new banner was unfurled by John Johnson.[568] On one side was a portrait of Gladstone, with the motto, 'Thrice armed is he who hath his quarrel just'. The reverse carried a Good Samaritan scene, 'Go thou and do likewise'. The banner was red silk, with a blue border and gold lettering, and was produced by G. Tutill.

The 1924 banner was unfurled at the Miners' Hall.[569] The front carried portraits of Ramsay MacDonald, Philip Showden, Keir Hardie, Joseph Hopper and Thomas Hepburn, with the motto, 'Something attempted, something done; our aims are one – the welfare of all'. The reverse carried a 'Sunshine of Liberty' scene, with the quotation, 'These things shall be, a loftier race than e'er the world hath known shall rise, with flame of freedom in their soul, and light of knowledge in their eye'. The banner was damask silk, 10 ft × 9 ft (305 × 274 cm), coloured red and yellow.

The 1938 replacement carried portraits of A.J. Cook, Peter Lee and Keir Hardie, with the reverse showing Conishead Priory. The banner was a red and purple damask silk, from Tutill's City Road works. It was later transferred to the Durham Cokemen (q.v.).

On the closure of Lambton colliery (q.v.) in 1965, 120 miners were transferred to Silksworth, along with their Hugh Gaitskell – Michael Doyle / 'Christ walking on the water' banner.[570] The portrait side of the banner was overpainted by 'Young and Redshaw', with a view of the colliery pithead. *Location*: Red Hill.

The lodge later acquired a Ryhope banner (q.v.), showing aged miners' homes and Conishead Priory. This was transferred to Eppleton (q.v.) in 1973.

## SLEETBURN

*See* New Brancepeth.

## SOUTH BRANCEPETH

*See* Pagebank.

## SOUTH DERWENT

The main sinking, the Hutton pit, lay close to Annfield Plain and was operating in 1856,[571] with the Stewart shaft near the Smith's Arms, Catchgate, and a staple at Carmyers. Certainly in the 1880s South Derwent was operated by R. Dickinson & Partners, along with the West Shield Row pit.[572] The Willie was sunk, north of the Hutton, between 1856 and 1884, and closed in March 1950.

The 1873 Gala banner showed a miner standing on a stone in a valley, and a master looking down on him from a hillside. Workmen hauling a pulley aim to raise the miner to the level of the master:

> Ye proud and wealthy let this theme
> Teach humbler thoughts of you;
> Since such a union has its gem,
> Can boast its splendour too.

The reverse bore the bundle of sticks fable, with the motto, 'Union is strength'.

## SOUTH DURHAM

There were two pits, Eldon Old Colliery, known as the John Henry pit, operating in 1856, and South Durham.[573] In the 1880s the operation was run by the South Durham Coal Co., which also worked Eldon (q.v.).[574] Confusingly, by 1920 South Durham colliery was known as Eldon.

A damask silk DMA banner shows a female figure, probably Britannia, with her Union shield, accompanied by a negro, Red Indian, Indian, the female figures of Friendship, Love and Truth, a lion, beehive, cornucopia, and tiny children, all set under an all-seeing eye, with the motto, 'Behold how good it is to dwell in unity'. The reverse shows a well-dressed child

presenting an open book to a miner's son, indicating 'I go to school' and 'I go to work', with the title, 'Miners unite to protect yourselves and your children'. This banner was certainly at the 1913 Gala.[575] It is red and orange damask silk with a purple-blue border, but is now fragmentary, measuring 8 ft 9 in × 5 ft 9 in (267 × 175 cm).
*Location*: Beamish (1984-10-18).

## SOUTH HETTON

The pit was sunk by the South Hetton Coal Co. Ltd in 1831–3, with both shafts to the Hutton. In the latter half of the nineteenth century mining concentrated on the Five Quarter, Main and Hutton (known on the market as South Hetton Wallsend). It was later operated by South Durham Steel & Iron Co. Ltd. A general decline was halted following nationalization, with a modernization programme, completed in 1953, involving electrification, the construction of new concrete headgear, winder-house and heapstead. A drivage was made to connect with Hawthorn (sunk 1958), but although the proposal to merge with the Hawthorn combine was put forward in 1965, this was not achieved until 1983. The output of High Main coal was drawn and processed at Hawthorn.

The banner at the 1872 Gala was described as 'worn', and it did not appear to have carried an illustration. It bore the inscription, 'United we stand, Divided we fall'.[576]

A new banner was displayed at the 1873 Gala.[577] It carried a representation of labour, with the line 'We live by our labour', and the verse,

> We'll bow to the sceptre of truth,
> Good will with justice and pure adoration,
> United we stand to the link of the chain,
> That forms this great demonstration.

A new banner was unfurled in July 1900 by G.R. Lindsay, the local schoolmaster, who had held several concerts to raise money for it.[578] The banner was produced at Tutill's City Road works and showed, on one side, Daniel in the lions' den, 'Be thou steadfast unto death', and on the reverse, two miners with their tools. It also bore the mottoes, 'Unity is Strength' and 'United to obtain the just reward for our labour'.

In 1932 the lodge purchased a banner showing 'Emancipation of Labour' on one side and the Gregson Terrace aged miners' homes, the 'Haven of Rest', on the other. The banner is orange and blue damask silk, with a red border, and measures 7 ft 8 in square (234 cm square). The banner was transferred to Adventure lodge (q.v.).

The 1956 banner was unfurled by J. Kelly, a union agent. It shows a scientist, fisherman, farmer and miner bringing gifts to the female figure of Humanity, with the title, 'Service to Humanity'. The reverse shows two miners in front of Red Hill. It is green with a red border.
*Location*: Blackpool Trades' Council.

South Hetton banner, showing a scientist, fisherman, farmer and miner offering gifts to 'Humanity'.

The 1980 banner, unfurled by Joe Gormley on 11 July, carries portraits of himself and Peter Lee, 'Not for an age, but for all time'.[579] The reverse shows a miner wearing a cap, sleeveless shirt and pit hoggers, holding a pick and safety lamp, on the left-hand side, and a modern miner, in overalls, with safety helmet and cap lamp, holding a spanner, on the right-hand side of the picture. In the background are the union headquarters at Red Hill. At the base of the roundel is the message, 'Sacrifice, Achievement and Gratitude'. It was produced by Turtle & Pearce (6.80) and is green with a red border. The banner measures 7 ft 2 in × 7 ft 10 in (218 × 232 cm).
*Location*: South Hetton Welfare Hall.

### SOUTH MEDOMSLEY

There is early evidence for mining, with the discovery of a wooden shovel in the Hutton seam in 1893.

The Ann pit was sunk in 1864, followed by the Mary in 1867.[580] Main and Busty were drawn at the Mary, and Hutton by drift. Certainly by the early 1880s the pit was worked by Owners of South Medomsley Colliery, and by 1887 they had opened the Five Quarter drift.[581] The Mary was linked to a drift in Pontop Low Wood by 1896. By 1921 the Main coal drift had been driven by the Pikewell Burn, with the Brass Thill drift east of Pontop Hall, and the Coronation drifts to the south-west. Most of these had been replaced with drifts to the Hutton, Low Hutton and Five Quarter by 1939. The pit closed in March 1963.

The banner at the 1872 and 1873 Galas showed a master and workman standing either side of a beehive.[582] The workman's comment is 'We make the honey', while the master replies, 'I have the power to take it from you!'. The reverse showed the bundle of sticks fable and the mottoes, 'Honour all men, but love the brotherhood' and 'United we stand, divided we fall'.

## SOUTH MOOR

There was certainly mining here in 1818.[583] Thomas Hedley & Bros sank Quaking House pit, north of Stanley, in 1845. The Annie was sunk in 1846, and the Mary in 1867.[584] Quaking House later became the Charley and Fan pits.[585] Other shafts included the Hedley and the William. Fire damaged the pithead at the Charley in 1911.[586] The operations merged with Morrison North and South in the 1950s. The group closed in 1973.

The 1873 Gala banner was designed by F. Oughton, a miner from Pelton Fell.[587] The obverse showed Tommy Ramsey displaying a yearly bond, attended by a miner with a pick, and another with a shovel, with the verse,

> Poor old Ramsey's dead and gone; he was the miners' friend;
> before he left this world of trials, he buried the yearly bond.

The reverse showed a master's weighman and a checkweighman correctly weighing coal:

> If man to man would still be just,
> Your weights and measures we would trust.
> A false balance is an abomination to the Lord, but a just weight is
> His delight.

The South Moor No. 1 lodge banner of 1921 shows portraits of J. Lawson, J. Herriotts and another person on the obverse, and miners shaking hands, accompanied by an angel, with the motto, 'United to obtain the just reward of our labour', on the reverse. There is some evidence of repainting.
*Location*: Beamish (1984-10-19).

The 1938 banner has a 'Sunshine of Liberty' theme over the inscription, 'These things shall be, a loftier race than e'er the world hath known shall rise with flame of freedom in their souls and light of knowledge in their

eyes'.[588] The reverse showed aged miners' homes, with the motto, 'and at eventide it shall be light'. It is red and orange damask silk, with a yellow border, 9 ft 1 in × 7 ft 7 in (277 × 231 cm), produced by Tutill at the City Road works. There are yellow rosettes in place of Tutill brass discs. Some tears have been patched with painted strips cut from another banner.
*Location*: Red Hill.

The lodge acquired the St Hilda Colliery banner (q.v.), showing South Shields pier, in 1959.
*Location*: Beamish (1984-10-20).

The NUM South Moor No. 2 Lodge banner carries a roundel scene showing an old miner in cloth cap, with a pick and lamp, extending the message, 'Now / it depends on / you', to a young miner wearing a safety helmet and holding a windy pick. At the base of the scene is the title, 'Progress'. The reverse shows a fallen miner being raised by the angel of Faith, with the figure of Justice standing close by. [589] This banner was at the 1947 Gala, and was later transferred to Hamsterley lodge (q.v.).

## SOUTH PELAW

Operations by the Perkins family began in 1860 with a 65 fathom shaft.[590] A new sinking to the Busty was made in 1890–1 for Thomas Gilchrist.[591] A large proportion of the higher seams were, at that time, still unworked. It was operated by the South Pelaw Coal Co. Ltd. The pit closed in January 1964.

The 1949 NUM banner was unveiled by Jack Lawson on 23 July.[592] It carries a panel showing a pit scene overlaid by eliptical portraits of Peter Lee and A.J. Cook, with the Hermitage on the reverse. It is pink, with a green border, and is 8 ft 9 in × 8 ft (267 × 244 cm). It was present at the 1962 Gala.[593]
*Location*: Red Hill.

## SOUTH TANFIELD

A pit was sunk in 1837 by Joseph Smith & Co. to work Main coal.[594] The 'C' pit was added in 1870–1. Further sinking was carried out in 1880, during which a sinker was killed while travelling in a kibble between the Hutton and Brass Thill. From the 1880s the operation was run by James Joicey, but closed in 1914–15.

The banner at the 1873 Gala showed a conference between masters' and workmen's agents, and the words,

People throughout the land join in one social band and save yourselves.
If you would happy be – free from all slavery, banish all knavery and
save yourselves.

The reverse carried a representation of the 'Triumph of Liberty' and the verse,

Onward ye delighted nations, progress is the rule of all;
Man was made for healthful effort, tyranny has crushed him long,
But he shall march from good to better, and do battle with the wrong.[595]

## SPRINGWELL

A sinking was carried out in 1824 by Lord Ravensworth & Partners and the first coal was taken to Jarrow Staithes on 17 January 1826.[596] There were two shafts, A and B. An explosion in the B pit on 9 May 1833 killed forty-seven in the Hutton seam and twenty-seven were killed in the same seam on 6 December 1837. Three were killed when the cage chain broke on 9 March 1840.[597] The pit was later operated by John Bowes & Partners Ltd, but was closed in 1931.

The 1873 Gala banner showed a Joint Committee meeting, with an unrecorded inscription, and, on the reverse, an illustration of Hartley colliery, with a master and workman shaking hands.[598]

A post-1915 DMA banner carries a panel showing John Wilson, accompanied by J. Johnson and W. House. Red Hill appears on the reverse, with the motto, 'Unity is Strength'. It is blue silk with a red border.
*Location*: Bowes Railway Museum, Springwell, Gateshead.

## STANLEY

A colliery north of Crook, sunk by Joseph Pease in 1857[599] and known as the Josephine. There was some drifting to the north of the site, but the operation closed in 1911.

The banner at the 1872 and 1873 Galas showed a scene of masters and men, with the words, 'May we ever be united, let us love one another'.[600] The reverse showed an emblem of charity and 'An evil [or false] balance is an abomination [to the Lord], but a just weight is His delight', 'Let brotherly love continue' and 'See that ye fall not out by the way'.

## ST HELEN'S AND TRIMDON COLLIERIES

The Engine pit was sunk to the Brockwell in 1830, and was followed by the Emma, to the Yard, in 1831, and the Catherine, to the Brockwell, in 1835.[601] A fourth shaft, the Tindale, worked the Harvey.[602] Mining was controlled by Joseph Pease & Partners, but flooding forced closure in 1924.[603]

At the 1872 Gala, a small bannerette was displayed, inscribed 'United we stand, Divided we fall'.[604]

A new banner was purchased for the 1873 Gala. It appeared to have the obverse divided into two sections, with a figure of Liberty and portraits of Ernest Jones and Fergus O'Connor on one side, and Henry Hunt and Thomas Paine on the other, with the words, 'Liberty the friend of progress'. On the reverse was the figure of Justice, with portraits of Crawford, Foreman, W.P. Roberts, MacDonald and the words, 'Let's not be weary in well doing, for in due season we shall reap, if we faint not'.[605]

## ST HILDA

Initial operations, known as Chapter Main colliery, were begun by S. Temple in 1810, but he was followed by a series of owners, including Messrs Brown and Messrs Devey. A shaft was sunk by Messrs Brandling in 1822, reaching the Bensham in 1825.[606] It subsequently passed to the Harton Coal Co. Ltd. An explosion on 28 June 1839 killed fifty-one. An outlying shaft at Westoe was sunk in 1909. The colliery closed in 1940, but the shaft continued to be used as an upcast to Westoe.

The 1873 Gala banner carried the large message, 'By commerce we live', on one side and a widow mourning at a grave on the other.[607]

A banner, in a photograph of *c.* 1920, shows South Shields pier, with an inset small roundel at the top depicting a building.[608]

Another banner, post-1930, also shows South Shields pier on the obverse and Conishead Priory on the reverse, with the motto, 'Help and Sympathy in Time of Sickness'. The banner was sent to South Moor (q.v.) in 1959. It is blue with a red border and has, at some stage, been shortened; it now measures 9 ft 10 in × 8 ft (300 × 244 cm).

## SUNNISIDE

The pit was sunk in 1866–8 for Joseph Pease.[609] There were several drifts and air shafts north towards the River Deerness. At the beginning of the twentieth century it was probably associated with Dicken House drift. Operations ceased in 1925.

The 1872 Gala banner carried a shield bearing the stanza, 'Success to all pitmen, their sweethearts and wives. May they never want money all the days of their lives'.[610]

A new banner was purchased in 1874.[611] On one side was a depiction of the colliery, with a verse on the advantages of union. The reverse carried representations entitled 'The Five Alls of the Nation', with a large arbitration scene in the centre. Below is the Queen, 'I rule all', with a bishop, 'I pray for all', a lawyer, 'I plead for all', a soldier, 'I fight for all' and a poor man, 'I pay for all'.

The banner used in 1893 may have carried a 'Good Samaritan' scene, with the motto, 'Bear ye one anothers burdens'.[612]

## SUNNYBROW

There was a short-lived period of mining activity when the Northern Coal Mining Co. sank Willington colliery in 1840, but this was subsequently worked by Straker & Love as the 'A' and 'B' pits. It was closed in 1925, and again later in June 1927 with the loss of 275 jobs, but reopened in February 1929.[613] The colliery closed in 1932.

Sunnybrow lodge had a large Tutill banner at the 1872 Gala.[614] On one side was Britannia, with the sea and a ship in the background, and on the reverse, the bundle of sticks fable.

A later DMA banner shows a man assisting a widow and orphans at a graveside, 'We succour the widows and orphans'. Flanking this scene are the portraits of John Wilson and William House. The reverse side shows the parable of the Good Samaritan. It is red with a blue border, the bottom part now damaged, and measures 9 ft 9 in × 8 ft 7 in (297 × 262 cm). Black rosettes are still attached near the top.
*Location*: Beamish (1984-10-21).

A new banner, but with the same illustrations, was unfurled by J. Swan in 1923.[615]

## TANFIELD LEA

The Engine pit was sunk in 1830–1, with the New pit to the west in 1839.[616] It was operated by the Marquis of Bute,[617] but was purchased by James Joicey in 1847, and was to form part of Lambton, Hetton & Joicey Collieries Ltd. The Margaret was sunk in 1903.[618] The colliery closed on 25 August 1962.

A DMA banner carries portraits of Keir Hardie and A.J. Cook on one side and a miner and sailor at a quayside shaking hands on the other, symbolizing 'Unity is Strength', under the motto, 'All men are Brethren'. This is red silk with a light blue border, 11 ft × 10 ft (335 × 305 cm) and bears the painted mark, 'G. Tutill – London'.
*Location*: Red Hill.

The lodge also had a banner which showed A.J. Cook and Peter Lee on one side and 'All Men are Brethren' on the other.

The NUM banner carried, on one side, two vertical elipses displaying portraits of 'C. Attlee' and 'A.J. Cook'.[619] The reverse bore the message, 'Organisation the Key to Economic Emancipation', around an illustration of a female charioteer driving four charging horses, with the message, 'Hail the Dawn'. At the base of the scene was the message, 'One Union for All'. The banner was present at the 1961 Gala.[620]

## TANFIELD MOOR

Tanfield Moor was won by the Earl of Kerry, with the first coals taken to Derwenthaugh Staithes on 14 June 1768.[621] The Willie pit closed in 1948.

The lodge had a light coloured banner, with dark central panel inscribed 'Tanfield Moor Branch / Liberty / Equality / Fraternity'.[622] The carrying poles had Tutill-type spearheads.

## TANFIELD UNITED COLLIERIES

The banner at the 1872 and 1873 Galas carried two texts:

> Why should kings forget that they are men,
> and men that they are brethren?

and

For a wit's a feather, a chief a rod;
But an honest man is the noblest work of God.

The reverse showed wakeful and sleeping schoolboys, 'Train up a child in the way he should go'.

## THORNLEY

Thornley was sunk in 1834–5 by John Gully & Partners to work the Harvey.[623] Fire broke out underground in June 1858 and the area was drowned to stop it.[624] Some work continued until the Harvey was laid in during 1861. It then passed to the London Steam Colliery & Coal Co. in 1865.[625] The company was renamed the Original Hartlepool Collieries Co. in 1868, and in 1870–2 sank Thornley New Winning to the Five Quarter.[626] The surface operations were destroyed by fire on 8 May 1875, and the company went bankrupt in 1877. They recovered, but finally collapsed in 1884.[627] The shaft was then filled in, but was reopened in 1888 by the Weardale Iron & Coal Co. The No. 2 shaft was sunk in 1904 and from 1914 became the main drawing shaft. In 1949 three men were drowned when water broke in from old Cassop Vale workings.[628] Following a reorganization in 1956, a new Baum washery and dry-cleaning plant were constructed. Production ceased on 9 January 1970, and the pit officially closed on 31 January.[629]

Thornley's banner was set above the platform at the first Gala in 1871, though no descriptive details were recorded.[630]

The banner at the 1872 and 1873 Galas showed an arbitration scene and the message, 'Blessed is the day when strikes die away'. The reverse showed a widow and orphans, 'Compensation we demand when life is sacrificed'.[631] It was produced by W. Whaite, of Manchester.

At the 1927 Gala the Thornley banner carried the motto, 'A fair day's work for a fair day's pay'.[632] A banner, possibly this one, was destroyed by fire in 1943.[633]

The subsequent banner, present at the 1947 Gala, shows the aged miners' homes, named after Arthur Greenwood, on one side and a scene of children playing in a park on the other, with the title, 'Peace and Prosperity'.[634] The banner is red with a yellow border and measures 8 ft 4 in × 7 ft 10 in (254 × 239 cm). This was damaged in the 1950s but subsequently repaired and given to Arthur Greenwood.[635]

*Location*: Thornley Community Centre.

The 1953 banner, produced by Tutill at Chesham, repeated the previous designs. It was unfurled by Arthur Greenwood at Thornley Welfare Hall on 17 July.[636] It is red with a yellow border and measures 8 ft × 7 ft 10 in (244 × 239 cm).

*Location*: Thornley Community Centre.

## THRISLINGTON

Borings were carried out in 1835 which proved the Bottom Hutton.[637] The colliery was in operation in 1843, and was sunk to the Main.[638] However, it was further opened out, as the Mary pit, in 1867 by the Rosedale & Ferryhill Iron Co. to supply the Ferryhill iron works, until recession led to the collapse of the company in 1879. It was then taken over by the Thrislington Coal Co. Most of the heapstead was destroyed by fire in 1911.[639] Around 1914 it passed to the North Bitchburn Coal Co., and to Henry Stobart & Co. in 1932. The workforce in 1930 totalled 1,005 and, though there was a drop in the number in the 1940s, the figure rose to a peak of 1,124 in 1950. It then fell to 805 in 1960, and the pit closed on 4 March 1967.

The banner carried at the 1873 Gala carried portraits of Nicholas Wilkinson, William Crawford, Tommy Ramsey and William Patterson, with the verse, 'Unity is strength / Knowledge is power'. The reverse showed a master and workman shaking hands.[640]

A post-1930 DMA damask silk banner shows a detail of Conishead Priory on one side and the 'Amicitia, Amor et Veritas' design on the other. The banner was produced by Tutill at the City Road works and is a grey-blue and pale red damask silk with a yellow border. It is now in five damaged pieces, measuring 8 ft 9 in × 8 ft 4 in (267 × 254 cm).
*Location*: Beamish (1984-10-22).

The lodge later acquired the Fenhall Drift banner (q.v.), which was subsequently transferred to Harton and Westoe lodge (q.v.).

## TRIMDON GRANGE

The Grange was sunk by Joseph Smith in 1845, initially to the Five Quarter in 1846, and in 1847 to the Main. Smith sold the pit to Matthew Forster in 1852 and the sinking was taken down to the Low Main in 1863, and the Harvey in 1872–3. In 1880 it was sold to Walter Scott, and the coking capacity at the site was expanded. On 16 February 1882 an explosion in the Harvey killed sixty-nine.[641] The pit was closed from 1930 to 1937 and reopened by East Hetton Collieries Ltd. Coking ceased in 1962, though the pit was graded in the long-life 'A' category. Unfavourable operating conditions, however, led to proposals for closure in 1967. This was deferred until 16 February 1968.[642]

The damask banner of *c.* 1910 carried a scene of an Englishman, Scot (bearded), Welshman and Irishman clasping hands.

The 1929 banner repeated the Four Nations theme. The reverse side carried the bundle of sticks fable, with the young warrior trying to break the bundle and the patriarch breaking the sticks individually. It was accompanied by the motto, 'Unity is Strength'.

On 19 July 1963 Harold Wilson unfurled a new banner showing an updated version of the four figures, with a clean-shaven Scot. The reverse shows the bundle of sticks image, with the motto, 'Unity is Strength'. It is blue with a red border.
*Location*: Trimdon Grange Community Association.

The Trimdon Grange banner, *c.* 1910, showing the Four Nations shaking hands in unity.

Mr D. Guy, NUM (NE Area) president, unfurled a DMA banner on 30 June 1996. It was produced by Chippenham Design, repeating the 1929 design, and is blue with a red border.
*Location*: Trimdon Grange Church Hall.

### TUDHOE AND TUDHOE GRANGE

Tudhoe Colliery was sunk in 1864–6 by the Weardale Iron Co. with three shafts, the East, West and Success.[643] Tudhoe Grange was sunk in 1869–70 by the same firm, but it only worked until 1885. An explosion on 18 April 1882 killed thirty-seven.[644] Output was principally directed to the local iron works. The pit closed in 1935, but reopened at the end of the Second World War, and was worked as Tudhoe Park Drift from 1948. Problems selling the coal led to closure on 23 May 1969.[645] Tudhoe Mill drift operated from 1954 to February 1965.

The 1872 Gala banner of Tudhoe and Tudhoe Grange showed a master and worker shaking hands, with the line, 'Masters, give unto your servants that which is just and equal, knowing that ye also have a Master', and the verse, 'Come let us grasp each other's hands, and cast away our fears; / And for the Miners' Union band let's give three hearty cheers'. The reverse carried the bundle of sticks fable.[646] At the 1873 Gala the banner was said to have lost some of its brilliance and beauty.[647]

A subsequent Tudhoe DMA banner, produced at Tutill's City Road works, carries a scene of the village green on one side and 'Emancipation

of Labour' on the other. This is a blue and gold damask silk banner, with a red border. The village green image was certainly on the banner at the 1955 Gala.[648] It measures 7 ft 6 in × 8 ft 10 in (229 × 269 cm).
*Location*: Red Hill.

The Ouston 'E' DMA banner was transferred to Tudhoe, probably in the 1950s. It is a Tutill City Road banner and shows 'Conishead Priory Convalescent Home for Durham Mineworkers' on one side and a view of the west end of Durham Cathedral, looking south-east, on the other. It is red and blue damask silk and measures 8 ft 5 in × 9 ft 6 in (256 × 290 cm).
*Location*: The banner was displayed at the Black Horse pub, Tudhoe, but sent to Red Hill in 1988.[649] It now hangs in Spennymoor Town Hall.

A banner for Tudhoe Park lodge was unfurled by Hugh Gaitskell on 18 July 1958.[650] One side showed Tudhoe Mill drift, in woodland, and the other side carries a scene of the Gala, with crowds and banners on the Racecourse.[651] The designs were created by Norman Cornish. A photograph taken in 1975 showed the banner, but a close-up shot showed the 'Park' roughly painted out. This banner was later presented to Boldon lodge (q.v.).

TURSDALE

Borings were carried out in 1854, and the pit was sunk in 1859–60.[652] It was taken over by Dorman, Long & Co. in 1923, and later combined with Bowburn (q.v.) as a man-riding shaft. It closed in 1968.

The DMA banner at the 1873 Gala showed figures of industry on one side and clasped hands, with the verse,

> For ever let our motto be
> Unity, Combination and Liberty.

It was described as 'Neat and unpretentious'.[654] This could be the banner now at Beamish, which has the same verse and, in the border, a seated woman teaching her daughter, two male standing figures and a female figure. The reverse shows a stepped framework, on which are a seated female figure, a beehive, a coiled serpent, a set square and a sextant, with scenes of a crane, blast furnace, colliery, sailing ship and factory chimneys. The banner comprises cream sheets on a blue central ground, with a red border, and measures 9 ft 4 in × 9 ft 9 in (285 × 297 cm).
*Location*: Beamish (1984-10-23).

The following banner shows a workman attempting to break a bundle of sticks, 'Forever let our motto be, Unity, Combination and Liberty'. The reverse follows the same design as the previous banner. The banner was also produced in the same way and measures 10 ft 5 in × 8 ft 8 in (318 × 264 cm). It is unclear whether this was the banner known to have been purchased around 1895[655] or an intermediate banner.
*Location*: Beamish (1984-10-24).

Tursdale banner, with the portrait of Joseph Hopper, the founding father of the Durham Aged Mineworkers' Homes Association, and a view of the local homes, opened in 1921.

The subsequent banner was unfurled in 1925 by R.D. Ayton, the lodge president, in the lodge room.[656] It carries a shield enclosing three portraits – the Rt Hon. J. Ramsey MacDonald, J. Keir Hardie and the Rt Hon. Philip Snowden – with the motto, 'The cause of labour is the hope of the world'. The reverse carries a small portrait of 'Mr Joseph Hopper', inset over a view of the three blocks of 'Tursdale Aged Miners' Homes'. The banner was produced by Tutill in London. It measures 10 ft × 8 ft 4 in (305 × 254 cm) and is a light blue silk with a red border.
*Location*: Red Hill.

## TWIZELL

Exploratory work to prove seams was carried out in 1795, but the main sinking, the Gate pit, was begun in 1842.[657] The pit was operated by James Joicey, but the rising costs of extraction led to its closure in 1934. The nearby Alma pit of West Pelton colliery (q.v.) closed in November 1958.

The DMA Alma and Twizell lodge banner in use around 1912 carried a central roundel surrounded by foliage, containing the portraits of two men, possibly lodge officials, with three lines of text in the lower segment.[658]

A DMA banner in use in the 1920s showed four seated figures in front of six standing men, possibly union officials.[659]

The banner at the 1947 Gala carried the themes, 'Unity is Strength', and 'He that would be free must strike the blow'.[660]

## TYNE MAIN

This pit was also called Friar's Goose colliery. The Engine pit was sunk in 1798–9. The High Main was abandoned in 1842, though pumping was maintained at Friar's Goose pit.[661] By 1860 Tyne Main and Woodside were worked by Messrs Losh & Co., with 3 shafts and 406 hands.[662] The pit closed in 1926.

The banner at the 1873 Gala showed a Good Samaritan scene on one side, with 'Go thou and do likewise', and a widow and orphan on the reverse.[663]

## URPETH 'C' PIT

A pit was sunk to the Hutton by William Coulson in 1831,[664] but Messrs Hunt, Perkins & Co. were also working at Urpeth in the early nineteenth century. The latter operation was subsequently run by the Perkins family, owners of Birtley iron works (subsequently renamed Owners of Pelaw Main Collieries Ltd in 1906, and Pelaw Main Collieries Ltd in 1926). In 1908 the heapstead was renewed, with a Blackett washery to clean Urpeth Busty and 'C' pit coal. A surface drift was also driven from the surface to the Shield Row.[665] The pit was merged with Ouston 'E' in 1957, but closed in 1959.

The 1921 banner carried the 'Two Sides of the Question' image. The reverse carried the motto, 'Unity is Strength'.

The lodge purchased a banner from Tutill in 1930.

## USHAW MOOR

Test drilling was carried out in 1857, 1867 and 1870, followed soon after by the sinking of a shaft. In 1873 the coal master was John Sharp. By 1879 the pit had been purchased by Henry Chaytor, but was sold to Pease & Partners in 1883 after a violent strike.[666] It was closed from 1927 to 1929. An explosion in the Victoria on 14 November 1932 killed two.[667] Proposals to close the pit were put forward in late 1959[668] and it finally closed in August 1960, with 5 million tons of coal remaining in the Harvey.[669]

A strike banner was present at the 1883 Gala.[670] *See* section on 'Strike and Sacked Miners' Banners' (p. 259).

From the 1930s the DMA banner bore a circle containing three linked portraits of Peter Lee, Isaac Finlay and J. Black. The banner was later torn. The painting of Finlay was cut from the banner, framed and presented to him on his retirement in 1944.[671]

The banner at the 1947 Gala showed Joseph Clake, Peter Lee and Isaac Finlay on one side and 'Unity is Strength' on the other.[672]

The NUM banner was unfurled by Mrs Attlee on the eve of the 1955 Gala.[673] It bears the portrait of Jack Joyce on one side and Red Hill on the other. After 1960 the banner was transferred to Kimblesworth (q.v.) and renamed, but the original lodge name was replaced for the 1995 Gala.

## USWORTH

The colliery was sunk in 1845–7 and worked by J. Johansson and Sir George Elliott, with two shafts, the Wellington East and West. The principal shaft, the Frederick, was sunk in 1874. The site was transferred to John Bowes & Partners *c.* 1882. At this time the Maudlin, Low Main and Hutton were worked. An explosion in the West pit on 2 March 1885 killed forty-one.[674] The engine-house was destroyed by fire in 1890. A boiler explosion at the Low Main haulage engine in 1891 killed three. The Victory shaft was sunk in 1910, and in 1959 the colliery was combined with Follonsby/Wardley (q.v.). In 1961 output was from the Maudlin, Hutton, Harvey and Busty, but the pit closed on 1 August 1974.

The 1873 Gala banner carried portraits of Bruce, MacDonald, W. Pickard, Crawford and Burt, with the verse,

> Long life attend our agents, and may they still prove true,
> Then one and all will acclaim they shall never have cause to rue,
> Remember what they have done for us for our liberty,
> They have laid aside the yearly bond through the strength of unity.

The reverse showed a man lying with a bleeding leg, 'Just look at this poor fellow got lamed by the fall of a stone'.[675]

The subsequent banner again shows MacDonald and Crawford on one side and the 'Amicitia, Amor et Veritas' design on the other. It measures 9 ft 11 in × 8 ft 6 in (302 × 259 cm) and is blue and red damask silk with a yellow border.
*Location*: Beamish (1984-10-25).

In January 1921 the lodge sought quotations for a new banner, but the 1921 strike intervened and it was not until 1923 that the purchase seems to have been completed.[676] There are no details of the designs. It was repaired in 1936.

On 24 July 1938 another banner was ordered and payment was being made in November, though, again, there are no details given in the lodge minutes.[677]

A DMA banner, perhaps that of 1938, carries a shoulder-length portrait of Keir Hardie on the obverse, with an 'Emancipation of Labour' design on the reverse. This pale blue and green damask silk is now set in a frame without its fabric border.

*Location*: Usworth and Washington Gardeners' Club.

On 10 October 1954 the lodge agreed to buy a new Tutill banner, with repeat designs (they actually sent it down for copying) and it was unfurled in July 1955.[678] This NUM banner[679] is light green silk with a pale blue border and measures 9 ft × 8 ft (274 × 244 cm). There was some repainting in 1974 by D. Brenen.

*Location*: Usworth and District Workmen's Club, Manor Road, Usworth.

A subsequent banner repeated the large roundel portrait of J. Keir Hardie, with the border of the illustration inscribed 'Equality', 'Fraternity' and 'United we Stand'. The reverse continued the 'Emancipation of Labour' scene. The cream and blue damask silk was woven at the City Road works, with a red border, though the painting was presumably done at Chesham. This banner was 'Presented by the Usworth Miners' Lodge of the National Union of Mineworkers Jan. 14th 1974' to the 'Trades Union Council, Chester-le-Street', with these details painted onto it by D. Brenan. It measures 8 ft 7 in × 8 ft 5 in (262 × 257 cm).

*Location*: Beamish (1980-887).


VANE TEMPEST

The decision by Londonderry to sink a shaft was made public in January 1923[680] and work began in December. Two shafts were sunk, the Vane and Tempest, using the freezing process, and were completed in 1926. The 'C' seam was developed inland in 1976. The pit was combined with Seaham (q.v.) on 11 July 1983. Dosco & Anderson roadheaders were used for main gate roadway drivage, and Eickhoff double-ended in-web shearers at the faces.[681] Run of Mine (ROM) was processed at Seaham, with smalls for power station blend. Vane Tempest was included by British Coal in a list of thirty-one pits to be closed, announced by Heseltine on 13 October 1992, and was subsequently listed with nine others as subject to the statutory ninety days consultation period. The last shift was worked on 23 October 1992, and the pit officially closed 4 June 1993.

An NUM banner of blue silk with a yellow border carried a central roundel painting of the traditional view of Durham Cathedral, 'Build your Association firmly and strong'.[682] The reverse showed Conishead Priory. This was at the 1947 Gala.[683]

In 1951 the lodge acquired the Byremoor banner showing Parliament and the Hermitage.

The 1982 NUM Durham Area banner was unfurled by Tom Urwin MP in Vane Tempest Welfare Hall.[684] It shows Durham Cathedral, while the reverse carries a roundel central shield containing an aerial view of the colliery, with 'Unity is Strength' at the bottom of the shield border. The banner was produced by Turtle & Pearce Ltd (no. 6.82) and is red with a yellow border.

*Location*: Vane Tempest lodge.

### VICTORIA GARESFIELD

The pit was sunk around 1860 and operated by several owners, including the Victoria Garesfield Colliery Co., until it was purchased by Priestman Collieries Ltd in 1899. It was closed on 13 July 1962.

A damask silk DMA banner carried a small portrait of Keir Hardie, over a 'Sunshine of Liberty' type scene, entitled 'Gain the Co-operative Commonwealth'. At the base of the scene was the inscription 'Producers of the Nation's wealth, unite! and have your share of the world'.[685]

### WALDRIDGE

Coal was won by William Jolliffe on Waldridge Fell in 1779 and shipped from Fatfield.[686] Another pit was sunk in 1831 and worked by Messrs Sowerby & Co. with two shafts.[687] In the 1870s the operators of the colliery were Christian Rudolph Ferdinand Thiedeman of Newcastle and Owen Wallis, a Northamptonshire farmer. The Busty was sunk in 1875.[688] They continued to operate the pit in the 1880s, but there were several owners in the 1890s. By 1896 the main working was by the 'A' and 'D' shafts. Waldridge Fell Old pit, which had been leased by Priestman Collieries Co. from Hylton Jolliffe, closed in 1911.[689] The 'A' pit closed in 1926, but the 'D' pit remained open until 1963. Subsequent drift mining at Smithy Dene, on Waldridge Fell, broke into early workings, where timbering, a sledge runner and fragments of a leather shoe were noted.[690]

A banner was purchased in 1871–2 and was present at the 1873 Gala. It showed a master and workman shaking hands on the obverse and an arbitration scene, the 'Final Appeal', on the reverse.[691]

A second banner was used from 1892 until it was damaged by the weather at the 1908 Gala.

A new banner was unfurled in 1909 by John Wilson.[692] It was produced by Tutill and bore a 'Lion and Lamb' scene on one side and the North Road Miners' Hall in Durham on the other.

### WARDLEY

*See also* Follonsby.

The 1873 Gala banner showed a master and workman on one side and a weeping widow at a grave on the other.[693]

## WASHINGTON

A new winning is recorded in 1776, and in 1828 fourteen were killed in the Eye pit of Washington colliery. Certainly some early operations were carried out by Mounsey, Backhouse, Cruddace & Co., but were abandoned *c.* 1862.[694] The Washington Coal Co. acquired royalties at Oxclose and Glebe pits, and sank the Nos 1 and 2 shafts in 1901–2.[695] An explosion on 20 February 1908 again killed fourteen.[696] By 1970 the pit was fully mechanized, using bi-directional shearers.[697] On the exhaustion of the Maudlin, work concentrated on the thin Hutton, but its declining quality made it unsuitable for CEGB use, leading to closure of the Glebe on 5 August 1972.[698]

The 1873 Gala banner carried portraits of Ernest Jones, William Crawford and John Bright, with a pair of suspended scales and the message, 'Masters give unto your servants that which is just and equal, knowing that ye have a master in heaven'.[699] The reverse carried the message, 'The husbandman that laboureth must be first partaker of the fruits'.

At the 1875 Gala the same banner was in use, but the portrait of John Bright was covered in a black veil.[700]

A banner in use around 1930–1 was a Tutill damask silk type, with portraits of Thomas Cann and two others, conceivably House and Lawson.

## WASHINGTON 'F' PIT

The 'F' pit was originally sunk in the late eighteenth century, but was subsequently operated by Washington Coal Co. until 1926. It was reopened by Matthew Henry Kellett, a mining engineer, in 1927. Kellett introduced electrification and windy picks. Power loading followed nationalization, with peak production in 1964–5 (486,000 saleable tons). Exhaustion of the Busty on 9 March 1968 and the Brass Thill on 21 June 1968 led to the pit's closure on 28 June 1968.

The DMA banner used in the 1930s carried paintings of Durham Cathedral and Conishead Priory.[701] This was present at the 1947 Gala.

The NUM banner, in use certainly by 1952, carried a painting of the west front of the Cathedral on one side and the Hermitage on the other.[702]

Another NUM banner has Durham Cathedral on one side and Conishead Priory on the other. This was produced by Tutill at Chesham (no. 962) and is yellow with a blue border. It measures 5 ft 10 in × 6 ft 5 in (178 × 196 cm). *Location*: Washington 'F' Pit Museum, Albany Way, Washington.

A new banner was purchased in 1962 from Sharps Studios of Hitchin.[703] It carried paintings of the Cathedral and Conishead Priory, produced by Pauline Trail.

## WASHINGTON GLEBE

The available lodge minute books for 1910–15 and 1920–6 indicate a banner (or banners) in use, but there is no reference to a purchase made during these time periods.[704] The 1925 minutes refer to two repairs done locally.[705]

A DMA banner of 1930 shows aged miners' homes on one side and two miners shaking hands, with the motto, 'All Men are Brethren', on the other. It carries the painted mark, 'Tutill – London', and is blue silk. Now damaged, it measures 11 ft 1 in (338 cm) in length, with a surviving height of 8 ft 10 in (269 cm). This was at the 1947 Gala.
*Location*: Red Hill.

The NUM banner showed two miners shaking hands, with an angel holding a scroll inscribed 'Unity is Strength'. At the base of the scene was the message, 'All Men are Brethren'. This was torn in 1962.

A new banner was unfurled in 1963 by James Callaghan. It carries a portrait of Nye Bevan, and the crest of the Washington family is incorporated in the four corners of the panel. The reverse shows a coal-plough working at the colliery. The banner carries the mark of 'Tutill – Chesham' (no. 263), but there is some evidence of repainting on the reverse, particularly in the overpainting of the maker's details, and the replacement of an elliptical base label with the present moulded form carrying the name, 'Nye Bevan'. The banner is blue silk and is now set in a frame, 5 ft 8.5 in × 6 ft 10.5 in (174 × 210 cm).
*Location*: Westwood Club, Washington.

WATERGATE

This colliery was operated by Priestman Collieries Ltd from the 1920s. It closed in August 1964.

A banner depicted two miners shaking hands in the presence of an angel and the motto, 'Unity is Strength'. The banner at the 1947 Gala carried, on both sides, themes relating to 'Unity is Strength'.[706]

A later banner carried paintings of the Big Meeting and Conishead Priory.

WATERHOUSES

Peases West Brandon was sunk in 1856–7, with the Mary as a second shaft, to work the Main coal,[707] though it was not until 1863 that the pit became productive. A series of drifts were driven – South Main in 1870, North Five Quarter in 1879, North Main and South Five Quarter in 1885, and Klondyke Five Quarter in 1899. In 1901 the Ladysmith drift was driven from the North Five Quarter to the Ballarat.[708] Main coal was also worked in the Rowley Gillett Royalty, and in 1919 the company acquired a lease to work baryta. Tests in the Oakenshaw Exchange Boundary Fault proved 96 per cent barium sulphate, and the South Ballaratt heading was driven to work it.[709] Kellets Main coal drift was driven in 1924. By the 1930s most of the output went to ICI Synthetics Products, Billingham, and Bankfoot cokeworks. Certainly by 1936 windy picks and scraper loaders were being used, and in 1954 a Gusto multi-plough was installed to work the thin seams. In 1963 Ivesley drift closed, and miners began to leave for the Midlands and Wales. By March 1964 drawing was reduced to one shift, with 146 men left.[710] The Victoria seam was worked, but roof difficulties, water and declining reserves led to closure in August 1966.

An early banner appears to have carried a portrait of Joseph Cowen, although the message, 'Not approved', had been added in prominent letters over the portrait when it was paraded at the 1885 Gala.[711]

A new banner was unfurled by William Patterson on 8 July 1892.[712] The front showed William Crawford seated at a table, quill-pen in hand, with Tommy Ramsey entering the office with his crake and declaring, 'They are all in the union now'. The reverse carried representations of Purity, Industry, Unity and Justice, with the motto, 'By industry we flourish, united we stand'.

This banner was replaced, around the 1920s, by one showing the seated figure of John Wilson, flanked by J. Johnson and W. House, both standing. The reverse shows the bundle of sticks fable, with the motto, 'Unity is Strength'. It is a blue and red damask silk with a yellow border and was produced at Tutill's City Road works. It measures 9 ft 6 in × 8 ft 8 in (290 × 264 cm).

*Location*: Hung in St Paul's Church, Waterhouses in 1984;[713] later transferred to Red Hill.

A NUM banner was purchased in 1951.[714] It shows the bundle of sticks fable on one side and the aged people's home and communal hall at Esh Winning on the other. It is a light green and red damask silk with a yellow border, from Tutill's City Road works, while the painting was done at Chesham. It measures 7 ft 2 in × 7 ft 8 in (218 × 234 cm).

*Location*: Esh Winning Community Centre.

WEARMOUTH

*See* Monkwearmouth.

WEST AUCKLAND

Test borings were carried out in 1826, but a pit was not sunk until 1838.[715] In the 1850s it was worked by Messrs Edmund Backhouse & Co.,[716] but by the 1870s was in the hands of Bolckow, Vaughan & Co.[717] They worked the Harvey, Brockwell and Busty in the 1890s. In 1914 they cleaned out a shaft sunk *c.* 1884 at the top of Bildershaw Bank. The principal Townend colliery closed in 1925 because of flooding, though small-scale drifting continued.[718] In the 1930s the Ramshaw Coal Co. Ltd was active here. Mining ceased in July 1967.

The banner carried into Durham for the 1872 and 1873 Galas showed an arbitration scene, with twelve men sitting around a table and the words, 'Unity, peace, law, and order is our motto'.[719] The reverse displayed two elements. On the left were 'Manhood Suffrage' and 'Household Suffrage

The West Auckland banner portrait of Arthur Horner, a member of the Central Committee of the Communist Party of Great Britain, appointed secretary of the NUM in September 1946.

for the Counties', with a scene of men pushing a wheel inscribed 'Reform'. On the right were portraits of Charles Bradlaugh and Joseph Cowen, with the message, 'Vote by ballot and no property qualification'. It was green with a red edge and gold border.

A later DMA banner showed the seated figure of John Wilson, with House standing to the right.[720]

The 1959 NUM banner was unfurled by Arthur Horner. It carries the portrait of 'A.L. Horner', with the motto, 'Unity is Strength', on one side and 'Red Hill, Durham' on the other. It was produced by Tutill at Chesham and is red with a blue border.

*Location*: Beamish (1967-943).

WESTERTON

This area had been mined by Edmund Backhouse & Co., but by 1841 it was worked by Nicholas Wood & Partners, who operated it as part of the Black Boy Coal Co.[721] The colliery then passed to Bolckow, Vaughan & Co. in the 1870s, and the High Main and Brockwell were principally worked. The colliery was closed in 1924, but was restarted in May 1928, though it became loss-making. The company was absorbed by Dorman, Long & Co. in 1929. The Merrington Lane drift was used and work continued until 1931.

A banner carries full-length paintings of Trevelyan, Alexander MacDonald and Lloyd Jones (named at the base of the panel) holding scrolls inscribed 'Franchise', 'Employers' Liability' and 'Arbitration'. The reverse side shows a Good Samaritan scene, with the motto, 'Go and do thou likewise'. This was produced by H. Hales of 10 Wellington Street, The Strand, London, and is pale grey and green damask silk with a yellow border. It measures 8 ft 5 in × 8 ft 8 in (257 × 264 cm).
*Location*: Beamish (1984-10-26).

The 1957 NUM banner was unfurled by A. Greenwood at Spennymoor Town Hall on 19 July. It showed a band, banner and crowd crossing Elvet bridge on its way to the Racecourse on Gala day, while the reverse showed a miner and an apprentice. The banner was transferred to Houghton lodge (q.v.).

WESTOE

*See also* Harton.

The Harton Coal Co. sank a shaft in 1909–11 as an outlier to the St Hilda colliery (q.v.), which remained as the main coal winding shaft. The pit took on its own identity in 1947, with work concentrating on the Yard seam using longwall. It was modernized in the 1950s to work undersea reserves, with a tower-mounted multi-rope friction drum winder set up over the new Crown shaft, 3.5 ton mine cars, and 12.5 ton battery locos.[722] Work concentrated on the Main, Maudlin and Brass Thill using 270 h.p. AM double-ended ranging drum shearers, the produce principally for the Blyth, Drax, Eggborough, Kingsnorth and Tilbury power stations.[723] The pit was included in the Heseltine closure list announced on 13 October 1992, although it had substantial proven operational reserves.[724] It was subsequently included in the moratorium on ten pits and was then closed in May 1993. Demolition was planned for 25 November 1993.[725]

The NUM banner was commissioned in 1976, although apparently produced in 1980. It was designed by E. Malcolm, the lodge secretary, and carries a panel with three roundel portraits of 'T. Hepburn', 'A.J. Cook' and 'Nye Beven', 'Pioneers of Social Justice'. The reverse carries two eliptical paintings of 'St Hilda's Colliery' and 'Westoe Colliery' (the Crown shaft) with the inscription,

We are the far off future of the distant past
We are that noble race of men for whom they dreamed and died.

The banner was produced by Turtle & Pearce (no. 6.80) and is red with a yellow border. It measures 6 ft 8 in × 8 ft (203 × 244 cm).
*Location*: South Shields Labour Party Headquarters, Ede House, Wentworth Terrace, South Shields. Transferred there in 1993.

The 1992 NUM South Shields banner reproduced the portraits and inscription used on the 1976 banner, but E. Malcolm and W.A. Lilley, the lodge treasurer, designed a new leading side.[726] The obverse carries a central panel with scroll edging, divided into three scenes. On the left is a scene of police cavalry charging a picket line – 'Orgreave June 18 1984'. The central roundel shows a half-length portrait of a miner, dressed in vest and pit helmet, holding his daughter in his right arm, while holding an open book in his left hand. The scene on the right side shows a fettered man, arms raised, breaking his chains – 'The enemy within'. Under the scenes, and within the panel, are the mottoes, 'Agitate', 'Educate' and 'Liberate'. Below the panel, on a scroll, is the inscription 'Eternal vigilance / the price of freedom'. The reverse shows the portraits of Hepburn, Cook and Bevan, but without the 'Pioneers of Social Justice' inscription. The banner was produced by Chippenham Design, Cromer, Norfolk. The mark, 'Chippenham 0263788221', is placed near A.J. Cook's portrait. The banner is red with a blue border and measures 6 ft 11 in × 7 ft 9 in (211 × 236 cm).
*Location*: South Shields Town Hall.

WEST PELTON

The colliery had two shafts, the Alma, near Grange Villa, and Handen Hold pit, at West Pelton. A series of banners are known under the collective term, West Pelton Collieries, but others exist for Handen Hold (q.v.) and Alma, in association with Twizell (q.v.).

The 1873 banner showed an arbitration scene on one side and men pushing a wheel on the other.[727]

A damask Tutill banner of West Pelton Collieries, in use *c*. 1895, showed Gladstone and MacDonald on one side and Crawford standing beside the seated figure of Ald. Fowler, mayor of Durham, on the other.[728]

A new banner was unfurled by James Robson in 1927.[729]

WEST STANLEY

The coal royalty of Charles Townley was leased to Messrs Clark, Rayne, Burn, Hawthorn and Anderson in 1842, but was operated principally by David Burn.[730] There were three shafts, the Kettledrum, sunk in 1859, the Lamp, of 1874, and the New pit, of 1876.[731] In the 1890s the Shield Row, Five Quarter, Low Main, Hutton and Busty were worked. Fire destroyed the pithead in 1891 and an explosion in 1909 killed 168.[732] The pit was later worked by the South Derwent Coal Co. Ltd, but closed in 1936.

BANNERS OF THE DURHAM COALFIELD

The DMA banner carried at the funeral of the victims of the 1909 disaster bore a 'Unity is Strength' image.

A later DMA banner shows a depiction of the 1909 disaster, with a miner kneeling in a seam, arms raised, with his lamp and pick on the floor. The explosion's cloud of smoke and gas swirls above him and is shown rising to the surface at the pithead. Houses and gardens are shown beside the pit and, above, an angel flies, carrying an olive branch. Attached to the underground scene is a scroll inscribed 'The Unknown Miner'. The reverse shows a miner and Britannia standing before Justice, negotiating 'A Fair Exchange'. The miner's belt is inscribed MFGB. The banner is blue with a red border and measures 10 ft × 8 ft 4 in (305 × 254 cm). *Location*: Beamish (1984-10-27).

WEST THORNLEY

This was a Weardale Iron Co. colliery. In the 1890s coal was worked by 350 hands from the Ballarat, Five Quarter, Top, Main and Three Quarter seams.[733] It closed in 1925 with the loss of 450 jobs, but reopened in 1937.[734] It finally closed on 6 November 1965.

The surviving DMA banner, produced by Slingsby & Son at Nuneaton, shows a roundel portrait of John Wilson set centrally over a panel depicting the North Road offices of the DMA, with all four statues in the windows. There are blank side panels. The reverse has clasped hands over a panel depicting two miners with tools, set either side of a representation of Justice. At the lower corners of the panel are circular scenes of the bundle of sticks fable and the Good Samaritan. The obverse painting would suggest a date between 1905 and 1915. *Location*: Red Hill.

WESTWOOD

The colliery was sunk by Consett Iron Co. in 1871 and worked the Bottom Busty, Three Quarter and Brockwell. It temporarily closed in 1901, because of a slump in coke sales, and finally closed in 1940.

The 1873 Gala banner carried a scene of Justice on one side, with the verse,

> Two years we have been established, which surely is not long,
> Yet now the miners' union is forty thousand strong.[735]

The reverse showed a master and workman shaking hands, and the lines,

> The Union they say is winding its way, and driving all fear,
> Yes, the old times are fled, the old bond is dead, and never a tear.

In 1895 a banner designed by a young local man, Mr Unwin, was unfurled.[736] On one side it showed Justice, surmounted by portraits of

West Thornley banner, by Slingsby & Son of Nuneaton, with images of Unity and Justice, the Good Samaritan and the bundle of sticks fable.

Gladstone, Lloyd Jones and William Crawford. On the other side was a portrait of Tommy Ramsey, with a view of Westwood colliery and scenes of pit life.

## WHEATLEY HILL

The pit was sunk in 1869, probably by the Thornley Coal Co., but on 19 January 1871 five men were drowned when water entered from Thornley. Within twenty years the pit had passed to the Original Hartlepool Collieries Co. Ltd. The firm operated under difficulties until final collapse in 1884. In 1885 it was taken over by the Weardale Iron & Coal Co. Ltd. Work on the Harvey started in 1892 and in 1900 a second-hand Dunlop & Meredith vertical winding engine was set up.[737] From 1956 coal was processed at Thornley.[738] Exhaustion of reserves led to the closure of the No. 1 pit on 11 December 1965 and the men were transferred to No. 2. The deteriorating quality of the coal and financial losses led to final closure on 3 May 1968.[739]

The 1873 Gala banner showed Capital and Labour, 'Let us reason together'. The reverse side showed a checkweighman at work, 'A just balance is our delight'.[740]

A later DMA banner carries a portrait of Peter Lee on one side and a 'Suffer little children to come unto me' image on the other. It is red and grey damask silk with a red border and measures 8 ft 9 in × 7 ft 3 in (267 × 221 cm). It was at the 1947 Gala.
*Location*: Wheatley Hill Community Centre.

The NUM banner repeated the images, although there is a small change to the New Testament scene. It was carried into the Cathedral for the 1968 Gala service[741] and is a red and purple damask silk, produced by Tutill at Chesham. In 1993 the silk below the central painting was missing. Length 5 ft (152.5 cm).
*Location*: Red Hill.

WHITE LEA

The colliery, near Crook, was sunk in 1840.[742] It was owned, in the early 1850s by Ralph Walters, but was operated from 1855 by Bolckow, Vaughan & Co. It was subsequently taken over by Pease & Partners in 1889.[743] The 1856 Ordnance Survey map shows Old White Lea, west of Billy Row, White Lea Colliery, north of Peases Bankfoot complex, and New White Lea, to the south-west.[744] White Lea drift closed in 1904.[745]

The banner at the 1872 and 1873 Galas displayed a beehive with the verse,

> In this beehive we are all alive,
> In heart we are joined together;
> And if you will our Union try,
> We'll live together.

The reverse side carried the words, 'Here's my hand, here's my heart; by our labour we live'.[746]. It was magenta and blue.

The banner at the 1874 Gala showed the North Road Miners' Hall 'Now being erected in this city'.[747]

WHITWELL

There were landsale workings of the royalty in the early eighteenth century by Abraham Teesdale and Mrs Ann Wilkinson.[748] The main colliery, east of Shincliffe, initially comprised two pits, 'A' (1836–7) and 'B' (1840), sunk to the Hutton and operated by the Whitwell Coal Co. (Messrs White, Robson and Ogden).[749] The 'C' pit was sunk in 1855–6.[750] By the 1860s it was operated by White, Panton, Robson & Co., with 200 hands.[751] It seems to have closed in the late 1870s, and in 1884 when the lease, held by J.M. Ogden, was due to expire, there were negotiations on a takeover, but there is little evidence of this happening.

The banner at the 1873 Gala bore emblems of Peace and Friendship, 'Do justice, love mercy, unite together'.[752] The reverse showed docks and ships, with the title, 'Colony and Commerce'.

## WHITWORTH PARK

The Durham County Coal Co. sank Whitworth Park colliery, reaching the Hutton in 1841, but the company closed it in 1842.[753] West Dock Co. then sank the Whitworth shaft, but it was sold to R.S. Johnson and T.M. Reay, who worked the Low Main.[754] Economic problems forced its closure in 1883. The plant was sold in 1885, with the heapstead going to Castle Eden colliery.[755] Mining was subsequently carried on by Messrs Brown & Oliver who continued with the Low Main in the 1890s. A new Whitworth Park colliery was opened in 1928, operated by Whitworth Park Coal Co. Following nationalization work concentrated on thin seams with hand-filling, but exhaustion of reserves forced closure on 26 July 1974.[756]

A banner was present at a meeting of miners and ironworkers at Tudhoe Grange on 29 June 1872 to discuss weekly pay.

The 1873 Gala banner carried representations of Labour and Capital, 'A fair day's pay for a fair day's work' and 'Masters, give unto your servants'.[757]

A DMA banner, probably from Pagebank, of *c.* 1910, shows John Wilson seated, wearing his Doctor of Civil Law robes, on one side and a scene with a miner and an owner on the other. The owner holds a scroll inscribed 'Land owner's coal rent ten pence per ton. To workman from hewing coal one shilling per ton tax on labour'. Below the figures are two inscriptions – for the owner, 'One colliery on my estate returns me £10,000 per year without risk of life or capital', and for the miner, 'The same colliery returns me £60 per year for labour and risk of life and limb every day'. The banner is gold and blue damask silk, with an orange border, and measures 8 ft 6 in square (258 cm square). It has a Chesham address label attached to the top fabric, which may be associated with the painting of the new lodge name.
*Location*: Red Hill.

A NUM banner showed a shoulder-length portrait of 'A.J. Cook'.[758]

A new lodge banner was unveiled by C.F. Gray, MP for Durham, at Byers Green on 22 July 1949.[759] It was designed by the local lodge delegate, Coun. T.M. Moult, and showed a miner holding the badge of the Labour Party, with the words, 'Let us face the future'. The reverse side showed the Miners' Memorial in Durham Cathedral. The banner was green, red, brown and gold.

A subsequent NUM banner shows A.J. Cook on the front and a scene on Palace Green, Durham Cathedral, with a band playing, entitled 'Gresford.

Lest we forget'. It was produced by Tutill at Chesham and is red with a blue border. It was repainted and renovated by D. Brenen in 1983 and measures 8 ft 8 in × 8 ft 1 in (264 × 247 cm).
*Location*: Red Hill.

The lodge then acquired the New Shildon lodge banner (q.v.) which shows 'Dr Hugh Dalton MP', seated at a desk, pen in hand. The reverse depicts aged miners' homes, 'Security in Retirement'. The banner was produced by Tutill at Chesham and is green with a yellow border.
*Location*: Spennymoor Town Hall.

## WINGATE

The pit was initially operated by Lord Howden & Partners, with the Lord shaft in 1839.[760] It was later worked by the Executors of John Gulley. A second shaft, the Lady, was also sunk. By the 1880s the Wingate Grange Coal Co. was in control. An explosion on 14 October 1906 killed twenty-four. Output was principally exported and known on the coal market as 'Caradoc'. The Lord served as the upcast, with the Lady as the downcast, ventilation being further assisted by the Marley shaft at Hutton Henry. By the 1950s Five Quarter and Main were abandoned and Harvey and Tilley were worked by longwall at hand-getting faces. The pit closed on 26 October 1962.

The 1873 Gala banner showed the bundle of sticks fable, 'How good and loving it is to dwell together in unity'.[761]

A subsequent DMA banner bore a large central portrait, flanked by two

The draped banner of Wingate lodge being carried at the funeral procession for the victims of the 1906 disaster.

small portraits. The reverse showed a landscape and portraits of Shakespeare, Robert Burns and another.

This was replaced by one carrying three circular linked portraits of 'A.J. Cook', 'Peter Lee' and 'J. Keir Hardie'. The reverse shows a 'Labour and Peace' image. It is cream and red damask silk with a red border. The banner was at the 1947 Gala.

*Location*: Wingate Community Centre.

## WITTON

The pit, formerly an element of Charlaw colliery, was sunk in 1859–60 to the Hutton and was operated from the 1890s by Charlaw & Sacriston Collieries Co. Ltd.[762] In 1882 the pit was linked by a drift to Sacriston colliery (q.v.). The Shield Row was worked from the 1920s by Nos 1 and 2 drifts, near Sacriston Heugh, with Sacriston colliery working the seam by the Coronation drift. Operations ceased on 8 January 1966.

Probably the first banner was unfurled in Front Street, Sacriston on 13 July 1902.[763] On one side were the mottoes, 'United we stand, divided we fall' and 'We unite to assist each other'. On the other side were portraits of John Wilson and Thomas Cann.

The 1923 banner was unfurled by T.H. Cann and J. Swan.[764] It carries portraits of Cann and J. Lawson, with John Wilson in the centre wearing Doctor of Civil Law robes. The reverse carries a 'Sunshine of Liberty' image, with the verse, 'These things shall be. A loftier race than e're the world hath seen shall rise, with flame of freedom in their souls, and light of knowledge in their eyes'. It is blue with a red border and has a patch of red and white damask silk, probably from an earlier banner, attached to the bottom right corner, which still retains part of a mark of Tutill's City Road works. The bottom section of the border is very damaged, and the banner now measures 8 ft 9 in × 8 ft 4 in (267 × 254 cm). It was in use in 1947.

*Location*: Beamish (1984-10-28).

A Witton Lodge banner was unfurled by Sam Watson on 14 July 1950, in the presence of Herbert Morrison and Lord Lawson.[765] It was produced by Tutill at Chesham and carries paintings of the aged miners' homes at Sacriston, 'A reward for their labours', on the front and the Hermitage on the reverse, with the motto, 'And they came to be healed of their wounds'. The banner is red and silver damask, with a red border and a Chesham address label on the heading strip. It measures 7 ft 8 in × 7 ft 2 in (234 × 219 cm).

*Location*: Sacriston Community Centre.

## WOODHOUSE CLOSE AND TINDALE (EMILY)

This colliery lay south-west of Bishop Auckland and was sunk around 1842 by Mr Flintoff to take remaining coal out of the disused Coppy Crooks colliery.[766] It later came into the possession of Thomas Vaughan & Co., Middlesborough ironmasters. The firm became bankrupt, and the colliery was sold in 1880.[767] Pease & Partners were certainly working

Tindale in 1885, and the lodge was linked with St Helen's, but the pit was abandoned by 1897. Between 1856 and 1897 Woodhouse Close New colliery was sunk, just to the south-west, near Tindale Crescent (which had developed close to Fylands Bridge gas works and engine sheds). It probably closed in the 1930s.

The 1873 Gala banner carried a depiction of the horrors of an explosion:

> The dangers that miners have to undergo,
> Are many and fearful, by this you may know.[768]

## WOODIFIELD

The colliery was sunk south-west of Crook in 1840–3 and was worked by Bolckow, Vaughan & Co, certainly in the 1850s.[769] It closed in 1884[700] and again in 1909.[771] Further mining was carried out in the 1930s by Steels House Colliery Co. Ltd.[772]

Two banners were carried into Durham for the 1873 Gala.[773] One showed emblems of a fair division of capital and labour. The second carried a portrait of William Crawford entering the Commons, 'We are resolved not to rest content, until a man to Parliament we have sent'. The reverse showed an arbitration scene, 'In justice we demand a fair share of the gain, which from the products of our labour you obtain'.

## WOODLAND

Messrs Sharp and Hardy worked the pit on a lease from the Duke of Cleveland until 1837. It was subsequently held by the assignees of the late Revd W.L. Prattman, and from 1867 was operated by Messrs Whitwell, Fryer, Grieveson & Dale (later termed Woodland Collieries Co. Ltd), with drifting to work Five Quarter and Main.[774] The firm also operated Crake Scar (1872) and developed Wigglesworth Colliery (exhausted 1901). The Cowley shaft was sunk in 1896.[775] The firm went into liquidation, and its operations at New Copley and Langleydale were sold to New Copley Collieries Ltd.[776] Woodland pit was taken over by Cargo Fleet Iron Co. Ltd and operated by them until 1921. Some small-scale mining took place up to *c.* 1926.

The banner at the 1874 Gala showed an arbitration scene – 'Come let us reason together, and do justice and love mercy'. The reverse showed a substantial house close to a field of corn, with a woman at the door holding out her hand to receive her miner husband home from work – 'Welcome my bonny pit lad'.[777]

A later DMA banner carries the 'Amicitia, Amor et Veritas' design on the obverse and two miners shaking hands by an overturned basket of coal on the reverse, with the motto, 'Unity is Strength'. It is blue and yellow damask silk with a red border and is now incomplete, the surviving piece measuring 9 ft × 6 ft 9 in (274 × 206 cm).

*Location*: Beamish (1984-10-29).

Another DMA banner repeats the 'Amicitia' design on the front and has miners shaking hands in front of an angel bearing a ribbon inscribed 'Unity is Strength' on the back. The latter scene carries the title, 'United to obtain the just reward of our labour'. The banner is blue and gold damask silk with a red border and was produced by Tutill at the City Road works. There is a repair to the name scroll. It is now in pieces and measures 8 ft 6 in × 7 ft 9 in (259 × 236 cm). This is probably the Woodland banner, recorded as having fallen to pieces at the 1969 Gala display of old banners, which was carried tied together with string.[778] *Location*: Beamish (1984-10-30).

WOOLEY

The colliery was sunk in 1864 by Joseph Pease & Partners, forming part of the Peases West complex of collieries. The coal hopper and washery were badly damaged by fire on 30 January 1911. The pit closed in June 1927, but reopened in 1929.[779] It closed again in September 1931, but restarted in 1937, when Pease & Partners agreed a long-term order to supply the total output to Dorman, Long and Co. for coking purposes. It was linked with Roddymoor and continued until final closure in August 1963.

The Tutill banner at the 1872 and 1873 Galas showed a view of the colliery, 'We live for the well-being of our fellow men, in order that they may live for ours'. The reverse showed an arbitration scene, 'My command is that ye love one another'.[780]

The 1938 banner depicts a miner, cap in hand, wearing jacket and pit hoggers, offering support to a weeping widow at a grave, with her three children – 'We succour the widows and orphans'. The reverse carries the pattern-book 'Labour and Peace' image. It was produced by Tutill at the City Road works and is red and blue damask silk, with a yellow border. The banner is now very fragile and measures 8 ft 10 in (269 cm) in length. *Location*: Red Hill.

# Area Banners

A simple banner was used in the 1970s, inscribed 'NUM / Durham Area'. It was carried at the London march against the Industrial Relations Bill in 1971.[781]

The NUM Durham Miners' Association banner was designed by Jack Davis, of Blackhall lodge, and Bill Dowding. It was unfurled by Joe Gormley at Durham Cathedral in 1981.[782] It carries a rounded shield containing paintings and date plaques of the room in the Market Hotel – Durham '1869'; the Miners' Hall in North Road '1876'; Red Hill '1915' – with the DMA 1869 shield, set on a background of clouds. The reverse carries a similar shield, with an illustration of the statues of Forman,

Patterson, MacDonald and Crawford on a grassy slope; a pithead is in the background. Below the shield is a ribbon inscribed 'A History of Loyalty'. The banner images were originally shown as sketches, but colour was later added. It is red with a yellow border and measures 8 ft × 6 ft (324 × 183 cm). *Location*: Red Hill.

The amalgamation of the Durham Miners' Association, Northumberland Miners' Association, Durham Colliery Mechanics' Association, the Northumberland Colliery Mechanics' Association and the Durham Winding Enginemen's Association to form the NUM North East Area in 1981 was marked by the purchase of a new area banner. This was produced by John Midgley of Chippenham Design, Norfolk, and was dedicated by the Rt Revd David Jenkins, Bishop of Durham, on 6 February 1991.[783] It was first used at the 107th Gala.

On one side of the banner are clasped hands, portraits of Thomas Hepburn and Martin Jude and scenes of Durham Cathedral and the Tyne bridge. The main illustration shows bands, crowds and banners emerging from the Miners' Hall at Red Hill, 'United we stand – divided we fall'. On the other side are two ribbons carrying the inscriptions, 'National Union of Mineworkers' and 'North East Area', with safety lamps hanging from the ends of the scrolls. The lower scroll is supported by a miner, shown with naked torso and wearing a safety helmet. Around the figure are scenes from the 1984–5 strike – a pithead and wheel, pickets, placards proclaiming 'Coal not dole' and 'Victory of the miners', and riot police, one wielding a truncheon. Initially a dividing grey band separated this scene from a lower image with two miners, wearing brown overalls and helmets, working in a seam, but later the inscription, 'Our fight is for the right to work', was added to the band. Below the illustrations is a scroll inscribed 'We struggle for justice and freedom'. There is a manufacturer's mark of a green disc inscribed 'Chippenham / TU / Design'. The banner is green with a red border and measures 7 ft 6 in × 9 ft 10 in (229 × 300 cm). *Location*: Red Hill.

# Colliery Officials and Staff Association (COSA)

COSA acquired the redundant Bowburn banner (q.v.) after the pit closed in 1967. The banner carries the inscription, 'National Union of Mineworkers COSA', on a scroll at the top with a lower scroll marked 'Colliery Officials and Staff'. The central panel shows an aerial view of 'Conishead Priory'. The reverse shows a Gala scene on the Racecourse, with the motto, 'Workers of all lands unite'. It was present at the 1982 Gala.[784] It is red with a blue border. *Location*: COSA, Sutton in Ashfield, Nottinghamshire.

# Durham County Colliery Enginemen's, Boiler Minders' and Firemen's Association

The Enginemen's Mutual Protection Society was formed in 1864, but collapsed in 1869. It was succeeded in 1871 by the Durham County Colliery Enginemen's Mututal Protection Association. The Boiler Minders joined the Association in 1893, and the Firemen in 1912.

The County of Durham Colliery Enginemen's Association banner had an elliptical central panel showing a committee meeting or arbitration case around a table, with the motto, 'Every man is a master and a servant'.[785]

The banner of 1900 was produced at the works of W. Elam, in Hackney

The 1900 banner of the Durham County Enginemen's and Boiler Minders' Association.

Road, London.[786] It bears scrolls inscribed 'Durham County Enginemen's and Boiler Minders' Association / Established 1871', with an elaborate central panel. At the top are three portraits – Mr Nicholson, the president, the central figure of W.H. Lambton, the general secretary from 1874, who had been one of the founders and early presidents of the Association, and W.B. Charlton of Hetton, the treasurer. Underneath them are the words, 'United we stand. Divided we fall'. Lower down are portraits of George Stephenson and James Watt, both seated, flanking a colliery scene of the pithead and a steam engine pulling trucks. Below are illustrations of a steam engine and a beam engine. At the bottom of the scene, on a scroll, is the text, 'There is no safe side but the side of truth'.[787] The reverse design was emblematic of the work of Friendly Societies. Under clasped hands and the motto, 'Industrial and provident we unite to assist each other', is a sickbed scene, flanked by the figures of Unity and Justice, with the title, 'I was sick and ye visited me'. Below the figures is an engine and two stokers standing by a row of boilers, with the motto, 'Honour all men but serve the brethren'. It is blue, with a red border and measures 8 ft 8 in × 9 ft 8 in (264 × 295 cm).

*Location*: Stored at County Hall, later transferred to Red Hill.

A new banner was unfurled by Edward Nicholson, the Enginemen's president, at the Town Hall in 1937.[788] On the obverse, within a large roundel, are two past secretaries, W.H. Lambton and W.B. Charlton, with their current secretary, George Peart. Below the portraits is an illustration of a winder house and pithead gear (probably Horden) and the motto, 'Organisation and Security'. The reverse shows Conishead Priory, 'We unite to assist each other'. The banner is a light blue and silver damask silk, with a red border, and measures 9 ft 1 in × 8 ft 9 in (277 × 267 cm).

*Location*: Red Hill.

# Durham Cokemen

Cokeworkers were represented by two organizations – The Durham Coke Burners' Association, for men considered to be in charge of the ovens and the burning process, and the Durham Coke Drawers' & Labourers' Association, which covered drawers, small runners, levellers, fillers, labourers and daubers.

The only located reference to a nineteenth-century banner for cokeworkers relates to the burners' association. At a mass meeting on the Batts, Bishop Auckland, in 1872, cokeburners from surrounding collieries marched onto the field preceded by a 'handsome new banner'.[789]

The banner of the NUM Durham cokemen (representing Derwenthaugh, Fishburn, Hawthorn, Lambton, Monkton, Norwood and Randolph) carries, on one side, a large roundel containing the interconnected portraits of A.J. Cook, Peter Lee and J. Keir Hardie, set against a background of a colliery scene, with a windy pick and shovel. The banner was originally produced by G. Tutill at the City Road works for Silksworth miners' lodge (q.v.) and, on transfer, the reverse scene of Conishead Priory was overpainted by Maurice White in 1975 and again by J. Doddsworth in 1980, to show a cokeworks. The illustration chosen is the complex at Lambton. This site had Semet Solvay waste heat, and Simplex regenerative ovens, built in 1907 and 1918 respectively. They were replaced in the latter half of the 1930s by Colins silica regenerative ovens. The banner is a purple and red damask silk with a light blue border and measures 7 ft × 6 ft 4 in (213 × 193 cm).

*Location*: Red Hill.

# Durham Colliery Mechanics

The first attempt at a union was the National Amalgamated Society of Colliery Mechanics, formed in 1874, which collapsed in 1878. It was succeeded by the Durham Colliery Mechanics' Association, which was registered in 1879. The union became part of the Durham County Mining Federation and, in 1918, became affiliated, through the DMA, to the MFGB.

The earliest surviving banner carries a central ellipse containing a portrait of 'J.W. Taylor Esq MP', with four flanking scenes showing workmen with various tools. The upper and lower scenes are divided by a horizontal strip decorated with a rose, thistle, leek and shamrock. The reverse shows the executive seated around a table, with the motto, 'United we stand, divided we fall'. The banner was produced by Tutill at the City Road works and is blue with a red border. It measures 12 ft 6 in × 10 ft (381 × 305 cm).

This banner was produced in the 1880s or early 1890s and originally carried a portrait of Launcelot Trotter, elected union president in 1880 and general secretary in 1881. Trotter was suspended in 1897 because of financial irregularities.[790] Initially Hetton-le-Hole lodge proposed that the banner be destroyed and a new one purchased, showing Mechanics' emblems, but no portraits; however, in 1899 it was resolved that one side should be repainted. Tutill replaced Trotter with the painting of John Taylor MP, general secretary from 1897 to 1923. Taylor became MP for the Chester-le-Street division in 1906, which implies either that the portrait repainting was delayed, or that the letters of his new title were added later.

*Location*: Beamish (1979-996).

An NUM Mechanics' banner was decorated with a large ellipse showing the traditional view of Durham Cathedral flanked by four small illustrations of machinery.[791] The other side carried a central illustration of a Dosco road-heading machine, with a mechanic standing beside it in blue overalls. This too was flanked by small illustrations of machinery, with a motto, 'The past we inherit, the future we build'. The banner was red with a yellow border.

BRADLEY SHOPS LODGE (LEADGATE)

The banner was unfurled by Aneurin Bevan in 1959.[792] The central panel, surmounted by the arms of the NCB, shows a mechanic with a spanner in his hand, handing over an Anderson Boyes 'Dreadnought' coal-cutter to a miner, to replace his hand pick. In the background are the area workshops, and with the scene is the motto, 'Nationalisation, Mechanisation, Realisation'. Flanking the panel are eight illustrations of tools indicative of the different trades – hacksaw and spanner (fitter), anvil and sledge hammer (blacksmith), trowel and spirit level (bricklayer), flash and pincers (electrician), saw and plane (carpenter), electric motor and cable (armature winder), face guard (spot welder), blow torch and cutter (plumber).

The reverse shows Christ with Joseph in the carpenter's shop, with the title 'The Perfect Craftsman'. The scene is also surmounted by the shield of the NCB, with the border illustrations of the trade tools. At the base of the panel are two illustrations – a low-loader carrying a bulldozer, representing the beginnings of NCB opencast mining at the Medomsley site, and a train with coal truck. Below this is a scroll carrying the sub-title, 'Author / Creator / Perfector'. The banner was produced by Tutill at Chesham (no 359) and is blue with a red border. It measures 7 ft 9 in × 7 ft 4 in (237 × 223 cm).
*Location*: Consett Civic Centre.

HORDEN MECHANICS

A banner was produced during the 1984–5 strike, and paid for by D. Robinson. Fabric was donated by factories in Peterlee, and the painting was done by D. Brennan. The central vertical panel is inscribed 'Horden / Mechanics / Lodge', over a shield labelled 'Durham Area', containing a roundel with a border inscribed 'National Union of Mineworkers'. Within the roundel is the Mechanics' logo of interlocked DCM, with a pitwheel over the M. Below the shield, on three V-shaped stripes, is the motto, 'Miners united will never be defeated'. The main fabric is green, with a painted light blue central panel. It measures 4 ft 4 in × 6 ft 4 in (132 × 193 cm). It is stylistically similar to the banners of the Houghton Mines Rescue Brigade (q.v.), Durham Miners' Support Group (q.v.), Burnhope Miners' Support Group (q.v.), the Confederation of Health Service Employees (Northern Area) and Worsboro Women Against Pit Closures.
*Location*: Private Owner.

TURSDALE MECHANICS

The Tursdale Mechanics' NUM banner is a post-1984–5 strike banner by Barry Ormsby. On one side it carries a central roundel showing a man

holding a baby, with a woman raising her hand to protect him from the truncheon of a police cavalryman who is wearing helmet and visor. The other side has a roundel with a scene showing a pair of hands putting together machine parts, set over a large wheel or fan blades and a stylized pithead. Around the border of the scene is the inscription, 'In our hands lies a power greater than their hoarded gold'. The banner is cotton duck, painted with acrylics, and is red with a green edging strip. It measures 6 ft × 6 ft 8 in (183 × 203 cm).
*Location*: Red Hill.

WESTOE

The 1984 banner was produced by Mrs Perry, with artwork by Michael Finnigan, and was first displayed at the 1985 Gala.[793] The obverse shows the colliery, viewed from the Westoe shaft towards the Crown shaft, with conveyers, washery, track and NCB Harton steel wagons. Below the scene is the motto, 'The past we inherit, the future we build'. Above and below the central panel is the Mechanics' logo of the interwoven letters DCM with a pulley wheel above the M. The reverse carries a view of the west end of Durham Cathedral, viewed from the south-west, and the same motto and logo. It is red with a blue border and measures 6 ft 8 in × 7 ft 6 in (203 × 229 cm).
*Location*: St Hilda's Church, South Shields.

WILLINGTON

A banner of 'Durham Colliery Mechanics' Association NUM No. 5 Area' carries a scene of Conished Priory in a panel surmounted by the label, 'Willington'. The reverse has an 'Emancipation of Labour' image. It was conserved in 1954.
*Location*: Beamish (1971-201).

Another banner showed, on one side, a 'Labour and Peace' image[794] and on the reverse, 'Emancipation of Labour', with the motto, 'Workers of the world unite you have only your chains to lose, you have a world to win'.[795]

# *National Association of Colliery Overmen, Deputies and Shotfirers (NACODS)*

The Durham Deputies Mutual Aid Association was formed in 1873, but was expanded as NACODS in 1945.

The first NACODS banner was unfurled at John Street, Durham City, by J.G. Sanderson, the former president for twenty-five years, in 1950.[796]

The unfurling of the 1950 National Association of Colliery Overmen, Deputies and Shotfirers' banner in John Street, Durham.

The motto, 'Unity is Strength', was displayed on a scroll over a central roundel showing a manager, deputy and miner clasping hands at a meeting station. In the background was a kist, drift entrance, office and the western towers of Durham Cathedral. On the rim of the roundel were the words, 'Rules and Regulations', 'Safety First' and 'First Aid'. The reverse had a scroll inscribed 'Combined efforts shall accomplish all things' over a roundel, with the inscription of 'National Assoc. Colliery Overmen Deputies and Shotfirers. Durham Area' around the rim. The central scene showed a deputy holding up a safety lamp to test for gas. The design was by R.W. Smith of 4 Park House Gardens, Sherburn. The banner was a red and black damask silk with a green border.

A new banner was unfurled by NACODS president, A. Keenleyside, in 1963.[797] It carries a roundel scene of a deputy, wearing white overalls and a black safety helmet, holding up a lamp to test for gas. The figure is standing in a working with curved roof girders. Below the roundel is a scroll inscribed 'Safety is our concern'. The reverse shows the frontage of 'The Sam Watson Rest Home, Richmond'. The banner was produced by Tutill at Chesham and is red with yellow border. It measures 6 ft 9 in × 7 ft 5 in (206 × 226 cm).
*Location*: NACODS, John Street, Durham City.

## Houghton Mines Rescue Brigade

A banner was purchased in 1983. It carries the name of the brigade at the top, over a DMA shield, overlaid with bands inscribed 'Thomas Hepburn

1796–1864' and the motto, 'Pioneer! O Pioneers'. At the bottom of the painted ground is the Latin motto, 'Labore et Honore, Clarior e Tenebris'. Also at the bottom right corner are the names of the banner makers, D. & F. Brenen. It is single-sided, with the painting applied to red fabric, and it measures 3 ft 7 in × 4 ft 1.5 in (109 × 126 cm). There are also red side hangings, both 9 in × 4 ft 1.5 in (23 × 126 cm). The carrying frame is much earlier, with pike heads bearing the embossed stamp of G. Tutill and the City Road address.
*Location*: Mr McGough, Houghton le Spring.

# Production Bannerettes

In July 1948 Tutills announced that they would present a banner on which would be recorded the name of the lodge of the colliery which produced the highest output between Galas.[798] The vertical rectangular bannerette was fastened to a cross bar, hung from a central carrying pole. At the top was a central scroll inscribed 'NUM / Durham Area', set over a panel showing a hand rising from clouds and holding a victor's garland, accompanied by the motto 'By the people / For the people'. This was flanked by sixteen originally blank scrolls and at the base was the title, 'Production Champions'. The name of the colliery champion was added annually to the scrolls.

No. 1

| | | | |
|---|---|---|---|
| East Tanfield | 1949–50 | Thrislington | 1957–8 |
| Kibblesworth | 1950–1 | Towneley Emma | 1958–9 |
| Deaf Hill | 1951–2 | Handen Hold | 1959–60 |
| Heworth | 1952–3 | Silksworth | 1960–1 |
| South Pelaw | 1953–4 | Marsden | 1961–2 |
| Follonsby | 1954–5 | Washington Glebe | 1962–3 |
| Tudhoe Park | 1955–6 | Ravensworth Ann | 1963–4 |
| South Hetton | 1956–7 | East Hetton | 1964–5 |

No. 2

| | | | |
|---|---|---|---|
| Chester Moor | 1965–6 | Vane Tempest | 1973–4 |
| Harton-Westoe | 1966–7 | New Herrington | 1974–5 |
| Houghton | 1967–8 | Murton | 1975–6 |
| Dawdon | 1968–9 | Seaham | 1976–7 |
| Ravensworth Ann | 1969–70 | Seaham | 1977–8 |
| Horden | 1970–1 | New Herrington | 1978–9 |
| Houghton | 1971–2 | Houghton | 1979–80 |
| Eppleton | 1972–3 | Houghton | 1980–81 |

The Production Bannerette coming onto the Racecourse at the 1949 Gala.

No. 3

This bannerette followed the same layout and design as 1 and 2, but the manufacturers details were changed to 'Presented by George Tutill & Turtle & Pearce Ltd. London SE1'.

South Hetton          1981–2
Vane Tempest          1982–3

# Strike and Sacked Miners' Banners

At the 1883 Gala the Ushaw Moor strikers came in with their lodge banner, accompanied by two women carrying a banner marked 'No Surrender'.[799]

At the 1897 Gala, Ouston lodge banner was marked 'On strike against non-unionists'.[800]

During the 1909–10 disturbances over the Eight Hour agreement, the South Moor lodge produced a banner attacking the DMA agent John Johnson. It was inscribed 'We are / the / South Moor miners / Down with / Johnson / the / three shift candidate / the miners ruination / Vote for / Elverston'.[801]

A white sheet with the message, 'To hell with bishops and deans, we demand a living wage', was seen at the 1925 Gala.[802]

After the 1984–5 strike 150 Durham mineworkers were sacked, the third largest group after Yorkshire[306] and Scotland.[206] A number of banners were produced to highlight the position of these men:

DURHAM AREA NUM

This is a blue fabric banner with a central, stylized, light green pithead, overprinted in yellow and red lettering, 'For All Sacked miners. Amnesty Now! Durham NUM'. It measures 6 ft 8 in × 5 ft 7 in (203 × 170 cm). *Location*: Red Hill.

EASINGTON

A plain sheet, strung from two carrying poles, bore the stencilled message, 'Easington's Victimised Miners'. It was carried at the 1986 Gala and was a reminder that five miners had been dismissed from Easington colliery and five were imprisoned.[803]

SACRISTON

This red banner was hung on a standard carrying frame and was inscribed in black and yellow lettering, 'DMA Sacriston Lodge. 40 Dismissed Miners from Private Drifts'.[804] In the upper corners were crossed picks and shovels.

A banner at the 1985 Gala highlighting the position of forty dismissed miners from private drifts.

## SPENNYMOOR AND DISTRICT TRADES UNION COUNCIL

The Spennymoor and District TUC Commemorative Banner, by Barry Ormsby, carries a portrait of Jeff Hartnell, of Tursdale workshops, who was victimized as a result of his active role in the 1984–5 strike. He died shortly afterwards, and the motto around this portrait reads 'Do not mourn for me, struggle for me'. The reverse carries a sunburst, the rays symbolizing Peace and Solidarity, set around a globe from which a clenched fist is raised. Below the globe is the quotation, 'Tyrants' chains are only strong / when slaves submit to wear them'. The paintings are on a red ground.
*Location*: Mr B. Gibson, Ferryhill.

# Durham Miners' Support Groups

## DURHAM AREA

A scroll, inscribed in yellow lettering, 'Durham Miners' Support Groups', is set over a roundel flanked by foliage, flower heads and pit lamps carrying the dates 1984 and 1985. Around the ring are the area details and the motto, 'United we Stand, Divided we Fall'. Within the roundel are a miner and a woman clasping the handle of a safety lamp, while holding a banner of the 'Miners' Support Group' aloft, set over a NUM symbol. At the base is the text, 'The more they suppress me, / the more united they'll

The Durham Miners' Support Group banner, by Davison Brenan.

find us'. The other side carries a similar top scroll and a roundel, the border marked 'Unity is Strength: Break the chains that bind you'. Within the roundel is a colliery scene and a raised fist, with broken manacle, under the scrolled motto, 'Equality'. The roundel is again flanked by foliage, flower heads and lamps. Below the roundel is a broad scroll inscribed 'Come! Join in the battle! / wherein no one can fail. / Living or dying, your deeds shall prevail'. The banner was produced by Davison Brenan in 1985 and is light blue with a red border. It measures 6 ft 3 in × 6 ft (191 × 183 cm).
*Location*: Red Hill.

### BURNHOPE

The scroll of 'Burnhope Miners' Support Group' is set over a roundel whose border is inscribed 'Durham Area' and 'Pioneers Oh! Pioneers'. Within the roundel is the DMA 1869 shield, surmounted by the letters NUM. Flanking the roundel are two plant trails, with small scrolls bearing names and dates – T. Hepburn 1798–1864, A.J. Cook 1885–1931, A.L. Horner 1894-1968 and W. Paynter, 1903–1984. At the base is the verse, 'Come! Join in the battle, where / in no one can fail. Living or / dying your deed shall always / prevail'.

The reverse carries the same group label, over a roundel showing a raised fist, with broken fetters, rising from a colliery, accompanied by the motto, 'Loyalty', an NUM logo and '1984 Strike 1985'. Flanking the roundel are two small circles containing pit lamps and four small scrolls inscribed 'Liberte', 'Egalite', 'Fraternite' and 'Solidarity'. Below the central roundel, in small black lettering, is 'Thomas Hepburn Boldon Fells 1831'. A broad lower scroll carries the verse, 'Tyrants chains are only strong / when slaves submit to bare [*sic*] them, / who will bind them on the throng, / determined not to wear them.'

Both sides carry the mark of 'Davison Brenan 1986'. The main designs are painted onto light blue fabric, with a red border. It measures 4 ft 8.25 in × 5 ft 8.5 in (143 × 174 cm) and follows the style of the Durham area support group banner.
*Location*: St John's Church, Burnhope.

A white sheet, attached to two carrying poles, was inscribed 'Burnhope / Women's / Support Group / Durham Area / Victory / to the Miners'.

### BURNMOOR

A white sheet attached to two carrying poles was inscribed 'Burnmoor / Miners' Wives / Support Group' and 'Coal not Dole'.

### EPPLETON

Within the angular frame of the central panel is the title, 'Eppleton Miners' Wives Support Group', and the motto, 'We shall be heard!' The

central scene shows, in the foreground, a family at a table about to have a meal. Behind is a street scene with women marching arm-in-arm, against a backdrop of pitheads. The panel is attached to red fabric, 3 ft 5 in × 5 ft (104 × 153 cm), with a black cord strung at the base. The painting has been signed by Arthur Scargill and Tom Callan.
*Location*: All Saints' Church, Eppleton.

### WASHINGTON

A bannerette was inscribed 'Washington / Miners' / Family / Support / Group'.

### WEARMOUTH

The banner was inscribed 'Wearmouth /Miners' Wives / Support Group'. Set between the second and third lines was the slogan, 'Coal not Dole'.

# Women Against Pit Closures (WAPC)

### SACRISTON

The Sacriston banner was a white sheet with red lettering, 'Sacriston Women Against Pit Closures'. The 'o' of Sacriston and Women is set out with a cross as a female symbol. The sheet is attached to two carrying poles, and the cloth at these points is inscribed 'Durham Area'.

### SEAHAM–VANE TEMPEST

The banner was inscribed 'Seaham Women Against Pit Closures', with a central roundel containing a stylized pithead and the border title, 'Vane Tempest'. Flanking the roundel were two female symbols.

A yellow dyed cotton banner, with the dominating black outline of the pithead, a top title, 'Vane Tempest Vigil' and the base details, 'Seaham Women Against / Pit Closures', was produced by Lottie Shankland in 1986. It measures 5 ft × 6 ft 4 in (152 × 193 cm).
*Location*: Red Hill

A white sheet inscribed 'WAPC Say Don't Give Up a Job' was also used at the Vane Tempest camp in 1992.

# Save Easington Area Mines (SEAM)

SEAM began as a local campaign group in 1983 to retain threatened collieries operating on the east Durham coast. It became actively involved as a miners' support group following a meeting on 8 May 1984.[805] The group also campaigned to retain services in the area.

The Seaham Women
Against Pit Closures
'Vane Tempest Vigil'
banner.

The banner was a horizontal rectangular blue plastic sheet, hung on a carrying frame, with the design divided into two horizontal bands. On the left side of the upper section, the lamp on a miner's helmet shines a beam across the sheet, which is overlain by the initials 'SEAM'. At the right side is the black outline of a pithead. Below a central dividing line is 'Save Easington Area Mines' and 'Coal not Dole'.

# Durham Aged Mineworkers' Homes Association

A specially commissioned banner was produced by Seaham community programme, with art-work by Walter Hudspith, senior lecturer in art and design at Sunderland Polytechnic. It was first displayed at the 100th Gala in 1983.[806] The Association's title, with the date of establishment, 1898, is carried on three scrolls over a central shield bearing clasped hands. On one side is a depiction of the Castlereagh aged miners' homes at Seaham, with the portraits of Dr John Wilson and Joseph Hopper, while on the other side is a modern home (similar to Gair Court, Kimblesworth), with portraits of Edward Cain and Jack Adair. The banner is purple with a yellow border and measures 6 ft 5 in × 8 ft 8 in (196 × 264 cm).
*Location*: DAMHA, Chester-le-Street.

# Associated Foreign Pennants, Banners and Bannerettes

### CHOPWELL

A red bannerette was presented by the Donbas miners of the Ukraine to Len Hawkshaw, Chopwell lodge chairman, in 1957.[807] In 1976 it was hanging in Chopwell Community Centre, but appears to have transferred to Red Hill where a red bannerette carries, on one side, the message, 'From the miners / of the Donbas coalfield / to their brothers / in labour – the miners / of Durham', with the text repeated in Russian Cyrillic on the other side. On the latter side is an elaborately embroidered Soviet miners' emblem. It measures 1 ft 7.75 in × 2 ft 5.5 in (50 × 75 cm).

### DEAN AND CHAPTER

At the 1956 Gala the lodge banner was draped with a Soviet bannerette, sent as a gift from a delegation who had attended the 1955 Gala.[808] On one side is the message, 'Fraternal greetings to the miners of Durham from the miners of the Soviet Union', while on the other side is the same message

A Soviet miners' bannerette, 'From the miners of the Donbas Coalfield to their brothers in labour – the miners of Durham', Red Hill.

in Russian Cyrillic, surmounted by an elaborately embroidered Soviet miners' emblem. It is red satin, with a yellow fringe and looped hanging cord, and measures 1 ft 7 in × 2 ft 4.5 in (48.5 × 72 cm).
*Location*: Private owner.

DURHAM

At the 1955 Gala, Ivan Rossochinsky, leader of a Soviet miners' delegation, presented Sam Watson with a bannerette, inscribed on one

Easington lodge banner
with the Yugoslav
pennant.

side, 'Best wishes and greetings from the Soviet miners and their families to the miners of Durham and their families'.[809] The message was repeated in Russian Cyrillic on the reverse.

EASINGTON

From 1951 onwards a Yugoslav pennant (a blue-white-red tricolour with red star) has been attached to the lodge banner. This is 2 ft 11.5 in × 7.5 in (90 × 19 cm).
*Location*: Easington Welfare Hall.

SOUTH AFRICA

An anti-apartheid banner by Lottie Shankland repeated the Vane Tempest vigil design of a black pithead on a yellow ground, with two attached labels inscribed, 'Save our Pits' and 'Ban SA Coal'. It was produced in 1985 and was carried on several occasions, such as at the closure of Murton colliery, until the election of Nelson Mandella and the end of apartheid. It is a dyed cotton sheet, 7 ft 3 in × 4 ft 10 in (221 × 148 cm).
*Location*: Durham Anti-Apartheid Group.

# Sources of Illustrations

The following list indicates by page number the sources for all the illustrations reproduced in the book.

| | |
|---|---|
| 64. | Beamish. |
| 65. | Durham University Library, Edis N36. |
| 66, 67. | Author. |
| 68. | Beamish. |
| 71. | Author. |
| 73. | DCRO D/X1116/5, Mrs Burch. |
| 75. | DCRO D/MRP75/19, Miss J. Wade. |
| 77. | D. Scott. |
| 78, 79. | Author. |
| 82. | Gateshead Libraries and Arts Service. |
| 83. | Scorpion Cavendish Ltd. |
| 84. | *Northern Echo* collection, Newsquest (North East) Ltd. |
| 87, 88. | Author. |
| 98. | Sedgefield Borough Council. |
| 100, 102. | Beamish. |
| 103, 104. | Author. |
| 105. | D. Scott. |
| 105. | DCRO NCB25/34, Newsquest (North East) Ltd. |
| 107, 109, 110. | Author. |
| 111. | Beamish. |
| 112. | D. Scott. |
| 115. | DCRO NCB25/29/28, Newsquest (North East) Ltd. |
| 116. | *Northern Echo* collection, Newsquest (North East) Ltd. |
| 120, 121, 122, 141, 143. | Author. |
| 145. | A. Thompson. |
| 156. | Author. |
| 166. | *Sunderland Echo.* |
| 169, 174, 180. | Author. |
| 192. | DCRO NCB25/29/22, Newsquest (North East) Ltd. |
| 197, 198, 212, 221. | Author. |
| 229. | Sedgefield Borough Council. |
| 231. | Author. |
| 239. | Beamish. |
| 243, 246, 251. | Author. |
| 256. | DCRO NCB25/29/26, Newsquest (North East) Ltd. |
| 258. | DCRO NCB25/29/23, Newsquest (North East) Ltd. |
| 260. | NUM (NE Area). |
| 260, 263, 265, 266. | Author |

# References

The following abbreviations have been used:

DA     *Durham Advertiser*
DC     *Durham Chronicle*
DCRO   Durham County Record Office
DMA   Durham Miners' Association
NMLH   National Museum of Labour History, Manchester
PP     Parliamentary Paper
PRO   Public Record Office

References are included in full in the Bibliography.

## Introduction

1. DC 28.6.1872.
2. DC 9.5.1879.
3. DA 5.7.1957.
4. DC 2.7.1880.
5. *Northern Echo* 6.7.1994.
6. Tickner, L. 1989, 60–73, 254–61.
7. Thalia, C. & Wilson, M. 1994.
8. Several banners survive – Esh Winning and Witton Gilbert banners, for instance, now hang in the office of Gerry Steinberg MP. Durham City banner is held by Durham County Record Office (D/X1048/65). Documented examples include New Seaham (DC 5.7.1929) and Rowlands Gill (*Blaydon Courier* 10.6.1955). For illustrations see DCRO D/X1048/48, 52 and 123.

## Chapter 1

1. Gorman, J. 1986, 48; Weedon, G. & Ward, R. 1981.
2. Kelly & Co. 1857, 1573.
3. Kelly & Co. 1859, 1396.
4. Gorman, J. 1986, 50.

5. Rothstein, N. 1987, 125–40, and 1989, 33–47.
6. PP 1857 (94 sess. 2) xxxviii, 439.
7. Collins, L. 1989, unpag.
8. Patent Office, patent no. 1728.
9. Rothstein, N. 1977, 281–9.
10. PRO RG9/141, f. 88–9; RG 10/1629, f. 25.
11. Somerset House, Probate 21.3.1887, vol. 6, 1887.
12. Greater London Record Office, AR/TP51.
13. Companies House 00369605.
14. Kelly & Co. 1866, 1009.
15. Kelly & Co. 1874, 1523.
16. Kelly & Co. 1904, ii, 20.
17. Kelly & Co. 1857, 1972.
18. Kelly & Co. 1864, 1057.
19. Ibid.
20. DC 20.6.1873.
21. Manchester Library. Whaite, H. 1883.
22. Slater, I. 1910, 1476.
23. PP 1818, ix, 11.
24. *The Gentleman's Journal and Gentlewoman's Court Review* 3.4.1903, 18.
25. *Nuneaton Chronicle* 15.10.1943.
26. Airey, A. & J. 1979.
27. Whellan, W. 1865, 581.
28. Whellan, F. 1894, 1137.
29. Kelly & Co. 1897, 337.
30. Not recorded in Kelly & Co. 1890, but listed in 1894 ed., 299.
31. Kelly & Co. 1897, 331.
32. Beamish Museum 1986.118.1.
33. DC 5.7.1872.

## Chapter 2

1. Beamish Museum 1962.225 /W3.05.
2. Northern Film and Television Archive NCB 1/18/3.

3. Leesom, R.A. 1971, 23–4.
4. Cornish, N. 1989.
5. Jim Perry, Durham Colliery Mechanics, Westoe Branch, pers. comm.
6. Kemp, B. 1980, 125.
7. Bell, R.E. 1991, 117.
8. NMLH 1–234.
9. NMLH 1–230.
10. NMLH 1–9.
11. NMLH 1-118.
12. NMLH 1–111 and 1–122.
13. Handford, S.A. 1964, 177.
14. Yorkshire Mining Museum, Caphouse Colliery, Overton.
15. NMLH 1–42.
16. NMLH 1–40.
17. NMLH 1–17.
18. NMLH 1–179.
19. Temperance panel, unprovenanced, Tyne and Wear Museums, Newcastle Discovery, Blandford Square, Newcastle.
20. NMLH 1–17.
21. Page, F. 1970, 206.
22. Piggott, S. 1968.
23. Rosemary Preece, Yorkshire Mining Museum, pers. comm.
24. NMLH 1–124.
25. Wells, S. & Taylor, G. 1992, 77.
26. Ibid., 1214.
27. Kinsley, J. 1969, 121.
28. Davis, T. 1990, 182.
29. Bartlett, J. 1968, 785; Drabble, M. 1991, 957.
30. Bradley, S. 1953, 193.

## Chapter 3

1. DC 12.6.1891.
2. DC 15.7.1892.
3. DC 21.7.1911.
4. DCRO D/DMA 334/25.
5. DC 13.7.1906.
6. DC 3.8.1923.
7. DC 23.7.1937.
8. *Stanley News* 16.6.1955.
9. DC 20.7.1883.
10. DC 17.7.1908.
11. DA 27.7.1951.
12. Abbott, H. 1984, 14.
13. DMA Gala notice 17.6.1878.
14. DMA Gala notice 25.7.1881.
15. DC 3.7.1914.
16. DCRO D/DMA 308/1, 6.8.1925, 66.

17. NUM Durham Area 1959, 1950.
18. WNS 1953, 170–1; Johnson, P. 1991, 626–8.
19. DC 14.6.1872.
20. DC 14.6.1872.
21. DA 24.7.1970.
22. DC 2.7.1937.
23. Dean & Chapter, Durham, Add. Ms. 48.
24. Dean & Chapter, Durham Minutes 6.3.1954.13.
25. Dean & Chapter, Durham, The Eighty-Sixth Miners' Festival Service 1995, 5.

## Chapter 4

1. Clack, P. 1985, 78.
2. DA 23.5.1818.
3. DA 14.11.1829.
4. Dougan, D. & Graham, F. 1969, 42–4.
5. Richardson, M.A. 1844, 82.
6. Richardson, M.A. 1844, 91–2; DA 19.8.1831.
7. Fynes, R. 1923, 56.
8. PRO HO 45/644, f. 148.
9. DC 13.11.1863.
10. DC 4.6.1869.
11. Challoner, R. 1990; *Sunderland Times* 22.6.1869.
12. *Sunderland Times* 6.7.1869.
13. *Sunderland Times* 13.7.1869.
14. *Sunderland Times* 17.7.1869.
15. *Sunderland Times* 27.7.1869.
16. DC 3.9.1869.
17. DC 1.10.1869.
18. DC 26.11.1869.
19. DC 18.2.1870.
20. DC 4.7.1890.
21. DC 7.9.1900.
22. DC 24.7.1896.
23. DC 16.5.1873.
24. DA 21.7.1933.
25. DC 6.5.1873.
26. DC 9.6.1876.
27. DC 9.7.1875.
28. DC 23.6.1905.
29. Webb, S. 1921, 58.
30. DCRO Q/D/SB1; *see also* Turner, J.J, 1985, 22–36.
31. The banner is now hung at Tow Law Community Centre.
32. DC 21.5.1875.
33. Hutchinson, W. 1987, 228.
34. Jones, B.E. 1950, pl. vi.
35. Atherley Jones, L.A. & Bellot, H. H. L. 1904, 15.
36. Wilson, J. 1908, 131–2; Charlton, W.B. 1925, 59–62.

37. DC 15.7.1881.
38. Challoner, R. & Ripley, B. 1990; Wilson, K. 1986, 81–104.
39. DC 18.4.1873.
40. DC 1.7.1881.
41. DC 5.8.1881.
42. Wilson, J. 1908, 192.
43. *Auckland Chronicle* 8.7.1890.
44. Wilson, J. 1910.
45. DC 6.1.1911.
46. DC 18.7.1913, 10.5.1924.
47. DC 11.5.1917.
48. DC 1.8.1913.
49. DC 10.4.1926.
50. Pelling, H. 1979, 179.
51. *Fabian News*, November 1896, 38.
52. DC 26.7.1901.
53. DC 28.9.1906.
54. DC 21.12.1906.
55. DC 17.12.1909.
56. DC 21.1.1910.
57. Walker, G. 1983, 21–4.
58. DCRO D/X1118/2, 4.9.1912.
59. Lawson. J. 1946, 118.
60. DCRO D/MRP 58/2.
61. Labour Party LP/ORG/14/2/3–4.
62. Labour Party LP/ORG/14/2/23.
63. Wilson, J. 1907, plate facing p. 182.
64. *Durham University Calendar 1912–13*, 501.
65. DMA 1915; DC 29.10.1915.
66. DC 14.7.1916.
67. DC 31.7.1914.
68. DC 17.4.1926.
69. DC 10.5.1907.
70. Davis, H.W.C. & Weaver, J.R.H. 1927, 100–1.
71. DC 2.9.1921.
72. NMLH 1–41.
73. Beamish Museum 1973.511.
74. DC 15.8.1919.
75. Adamson, J. 1970, 29.
76. DCRO D/DMA 248, 81.
77. Kendall, W. 1969, 109; Ripley, B.J. & McHugh, J. 1989.
78. *Newcastle Daily Chronicle* 21.5.1926.
79. DC 26.7.1924.
80. DC 30.8.1924.
81. Levenson, S. 1973; Ransom, B. 1980.
82. DC 9.3.1928.
83. Davies, P. 1987.
84. DC 28.3.1925, 11.4.1925.
85. DA 13.2.1931.
86. DCRO D/X1118/4, 7.2.1923, 109.
87. Lawson, J. 1936.
88. Lawson, J. 1946.
89. Deacon, R. 1969, 256; *see also* PRO HO 45/13798, file 521000.
90. Chadwick, O. 1983, 16; DC 1.8.1925; Wild, J.H.S. 1977–8, 17–18.
91. *North Mail & Newcastle Daily Chronicle* 22.5.1926.
92. Burns, E. 1926, 152.
93. *Stanley News* 7.10.1926.
94. *Auckland Chronicle* 29.5.1926.
95. Ball, S. 1992, 88.
96. DCRO/ D/MRP21/3.
97. *Stanley News* 29.7.1926.
98. PP 1927, 1123.
99. *Stanley News* 2.9.1926.
100. *Stanley News* 5.8.1926.
101. *Stanley News* 14.10.1926.
102. Klugman, J. 1968, 163 & 345.
103. *Auckland Chronicle* 4.11.1926.
104. *Stanley News* 22.7.1926.
105. *Stanley News* 18.11.1926.
106. Ibid.
107. Emery, N. 1992, 131.
108. DCRO Sam Watson Papers, The Non-Political Miners' Journal 16, no. 2, Sept. 1928.
109. DC 27.1.1928, 3.2.1928.
110. Page-Arnot, R. 1953, 522–3; DC 19.8.1927.
111. MacFarlane, L.J. 1966, 195–220.
112. DC 2.3.1928.
113. DC 28.7.1928.
114. DCRO Sam Watson Papers.
115. DCRO Sam Watson Papers, 'Durham Woman'.
116. DC 20.7.1928.
117. DC 3.8.1928.
118. DC 10.8.1928.
119. DC 26.4.1929, 13.9.1929.
120. DC 16.3.1928, 4.5.1928.
121. Mahon, J. 1976, 156.
122. Howard, S. 1987, 3–16.
123. DC 10.5.1929.
124. PP 1926, 742.
125. DC 3.5.1929.
126. DA 29.7.1932.
127. DCRO D/EBF 46.
128. DC 194.1929, 26.7.1929, 22.11.1929.
129. DC 30.1.1931.
130. Bean, P. & Melville, J. 1990.
131. DA 27.3.1931.
132. DA 18.1.1935.
133. Ibid.
134. DCRO D/MRP 8/4.
135. DC 1.2.1929.
136. DA 29.7.1932.
137. DA 22.7.1932.
138. Turner, I. 1984, 46.

139. Kingsford, P. 1982, 184–5.
140. DA 9.3.1934.
141. DA 30.11.1934.
142. DA 1.3.1935.
143. DA 15.2.1935.
144. DA 26.4.1935.
145. DA 16.10.1936.
146. Todd, N. 1995.
147. DA 9.10.1936.
148. DA 16.10.1936.
149. Graham, F. 1987.
150. DA 18.6.1937.
151. DA 30.4.1937.
152. DA 5.11.1937.
153. DA 23.9.1938.
154. DA 11.11.1938.
155. DA 18.11.1938.
156. DA 26.7.1946.
157. Temple, D. 1988, 8.
158. Cole, M. 1949.
159. Woodhorn Colliery Museum, Ashington Federation banner.
160. Slowe, P. 1993, 216–27.
161. DC 23.7.1948.
162. Harris, K. 1982, 450.
163. DA 2.5.1967.
164. Dorritt, S. & Ramsay, R. 1992, 14, 16–17, 22, 30.
165. *Blaydon Courier* 23.7.1954.
166. Pickard, C. 1976, 24–6.
167. *Tyneside Chronicle* 25.7.1958.
168. DA 22.7.1955.
169. Leslie, R.F. 1980, 349–54.
170. DA 20.7.1956.
171. DA 29.8.1930.
172. DA 30.6.1944.
173. DA 2.6.1961.
174. DC 23.7.1948.
175. DA 29.7.1949.
176. Dean & Chapter Minute Book 1939–47, 325.
177. Ibid., 333
178. DA 28.2.1947.
179. DA 27.7.1951.
180. PP 1936–7, 733.
181. DA 27.7.1956.
182. DA 28.7.1950.
183. DCRO D/DMA 328/4.
184. DA 25.7.1969.
185. Gormley, J. 1982, 61–2.
186. Beynon, H., Hudson, R. & Sadler, D. 1991.
187. Hudson, R., Peck, F. & Sadler, D. 1984, 10, 13.
188. Campaign Group of Labour MPs 1986, 29–34; 'Coal Industry Dispute (Police Operations)' debate of 10 April 1984 in *Official Report (Hansard)*, 1983–4, 55, 203–44.
189. Milne, S. 1994.
190. *The Durham Striker* March 1985.
191. Workers' Revolutionary Party 1985, 138.
192. Fynes, R. 1923, 36.
193. 105th Durham Miners' Gala Souvenir Programme 15 July 1989, 22–3.
194. *Coal News* (375) November 1992, 24.
195. *Coal News* (366) February 1992, 3, quoting Neil Clarke, in evidence to the Commons Energy Select Committee.
196. *Coal News* (371) July 1992, 14.
197. *The Observer* 1.11.1992.
198. *Northern Echo* 17.5.1992.
199. *The Observer* 25.10.1992.
200. *The Times* 21.10.1992.
201. North East Trade Union Studies Information Unit (NETUSIU) 1986, 9, quoting North-East NCB 'Plan for the Hawthorn Combine, August 1985'.
202. Mr Atkinson, Area Industrial Relations Officer, in reply to DMA, in NETUSIU 1986, 10.
203. Beynon, H., Hudson, R. & Sadler, D. 1991, 37–83.
204. *Mail on Sunday* 18.10.1992.
205. *The Fed* 4, 18.11.1991.
206. *The Observer* 18.10.1992.
207. *Northern Echo* 18.9.1992.
208. House of Commons Trade and Industry Committee 1992–3, 82–3, 88
209. House of Commons Employment Committee 1992–3, viii, B20.
210. Ibid., note 209, viii, C22.
211. *Official Report (Hansard)* 212, c. 205–36, 19.10.1992.
212. *Official Report (Hansard)* 212, c. 216, 19.10.1992.
213. Lexis on-line database. R v. British Coal Corporation and Secretary of State for Trade and Industry ex parte Vardy and others, 21.12.1992.
214. *Northern Echo* 24.10.1992.
215. *The Times* 24.10.1992.
216. *Northern Echo* 28 and 29.10.1992.
217. House of Commons Trade and Industry Committee 1992–3, 76–7, tables 22 (a) and (b).
218. White Paper. 1993 The Prospect for Coal: Conclusions of the Government's Coal Review.
219. *Northern Echo* 2.6.1993.
220. *Northern Echo* 17.7.1993.
221. *Coal News* (267) October 1983, 11.
222. *Coal News* (366) February 1992, 6.
223. Ibid.
224. *Northern Echo* 23.11.1994.
225. *Northern Echo* 10.12.1993, 5.1.1994, 20.1.1994.
226. *Northern Echo* 25.3.1994, 1.4.1994.
227. 110th Durham Miners' Gala, Saturday 9 July 1994, hand-bill.

# Chapter 5

1. Whellan, F. 1894, 1270.
2. DC 20.6.1873.
3. Fordyce, W. 1860, 45; Whellan, F. 1894, 316.
4. DC 23.5.1873.
5. DC 20.6.1873.
6. Louis, H. 1907, 331.
7. Reid & Co. 1934, 32.
8. DA 27.7.1951.
9. Fordyce, W. 1860, 90–1.
10. Whellan, F. 1894, 1206.
11. DCRO Mine Abandonment Plan 10165.
12. DCRO Mine Abandonment Plan 12190.
13. Red Hill photograph.
14. DCRO D/X411/97.
15. OS map 1856 VI.14.
16. Whellan, F. 1894, 1262.
17. DC 23.5.1873.
18. DCRO D/EBF/54.
19. NCB No. 4 Area n.d.
20. DCRO D/X411/97.
21. Beamish Museum 4.2121.55 (1974.135).
22. Anon. 1900–1, 269.
23. DC 30.7.1897.
24. DC 9.7.1909; DCRO D/X1116/5.
25. DA 27.7.1951.
26. Richardson, M.A. 1843, 80, 98.
27. Letch, H. 1970, 37.
28. Goodley, H. 1975, 3.
29. DC 20.6.1873.
30. DC 19.7.1901.
31. Whellan, F. 1894, 356.
32. DC 12.10.1906.
33. J. Tuck, pers. comm.
34. Whellan, W. 1856, 289.
35. Fordyce, W. 1860, 45.
36. Whellan, F. 1894, 359.
37. DC 21.6.1872.
38. DC 23.5.1873.
39. DC 17.1.1913, 13.8.1913; DCRO D/X411/94.
40. DC 24.7.1936.
41. DC 24.7.1936, 31.7.1936.
42. Jones, D. 1985; *Northern Echo* 16.7.1955.
43. DA 22.7.1977.
44. DA 17.7.1981.
45. DC 21.3.1930.
46. Whellan, F. 1894, 419.
47. OS map 1897–1921 XXV.4 & 11.
48. *Auckland Chronicle* 1.11.1906, 29.3.1906, 7.6.1906.
49. DC 21.6.1872, 20.6.1873.
50. DC 28.9.1894.
51. Richardson, M.A. 1844, 383.
52. Louis, H. 1907, 334; Winlaton & District Local History Soc. 1975, 81.
53. DC 20.6.1873.
54. Whellan, F. 1894, 1057.
55. DC 21.6.1872.
56. DCRO D/X411/97.
57. DC 27.7.1906.
58. DA 4.11.1932.
59. DA 27.7.1934.
60. DCRO D/X411/97.
61. *Northern Echo* 18.7.1959; DCRO D/Ph 53/3.
62. DA 21.7.1967.
63. *Northern Echo* Library 69/7/523.
64. Surtees, H.C. 1925, 24.
65. Temple, A. 1940, thesis, 311.
66. DC 20.6.1873.
67. DC 28.7.1893.
68. DC 3.7.1914.
69. Quinn, V. 1990, thesis, 45.
70. PP 1896, xviii, 501.
71. DC 21.6.1872, 20.6.1873.
72. Bishop Auckland Library photo 54; DC 24.7.1908.
73. DCRO D/DMA 326/3; DC 3.8.1923.
74. *Northern Echo* Library photo 15.7.1961.
75. *Northern Echo* Library photo 16.7.1960.
76. DCRO D/DMA 326/25.
77. Wear Valley District Council, framed photograph.
78. DC 9.9.1927.
79. DC 20.6.1873.
80. DC 21.8.1874.
81. DC 28.7.1893.
82. DA 15.7.1949.
83. Prof. E. Black, Brandon University, pers. comm.
84. Hair, T.H. 1844, 45; Fordyce, W. 1860, 92.
85. Kelly & Co. 1873, 354; PP 1884–5a, 459–63; DC 2.5.1890.
86. DC 21.6.1872.
87. DC 20.6.1873.
88. DC 9.7.1875.
89. DC 3.8.1894.
90. DC 20.6.1873.
91. DC 27.7.1900.
92. DC 21.7.1911.
93. OS map 1939, XLII.14.
94. Beamish Museum photograph 14241.
95. DA 22.7.1955.
96. DC 20.6.1873.
97. Anon. 1986, 33.
98. DCRO D/X411/97.
99. *Stanley News* 18.6.1959.
100. Whellan, F. 1894, 1184.
101. DC 21.6.1872. 18.4.1873.
102. DA 26.7.1946.
103. *The Times* 3.2.1904, 16.7.1904.

104. Whellan, F. 1894, 1262.
105. DCRO Mine Abandonment Plan 12263.
106. DC 21.6.1872.
107. DC 20.6.1873.
108. Red Hill photograph.
109. Temple, A, 1940, thesis, 366–7.
110. Whellan, F. 1894, 352.
111. DC 9.5.1873.
112. DCRO D/HH/5/5/313.
113. DC 20.6.1873.
114. Whellan, W. 1856, 608; Kelly & Co. 1879, 39.
115. DC 3.6.1881.
116. DC 30.1.1882.
117. DC 21.6.1872, 20.6.1873.
118. Louis, H. 1907, 343.
119. DC 2.8.1929.
120. DCRO D/X411/97.
121. Red Hill photograph.
122. *Northern Echo* Library photograph E23.7.62.
123. DC 16.5.1879.
124. DC 15.7.1881, 30.9.1881.
125. DC 21.1.1886.
126. DA 24.8.1934.
127. DC 21.6.1872.
128. DCRO D/X411/97.
129. Louis, H. 1907, 330–1; Fordyce, W. 1860, 89.
130. Kelly & Co, 1873, 354; Fordyce, W. 1860, 90.
131. DC 16.5.1913.
132. *Blaydon Courier* 2.3.1956.
133. DC 20.6.1873.
134. DC 26.7.1924.
135. DC 26.7.1924.
136. DC 30.8.19.24.
137. *Blaydon Courier* 29.7.1955.
138. *Tyneside Courier* 20.6.1958.
139. *Blaydon Courier* 23.7.1954.
140. Simpson, F.R. 1896–7, 193–9
141. Hall, A. 1991.
142. DCRO D/X411/97.
143. *Blaydon Courier* 16.7.1954.
144. OS map 1857, XXXIII.3.
145. DC 20.6.1873.
146. DC 28.7.1893.
147. DCRO B21.
148. DC 21.6.1872.
149. DC 18.4.1873.
150. DC 20.6.1873.
151. DCRO B21.
152. Durham City Library 821/L19.
153. Louis, H. 1907, 334.
154. DC 16.2.1872.
155. DC 21.6.1872.
156. DC 20.6.1873.
157. Fordyce, W. 1857, 2, 657.
158. *South Durham & Auckland Chronicle* 8.7.1909.
159. DC 28.7.1939.
160. *Northern Echo* Library photograph 1939.
161. Beamish Museum photograph 54930, 58675.
162. DA 23.7.1976.
163. DA 22.7.1977.
164. OS map XXXIII.8
165. Kelly & Co. 1879, 48.
166. DC 20.6.1873.
167. DA 17.2.1939.
168. OS map XI.14.
169. *Consett Chronicle* 21.1.1965.
170. *Stanley News* 5.8.1926; *Consett Chronicle* 12.8.1926.
171. *Blaydon Courier* 23.7.1954.
172. Kearney, T. 1990, 47.
173. Anon. 1902–3, 598–9.
174. DCRO NCB 24/20.
175. DA 21.7.1933.
176. Louis, H. 1907, 343.
177. DC 6.2.1885.
178. DC 27.9.1889.
179. *Northern Echo* 6.1.1967.
180. *Sunderland Echo* 2.4.1964.
181. DA 27.6.1946.
182. DC 1.8.1902.
183. Ferryhill Library photograph.
184. DC 23.7.1915.
185. DC 16.2.1924; Beamish Museum photograph 10372.
186. DA 26.7.1946.
187. Fordyce, W. 1860, 91.
188. Whellan, F. 1894, 1264.
189. DC 20.6.1873.
190. Red Hill photograph.
191. Red Hill photograph.
192. DCRO D/X411/94.
193. PP 1951–2, 867.
194. Commons, Trade & Industry Committee 1992–3, 76.
195. DA 22.7.1932.
196. DA 22.7.1977.
197. Louis, H. 1907, 334.
198. Louis, H. 1907, 339.
199. Whellan, F. 1894, 778–9.
200. DC 7.5.1897, 14.5.1897.
201. *Northern Echo* 15.6.1983.
202. DC 20.6.1873
203. DA 15.7.1932, 29.7.1932.
204. DA 27.7.1951.
205. DA 22.7.1977.
206. Whellan, F, 1894, 1212.
207. DC 9.8.1929.
208. *Stanley News* 21.7.1955.

209. Fordyce, W. 1860, 91.
210. DA 18.7.1980.
211. DC 26.8.1921.
212. DCRO D/DMA 334/24, 71–6, 81–3.
213. Whellan, F. 1856, 872; PP 1884–5a, 462.
214. Whellan, F. 1894, 291.
215. DC 18.4.1873, 20.6.1873.
216. DC 28.7.1905.
217. OS map 1897, XLII.8.
218. Surtees, H.C. 1923, 29.
219. DC 23.5.1873.
220. Ayris, I. 1979–80, 6–35.
221. PP 1887, 417–49.
222. *Sunderland Echo* 2.2.1974.
223. DC 20.6.1873.
224. DC 28.7.1939.
225. DCRO D/X1077/4.
226. Grant, P. 1971, thesis, 28–32; *see also* Johnson, G.A.L. & Richardson, G. 1990, 84–96.
227. DC 20.12.1907, 3.7.1908.
228. Woodward, P.G. 1984–5, 22–4.
229. DC 20.6.1873.
230. Richardson, M.A. 1844, 154.
231. PP 1952, 923.
232. Anon. 1960, 826–8.
233. DC 25.7.1925.
234. DC 25.7.1925.
235. Beamish Museum neg. 14346.
236. DA 25.7.1969, 22.7.1977.
237. Whellan, F. 1894, 273.
238. Anon 1900, 356–60.
239. Anon 1913, 81.
240. J. Rayner, Esh Winning, pers. comm.
241. Whellan, F. 1894, 273.
242. DCRO NCB4/63, 64, 66.
243. *Northern Echo* 29.6.1968.
244. DC 13.7.1894.
245. PP 1888, 547; OS map XLII.1.
246. DA 22.3.1935.
247. DC 23.5.1873, 20.6.1873.
248. DC 22.2.1884.
249. DC 28.3.1884.
250. DCRO D/Ph 236/1.
251. DC 20.6.1873.
252. Richardson, M.A. 1842, 60.
253. Liverpool Religious Tracts Society 1812.
254. Fordyce, W. 1857, ii. 750.
255. Whellan, F. 1894, 978.
256. DC 18.4.1873.
257. *Consett Chronicle* 31.12.1964.
258. DA 26.5.1961.
259. NCB Durham Div No. 4 Area n.d., 6.
260. *Evening Chronicle* 30.11.1973.
261. Whellan, F. 1894, 1061.
262. DCRO NCB 24/92.
263. *Sunday Sun* 30.9.1956; NCB Durham Div. No 1 (NE) Area 1961.
264. *Sunderland Echo* 6.1.1969.
265. DCRO D/X411/97.
266. *Northern Echo* 5.5.1988.
267. Louis, H. 1907, 335; DCRO D/Ph33/3–4.
268. Fordyce, W. 1860, 67.
269. DC 3.7.1908, 10.7.1908.
270. DC 9.11.1923.
271. DC 25.7.1925.
272. DC 20.6.1873.
273. OS map XLI.15; Kelly & Co. 1879, 42.
274. Beamish Museum photograph 20955.
275. DC 20.6.1873.
276. Temple, A,. 1940, thesis, 332.
277. OS map XXXIII.8.
278. DC 20.6.1873.
279. Louis, H, 1907, 344; PP 1884–5a, 442.
280. *Journal* 15.4.1966.
281. *Tyneside Courier* 27.6.1958.
282. Whellan, F. 1894, 284.
283. DC 21.8.1874.
284. DCRO D/DMA 237.
285. Cummings, J. 1909–10, 320–31.
286. DCRO NCB24/34.
287. *Northern Echo* 17.11.1967.
288. *Consett Guardian* 1.2.1968.
289. DC 18.4.1873.
290. NCB No. 5 Area Durham Div. n.d.
291. *Coal News*, Hobart House neg. T 1981.
292. DC 7.2.1913.
293. Hind, A.L. 1974, 35.
294. DC 20.6.1873.
295. DCRO D/Ph 53/2, D/X30/14.
296. Anon. 1909–10, 606.
297. DC 14.6.1895.
298. *Shields Gazette* 11.3.1969.
299. DC 18.4.1873.
300. DC 28.7.1893.
301. Louis, H. 1907, 331, 333.
302. Fordyce, W. 1860, 94.
303. Richardson, M.A. 1844, 247.
304. *Sunderland & Durham County Herald* 1844.
305. DC 6.8.1897.
306. DC 29.7.1904.
307. DC 18.4.1873, 20.6.1873
308. Fordyce, W. 1860, 78.
309. DC 18.4.1873, 20.6.1873.
310. DA 14.9.1906.
311. DC 20.6.1873.
312. Whellan, W. 1856, 915.
313. PP 1884–5a, 461; 1888, 547.
314. DC 20.6.1873.

315. Moyes, W.A. 1974, 145.
316. DA 25.7.1958.
317. DA 19.7.1984.
318. Banham, J.D. 1988, thesis.
319. DC 10.1.1913; Fordyce, W. 1860, 93.
320. Maynard, T.C. 1861.
321. DC 21.6.1872, 20.6.1873.
322. Richardson, M.A. 1842, 78.
323. DC 21.6.1872.
324. DC 28.7.1893.
325. DC 22.7.1904.
326. DC 28.7.1911.
327. Anon. 1906, 4–5.
328. PP 1954–58, 465.
329. NCB No. 3 Area Durham Div. 1966.
330. Beynon, H., Hudson, R. & Sadler, D. 1991.
331. *Sunderland Echo* 9.11.1985.
332. *Financial Times* 31.1.1986.
333. DA 22.7.1966.
334. Louis, H. 1907, 332.
335. *Sunderland Echo* 25.2.1960.
336. *Northern Echo* 5.3.1960.
337. DC 21.6.1872, 20.6.1873.
338. DC 28.7.1923.
339. DA 22.7.1932.
340. DA 22.7.1977.
341. Kelly & Co. 1873, 354.
342. DA 12.1.1912.
343. DC 18.4.1873, 20.6.1873.
344. Louis, H. 1907, 334.
345. Anon. 1902–3b, 602–4.
346. *Sunderland Echo* 13.7.1979.
347. DCRO D/X1069/2, 10.4.1960, 31.
348. OS map 1858, XXV.7; Louis, H. 1907, 341.
349. PP 1887, 1006; OS map 1897, XXV.7.
350. Reid, A. 1934, 28.
351. DC 21.6.1872.
352. DC 20.6.1873.
353. Louis, H. 1907, 335.
354. Fordyce, W. 1857, ii, 659.
355. Kipling, M. n.d.
356. DC 20.6.1873.
357. *Guardian* 12.2.1965.
358. *Northern Echo* 30.3.1973.
359. *Journal* 4.10.1974.
360. DC 18.4.1873, 20.6.1873.
361. DA 19.7.1984.
362. DC 5.9.1913.
363. *Sunderland Echo* 4.11.1967.
364. DC 3.8.1923.
365. DA 23.7.1948.
366. DA 30.7.1948.
367. DC 6.6.1913.
368. *Consett Chronicle* 28.1.1965.
369. DA 29.1.1965.
370. DC 21.6.1872.
371. DC 20.6.1873.
372. DCRO D/DMA 328/4.
373. DA 19.7.1935.
374. Red Hill photograph.
375. Mountford, C.E. 1975.
376. DCRO D/MRP 25/1.
377. DCRO D.X 702/3.
378. DA 29.7.1932.
379. DA 27.3.1954.
380. DA 26.7.1963.
381. DA 25.7.1975.
382. Louis, H. 1907, 337.
383. Whellan, F. 1894, 382.
384. *Illustrated Chronicle* 21.5.1912.
385. DC 13.7.1928.
386. Whellan, F. 1894, 1184.
387. DC 20.6.1873.
388. Louis. H. 1907, 34.
389. DA 11.12.1931.
390. DC 23.7.1909.
391. *South Durham & Auckland Chronicle* 22.7.1909.
392. DA 27.6.1946.
393. Marrs, H. 1993, 18.
394. DC 21.6.1872, 20.6.1873.
395. *Northern Echo* 4.11.1986.
396. OS map 1856, XX.6; DC 11.4.1884.
397. DA 21.7.1939.
398. DC 21.6.1872, 20.6.1873.
399. *Northern Echo* 16.7.1960.
400. DC 12.10.1906.
401. *Auckland Chronicle* 22.6.1967.
402. *Sunday Sun* 29.9.1968.
403. *Northern Echo* 4.12.1968.
404. DA 29.7.1949.
405. *Northern Echo* 21.7.1951.
406. Coia, A.J., Teesdale, J.G. & Wilcockson, B. 1990, 56, pl. 173.
407. Whellan, F. 1894, 1262.
408. DCRO NCB 24/58.
409. *Gateshead Post* 12.11.1981.
410. *Northern Echo* 4.3.1983.
411. DA 20.6.1873.
412. DC 28.7.1896.
413. DA 28.7.1946.
414. Daglish, J. 1882, 5–43.
415. Clark, D. 1992, 25.
416. Clark, D. 1992, 22–3.
417. DA 3.8.1934.
418. Louis, H. 1907, 344.
419. DCRO NCB 24/60.
420. *Evening Chronicle* 25.3.1970.
421. *Evening Chronicle* 6.10.1972.

422. *Stanley News* 16.6.1955.
423. Ibid.
424. OS map XXXIV.8
425. Gorman, J. 1986, 132.
426. DC 20.6.1873.
427. DA 27.7.1962.
428. DC 20.6.1873.
429. Bell, W.R. & McGowan, E. 1895–6, 221–6.
430. Fordyce, W. 1856, 73.
431. Trade and Industry Committee 1992–3, 76.
432. DC 18.4.1873.
433. DA 13.3.1931.
434. *Northern Echo* 8.6.1985.
435. A. Mardghum, lodge secretary, pers. comm.
436. PP 1947–8, 697.
437. Anon. 1923–4, 134–6.
438. *Northern Echo* 6.10.1973.
439. DA 23.7.1971.
440. *Northern Echo* 11.3.1993.
441. Potter, E. 1856–7, 43–61.
442. DC 18.8.1848.
443. PP 1942–3, 31.
444. *Northern Echo* 30.11.1991.
445. DC 21.6.1872, 18.4.1873, 20.6.1873.
446. DC 11.7.1884.
447. DC 25.7.1925.
448. Whellan, W. 1856, 876; PP 1884–5a, 460; PP 1888, 544.
449. *Northern Echo* 7.6.1974; *Journal* 27.9.1974; *Evening Chronicle* 28.9.1974.
450. DC 20.6.1873.
451. DCRO D/MRP77/1.
452. DC 24.6.1953.
453. DC 21.6.1872.
454. DA 27.6.1946.
455. DCRO D/Ph 182/1.
456. Whellan, W. 1856, 297.
457. Kelly & Co. 1873, 354.
458. Whellan, F. 1894, 354.
459. DC 21.8.1874.
460. Louis, H. 1907, 342.
461. NCB No. 2 Area Div 1958.
462. DA 27.7.1956.
463. Whellan, F. 1894, 385.
464. DC 12.7.1929.
465. DC 23.5.1873.
466. PP 1884–5a, 462.
467. DC 20.6.1873.
468. Richardson, M.A. 1842, 223–4.
469. Taylor, P.M. 1983, 13.
470. DC 23.5.1873, 20.6.1873.
471. DC 20.6.1873.
472. Ibid.
473. Richardson, M.A. 1842, 144.
474. Durham City Library 338.272/L185.
475. DC 3.8.1900.
476. DC 21.8.1874.
477. DC 21.6.1872, 20.6.1873.
478. Grant, P.A. 1973, 6.
479. DC 21.6.1872, 20.6.1873.
480. DC 20.6.1873.
481. DC 28.7.1893.
482. Richardson, M.A. 1843, 180.
483. DC 14.4.1914.
484. DC 26.5.1916.
485. DC 6.1.1928.
486. DC 30.7.1897.
487. Red Hill photograph.
488. DC 1.10.1858.
489. Temple, A. 1940, thesis, 392.
490. DC 21.6.1872, 20.6.1873.
491. DC 11.7.1884.
492. DC 20.6.1873.
493. Fordyce, W. 1860, 74.
494. DC 22.11.1866.
495. PP 1884–5a, 460.
496. DC 30.3.1928.
497. DC 7.6.1929.
498. DA 1.7.1932.
499. DC 21.6.1872, 20.6.1873.
500. Louis, H. 1907, 333.
501. DC 21.6.1872, 20.6.1873.
502. DC 21.6.1872.
503. DC 21.3.1913.
504. DC 20.6.1873.
505. OS map XI.12.
506. Reid, A. 1934, 35.
507. DC 20.6.1873.
508. Ibid.
509. Baker, J. 1900, 91–6
510. Richardson, M.A. 1842, 70.
511. DC 20.6.1873.
512. DCRO D/X411/97.
513. Taylor, P.M. 1983, 13.
514. DC 23.5.1884.
515. DC 20.6.1873.
516. DCRO D/X411/97.
517. Louis, H. 1907, 339.
518. DC 20.6.1873.
519. AC 11.7.1890.
520. DC 18.4.1913.
521. DA 27.1.1933.
522. Department of Employment & Productivity 1970, 14.
523. *Journal* 26.11.1966.
524. DC 20.6.1873.
525. DC 1.8.1925.
526. DCRO D/X411/97.

527. DA 25.7.1958.
528. Louis, H. 1907, 335; DCRO M40.1.
529. DC 27.11.1903.
530. *Northern Echo* 14.10.1985.
531. *Journal* 16.11.1985.
532. DC 21.6.1872, 20.6.1873.
533. DA 31.7.1931.
534. DA 26.7.1957.
535. DA 15.7.1983.
536. Fordyce, W. 1860, 71–3.
537. PP 1881, 477; McCutcheon, J.E. 1955, 66–72, 81–94. There are memorials to the victims of both explosions at New Seaham churchyard.
538. DC 20.6.1873.
539. Armstrong, K. 1994.
540. DC 9.1.1914.
541. DC 21.6.1872.
542. Louis, H. 1907, 333.
543. DC 9.1.1914.
544. DA 22.1.1965.
545. *Northern Echo* Library photograph 1939.
546. DA 26.7.1946; DCRO D/X411/97.
547. DA 24.7.1953.
548. DCRO/X30/10.
549. DA 23.7.1965.
550. DC 10.5.1929.
551. *Northern Echo* Library photograph 1939.552.
552. Louis, H. 1907, 333.
553. Louis, H. 1907, 340; Kelly & Co. 1873, 364; Whellan, F. 1894, 394.
554. DC 31.7.1908.
555. DC 21.6.1872.
556. Richardson, M.A. 1846, 215.
557. Whellan, F. 1894, 300.
558. DC 20.6.1873.
559. DC 4.7.1913.
560. *Northern Echo* 4.3.1959.
561. *Hartlepool Mail* 1.9.1972.
562. DC 21.6.1872.
563. DC 20.6.1873.
564. DC 23.7.1939.
565. Louis, H. 1907, 341.
566. *Sunderland Echo* 1.12.1959.
567. W. Calvert collection.
568. DC 23.7.1909.
569. DC 20.9.1924.
570. DCRO/D/DMA 328/4.
571. OS map 1856, XII.9
572. PP 1884–5a, 442.
573. OS map XLII.7–8.
574. PP 1884–5a, 462.
575. Chapman, V. 1994, 63.
576. DC 21.6.1872.
577. DC 20.6.1873.
578. DC 19.7.1900.
579. *Coal News* August 1980, 5.
580. Louis, H. 1907, 340.
581. PP 1888, 537.
582. DC 21.6.1872, 20.6.1873.
583. Richardson, M.A. 1843, 192.
584. Hardy, G.M. 1986, 37.
585. OS map XII.9.
586. DC 22.9.1911.
587. DC 20.6.1873.
588. DA 26.7.1946.
589. Red Hill photograph.
590. Fordyce, W. 1860, 45.
591. Louis, H. 1907, 343; DC 17.9.1891.
592. DA 29.7.1949.
593. DCRO/ D/Ph53/1.
594. Richardson, M.A. 1844, 367.
595. DC 20.6.1873.
596. Richardson, M.A. 1843, 321–2.
597. Richardson, M.A. 1846, 156.
598. DC 20.6.1873.
599. DC 22.5.1857.
600. DC 21.6.1872, 20.6.1873.
601. Louis, H. 1907, 333.
602. Whellan, F. 1894, 320.
603. Temple, A. 1940, thesis, 203.
604. DC 21.6.1872.
605. DC 20.6.1873.
606. Hobson, G.B. 1903, 373; Fordyce, W. 1860, 70.
607. DC 20.6.1873.
608. Clark, D. 1992, 63.
609. Taylor, P.M. 1983, 19.
610. DC 21.6.1872.
611. DC 21.8.1874.
612. DC 28.7.1893.
613. DC 14.6.1929.
614. DC 21.6.1872.
615. DC 3.8.1923.
616. Louis, H. 1907, 332, 335.
617. Fordyce, W. 1860, 45, 76.
618. Louis, H. 1907, 345.
619. *Northern Echo* Library photograph.
620. DA 27.7.1961.
621. Richardson, M.A. 1842, 170.
622. Beamish Museum photograph 66025.
623. Whellan, M. 1856, 610.
624. Wilson, W.B. 1901–2, 72–3.
625. DCRO D/X832/1.
626. DC 21.1.1872.
627. *Northern Daily Mail* 1.4.1959.
628. *Journal* 4.11.1963.
629. *Hartlepool Mail* 28.1.1970.
630. DC 18.8.1871.
631. DC 21.6.1872, 20.6.1873.

632. DC 19.8.1927.
633. *Coal News* August 1983, 7.
634. DCRO/ D/X411/97.
635. Ibid., note 633
636. DA 24.7.1953.
637. Louis, H. 1907, 333.
638. Bell. J.T.W. 1843, map.
639. DA 1.12.1911.
640. DC 20.6.1873.
641. PP 1882a, 257.
642. *Northern Echo* 17.2.1968.
643. Surtees, H.C. 1925, 18; Louis, H. 1907, 340.
644. PP 1882c, 273.
645. *Evening Gazette* 12.4.1969; *Northern Echo* 22.8.1969.
646. DC 21.6.1872.
647. DC 20.6.1873.
648. DA 22.7.1955.
649. *Northern Echo* 7.7.1988.
650. DA 25.7.1958.
651. DCRO D/X30/1; D/PH 53/4.
652. Louis, H. 1907, 339.
653. Whellan, F. 1894, 260.
654. DC 20.6.1873.
655. DC 25.7.1925.
656. Ibid.
657. Louis, H. 1907, 330; Purdon, G. 1977.
658. NUM 1989, 20, pl. 35.
659. Purdon, G. 1977, 36.
660. DCRO D/X411/97.
661. Louis, H. 1907, 337.
662. Fordyce, W. 1860, 45.
663. DC 20.6.1873.
664. Louis, H. 1907, 333.
665. DC 17.7.1908.
666. Emery, N. 1987, 44–6.
667. DA 18.11.1932.
668. DA 27.11.1932.
669. DA 5.8.1960.
670. DA 20.7.1883.
671. DA 26.7.1957.
672. DCRO D/X411/97.
673. DA 22.7.1955.
674. PP 1884–5b, 1015.
675. DC 20.6.1873.
676. DCRO D/DMA 322/12.
677. DCRO D/DMA 322/15.
678. DCRO D/DMA322/22.
679. DA 27.7.1956.
680. DC 15.12.1923.
681. Boyd, J.T. 1993 Report 2265.7, 9.3.
682. Red Hill photograph.
683. DCRO D/X 411/97.
684. *Coal News* August 1982, 4.
685. Red Hill photograph.
686. Richardson, M.A. 1844, 91.
687. Fordyce, W. 1860, 45, 91.
688. Louis, H. 1907, 342.
689. DC 6.1.1911.
690. Emery, N. & Thomas, C. 1992, 85–6.
691. DC 20.6.1873.
692. DC 9.7.1909.
693. DC 20.6.1873.
694. Fordyce, W. 1860, 45.
695. Ford, M. 1902–3, 293–306.
696. PP 1908, 315.
697. *Shields Gazette* 21.1.1970.
698. *Sunderland Echo* 5.8.1972.
699. DC 20.6.1873.
700. DC 9.7.1875.
701. DA 2.8.1935.
702. DA 1.8.1952.
703. DA 22.7.1966.
704. DCRO D/X1118/1–5.
705. DCRO D/X1118/5, 137, 24.6.1925.
706. DCRO D/X411/97.
707. NEIMME 1885, 205–7.
708. DCRO NCB4/136.
709. DCRO D/Br/B112; NCB 4/59.
710. DA 28.2.1964.
711. DC 31.7.1885.
712. DC 15.7.1892.
713. DA 19.7.1984.
714. DA 27.7.1951.
715. Louis, H. 1907, 335; Surtees, H.C. 1924, 32.
716. Whellan, W. 1856, 294.
717. Kelly & Co. 1873, 354.
718. Temple, A. 1940, thesis, 195, 203.
719. DC 21.6.1872, 20.6.1873.
720. Beamish Museum photograph 2342.
721. Whellan, W. 1856, 299; Fordyce, W. 1860, 45; Richardson, M.A. 1846, 272.
722. Widdas, C.G. 1958, 3–16.
723. Boyd, J.T. 1993, Report 2265.6, 4.20–4.21.
724. Westoe Colliery Campaign Group 1993; Trade & Industry Committee Report 1992–3, 76.
725. *Northern Echo* 15.10.1993.
726. E. Malcolm, lodge secretary, pers. comm.
727. DC 20.6.1873.
728. Beamish Museum 1962.225/W3.05.
729. DC 28.7.1927.
730. Fordyce, W. 1860, 9.
731. Louis, H. 1907, 339, 342.
732. PP 1882b, 331; Forster, E. 1969; Pearce, K. 1985, 32–7.
733. Whellan, F. 1894, 418.
734. Temple, A. 1940, thesis, 289, 291.
735. DC 20.6.1873.

736. DC 2.8.1895.
737. Harrison, J.K. 1970, 7–14.
738. *Sunderland Echo* 2.3.1956.
739. *Northern Daily Mail* 2.5.1968.
740. DC 20.6.1873.
741. DA 26.7.1968.
742. Taylor, P.M. 1983, 13.
743. Whellan, F. 1894, 263.
744. OS map 1856, XXV.16.
745. Taylor, P.M. 1983, 27.
746. DC 21.6.1872, 20.6.1873.
747. DC 21.8.1874.
748. Fordyce, W. 1857, 400–1.
749. Fordyce, W. 1860, 66; Whellan, F. 1894, 299; Louis, H. 1907, 334–5.
750. Louis, H. 1907, 339.
751. Fordyce, W. 1860, 45.
752. DC 20.6.1873.
753. Louis, H. 1907, 335; Dodd, J.J. 1897, 110; Abley, R.S. 1991.
754. Dodd, J.J. 1897, 110.
755. DC 30.1.1885.
756. *Journal* 26.7.1974.
757. DC 20.6.1873.
758. *Northern Echo* Library photograph E17/7/67.
759. DA 29.7.1949; Northern Echo 23.7.1949.
760. Fordyce, W. 1860, 45, 77; Whellan, F. 1894, 792.
761. DC 20.6.1873.
762. DCRO M40/1.
763. DC 17.7.1903.
764. DC 3.8.1923.
765. DA 21.7.1950.
766. Fordyce, W. 1857, 604.
767. DC 13.8.1880.
768. DC 20.6.1873.
769. Whellan, W. 1856, 240.
770. Lloyd, E. 1916, 27.
771. Taylor, P.M. 1983, 27.
772. Reid & Co. 1934, 35.

773. DC 20.6.1873.
774. Whellan, W. 1856, 440; Temple, A. 1940, thesis, 145–6.
775. Louis, H. 1907, 344.
776. DC 25.4.1913.
777. DC 21.8.1874.
778. DA 25.7.1969.
779. DC 14.6.1929.
780. DC 21.6.1872, 20.6.1873.
781. NUM 1989, 91, pl. 157.
782. *Coal News* December 1981, 7.
783. DMA 1991, 22.
784. DA 16.7.1982.
785. DCRO D/EBF/57.
786. DC 3.8.1900.
787. DCRO D/EBF/49.
788. DC 30.7.1937.
789. DC 2.8.1872.
790. Hall, W.S. 1929, 22; J. Perry, branch secretary, pers. comm.
791. Red Hill photograph.
792. DA 27.7.1962.
793. J. Perry, pers. comm.
794. *Northern Echo* Library photograph 15/7/61.
795. *Northern Echo* Library photograph D2/7/75.
796. DA 28.7.1950.
797. DA 26.7.1963.
798. DC 23.7.1948.
799. DC 20.7.1883.
800. DC 30.7.1897.
801. DC 21.1.1910.
802. DC 1.8.1925.
803. DA 18.7.1985.
804. Red Hill photograph.
805. Mrs M. McPherson, pers. comm.
806. DA 15.7.1983.
807. Pickard, C. 1976, 25.
808. DA 27.7.1956.
809. DA 22.7.1955.

# Bibliography

## *British Government Publications*

### COMMAND PAPERS

**1881** Report by R.S. Wright on the explosion which occurred at the Seaham Colliery on 8 September 1880 (c. 2924) xxiv, 477.

**1882a** Report by T.W. Snagge on the explosion which occurred at Trimdon Grange Colliery on 16 February 1882 (c. 3319) xvii, 257.

**1882b** Report by Arnold Morley MP upon an inquiry into the causes of a fatal explosion which occurred on 19 April 1882 at the West Stanley Colliery, Chester-le-Street (c. 3331) xviii, 331.

**1882c** Report by Arnold Morley MP upon the circumstances attending a fatal explosion which occurred on 18 April 1882 in the Brockwell seam of Tudhoe Colliery, in the County of Durham (c. 3327) xvii, 273.

**1884–5a** Mining and Mineral Statistics of the United Kingdom of Great Britain and Ireland for 1884 (c. 4430) lxxxxv, 459.

**1884–5b** Report to the Right Hon. the Secretary of State for the Home Department on the circumstances attending an explosion which occurred at Usworth Colliery on 2 March 1885, by Hon Alfred Lyttelton (c. 4549) xiv, 1015.

**1887** Report on the circumstances attending an explosion which occurred at the Elemore Colliery on 2 December 1886, by Haden Corser (c. 5065) xvii, 417.

**1888** Mining and Mineral Statistics of the United Kingdom for the year 1887 (c. 5464) cvii, 369.

**1896** Report on the circumstances attending an explosion which occurred at the Brancepeth Colliery in the County of Durham on 13 April 1896, by J. Edmonson Joel and R. Donald Bain (c. 8174) xviii, 501.

**1907** Report by HM Secretary of State for the Home Department on the circumstances attending an explosion which occurred at Wingate Grange Colliery, Wingate on 14 October 1906, by A.H. Reugg, R.D. Bain and J.B. Atkinson (cd. 3379) xiii, 691.

**1908** Report on the circumstances attending an explosion which occurred at Washington 'Glebe' in the County of Durham on 20 February 1908, by J.B. Atkinson (cd. 4183) xii, 315.

**1926** Communist Papers. Documents selected from those obtained on the arrest of the Communist leaders on 14 and 21 October 1925 (cmd. 2682) xxiii, 585.

**1927** Chester-le-Street Union. Report of the Board of Guardians on the Administration for the period of 30 August 1926 to 31 December 1926 (cmd. 2818) xi, 1123.

**1936–7** Report on the causes of, and circumstances attending, an explosion at Gresford Colliery, Denbighshire, on 22 September 1934, by Sir Henry Walker, Mr John Brass and Mr Joseph Jones (cmd. 5358) xiii, 733.

**1947–8** Report on the causes of, and circumstances attending, the explosion which occurred at Louisa (including Morrison Old Colliery, Durham, on 22 August 1947, by R. Yates (cmd. 7347) xiii, 697.

**1951–2** Report on the causes of, and circumstances attending, the explosion which occurred at Easington Colliery, County Durham, on 29 May 1951, by H.C.W. Roberts (cmd. 8646) xvi, 867.

**1952** Report on the causes of, and circumstances attending, the explosion which occurred at Eppleton Colliery, Durham, on 6 July 1951, by R. Yates (cmd. 8503) xvi, 923.

**1954–5** Report on the causes of, and circumstances attending, the explosion which occurred on 23 March 1953, at Horden Colliery, Co. Durham, by W. Brown (cmd. 9399) vi, 465.

## REPORTS OF COMMITTEES

**1818** Report from the Select Committee to whom the Several Petitions of Ribbon Weavers of Coventry and Leek, of Silk Weavers of Macclesfield and Reading, and of Silk Manufacturers of Macclesfield were referred (398) ix, 1.

**1821** The Select Committee of the House of Lords appointed to inquire into the means of extending and securing the foreign trade of the country. Second Report relative to the silk and wine trade (703) vii, 421.

**1857** A return of the quantities of Silk of the various kinds imported into the UK from various countries from 1842 to 1856 (94 sess. 2) xxxviii, 439.

**1992–3** Trade & Industry Committee: First Report. British energy policy and the market for coal. Session 1992–3 (HC 237).

**1992–3** Employment Committee: Second Report. Employment consequences of British Coal's proposed pit closures. Volume 1: Report and Proceedings of the Committee. Session 1992–3 (263.I).

## DEPARTMENT PUBLICATIONS

**1970** Department of Employment & Productivity 1970. Ryhope: a pit closes. A case study in redeployment (London).

**1993** Independent Analysis. 21 Closure Review Collieries, British Coal Corporation, United Kingdom. John T. Boyd Company. Report 2265.6, January 1993 for DTI Coal Review Team (London).

**1993** Independent Review. 10 Collieries under Consultation, British Coal Corporation, United Kingdom. John T. Boyd Company. Report 2265.7, March 1993 for DTI Coal Review Team (London).

## WHITE PAPERS

**1993** The Prospects for Coal: Conclusions of the Government's Coal Review. Cm 2235.

## OFFICIAL REPORTS (HANSARD)

Commons 1983–4, 55.
—. 1992, 212.

# Newspapers

*Auckland Chronicle*
*Blaydon Courier*
*Coal News*
*Consett Chronicle*
*Durham Advertiser*
*Durham Chronicle*
*Durham Striker*
*Evening Chronicle*
*Evening Gazette*
*Financial Times*
*Gateshead Post*
*Guardian*
*Hartlepool Mail*
*Illustrated Chronicle*
*Illustrated London News*
*Journal*
*Mail on Sunday*
*Northern Daily Mail*
*Northern Echo*
*Nuneaton Chronicle*
*Observer*
*Shields Gazette*
*Stanley News*
*Sun*
*Sunday Sun*
*Sunderland Echo*
*Sunderland Times*
*The Fed*
*The Times*
*Tyneside Chronicle*

# Durham County Record Office

**B21** Ayre, T.T. Cornsay Colliery. Portrait of a Durham Mining Village. 1975. Bound typescript.
**D/Br/B112** Brancepeth Estate Papers. Counterpart deed, 28.1.1919, empowering the working of baryta in the estate royalty.
**D/Br/C18** Brancepeth Estate Papers. Leases to Pease and Partners 1858–1942.
**D/DMA 237** Hamsteels lodge minutes 1892–6.
**D/DMA 308/1** Murton lodge minutes 1921.
**D/DMA 322/12** Usworth lodge minutes 1921–3.
**D/DMA 322/15** Usworth lodge minutes 1937–9.
**D/DMA 322/22** Usworth lodge minutes 1954–6.
**D/DMA 326/3** Brancepeth No. 2 lodge minutes 1923–5.
**D/DMA 326/25** Brancepeth lodge minutes 1964.
**D/DMA 327/7** Marsden lodge minutes 1914–15.
**D/DMA 328/4** Lambton lodge, scrap book.
**D/DMA 334/25** Eden lodge minutes 1961–3.
**D/DMA** Sam Watson Papers.

**D/EBF/46** The Coal Crisis 1931: A speech to Special Conference 23 June 1931, by A.J. Cook.

**D/EBF/49** Photograph, Durham County Colliery Enginemen's banner, 1871.

**D/EBF/54** Photograph, garden party given by Bishop Moule for aged miners and their wives, with Auckland Park banner displayed, 1910.

**D/EBF/57** Photograph, Durham County Colliery Enginemen's banner, n.d.

**D/HH/5/5/313** Particulars of sale of New Carterthorne Colliery, 1887.

**D/MRP 8/4** Letter from Andrew Lawther to Sam Watson re. Harton workhouse march, 1925.

**D/MRP 21/3** E. Fairbridge 1973 'Recollections of Stanley', typescript.

**D/MRP 25/1** Description by Matthew King of the collapse of coke ovens at Langley Park, 1904, and building of new ones.

**D/MRP/ 58/2** Notebook of Henry H. Robson, 1892.

**D/MRP 77/1** Joseph Pease to Brodie Cochrane, lease of 500 acres of coal royalty near Brandon, 22.10.1856.

**D/PH33/3–4** Letters from Northern Coal Co. offices re. affairs of Framwellgate Colliery, 1841.

**D/Ph 53/1–4** Photographs of Durham Miners' Gala 1959–62.

**D/Ph 182/1** Photograph, New Brancepeth banner at 1950 Gala.

**D/Ph 236/1** Articles of agreement re. purchase of Evenwood and Tees Hetton collieries, 1891.

**D/X30/1, 10** 14 Miners' Gala photographs, 1962.

**D/X411/94** NCB information sheets, post-1956.

**D/X411/97** List of banners, Miners' Gala 1947.

**D/X702/3** Langley Park lodge minutes 1881–8.

**D/X832/1** Minutes of meeting re. formation of London Steam Colliery & Coal Co., 1865–7.

**D/X1048/48** Photograph, Durham Labour Women's procession, 1950s.

**D/X1048/52** Photograph, Hunwick Women's Section procession, 1950s.

**D/X1048/65** Durham City Labour Party Women's Section banner.

**D/X1048/123** Photograph, London national conference of Labour Women.

**D/X1069/2** Hylton lodge minute book 1959–62.

**D/X1077/4** Photograph of banners at the Gala, 1965.

**D/X1116/5** Group photograph with Bearpark banner, *c.* 1920s.

**D/X1118x1** Washington Glebe lodge minute book 1910–12.

**D/X1118/2** Washington Glebe lodge minute book 1912–15.

**D/X1118/3** Washington Glebe lodge minute book 1920–1.

**D/X1118/4** Washington Glebe lodge minute book 1922–4.

**D/X1118/5** Washington Glebe lodge minute book 1924–6.

**M/NBD 64** Waterhouses Bourne Methodist Church, Trustees' meetings, minutes.

**M40.1** The Sacriston colliery complex and other material by W. Thompson. Microfilm.

**Mine Abandonment Plans Catalogue**

**NCB 1/JB/1185** John Reay to John Buddle re. the Boldon Fell meeting, and the trial of pitman over the Waldridge Fell outrage, 1832.

**NCB 4/59** Deerness Valley collieries, Managers' monthly reports, 1918.

**NCB 4/63** Report of Deerness Valley Collieries 1926–34.

**NCB 4/64** Papers re. Deerness Valley unification scheme.

**NCB 4/66** Deerness Valley, proposed unification 1929–31.

**NCB 4/78** Esh Colliery, annual reports.

**NCB 4/101** Esh Colliery, papers concerning reopening 1935.

**NCB 4/136** Deerness Valley collieries, Reports, estimates and statistics, 1902–18.

**NCB 24/34** NCB Public Relations Office file, Hamsterley colliery 1963–78.

**NCB 24/58** NCB Public Relations Office file, Marley Hill *c.*1960.

**NCB 24/60** NCB Public Relations Office file, Medomsley colliery 1959–72.

**NCB 24/92** NCB Public Relations Office file, Wardley colliery, 1958–75.

**Q/D/SB 1** List of Friendly Societies 1785–1874.

# *Other Primary Sources*

## BEAMISH MUSEUM

Tutill, G. 1895 Annual Catalogue. 1962.225/W3.05.
Photographs: Bearpark (4.2121.55), Brusselton (14242), Craghead (54930, 58675), Dean & Chapter (10372), Eppleton (14346), Gordon House (20955), Tanfield Moor (66025), West Auckland (23429).

## BISHOP AUCKLAND LIBRARY

'Flashbacks', photograph 54, neg. 11, Mayor of Darlington unveiling the Thomas Barton memorial, Willington, 22 July 1908.

## COMPANIES HOUSE

00369605 George Tutill Ltd.

## DEAN AND CHAPTER, DURHAM CATHEDRAL

Additional Ms. 48.
D & C Minute Book January 1939 – 14 June 1947.
D & C Minute Book January 1954 – 29 December 1958.
The Eighty-Sixth Miners' Festival Service, 8 July 1995, service sheet.

## DURHAM CITY REFERENCE LIBRARY

**829/L19** Lines on the unfurling of Cornsay Colliery lodge banner.
**338.272/L185** Particulars, plan and conditions of sale of Norwood colliery, near Evenwood. Sale catalogue 10 March 1898.

## FABIAN SOCIETY

*Fabian News* vi, no. 9, November 1896.

## FERRYHILL LIBRARY

Photocopied photograph of unfurling of first Dean and Chapter banner at Ferryhill.

## GREATER LONDON RECORD OFFICE

**AR/TP51** Bomb damage map.

## LABOUR PARTY

**LP/ORG/14/2/3.4** National Organiser to W. Holmes, 15 April 1914.
**LP/ORG/14/2/23** Letter to W. Holmes, 21 May 1914.

## MANCHESTER LIBRARY

Annual Spring Exhibition, 1883. Catalogue of the Twenty-Third Exhibition of paintings in oil, watercolour drawings, sketches, crystoleum and chromatographic pictures etc. Now on view at Whaites Fine Art Gallery.

## NATIONAL UNION OF MINEWORKERS (NE AREA)

DMA Gala Notice, 17.6.1878; 25.7.1881.
NUM Durham Area 1959 National & District Agreements (Durham Area) to Dec. 1956 (Durham).
NUM (Durham Area) 1980 Rules (including Political Fund Rules), Durham.
NUM (NE Area) 1988 Rules and Standing Orders. Sheffield.
105th Durham Miners' Gala Souvenir Programme 1989.
107th Durham Miners' Gala Souvenir Programme 1991.
110th Durham Miners' Gala 1994, hand-bill.
Photographs: Allerdene, Byermoor, Chester Moor, Derwent, Lambton, Ouston, South Moor, Vane Tempest, Victoria Garesfield, NUM Mechanics, Willington Mechanics, DMA Sacriston lodge, forty dismissed miners from private drifts.

## *NORTHERN ECHO* LIBRARY

Photographs: Bowburn (69/7/523), Brancepeth (16/7/1960, 15/7/1961), Chester Moor (E23/7/62), Sherburn Hill (1939), Sherburn House (1939), Tanfield Lea, Whitworth Park (E17/7/67), Willington Mechanics (15/7/61, D2/7/75).

## NORTHERN FILM AND TELEVISION ARCHIVE

**NCB 1/18/3** NCB Film Unit, 1963 Mining Review, Sixteenth Year, No. 10, 'Pride of the Lodge'. U-matic black & white copy from 35 mm.

## PATENT OFFICE

**No. 1728** Letters Patent to George Tutill, of No. 83 City Road, in the County of Middlesex, for the invention of 'Improvements in treating materials for the manufacture of banners and flags', 6 July 1861.

## PUBLIC RECORD OFFICE

*Chancery Lane*
**RG9/141** Census enumerators' returns.
**RG10/1629** Census enumerators' returns.

*Kew*
**HO 45/644 f. 148** Disturbances, Durham, 1844.
**HO 45/13798 file 521000** Papers relating to the Zinoviev Letter.

## SOMERSET HOUSE

George Tutill, Probate 21.3.1887, vol. 6, 1887.

## WEAR VALLEY COUNCIL, CROOK

Framed photograph, Brancepeth lodge banner.

# Books and Articles

**Place of publication is given only if outside London.**

Abbott, H.C., Murton Pit and People 1838–1984. Murton, 1984.

Abley, R.S. *Whitworth Park Colliery 1836–1855*. Spennymoor, 1991.

Adamson, J. 'The General Strike in the North East. Tape Recording. A comment by James Stephenson of Winlaton', *North East Labour History* 4, 1970, pp. 25–32.

Airey, A. & J. *The Bainbridges of Newcastle. A Family History 1679–1976*. Newcastle, 1979.

Anon. 'College Notes', *Ushaw Magazine* 10, 1900, pp. 356–60.

Anon. 'Bearpark Colliery', *Transactions of the Institute of Mining and Mechanical Engineers (TIME)* 21, 1900–1, p. 269.

Anon. 'Dawdon Colliery', *North of England Institute of Mining and Mechanical Engineers (NEIMME)* 24, 1902–3a, pp. 598–9.

Anon. 'Hylton Colliery', *TIME* 24, 1902–3b, pp. 602–4.

Anon. 'Horden Colliery', *NEIMME* 32, 1906, pp. 4–5.

Anon. 'The Harton Coal Company Ltd', *TIME* 38, 1909–10, pp. 605–11.

Anon. 'College Notes', *Ushaw Magazine* 33, 1913, p. 81.

Anon. 'Visit to the sinking of the Morrison Busty Pits, Annfield Plain, Co. Durham', *TIME* 66, 1923–4, pp. 134–6.

Anon. 'Hawthorn combined mine', *The Engineer* 210, no. 5469, 1960, pp. 826–8.

Anon. Burnhope Miners Gala Diamond Jubilee Souvenir. 1986.

Armstrong, K. (ed.) *The Big Meeting. A People's View of the Durham Miners' Gala*. Newcastle, 1994.

Atherley Jones, L.A. & Bellot, H.H.L. *The Miners' Guide to the Coal Mines Regulation Acts and the Law of Employers and Workmen*. 1904.

Ayris, I. 'Elemore Colliery and the South Hetton Coal Co.', *Industrial Archaeology Review* 4, 1, 1979–80, pp. 6–35.

Baker, J. 'Randolph Colliery', *Trans. Weardale Naturalists Field Club*, 1, pt. 1, 1900, pp. 91–6.

Ball, S. (ed.) *Parliament and Politics in the Age of Baldwin and MacDonald. The Headlam Diaries 1923–1935*. 1992.

Bartlett, J. *Bartlett's Familiar Quotations*. 1968.

Bean, P. & Melville, J. *Lost Children of the Empire. The Untold Story of Britain's Child Migrants*. 1990.

Bell, R.E. *Women of Classical Mythology*. Oxford, 1991.

Bell, W.R. & McGowan, E. 'Haulage at Wearmouth Colliery', *TIME* 9, 1895–6, pp. 221–6.

Beynon, H., Hudson, R. & Sadler, D.A. *Tale of Two Industries: The Contraction of Coal and Steel in the North East of England*. Buckingham, 1991.

Bradley, S. *Walt Whitman. Leaves of Grass and Selected Prose*. New York, 1953.

Burns, E. *The General Strike May 1926: Trades' Councils in Action*. 1926.

Campaign Group of Labour MPs. *Justice. The Miners' Stike 1984–85*. 1986.

Campbell, T. & Wilson, M. *Each for All and All for Each. A Celebration of Co-operative Banners*. Rochdale, 1994.

Chadwick, O. 'Hensley Henson and the Durham Miners', Durham Cathedral Lecture. Durham, 1983.

Challoner, R. *A Radical Lawyer in Victorian England. W.P. Roberts and the Struggle for Workers' Rights*. 1990.

Challoner, R. & Ripley, B. *The Miners' Association – A Trade Union in the Age of the Chartists*. Whitley Bay, 1968.

Chapman, V. *Around Shildon*. Bath, 1994.

Charlton, W.B. *A Fifty Year History of the Durham County Colliery Enginemen's, Boiler-Minders' and Firemen's Association*. Durham, 1925.

Clack, P. *The Book of Durham City*. Buckingham, 1985.

Clark, D. *We do not want the Earth. The History of South Shields Labour Party*. Whitley Bay, 1992.

Coia, A.J., Teesdale, J.G. and Wilcockson, B. *Spennymoor and District: a Pictorial Recollection*. Spennymoor, 1990.

Cole, M. *Miners and the Board. Based on the Report of a Fabian Research Group*, Research Series 134. 1949.

Collins, L. *Silk Museums in Macclesfield*. Huntington, 1989.

Cooper, E. *People's Art. Working Class Art from 1750 to the Present Day*. Edinburgh, 1994.

Cornish, N. *Norman Cornish, a Slice of Life*. Wallingford, 1989.

Cummings, J. 'Sinking the John shaft at Hamsterley Colliery, through sand and gravel, by means of underhanging tubbing', *NEIMME* 38, 1909–10, pp. 320–31.

Daglish, J. 'On the sinking of the shafts at Marsden for the Whitburn Coal Co.', *Proc. Institute of Civil Engineers*, 71, 1882, pp. 5–43.

Davies, P. *A. J. Cook*. Manchester, 1987.

Davis, H.W.C & Weaver, J.R.H. (ed.) *The Dictionary of National Biography 1912–1921*. Oxford, 1927.

Davis, T. (ed.) *Oliver Goldsmith. Poems and Plays*. 1990.

Deacon, R. *A History of the British Secret Service*. 1969.

Dodd, J.J., *The History of the Urban District of Spennymoor*. Spennymoor, 1897.

Dorritt, S. & Ramsay, R. *Smear! Wilson and the Secret State*. 1992.

Dougan, D. & Graham, F. *Northumberland and Durham. A Social Miscellany*. Newcastle. 1969.

Drabble, M. (ed.) *The Oxford Companion to English Literature*. Oxford, 1957.

Durham Miners' Association, Opening of New Hall and Offices, Red Hill, Durham, Saturday, October 23, 1915. Programme. Durham, 1915.

Durham University. *Durham University Calender*. Durham, 1912–13.

Emery, N. 'The Ushaw Moor miners' strike and evictions, 1881–3', *North East Labour History Bulletin* 21, 1987, pp. 44–6.

—. *The Coalminers of Durham*. Thrupp, 1992.

Emery, N. & Thomas, C. 'Leather from Waldridge Fell drift mine', *Durham Archaeological Journal* 8, 1992, pp. 85–6.

Ford, M. 'Sinking by the freezing method at Washington, County Durham', *NEIMME* XXIV, 1902–3, pp. 293–306.

Fordyce, W. *History of Antiquities of the County Palatine of Durham*. Newcastle, 1857.

—. *A History of Coal, Coke, Coalfields and Iron Manufacture in Northern England*. Newcastle, 1860. (Reprinted 1973.)

Forster, E. *The Death Pit: The Story of the West Stanley colliery explosion 1909*. Newcastle, 1969.

Fynes, R. *History of the Northumberland and Durham Miners*. Durham, 1923.

*Gentleman's Journal and Gentlewoman's Court Review*. Supplement, *Town and Country Illustrated*, 3 April 1909.

Gervers, V. (ed.) *Studies in Textile History. In Memory of Harold B. Burnham*. Toronto, 1977.

Goodley, H. *Bewicke Main, the Colliery Village which Disappeared*. Gateshead, 1975.

Gorman, J. *Banner Bright*. 1973.

—. *Banner Bright*. 1986.

Gormley, J. *Battered Cherub. The Autobiography of Joe Gormley*. 1982.

Graham, F. *Battle of Jarama 1937. The Story of the British Battalion of the International Brigade in Spain*. Newcastle, 1987.

Grant, P.A. *The Coalmines of Durham City*. Department of Geography, Durham University, Occasional Paper, n.s. 2, 1973.

Hair, T.H. *A Series of Views of the Collieries in the Counties of Northumberland and Durham*. 1884.

Hall, A. *Coal Mining. A Technological Chronology 1700–1940*. Sheffield, 1991.

Hall, W.S. *A Historical Survey of the Durham Colliery Mechanics' Association 1879–1929*. Durham, 1929.

Handford, S.A. *The Fables of Aesop*. Harmondsworth, 1964.

Hardy, G.M. *The Dipton Story: a Souvenir of the Centenary of Dipton Parish Church*. 1986.

Harris, K. *Attlee*. 1982.

Hind, A.L. *History of Fatfield and Harraton*. 1974.

Hodgson, G.B. *The Borough of South Shields. From the Earliest Period to the Close of the Nineteenth Century*. Newcastle, 1903.

Howard, S. 'Dawdon in the "Third Period": The Dawdon dispute of 1929 and the Communist Party', *North East Labour History* 21, 1987, pp. 3–16.

Hudson, R., Peck, F. & Sadler, D. *Undermining Easington: Who'll pay the price of pit closures?* Department of Geography, Durham University for Easington District Council, 1984.

Hutchinson, W. *The Spirit of Masonry*. Wellingborough. 1987, reprint of 1775 edition.

Johnson, G.A.L. & Richardson, G. 'Coal Measures of the River Wear Gorge at Durham, England', *Transactions of the Natural History Society of Northumbria* 55, pt. 2, pp. 84–6.

Johnson, P. 'The Big Meetin', *The Railway Magazine*, September 1991, pp. 626–8.

Jones, B.E. *Freemasons' Guide and Compendium*. 1950.

Jones, D. *Durham Miners' Banners*. Durham, 1985.

Kearney, T. *Painted Red: A Social History of Consett*. Consett, 1990.

Kellet, A.H. *Herrington Colliery. NCB No. 2 Area Division*. 1958.

Kelly & Co. *Kelly's Post Office Directory of London*. 1857.

—. *Kelly's Post Office Directory of London*. 1859.

—. *Kelly's Post Office Directory of London*. 1864.

—. *Kelly's Post Office Directory of London*. 1866.

—. *Kelly's Post Office Directory of Durham*. 1873.

—. *Kelly's Post Office Directory of London*. 1874.

—. *Kelly's Post Office Directory of Durham*. 1890.

—. *Kelly's Post Office Directory of Durham and Northumberland*. 1894.

—. *Kelly's Post Office Directory of London*. 1904.

Kemp, B. *English Church Monuments*. 1980.

Kendall, W. *The Revolutionary Movement in Britain 1900–21. The Origins of British Communism*. 1969.

Kingford, P. *The Hunger Marchers in Britain 1920–1940*. 1982

Kingsley, J. (ed.) *Burns. Poems and Songs*. Oxford, 1969.

Kipling, M. *Iveston. History, Memories and Legends*. n.l., n.d.

Klugman, J. *History of the British Communist Party: 1 Formation and Early Years*. 1968.

Lawson, J. *Peter Lee*. 1936.

—. *A Man's Life*. 1946.

Leesom, R.A. *United We Stand. An Illustrated Account of Trade Union Emblems*. Bath, 1971.

Leslie, R.F. (ed.) *The History of Poland since 1863*. Cambridge, 1980.

Letch, H. *Birtley. Gleanings from the History of Birtley*. Newcastle, 1970.

Levenson, S. *James Connolly. A Biography*. 1973.

Liverpool Religious Tracts Society. *Narrative of a Dreadful Occurrence at Felling Colliery on the 25th of May 1812*. Liverpool, LRTS 166.

Louis, H. 'Mining', in Page, W., 1907, pp. 330–48.

Lloyd, E. *The Story of Fifty Years of Crook Co-operative Society*. Pelaw, 1916.

McFarlane, L.J. *The British Communist Party. Its Origin and Development until 1929*. Worcester, 1966.

Mahon, J. *Harry Pollitt. A Biography*. 1976.

Marrs, H. *The Dying Breed*. Durham, 1993.

Maynard, T.C. *An Authentic Copy of the Evidence taken on the Investigation into the Nature and Causes of the recent Hetton colliery explosion.* Durham, 1861.

McCutcheon, J.E. *Troubled Seams.* Seaham, 1955.

Milne, S. *The Enemy Within. MI5, Maxwell and the Scargill Affair.* 1994.

Mountford, C.E. *Langley Park Colliery: Centenary 1875–1975.* Chester-le-Street, 1975.

Moyes, W. *Banner Parade: A Selection of Lodge Banners of the Durham Miners' Association on Exhibition at the DLI Museum and Arts Centre, January/February 1973.* Newcastle, 1973.

—. *The Banner Book.* Newcastle, 1974.

NCB No. 5 Area Durham Division. *Beamish Mary Colliery.*

NCB No. 4 Area Durham Division. *Fishburn Colliery.*

NCB No. 5 Area Durham Division. *Handen Hold Washery.*

NCB No. 2 Area. *Herrington Colliery.* 1958.

NCB No. 3 Area Durham Division. *Horden Colliery.* 1966.

NCB NE Area. *Marley Hill Colliery.*

NCB No. 1 (NE) Area Durham Division. *Wardley–Usworth Combined Mine.* 1961.

National Union of Mineworkers. *A Century of Struggle. Britain's Miners in Pictures 1889–1989.* Sheffield, 1989.

North of England Institute of Mining and Mechanical Engineers. *An Account of the Strata of Northumberland and Durham as proved by Borings and Sinkings.* Newcastle, 1885.

Page, F. (ed.) *Byron. Poetical Works.* Oxford, 1970.

Page, W. (ed.) *The Victoria History of the Counties of England. Durham 3.* 1907.

Page-Arnot, R. *The Miners: Years of Struggle.* 1953.

Pearce, K. 'Pit Deaths in Stanley 1909', *North East Labour History* 19, 1985, pp. 32–7.

Peck, F. 'Horden Colliery: The Costs of Closure', *Northern Economic Review* 11, 1985, pp. 42–50.

Pelling, H. *A History of British Trade Unionism.* Hardmondsworth, 1979.

Pickard, C. 'Chopwell – "Little Moscow"', *NE Group for the Study of Labour History* 10, 1976, pp. 24–6.

Piggott, S. *The Druids.* Harmondsworth, 1968.

Potter, E. 'On Murton Winning in Co. Durham', *NEIMME* 5, 1856–7, pp. 43–61.

Purdon, G. *Twizell Pit Village.* Beamish, 1977.

Ransom, B. *Connolly's Marxism.* 1980.

Reid. *Reid's Handy Colliery Guide for Northumberland, Durham, Cumberland and Westmorland.* 1934.

Richardson, M.A. *The Local Historians Table Book.* Historical Division 2, 1842; 3, 1843; 4, 1844; 5, 1846.

Ripley, B.J. & McHugh, J. *John MacLean.* Manchester, 1989.

Rothstein, N. 'The Introduction of the Jacquard Loom to Great Britain', in Gervers, V., 1977, pp. 281–9.

—. 'Huguenots in the English Silk Industry in the Eighteenth Century', in Scouladi, I., 1987, pp. 125–40.

—. 'Canterbury and London: The Silk Industry in the Late Seventeenth Century', *Textile History* 20(1), 1989, pp. 33–47.

Scouladi, I. (ed.) *Huguenots in Britain and their French Background, 1500–1800.* 1987.

Simpson, F.R. 'Notes on the sinking of two shafts at Claravale Colliery, near Wylam upon Tyne', *TIME* 13, 1896–7, pp. 193–9.

Slowe, P. *Manny Shinwell: An Authorised Biography.* 1993

Sturgess, R.W. (ed.) *Pitmen, Viewers and Coalmasters: Essays in North-East Coalmining in the Nineteenth Century.* Bishop Auckland, 1986.

Surtees, H.C. *History of the Parish and Township of Evenwood, and the Parish of Eldon.* Mainsforth, 1923.

—. *The History of the Parish and Township of St. Helens Auckland together with the Township of West Auckland.* Mainsforth, 1924.

—. *The History of the Parishes of Tudhoe and Sunnybrow in the County Palatine of Durham*. Mainsforth, 1925.

Taylor, P.M. *The Growth and Development of the Town of Crook*. 1983.

Temple, D. *British Miners and the Capitalist Crisis*. 1983

Thalia, C. & Wilson, M. *Each for All and All for Each. A Celebration of Co-operative Banners*. 1994.

Tickner, L. *The Spectacle of Women. Imagery of the Suffrage Campaign 1907–14*. 1989.

Todd, N. *In Excited Times. The People Against the Blackshirts*. Whitley Bay, 1995.

Turner, I. 'Civil disorder in the North East between the Wars', *North East Labour History* 18, 1984, pp. 40–7.

Turner, J.J. 'The growth and development of Friendly Societies in Cleveland and Teeside *c*. 1835–1914: A preliminary research note', *Cleveland and Teeside Local History Soc.* 48, 1985, pp. 22–36.

Walker, G. 'George Harvey and Industrial Unionism', *North East Labour History* 17, 1983, pp. 21–4.

Webb, S. *The Story of the Durham Miners 1662–1921*. 1921.

Weedon, G. & Ward, R. *Fairground Art*. 1981.

Wells, S & Taylor, G. *William Shakespeare. The Complete Works*. Oxford, 1992.

Westoe Colliery Campaign Group. *Westoe Colliery. The Case against Closure. Final Report*. Westoe, 1993.

Whellan, F. *Directory and Topography of the County of Durham*. 1894.

Whellan, W. *Directory and Topography of the County of Durham with Newcastle upon Tyne*. Preston. 1865.

Widdas, C.G. 'Westoe Colliery reconstruction', *Iron and Coal Trades Review*, 1958, pp. 3–16.

Wild, J.H.S. 'Dean Welldon and the Miners' Wives', *Friends of Durham Cathedral Annual Report*, 45, 1977–8, pp. 17–18.

Wilson, J. *A History of the Durham Miners' Association 1870–1904*. Durham, 1908.

—. *Memories of a Labour Leader: The Autobiography of John Wilson JP, MP*. 1910.

Wilson, K. 'Chartism and the North-East Miners: A reappraisal', in Sturgess, R.W. (ed.), 1986, pp. 81–104.

Wilson, W.B. 'Tapping drowned workings at Wheatley Hill Colliery', *TIME* 23, 1910–12, pp. 72–84.

Winlaton and District Local History Society. *A History of Blaydon*. Gateshead, 1975.

WNS. 'Durham Miners' Gala', *British Railways Magazine* 9, (4) September, 1953, pp. 170–1.

Woodward, J.H.S. 'Stalactites and Stalagmites in the River Banks', *Friends of Durham Cathedral Annual Report* 45, 1984–5, pp. 22–4.

Workers' Revolutionary Party. *The Miners' Stike 1984–5 in Pictures*. 1985.

# *Theses*

Banham, J.D. Arthur Mowbray and the Hetton Coal Company – A Study of Early Nineteenth-Century Business Relationships. MA thesis, Sunderland Polytechnic, 1988.

Grant, P.A. The Coal Mines of Durham City. A Study of the History and Effects of Coal Mining in Durham City. BA thesis, Department of Geography, Durham University, 1971.

Quinn, V. Willington: A Study of the Industrialisation of a Durham Mining Village 1840–1914. MA thesis, Durham University, 1991.

Temple, A. The Derelict Villages of Durham County. M.Litt. thesis, Durham University, 1940.

# On-Line Database

**Lexis database**. R v British Coal Corporation and Secretary of State for Trade and Industry ex parte Vardy & Others. Queen's Bench Division (Crown Office List) [1993] ICR 720, [1993] IRLR 104. 21 November 1992.

# Maps

Bell, J.T.W. Plan of the Hartlepool Coal District of the County of Durham, 1843.
Ordnance Survey, 25 in maps, County Durham, 1856–1939.

# Index